The Language Arts

An Integrated Approach

Sharon E. Fox
The Ohio State University

Virginia Garibaldi Allen
The Ohio State University

Holt, Rinehart and Winston
New York Chicago San Francisco Philadelphia
Montreal Toronto London Sydney
Tokyo Mexico City Rio de Janeiro Madrid

Each of our lives has been blessed and made joyful by the support and devotion of our families. We dedicate this book to them with a depth of gratitude and love that cannot be put into words.

To G. N. and M. W. Fox
and my sister Audrey
and her family.

S. E. F.

To my sons Patrick and Brett
and to Ed

V. G. A.

Library of Congress Cataloging in Publication Data

Fox, Sharon E.
   The language arts.

   Bibliography: p.
   Includes index.
   1. Language arts (Elementary)   I. Allen, Virginia
Garibaldi.   II. Title.
LB1576.F67 1983   372.6′044   82-23293

ISBN 0-03-054046-1

Copyright © 1983 by CBS College Publishing
Address correspondence to:
383 Madison Avenue
New York, N.Y. 10017
All rights reserved
Printed in the United States of America
Published simultaneously in Canada
   4 5 6 7   038   9 8 7 6 5 4 3 2

CBS COLLEGE PUBLISHING
Holt, Rinehart and Winston
The Dryden Press
Saunders College Publishing

Preface

This book has grown out of our firm convictions about how children process language and our strong commitment to developing language-arts programs that help children gain in their communicative competencies. But language is used not only to communicate with others; language is also used to learn. We have included both aspects in our text.

Research and practice have been separated for many years, creating a false picture of professors in their "ivory towers" and teachers in the "real world." Such stereotypical characterizations are divisive. More and more, language research is based upon language produced in such natural settings as home, nursery center, or classroom. Investigators study the "real world" to answer questions about how language is used to meet a variety of intents within a social situation. Many of the classroom teachers we have taught work to keep abreast of the newer information being distributed. Some check researchers' findings in their own classrooms to see whether the results apply. These teachers continue to take classes, attend professional meetings, and add to the body of knowledge by making presentations and writing articles on incidents and teaching experiences in their own classrooms.

From our work with teachers, we have seen that the gulf between research and practice may be bridged. The classrooms reflecting this link have stimulated children who build with their teachers a positive context for learning. With the exception of the first chapter, in which a dialogue was constructed from an incident we saw but did not record, all the written and oral language protocols are true.

A major purpose of this book is to help students develop a theoretical framework that will allow them to make cohesive instructional decisions and plan integrated programs, and to that end we have cited research to support our main theses. From our experiences with undergraduates we know that names are less important to them than are ideas that make a difference in teaching; therefore our intention was not to present a survey of current

iv *Preface*

research. A number of studies that we know to be available and consider worthy are not discussed.

We wish to thank our past students who have become our present classroom teacher colleagues. They have supported the development of this text in many ways—as students who prodded us for reasons why and ways to, as teachers who invited us into their classes and shared their students' work, and as friends who offered to help and queried gently when the book would be finished. In particular the college teaching experiences in EPIC, an alternative undergraduate teacher-education program based on informal education theory and practice, and the experience of teaching in the Alternative Reading Masters Program, Integrating the Language Arts, formed the nucleus of such student/teacher support.

We are appreciative of cooperative school principals and staff who welcomed our visits and allowed us to take pictures. They include Highland Park Elementary School, Southwestern School District, Grove City, Ohio; Alternative Informal Classroom System, Upper Arlington, Ohio; and Douglas Alternative and Cranbrook Elementary Schools, Columbus, Ohio.

Our colleagues have supported the writing of this text. In particular, Charlotte Huck has encouraged us every step of the way—giving counsel when asked, explaining the intricacies of publication, and listening to our concerns. C. Ray Williams, our faculty chair, found ingenious ways to assist us during this project, including lightening of committee assignments. Carole Edelsky, Arizona State University; Dianne L. Monson, University of Minnesota; and Elizabeth Rosen, University of Illinois took time to give detailed, thoughtful comments that we found most helpful. To MaryAnne Hall of Georgia State University, who reviewed the final manuscript, we express our special appreciation. She understood our intent, philosophy, and organization, and her advice helped us sharpen and highlight aspects of the manuscript.

Barbara Fincher worked steadily on the manuscript, reading and typing revisions that decorated the margins, alphabetizing bibliographic entries when we were too rushed to do so, and reminding us of schedules we would rather have ignored. These tasks she performed not only professionally but also graciously, and we are most appreciative. In addition we express our gratitude to Fred Burton and Regis Goggin, who worked so painstakingly on the photographs.

Diane Driessen, one of our doctoral students, took the major role in developing chapter 11. We asked her to do this because of her special expertise which came from a background in library science and interest in children's literature. She also helped us by verifying sources and compiling a topic bibliography. We are indeed grateful for her willing contributions.

Two editors at Holt have been extremely helpful. David Boynton offered support and encouragement from the very beginning of the project, and H. L. Kirk gave care and attention to every aspect of transmuting the manuscript into a book. To both we offer heartfelt thanks.

S. E. F.
V. G. A.

In addition to the credits that appear in the text, we acknowledge here the permission of the authors and publishers indicated to reproduce the following material:

Chart, "Types of Teacher Talk," and list of discussion techniques from *Language Across the Curriculum* by Michael Marland (pages 78, 133–136), published 1977 by Heinemann Educational Books, Inc., Exeter, New Hampshire.

List of audience characteristics from *From Communication to Curriculum* (Penguin Education, 1976) by Douglas Barnes (page 109). Copyright © Douglas Barnes, 1975. Reprinted by permission of Penguin Books, Ltd., London.

"Questions" from *That Was Summer* by Marci Ridlon McGill, published 1969 by Follett Publishing Co., New York.

Interactional Competency Checklist from "There's More to Language Arts than Meets the Ear: Implications for Evaluation" by Janet K. Black, *Language Arts,* May, 1979. Copyright © 1979 by the National Council of Teachers of English. Reprinted by permission of the publisher and the author.

"Go outside . . ." from *The Way to Start a Day*. Copyright © 1976, 1977 by Byrd Baylor. Reprinted with the permission of Charles Scribner's Sons, New York.

Excerpt from *Swimmy* by Leo Lionni, copyright 1963 by Pantheon Books, a division of Random House, Inc., New York.

"Flashlight" from *Flashlight and Other Poems* by Judith Thurman. Copyright © 1976 by Judith Thurman (New York: Atheneum, 1976). Reprinted with the permission of Atheneum Publishers.

Excerpt from *Goodnight Moon* by Margaret Wise Brown. Copyright 1947 by Harper & Row, Publishers, Inc.; renewed 1975 by Roberta Brown Rauch. By permission of Harper & Row, Publishers, Inc.

"Winter Alphabet" from *Outloud* by Eve Merriam. Copyright © 1973 by Eve Merriam. Reprinted by permission of the author.

Excerpt from *A House Is a House for Me* by Mary Ann Hoberman, illustrated by Betty Fraser. Text copyright © 1978 by Mary Ann Hoberman. Reprinted by permission of Viking Penguin, Inc., New York.

Contents

Preface iii

PART 1 Foundations of the Language Arts

1 An Integrated Language-Arts Program: A Rationale 3

An Example of Integration 4

Child as Learner, Teacher as Learner 5 Teacher Planning 6

Framework of the Text 10

Theoretical Base for the Text 11
Interrelationships of the Language Arts 11 *Study of Discourse* 15 *How Children Develop and Learn* 18

How to Use the Book 21 Overview of the Chapters 23

Suggested Learning Experiences 26

Recommended Readings 26

References 27
Professional Literature 27 Children's Literature 27

2 Language Learning: A Powerful Force 29

The Nature of Language 32

Language Systems 33
Phonology 33 Morphology 35 Semantics 36

How Oral Language Is Learned 37

Language Development of Young Children 37 Language Development of School-Age Children 41 Summing up the Process 45

Written Language Development 45

Scribbling 46 Message Writing 46 Writing Explorations 48 Beginning to Spell 50 The Developing Writer 51 Summing up the Process 54

Implications of Oral and Written Language Development 55

Language Usage Varies 57

Functions of Language 58 Register 63 Dialect 64 Second-Language Learners 66 Implications of Language Variation 67

Summary 68

Suggested Learning Experiences 69

Recommended Readings 69

References 71
Professional Literature 71

3 Child Development: One Basis for Instructional Decisions 75

Cognitive Development 76

One Child's Representation of Her World 76 Major Principles of Piaget's Theory 78 Piaget's Stages of Development 83 Cognitive Development and the Language-Arts Teacher 87

Moral Development 89

Some Children's Ideas about Justice 89   Moral Development and the Language Arts 89   Cognitive Theories of Moral Development 90   Emotional Theories of Moral Development 94

Social Development 96

Interaction among a Group of First-Grade Children 96   Knowledge of the Social Situation and Language Development 97   Social Development and Personality 97   Stages of Social Development 99
Early Childhood 99   Middle Childhood 101   Puberty 102
Role of the Teacher in Grouping Children 104

Summary 105

Suggested Learning Experiences 105

Recommended Readings 106

References 107
Professional Literature 107   Children's Literature 108

PART 2 Integration of the Language Arts

4 Listening and Speaking 113

A Book Discussion: An Act of Discourse 114

Early Studies in Listening and Speaking 120
Research on Listening 120   Research on Speaking 120

Discourse 121
Discourse, a Contribution to Learning 121   Basic Competencies in Discourse 123
Identifying and Using the Context 123   Directing Speaking and Listening for Specific Purposes 125

Social Conventions of Speaking 126
Usage 127

Listening Aspects of Social Conventions 128
Chart of Basic Competencies in Discourse 129

Planning for Growth in Student Discourse 130
The Teacher's Role 130   Organizing into Groups for Discussion 133   Activities that Encourage Discourse 136
Sharing 136   Projects and Field Trips 137   Choral Reading 139   Drama 141
The Classroom Environment 142

Assessment 144
Spontaneous Language Observations 145   Story Retelling 148

Summary 150

Suggested Learning Experiences 151

Recommended Readings 151

References 152
Professional Literature 152   Children's Literature 154

5 Writing and Reading: The Beginnings 157

Literacy Begins in the Home 159

Ways in Which Children Begin to Organize Print 161
Beginning Writing 161
The Development of Writing Skills 164   The Role of the Teacher 168
Signs of Reading Knowledge in the Classroom 170
Decisions Based upon Observations 171

Beginning Writing and Reading, Teacher-initiated 172
Accepting Dictation 172   Ways of Using Children's Dictation 176   Word Banks 180   Learning from Children's Attempts to Read 181

Conventions of Print 184
Handwriting 184   Spelling 192

x Contents

Building a Literacy Context 195

Summary 197

Suggested Learning Experiences 198

Recommended Readings 199

References 199
Professional Literature 199   Children's Literature 201

6 Reading and Writing: On the Way 203

An Example of Self-initiated Writing 204

The Relationship Between Reading and Writing 205

The Writing Process 207

Sources of Writing 210
Concrete Experiences 210   Drama 212   Literature 215
Reading Aloud 215   Books as Themes 218   Books that
Children Read Themselves 223
Peer Influence 225

Writing Conferences 226
Purposes 226   Types of Conferences 227

Looking at the Writing Product 228
The Role of Revision 228   Responding to Writing 229
Evaluating Writing 231 Recordkeeping and Evaluation
Forms 234 Student Self-evaluating of Writing 239

Writing Context 242

Skills of Writing 244
Handwriting 244   Spelling 250   Report Writing 259

Summary 265

Suggested Learning Experiences 265

Recommended Readings 266

References 267
Professional Literature 267   Children's Literature 268

Contents xi

7 Language Arts in the Content Areas 271

Rationale 272

How to Integrate Language Arts in a Content Area 273

Selecting a Topic or Theme 273   Planning for the Theme 276   Organizing for Work 278
Grouping for Work 279   Managing Space and Time 279
Recordkeeping 280   In-class Experiences and Activities that Serve to Integrate 284   Out-of-class Experiences and Activities that Serve to Integrate 286
Study Trips 287   Study Trip Booklets 288   Materials 288
Interpreting the Experience 294   Sharing Experiences 296   Opportunities for Assessing 298

Language as a Content Area 303

What Teachers Need to Know About Grammar 303   What Children Could Learn About Language 305
Language Explorations for Primary-grade Children 305   Language Explorations for Middle-grade Children 307
What Children Can Learn About the Difference Between Oral and Written Language 309   Choosing Words to Shape Thought 311
Persuasive Language 311   Metaphor 312
What Children Should Learn About Words 313

Summary 316

Suggested Learning Experiences 316

Recommended Readings 319

References 320
Professional Literature 320   Children's Literature 320

8 Literature-Based Language Extensions 323

One Child's Version of a Well-known Tale 324

Reasons for Literature in the Language Program 327
Literature as Input to Language 327   Literature as Experience 328   Literature as a Stimulus to Language Output 330

Literature in the Classroom 331
Listening to Literature 331
Selecting Literature 333   Sharing Literature 337
Reading in Literature 338
Selecting Books for the Classroom Library 338   Setting Up a Context for Reading 341
Talking About Literature 347
Story Retelling: An Oral Response 347   Stages in "Book Talk" 349   Book Discussions 350   Activities with Books that Can Lead to Talk 353   Dramatic Expressions 356

Writing from Literature 359
Books that Provide a Story Frame 359   Books that Extend Children's Use of Words 362   Books that Motivate Writing 363

Integrating Literature into the Language-Arts Program 365
An Example of a Literature Web 365   Assessment 367

Summary 371

Recommended Readings 371

Suggested Learning Experiences 372

References 373
Professional Literature 373   Children's Literature 375

9 Second-Language Learning and the Language Arts 381

One Second-Language Learner in a Classroom 382

The Need for All Teachers to Know About Second-Language Learning 383

Bilingual Approaches to Helping Second-Language Learners 384

A Framework for Helping LEP Children 385
Cultural Considerations 385 Linguistic Considerations 388
Social Considerations 391

Role of the Classroom Teacher 392
Input 392 Environment 396 Concrete Experiences 399

Assessment of Oral Language 401

The Role of the ESL Teacher 407

Moving into Print 410
Learning to Read a Second Language 410 A Writing Experience in One Bilingual Classroom 412 Selecting Books for LEP Children 416 Suggestions of Books for LEP Children 416
Books that Develop Concepts and Vocabulary 416 *Books Whose Illustrations Tell the Story* 417 *Books with Repetitive Language* 418 *Wordless Picture Books* 419 *Informational Books* 420 *Books in the Child's Native Language* 420 *Books in English about the Child's Native Culture* 421

Summary 422

Recommended Readings 422

Suggested Learning Experiences 423

References 424
Professional Literature 424 Children's Literature 425

PART 3 Organization and Evaluation of the Language-Arts Program

10 Program Planning and Evaluation 429

Rationale for Planning 430

Developing Long-term Plans 431
An Example from One School District 432 An Example of One Teacher's Focus 433

Developing Short-Term Plans 435
An Example of One Class's Plans 436 Role of Weekly Plans 439

Developing an Integrated Program 439
The Beginning 439 Differences Between a Unit and a Theme 441

Communicating the Language-Arts Program 443
Other Teachers and the Principal 443 Parents 444
Newsletters 444 *Homework* 447 *Conferences and Notes* 449

Evaluating the Program 449
Plans 449 The Ongoing Program 450

NCTE Guidelines 451

Summary 465

Suggested Learning Experiences 466

References 466
Professional Literature 466 Children's Literature 467

11 Instructional Resources 469

[Developed by Diane Driessen]

Role of the Teacher 470

The Teacher as a Resource 470   The Teacher as a Professional 472

Professional Resources 472

Journals 473   Books 476   Children's Literature Textbooks 480

Children's Classroom Resources 483

Language-Arts Textbooks 483
Criteria for Assessing Language-Arts Textbooks 483   Using a Textbook 484
Magazines 490   Newspapers 492   Book Clubs 493   Book Fairs and Book Stores 493

Resources from Outside the Classroom 494

Television 494   Parents and Grandparents 494   Library Media Centers 495

Summary 497

Suggested Learning Experiences 497

Index 499

PART 1
Foundations of the Language Arts

An Example of Integration
Child as Learner, Teacher as Learner
Teacher Planning

Framework of the Text
Theoretical Base for the Text
How to Use the Book
Overview of the Chapters

Suggested Learning Experiences

Recommended Readings

References
Professional Literature
Children's Literature

Chapter 1
An Integrated Language-Arts Program: A Rationale

We think children learn best when they are involved in activities of genuine interest to them; when learning is interrelated; when instruction in communication skills extends to all areas of the curriculum; and when learning possibilities are both rich and flexible—rich in the scope and variety of resources, flexible in terms of responding to the unique demands of individual children. This kind of learning can be illustrated by an incident that we observed in a classroom.

An Example of Integration

The principal, Mr. Bush, stopped in to see Mrs. Driggs, who had asked him to look at the work her fourth graders were doing on their unit on time. One group of children was studying how quickly mice can run a maze. As Mr. Bush entered the room, the teacher greeted him and led him to the mouse cage where a student, Barbara, was engrossed in watching the two mice.

Mrs. Driggs: I brought Mr. Bush over to meet the mice, Barbara.

Barbara: Hi, Mr. Bush.

Mr. Bush: Hi, Barbara. So these are the famous mice! They look dead to the world.

Mrs. Driggs: I'm not surprised; they had a busy morning.

Barbara: Yeah. They're tired. You know, we had this maze box and the mice had to go through it and then they'd get food pellets at the end and we timed them with a stopwatch so we could see who was the fastest one. We wrote the names and the times on a chart.

Mrs. Driggs: There's the chart. They really kept careful records.

Mr. Bush: Sleepy and Dancer—are those their names?

Barbara: Uh huh. Sleepy sleeps a lot. He's the one with the sandy spot on his tail. Can you see it? Dancer's tail is thinner.

Mr. Bush: Sleepy was the fastest and Dancer was the slowest. Hey! That doesn't sound right! It should be the other way around.

Barbara: Well, Dancer, you see, when he got to a place in the maze where he had . . . where there was like a corner or a wall, well, he'd kind of jump back and forth like a dancer. Kevin said we should name the mouse Dancer and we did, but I wanted another name. I wanted to call him Walter.

Mr. Bush:	Walter?
Barbara:	You know, Walter, like in *Walter the Lazy Mouse*.
Mr. Bush:	I had a white mouse when I was a kid, but he didn't have a nice cage like this. Your mice have a much better life than my mouse did—fancy cage, fancy food—even toys!
Barbara:	Well, we have this book that tells all about mice—their habitats and how to take care of them and stuff. Want to see a picture of a mouse that looks just like Dancer? (Barbara pulls a book from the shelf and starts leafing through it.) Oh look! Here's a neat kind of mouse—a pocket mouse. I can't find the house mouse that looks like Dancer. Wait a second—no—just a minute. (Barbara turns to the index and slides her finger along the columns.) Here . . . yes . . . here it is, page 18. See, doesn't it look like Dancer?

Child as Learner, Teacher as Learner

As we observed this brief incident in the classroom, we were aware that two kinds of learning were taking place. Barbara was learning a great deal about mice, and Mrs. Driggs was learning a great deal about Barbara. If we had asked Barbara what she had learned, she probably would have said:

Dancer and Sleepy are not exactly alike.

I found some good books about mice.

I know the names of some different kinds of mice.

I can tell you what house mice look like and what pocket mice look like.

I'm learning how to take care of mice.

If we had asked the teacher what she had learned from that short incident, she might well have responded:

Barbara is extending her interest in animals beyond her pets at home. This is a sustained interest. For the past several days she has been watching the mice and reading books displayed next to the mouse cage.

Barbara is becoming a careful observer, able to note small differences in the two mice. Furthermore, she is able to use language in a precise way, which helps others to see and understand what she has observed.

Barbara is able to use language in appropriate and confident ways when she speaks with an adult.

Barbara is using the new vocabulary she has learned in her reading, and will use the index of a book to locate information.

As you can see, Barbara's interest in the mice is leading her into a new learning situation. She is sharpening her observation skills and is able to contrast how the two mice differ in both appearance and habit. On her own, Barbara is using books as a resource and her reading is extending her vocabulary. Not only is she able to name the mice and place them in the category of house mice, but she is also using words such as "habitat" and "pellets." She knows how to use an index to locate the information she needs. She obviously enjoyed reading *Walter the Lazy Mouse* (Flack) since she wanted to name a mouse Walter. Mr. Bush's genuine interest lets Barbara share both her enthusiasm and her newly acquired knowledge in a purposeful way.

While Barbara was observing the mice with studious care, her teacher was observing Barbara with thought and meticulous attention. She was able to see some of the things that Barbara was doing, such as sharing information with an adult, enjoying the mice, exploring books, and expanding her vocabulary. She also realized that, although Barbara had read and talked about mice, she had not yet done any writing. She therefore took a minute to jot a note to herself so that she would not forget the details of what she had just learned.

Barbara   February 7

Really interested in mice! Enjoyed talking with Mr. Bush. Read *Walter the Lazy Mouse* on her own. Used index. Check with Barbara about keeping a journal for the mice. Show her Brady's journal, *Wild Mouse*. Get *Once a Mouse* and *Frederick*. Read *Amos and Boris* aloud.

Teacher Planning

The incident of the mice did not end with Mrs. Driggs's notes. When we went back to the classroom after lunch, she had added *Once a Mouse* (Brown), *Frederick* (Lionni), and *Wild Mouse* (Brady) to the collection of books on the table beside the mouse cage. Later that afternoon Barbara and four other children fed the mice and explored the new books. The children's enthusiasm suggested to their teacher that there might well be a group interest in mice that could be extended in some exciting and meaningful ways.

The consideration of using mice as a theme made Mrs. Driggs realize that she knew very little about mice. If mice were to be studied, then she would have to become a learner about mice herself. The encyclopedia was a handy reference but some filling-out was needed. Mrs. Driggs promised herself to read all the books on mice placed in the classroom so she could direct youngsters asking concrete questions to appropriate informational books. She asked the school librarian to check to see that a good selection of mouse books was available to the class. That evening she thought through some of the possibilities of studying mice by developing a web.

What is a web? The creation of a web is a way for teachers to organize ideas around a theme or topic. A web can grow from children's concerns and interests or it can be initiated by a teacher. All webs are a product of both the teacher's and children's ideas and suggestions. Some individuals call a web "a plan of possibilities." Because new areas or concepts may be added by drawing lines from the center, the plan never becomes static. New extensions may always be included whether the ideas stem from the teacher or the student. This planning process encourages linking one area to another, providing opportunities for an integrated curriculum. A web represents long-term planning and creates a framework for short-term plans. Further discussion of the webbing process may be found in chapters 8 and 10.

Good planning reflects what the teacher knows about child development, the language-learning process, and content knowledge in general. By studying the web, a teacher can determine whether a balance of opportunities among all the language arts is present. Specifically, the planning is based upon the teacher's awareness of student interests, levels of development, and needs for growth. By looking at Mrs. Driggs's web we can see how it represents her general knowledge about children in the fourth grade, her specific awareness of Barbara's interests, development, and needs, and how an integation of all the language-arts areas is to be achieved.

The teacher's first decision was to follow an interest in mice. Why? Many interests are probably displayed by her students every day. However, mice are a particularly rich topic because not only were the animals already available as a concrete resource in the classroom, but also many fine children's books about mice—fiction, nonfiction, and poetry—are available. Mrs. Driggs's general knowledge of children's literature assisted her in this topic choice. Some other topics might not have as rich an array of literature available as does the topic of mice. For example, although children are commonly interested in caterpillars, few children's books have been written about them—or about butterflies, a similar topic. In order to support the study of caterpillars in fictional literature, an expanded theme would need to be selected, such as "change."

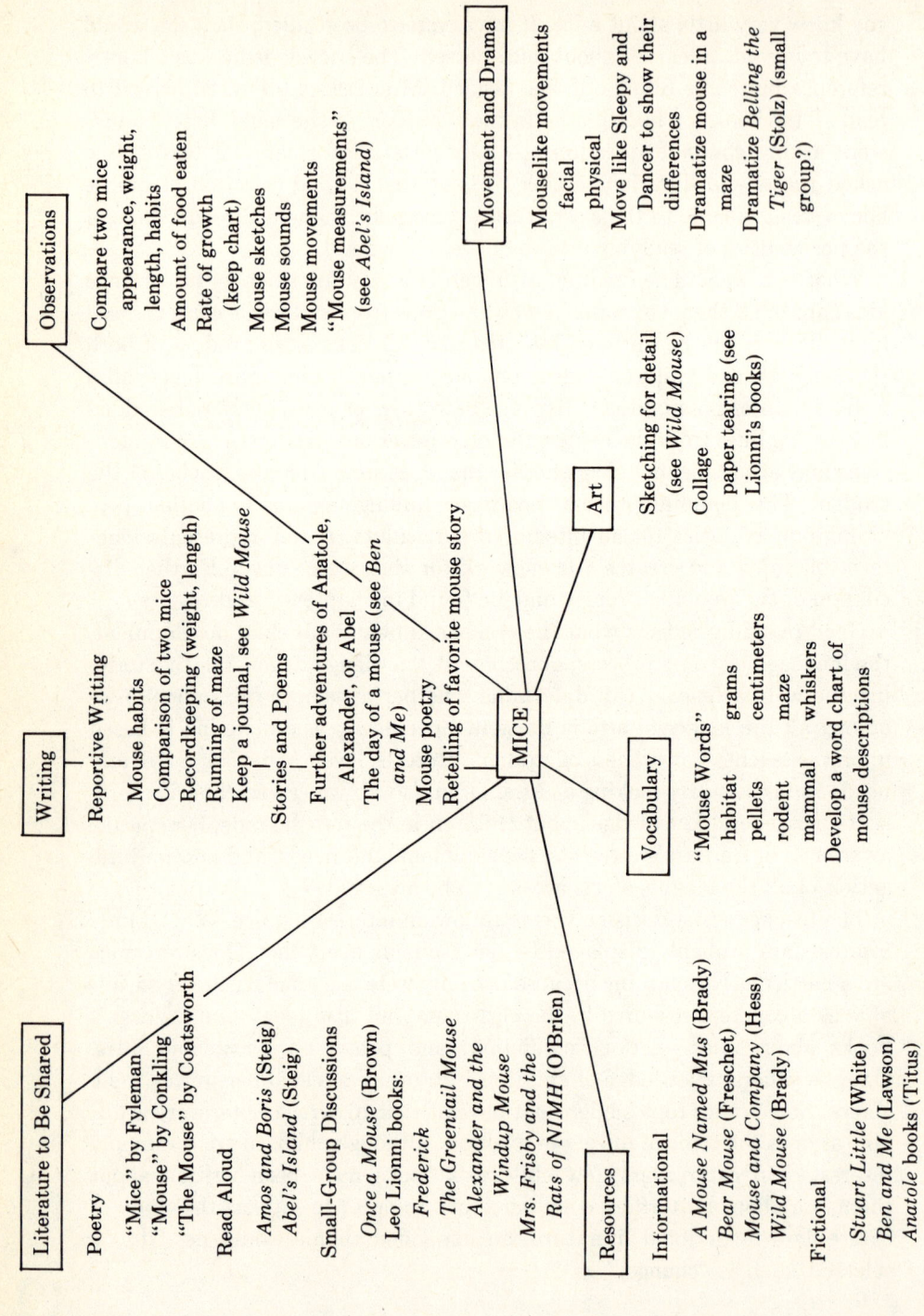

The variety of experiences present in the web encourages children to share oral language in many situations for differing purposes. As children observe, they will describe their findings for a comparison between the two mice. Recordkeeping charts made by small groups require planning language. Drama incorporates language for characterization. Oral retelling of a favorite mouse story involves narrative language. As a group investigates mouse measurements, an idea from the book *Abel's Island,* they must propose and agree upon which things to record in this fashion. Informal working situations such as art and movement can provide a time for personal interaction among students. Listening is an integral part of each of these learning situations for, to participate fully, the children must receive and provide feedback from and to others.

The other language arts appear quite naturally in these activities. Writing can grow out of oral discussions such as reports and group-made charts. Personal reading experiences may be shared orally, used for retelling, or become a basis for developing a dramatic exchange with others.

Children within the same age group read at different levels of difficulty. Mrs. Driggs's selection of books illustrates her expectation of a wide range of abilities. She includes both picture books such as *Once a Mouse* and *Frederick* and longer books such as *Abel's Island* and *Mrs. Frisby and the Rats of NIMH.* The small-group book discussions also reflect these differences. For some, reading one picture book in depth is enough; others might read several books by the same author and compare them. More advanced youngsters could tackle a book with longer chapters for a detailed discussion. By planning to read aloud and by holding small-group discussions, the teacher is structuring opportunities for her students to listen to stories and to each other, orally relate their understandings of literature, and participate in a shared reading experience.

The variety of writing activities proposed allows children to work at different levels of development. Extending the adventures of Anatole or Alexander would require not only general storytelling skills, but also the ability to generalize, infer, and transpose. For some youngsters, however, simply retelling the story in their own words would be a valuable experience. In these instances, writing evolves from reading. Other writing is based upon observations that may be shared orally among two or three children before actual wording is chosen.

Does the web contain any indication that Mrs. Driggs has thought of Barbara in her planning? We know that Barbara read *Walter the Lazy Mouse* on her own. Perhaps the teacher thought to extend Barbara's reading vocabulary and understanding of the theme through a comparison of the Lionni books. In the anecdotal record on Barbara, Mrs. Driggs thought of suggesting a journal as a writing experience, and this activity is listed in the web. *Wild Mouse,* a book written in journal form, is cited as an example. More specific information about Barbara is not available, but by studying the web itself, we can see that the teacher has planned a wide range of experiences for Barbara and the other children. The web on mice that Mrs. Driggs prepared illustrates how a teacher may use children's interests as a focal point in planning a rich variety of activities that will include all of the language arts, relate to developmental abilities of children, and also meet specific needs of the individual children in her class.

Framework of the Text

Our purpose in writing this book is to enable our readers to develop the ability to plan and implement an integrated language-arts program. The initial consideration in achieving this goal is the context in which language learning is to occur. The Rosens (1973) describe the difference between a traditional democratic classroom and a classroom where the teacher's concern is developing a supportive learning context.

> It has been fashionable for a long time to talk of "classroom climate" as a decisive factor in learning and the same very limited experiments are cited again and again as evidence that a "democratic" climate is the most desirable. Yet this seems to miss the point. The most successful classrooms are not ones ruled by majority decisions or their equivalents but ones which create a context in which a rich variety of language can flow with ease. For that to happen speakers must share a past, must share meanings, must have knowledge in common, must be able to make assumptions about each other and must have built their own network of conventions within which there is room for all those negotiations which makes language possible, facilitates and fosters (p. 39).

When teachers have a knowledge of language—how it is acquired as well as how it is used and shaped for a variety of purposes—they will be able to develop an environment that fosters language growth. This linguistic knowledge, coupled with an understanding of how children grow and develop, will permit teachers to build a framework within which they can make instructional decisions in order to meet the specific needs of individual children.

The classroom contains more than student learners. Children and teachers learn individually, learn together, and learn from each other. How and what each learns reflects and affects views of self, of others, and of the world. This interactive learning is a part of the context developed in the classroom. Children learn the nature of disciplines, learn about each other, and learn how to use language to engage in projects to reach personal and group goals. Teachers learn about the group dynamics of the children in the class, learn about each child's unique exploration of the world encountered, and learn how they as adults can assist children's growth. In addition, teachers continue building upon their own knowledge of the world about them. Teachers are scholars (that is, learners) also.

Theoretical Base for the Text

The framework that supports the thesis of this text has three components. The first is the interrelationships of the language arts; the second is a study of discourse; and the third is an examination of how children develop and learn. Each of these components will be discussed as they relate to language arts instruction.

Interrelationships of the Language Arts. Traditionally, the language arts are divided into four areas: listening, speaking, reading, and writing. This can be demonstrated by even a cursory glance through language-arts texts and curriculum guides. Such a division permits an in-depth analysis of each area and helps assure that each will receive a fair and balanced amount of consideration. Organizing material within the separate strands can allow for precision and clarity of presentation since it narrows the focus. Children's development in each specific area may be shown sequentially.

However, most people who work with children and language feel that listening, speaking, reading, and writing are deeply related. They cite the need to integrate the language arts, both with each other and with other areas of the curriculum. The teacher is left with the often frustrating task of fitting the pieces together. A curriculum guide that separates the language arts in its presentation often results in a school day in which twenty minutes is given to spelling, fifteen to handwriting, and sixty to reading.

Instead of starting with an examination of each separate strand in turn, we propose to demonstrate how these strands are actually woven into a cohesive whole. The commonalities and relationships of the four basic areas of the language arts may be seen quite easily in the following diagram:

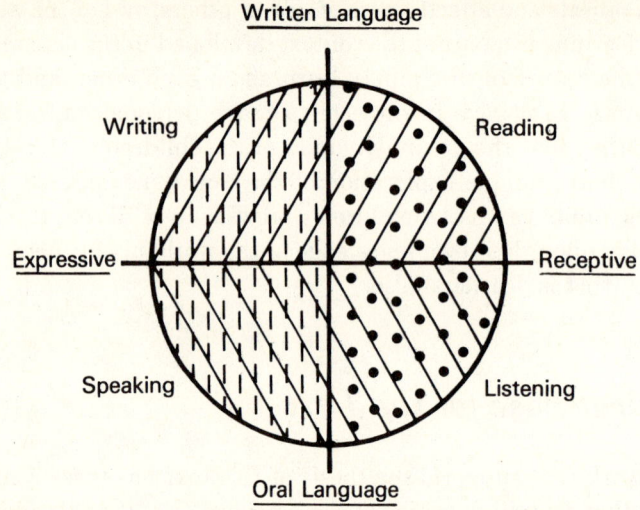

Written language, represented by the top half of the circle, includes both writing and reading. Oral language, the lower half of the circle, includes both speaking and listening. But the processes of the langauge arts can be divided in another way. Writing and speaking are expressive aspects of language that comprise the left half of the circle. Reading and listening, as the receptive aspects, complete the circle on the right.

By looking at this diagram, we can see how the typical language-arts curriculum in texts and for schools is developed. Clearly, the frustration of separating each area becomes visible. No one section may be removed without drawing the others with it. For example, if writing is pulled out for examination, reading, the other written-language component, must be dealt with if only in the sense of rereading. Writing suggests the reading of one's compositions by others and the input that reading experiences can give to written language. In addition, speaking will be drawn out with writing because it is the other expressive skill. Since oral language initially precedes written language, experiences in oral composition influence success in written composition. Listening, the remaining segment, is firmly attached to speaking and reading and also must be included. This makes sense because the language that one hears, especially the "story language" one hears when books are read aloud or when stories are told, is another source of written expression.

Just as language is not used in separate strands (as has been taught in the past) it is not learned in separate strands. Children learn language to fulfill meaningful functions in their lives. This contextual and integrated nature of language learning has strong implications for the way language arts should be taught in school. Shuy (1981) states:

> Research shows that good language learners begin with a function, a need to get something done with language, and move gradually toward acquiring the forms which reveal that function. They learn holistically, not by isolated skills. Such learners worry more about getting things done with language than with the surface correctness of it. They hold innately and naturally the perspective of the learner. They have an underlying and perceived belief that there is a system in the world. They experiment freely and try things out unashamedly. They adjust to contextual variables, even at an early stage of learning. This appears to be the way we all learned our native languages—the natural way (p. 106).

The circle representing the language arts on page 12 may be misleading, for language occurs within a physical and social context that serves as a basis for meaning. The significance of physical context may be seen in the following situation. If you heard someone say "They're running!," you might think the individual was referring to a field of participants in a race, such as the Boston Marathon. But if you knew this exclamation came from an individual looking into the waters of the Columbia River, you would realize the subjects were salmon. In the same way, the social situation provides a context for meaning. Sentence fragments, obscure antecedents, and ambiguous statements occur frequently with no loss of meaning in oral interactions.

In addition, the content of language arts is derived from concrete and abstract experiences. Barbara, working with her mice, had both kinds of experience. Her observations of Dancer and Sleepy are examples of concrete experience. Her reading about mice takes her a step further from reality and is more abstract.

Thus, the language-arts skills rely upon experiences leading to their use and the situations in which they occur. This concept may be visualized as the language-arts skills within a universe of concrete and abstract experience:

Shared experiences form a commonality on which to base interactions. After a baseball game, teammates will enjoy rehashing the points scored and the plays made. In contrast, new situations, if not too far removed from the audience's prior experience, can provide a real purpose for interaction. For example, if one of those team members wishes to tell another person about that baseball game, that person must have had some experience with baseball or at least share a partial vocabulary in order to understand the communication. Children need to have both kinds of experiences, shared and

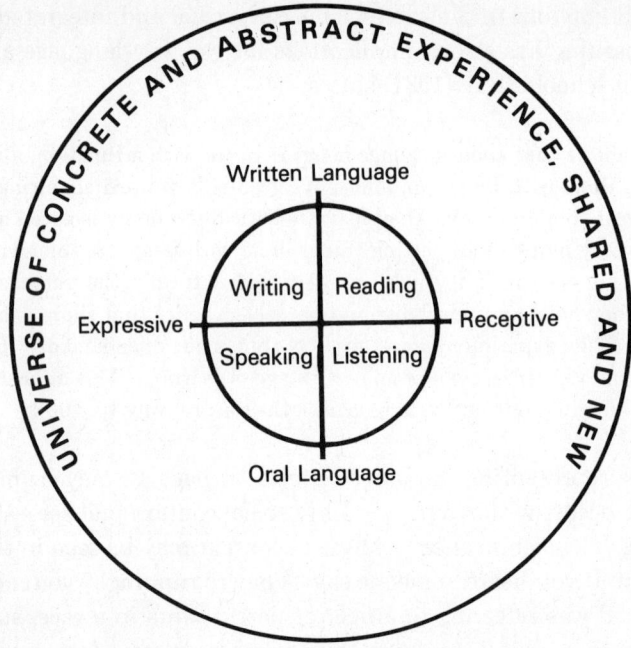

new. Platt (1979) describes the role of shared and new experiences in a classroom:

> The schools, then, need to foster the creation of such a shared life, one which provides a supportive context for early language use and thinking.... Schools also need to help children become independent of this supportive context. Eventually, children should not only be able to use language appropriately in a variety of contexts, with focus on meaning, but should also be able to focus objectively on that language itself. In this way they will be in control of their own language and thinking in the service of problem-solving, hypothesizing, and constructing reality in a new way.
>
> How can schools provide a supportive yet liberating context? A guiding principle would seem to be to balance familiar with the new. The school can make a connection with the home by providing a homelike context while extending this to carry children beyond the limits of the known into new, interesting, and challenging territory (p. 622).

The quality of the experience influences the quality and type of language used. Contrived school experiences result in contrived language with no real purpose for communication except to please the teacher. A familiar example of this is the "My Summer Vacation" theme. On the other hand, students' explanations of the city they have just constructed with blocks will involve more purposeful and elaborate language because they will have a real audience of other students and the teacher interested in the project.

Study of Discourse. The term *communication* implies that there is someone sending a message and someone receiving that message. The message may be shared orally—a storyteller to a listening child, a bit of gossip whispered to a friend, an anecdote recounted to one's dinner companions, or a speech presented to a large audience. The message may be shared through written language—a grocery list written to oneself, a letter to a parent, grafitti written for chance passers-by, or a novel shaped and polished for an anonymous audience. The message may be a nonverbal one—a shrug or a nod of the head in response to someone's comments, or the formally structured movements of ballet. The communication act does not occur in a vacuum but within a context that is a part of the message. This exchange of a message between a speaker and a listener, a writer and a reader, or a dancer and an audience and the context in which it occurs are what make up discourse.

Context undergirds the total communication act but for now let us focus upon three elements within that act: the sender, the receiver, and the message. If each is studied, we can begin to understand a great deal about the structure of discourse. For example, a speaker must make selections about the information to be sent. These decisions are based upon the purposes for sending the message as well as knowledge about the audience and the speaker's distance from that audience.

The person for whom the message is intended is not a passive receiver who simply absorbs a message the way a sponge blots up water. The receiver actively reconstructs the information that is sent out, comprehending and interpreting it in light of his or her own knowledge and experience.

These relationships among sender, receiver, and information to be shared shape the form taken by the message. The following hypothetical situation illustrates how different relationships can shape, enlarge, or structure a message. Don and Bill walked out of Dr. Smith's classroom together after taking their midterm examination in child development. The following dialogue ensued:

Don: Boy, was that rotten! Didn't ask us one thing about formal operations.

Bill: Yeah, just covered the book.

Don: He always pulls something like that! Makes you mad!

That evening Don's mother called. The phone conversation started off this way:

Mother: How has your week been?

Don: Okay, I guess. I had an exam from Smith in child development. Boy, did he pull a fast one! All the questions on the book, not a single one on his lectures. And I spent all kinds of time going over the darn notes.

Mother: Didn't you know he'd ask questions about the book?

Don: All he said was that the exam would be multiple-choice.

Mother: What do you mean, multiple-choice?

Don: You know. You choose the right answer and mark a, b, c, d, or e.

Mother: Don't worry. You read the book, so you must have remembered a little something.

Don: Well, I sort of read it. It's hard to keep up with everything.

Mother: Maybe you should spend a little less time with Suzanne and a little more time with your books.

At the end of the term the students were asked to turn in written evaluations of their instructors. This is an excerpt of Don's evaluation of Professor Smith:

> As for Professor Smith's examinations, I found them to be extremely unfair. For example, the midterm was based entirely upon the readings assigned in the textbook. Materials discussed in the lectures were not included. I feel strongly that the examination should reflect the total content of the course and not just certain aspects of it.

The department head wrote a note to herself: "Student with a low grade? Check this out with Smith. Several students have been complaining about the kinds of exams he gives."

The preceding incidents illustrate several things about the structure of discourse. First, the distance between the sender and the receiver makes a difference in which kinds of information are shared and how the message is shaped. In the conversation between Don and Bill, when Don said "Boy, was that rotten," both students knew that he was referring to the exam they had just taken. Don assumed that Bill would understand and share his irritation with the exam and the professor. But Don's conversation with his mother shows some differences. There is a greater distance between the speaker and the listener. Don needed to explain who Professor Smith was and to justify his view that the exam was unfair. The distance between the sender and receiver became even greater when Don had to write to an unknown evaluator. Don chose different vocabulary and arranged his words in a more formal manner to express the same message.

In looking at the other side of the coin, the task of the receiver of the message changes with each of the previous examples of discourse. Bill and Don have just shared the experience of taking an exam. Bill immediately understands the message Don is sending. Bill's comments are simply offered to show that he shares Don's feelings. Since Don's mother did not have much information about the exam or the professor, she needed to ask some questions to learn more. She did, however, have a vast background of knowledge about Don. When she put her new information together with her past experiences, she quickly concluded that Don's social life was getting in the way of his scholastic life. The department head interpreted Don's evaluation in light of her past experiences with Professor Smith and with many other students.

Moffett and Wagner's model of discourse (page 18) shows us how the sender of a message abstracts and selects information which is then shaped to his or her purposes to share with a particular audience. The receiver then reconstructs and interprets the message that has been sent.

One vital element of discourse mentioned by Moffett and Wagner in their discussion but not made explicit in the model is the role of feedback. The questions, comments, and replies that occur between the speaker and the listener or the writer and the reader determine the ongoing communication. Nonverbal messages and even silences are also a part of the feedback a speaker receives and can serve to encourage or discourage elaboration. Through this interaction the message can be developed, expanded, formed, and reformed. Feedback changes messages from static entities to part of a dynamic discourse.

The need for feedback often occurs when there is a gap between the experiences, knowledge, perceptions, or understandings of the sender and those of the receiver. For example, Don's mother did not know Professor Smith, the materials studied, nor the term "multiple-choice." She needed to ask questions. When she had received what she felt was sufficient information, she formed some conclusions. The department head was unable to get immediate feedback, but made a note that more information was needed. Feedback, then, is one way of making sure that the message being sent is the same message that is being received.

There is also another aspect to feedback that has great significance. Feedback offered by the receiver can help shape the message being sent. In its simplest form, for example, a person may start to recount an event. A listener whose questions show a delighted response will draw forth a more elaborated and detailed narration than was originally intended. At its best feedback can

18   *Foundations of the Language Arts*

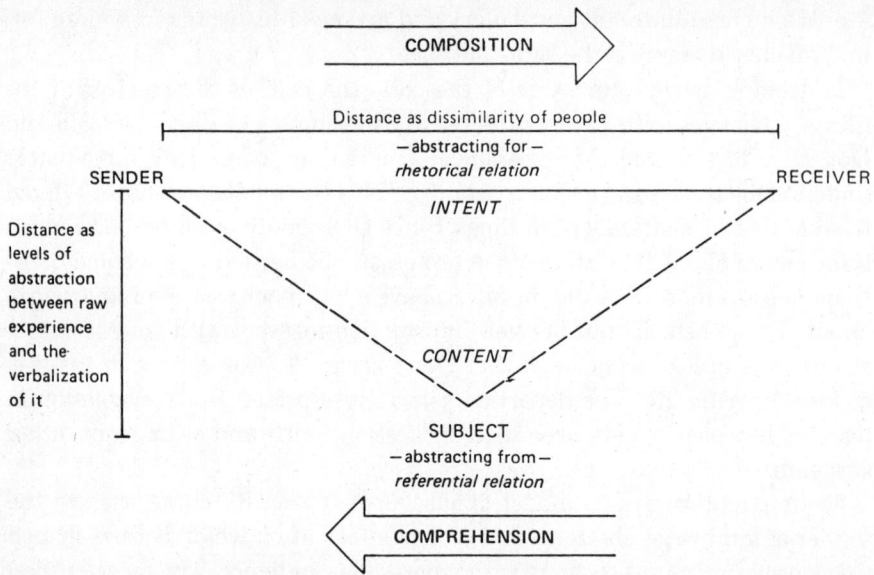

James Moffett and Betty Jane Wagner: *Student-Centered Language Arts and Reading, K–13,* 2nd ed., p. 15. Copyright © 1976 by Houghton Mifflin Company. Used by permission.

allow the sender and receiver to mesh their experiences, knowledge, and perceptions. This kind of dialogue permits the sender and receiver to exchange roles as they seek to broaden and deepen the area of shared meaning.

The notion of feedback has particular importance for a teacher. It is a vital part of communication. In setting up a classroom, the teacher must plan situations that will lead children to talk together in order to explore, define, and clarify ideas, as they provide feedback to each other. While talking with children, the teacher can offer the kinds of feedback that will encourage them to elaborate, focus on sequence, or describe precisely. At the same time, children's feedback will relay information that will deepen the teacher's knowledge about their concerns, abilities, and special strengths. Feedback, then, is an interactional process that permits both teacher and child to learn and develop new understandings from and about each other.

How Children Develop and Learn. The third area of our language-arts decision-making framework is how a child learns. Just as the sender constructs a message and the receiver actively works to reconstruct that message, so the child actively organizes experiences to develop a personal model of the world.

John, eighteen months old, was playing with his aunt in her garden when they heard the barking of the dog next door. "Doggie! Doggie!" cried John.

He raised his arms, gesturing for his aunt to lift him up so that he could see over the high hedge that separated her lawn from her neighbor's. When John caught sight of an enormous sheepdog his eyes grew wide. "Horsie?" he queried. The sheepdog barked again. "Doggie?" John asked, his forehead wrinkling with effort as he tried to attach a label to this large, four-footed, barking animal.

The sheepdog did not fit neatly into John's organization of prior experiences. He had assimilated the facts that although both dogs and horses have four legs, dogs bark and horses are large. What would a large, four-legged, barking animal be? John needed to accommodate his prior categorization schema to meet a new situation.

Even if his aunt tells John that what he is seeing is a dog, not a horse, his concept development will not be complete. His categories of dogs and horses were built upon hearing and seeing these animals in a variety of settings and from looking at pictures of them in books. John will need to see many large dogs and many small ponies and colts before he will have a fully developed understanding of what constitutes "horseness" and "dogness." This has implications for the teacher. If we examine the research of Piaget, which demonstrates that children actively seek information that they use to construct their own model of reality, we can see the need for many concrete experiences in the classroom.

Just as children develop concepts through experiences with which they organize and reorganize their version of the world, so do they develop an understanding of language. Language is acquired within a physical and social context of meaning in which children actively seek to abstract information about its nature. When children enter school, they know a great deal about language, its systems and functions. They know not only where and when they can speak, but also which kinds of language are appropriate for formal and informal situations.

Because the language experiences of different children can differ greatly, in any one classroom we can expect to find children who speak different dialects of English and some who are acquiring English as a second language. These language variations can create difficulty in understanding as the distance between speakers and listeners widens. This distancing is not limited to communication between one child and another but often includes the communication between a child and teacher. Through a series of shared experiences that are both concrete and abstract, a teacher can do much to shorten the distance between listener and speaker.

Child development forms a major component for language-arts curriculum planning. Teachers have to consider the physical abilities and characteristics of youngsters when deciding upon classroom seating arrangements, determining length of time spent in confining activities, and selecting tasks appropriate to the physical development of the child. For example, many first graders find painting at an easel with large brushes a successful way to express their thoughts. Few, however, would find such success in constructing mosaics, which requires fine motor control, a skill yet to be developed.

Children gain control in manipulating concepts as they develop cognitively. Teachers' selection of books, choice of extending activities, and expectations for children need to be in accord with what they know about the way in which their students perceive the world about them. Intermediate-grade students enjoy assuming a different point of view to retell a story, such as the wolf's version of *Little Red Riding Hood*. Young children adhere steadfastly to the original tale and many begin their retelling with the end of the story since that is most recent and, hence, most vivid in their minds.

Socially, children mature in establishing relationships with one another and with their teachers. Young children look to their teacher as the final authority—a vertical direction of power. Older children look to each other as peer groups gain authority—a horizontal direction of power. Teachers, aware of this shift, can apply students' sources of influence to extend interests. Reading-interest clubs for upper grades may build upon this aspect of social development as peers share books with each other.

Emotional development ties into social growth. As children approach adolescence, trying to find out who they are and where they belong in the world, their emotional security becomes unsettled. Peer perceptions become increasingly important and good social interaction a necessity. Projects that require cooperative efforts build upon youngsters' social skills and help them to view themselves as constructive members of a group.

Children's ability to use language continues to grow during their school years. They develop greater sensitivity to the way in which language functions in a variety of situations. Their vocabularies expand; syntax becomes more complex; conventions of written language are acquired; and reading fulfills continually advancing needs. Children develop in their ability to negotiate with language, argue and pursuade others, and to manipulate language to meet their own widening intentions. The learning context established in the classroom is central to continuing language development.

Thus, when considering child development as one of the components in establishing a framework for the language-arts curriculum, the entire realm of growth must be applied. Physical, cognitive, social/emotional, and language developmental patterns imply educational consequences for the teacher. Since children progress at different rates within these areas, individual assessment for teacher planning becomes an inherent part of the language-arts curriculum.

These youngsters developed a space station complete with landing site, living areas, and fuel supply banks. The language used in developing this project and explaining it to others was most complex, and they even developed a mural showing a space battle conflict. (Mrs. Kerstetter's classroom, Highland Park Elementary School, Grove City, Ohio)

How to Use the Book

Since the focus of the book is integration, we have organized the chapters so that no language-arts component is discussed alone. Therefore, writing and reading are woven together, as are listening and speaking. This format will support the reader by making clear both why integration is vital and how it can be achieved.

The organization of our book is not like the traditional text in this field. For example, it may seem strange to have to look for drama in the chapter on "Listening and Speaking," the chapter on "Reading and Writing," and the chapter on "Literature-Based Language Extensions." But the fact is, we really do believe that learning is an integrated act. Therefore, we cannot segment learning in order to present it to you and then ask that you find a way to integrate learning for children. Drama is in "Listening and Speaking" because it provides a need to listen to others, to take on new speech roles, and to focus on ways of using the voice. Drama is in the chapter on "Reading and Writing" because it permits the child to compose orally with the support of others and thus provides a strong base for written composition. The chapter on "Literature-Based Language Extensions" includes drama because drama assists children to explore a book in greater depth and to respond to that book in appropriate and satisfying ways.

Like drama, the subject of grouping is discussed in a number of places. We feel that grouping is basic to the language arts, for it is as children interact that language grows. Group experiences may be of many kinds—talking about books, constructing a model, composing a story, sharing information, and researching a report. Thus grouping is discussed in several contexts. However, you may wish to look at the subject of grouping in an in-depth way. Subject headings in the table of contents are designed to let you see at a glance in which chapters grouping is discussed at some length. The index will assist you in finding additional briefer comments.

A number of books offer a smorgasbord of ideas and present games to make learning fun. We do not believe that you have to "make" learning fun. Children love to learn and work very hard at it: just watch babies as they learn how to open a latch or sixth-graders mastering chess. Children are active learners who work diligently and with concentration on tasks that meet their needs and purposes and spring from their interests and concerns. So, while you will not find rules for spelling relay races or lists of "story starters" here, you will find, for example, ideas presented for assessing individual children's spelling errors so that you can base learning experiences on what children have shown that they need to know. Sections of the book contain suggestions for both oral and written language use that grow out of authentic rather than contrived experiences.

We have included much children's work, not just children's writing, but also transcriptions of conversations, discussions, and story retellings as well as artwork and classroom displays. These samples comprise a significant part of our text. We have based many of our discussions on children's language and other work. Thus the reading of dialogues or compositions becomes necessary to your understanding of the text. We believe that if teachers are to have the ability to build on children's knowledge, they need many opportunities to examine children's oral and written language and reflect upon what they discover there. Much of the work included is in the child's own handwriting, because this is what you, as teachers, will see in the classroom. In nearly all cases we have left work just as it was except in those few cases when misspelling or a lack of punctuation might have misled you.

We have analyzed what children have produced either orally or in writing not merely so that you can see what children have accomplished but so that you will also be able to view their work to decide for yourself what each child is focusing upon and therefore be better able to support his or her efforts. The artwork that accompanies some of the writing is important, for, through studying this type of expression, a teacher can see how a youngster is thinking about a concrete or abstract experience. The artwork can serve as a way to organize ideas or tender possible interpretations.

Ways of assessing and evaluating children's progress in language are included in each of the methodology chapters. Sometimes a list of questions is given; at other times a chart or grid is provided. In several instances a child's language, either oral or written, is analyzed to demonstrate how a teacher might evaluate the child's growth. For example, in Chapter 4, "Listening and Speaking," two protocols of children's storytelling are discussed to reveal what each child knows about language and about stories. Since one is a young child, age five, and the other an intermediate-level child, a comparison may be made between age levels.

There are several different kinds of activities at the end of the chapters. Some are designed to encourage you to interact with children in ways that will develop a deeper and a sharper awareness of what children are able to do. Other activities focus upon helping you understand processes such as language acquisition, writing, spelling, and responding to literature. Certain activities have been included to encourage interaction with other students, for, just as children learn by explaining, discussing, questioning, and sharing, so too do university students.

The list of annotated readings that concludes each chapter has been selected because it extends the ideas in the chapter in a way that we felt would interest many students. The list of professional references at the end of each chapter is longer and can serve as a resource for those who wish to explore a topic in greater depth. Children's books have been separated from the other references for easy referral.

Overview of the Chapters

The text has been divided into three major components. The first, "Foundations of the Language Arts," deals with the theoretical framework for integrating the language-arts strands, the need to build a supportive learning context, and the content knowledge teachers of the language arts must know. The second component, "Integration of the Language Arts," contains chapters that include descriptions of how to teach aspects of the language arts in an integrated curriculum. The final component, "Organization and Evaluation of the Language-Arts Program," contains professional resources for teachers and ways of planning and evaluating a program within a school district's guidelines.

A brief discussion of the intent behind each chapter is provided to help you better understand the text and how it may assist in your teaching. By gaining an overview of the book, you can develop certain expectations that can aid your reading.

Chapter 1 ("An Integrated Language-Arts Program: A Rationale") attempts to demonstrate how an integrated language-arts curriculum is initiated and planned. We present a rationale for teaching in this manner, showing that language occurs in a context that involves individuals' mutual interactions, their intents, and the shared environment in which their communication takes place. We present a discussion of the importance of an understanding of child development, language acquisition, and the nature of language itself.

Chapter 2 ("Language Learning: A Powerful Force") compares oral language development with development in writing. Although the oral and written language systems differ, their process of acquisition has similarities. The purpose of this chapter is to help teachers recognize growth in language skills and to understand the nature of language learning.

Chapter 3 ("Child Development: One Basis for Instructional Decisions") reveals how the developmental level of youngsters affects their responses to and perceptions of situations. One classroom may have students of a similar age but the spectrum of behaviors will have a wide range. Three aspects of development—cognitive, moral, and social—are examined in light of their implications for teachers of the language arts.

Chapter 4 ("Listening and Speaking") is the first of our methodology chapters and combines two strands of the language arts in its presentation. This chapter focuses upon the act of discourse, which involves both listening and speaking, and the significance of the context in which the discourse occurs. A chart of basic competencies in discourse is provided. In addition, the difference between language to communicate and language to learn is discussed.

Chapter 5 ("Writing and Reading: The Beginnings") reveals the growing awareness of print, which children acquire by listening to stories, looking at books, and observing the printed word around them. The relationship between writing and reading may be seen in the title of this chapter, for many children begin to write before they read. Initial work on the conventions of print such as spelling and handwriting are described, as well as the development of one child's writing over a year's time.

Chapter 6 ("Reading and Writing: On the Way") looks at the children who have acquired some degree of fluency in literacy. Once again the title reflects the stage of development, for these youngsters are able to use their reading experiences in their writing, not just for topic ideas but also for more subtle input, such as style and sentence structures. The role and value of conferences are discussed, as are ways to respond to writing.

Chapter 7 ("Language Arts in the Content Areas") takes one theme, weather, as an example and shows how language arts can become an integral part of the subject area curriculum. How to web, keep records, and organize for work are described. The second part of this chapter discusses language as a content area. We have delineated concepts of language that are important for children to understand and have included ways to help children become aware of them.

Chapter 8 ("Literature-Based Language Extensions") focuses on extensions from literature rather than the content of children's literature. Drama, writing, oral responses, and reading are described as an outgrowth of literary experiences. Themes derived from one book are discussed and an illustration is given. A guide for observing children's interaction with books is included.

Chapter 9 ("Second-Language Learning and the Language Arts") contrasts the acquisition of a first and a second language as one way of assisting the teacher of a child who does not yet speak English. Many regular classroom teachers are faced with the arrival of some children who speak a language other than English. An awareness of the difference between "learning a second language" and "acquiring a second language" can free the teacher from the need to teach English as a second language in a formal way and instead develop a classroom rich with opportunities for language growth.

Chapter 10 ("Program Planning and Evaluation") recognizes the need to work within the school district's guidelines and move from a separate subject curriculum toward an integrated school day. Objectives from one district are presented as an example and then used to show how they might be applied within an integrated curriculum. Ways of communicating the program with others are discussed and examples of classroom newsletters are given. Evaluating the language-arts program constitutes a major portion of the chapter, for evaluation is an important basis for teacher and child growth.

Chapter 11 ("Instructional Resources") acknowledges the wide variety of resources available to the teacher. Ways of developing as a professional are given as well as sources for selecting books for children. Criteria in the form of questions to evaluate children's language-arts textbooks are listed with a discussion of samples from two texts.

Suggested Learning Experiences

1. In small groups discuss the kinds of language-arts program you had in elementary school. What opportunities for speaking did you have? for listening? for writing?

2. Think of the classes you are taking presently. In which classes do you feel most free to talk? In which classes are you most reluctant to speak? What are the reasons for the difference?

3. What questions do you have about how children learn language? Jot them down before you read the next chapter and see if they are answered. If not, look at the resources at the end of the chapter or ask your instructor.

Recommended Readings

Shuy, Roger W., "What the Teacher Knows Is More Important Than Text or Test." *Language Arts,* 58:919–930, November/December, 1981.
    Shuy's article addresses the issue of what teachers should know if they are to provide effective instruction. In this age of brightly packaged learning programs, Shuy points out why no program, no matter how painstakingly designed or carefully sequenced, can ever replace the knowledgeable teacher. His discussion of the kinds of knowledge a teacher needs will be especially thought provoking to those embarking on a course of professional studies.

Platt, Nancy G., "Social Context: An Essential for Learning." *Language Arts,* 56:620–627, September, 1979.
    A journey to England to visit informal classrooms provided the impetus for this article. The author was struck by the many ways in which teachers were able to bring the familiar home experiences into the classroom to provide a link to new learnings. Platt's numerous examples and clear discussion will show the reader how such a classroom allows children to continue to develop their language as they do at home, naturally and purposefully.

Genishi, Celia, "Language Across the Contexts of Early Childhood." *Theory into Practice,* 20:109–115, Spring, 1981.
    From the chapter you have just read, it is evident that language is embedded in context. Genishi summarizes the research that has been done on the contexts that surround young children as they develop language in both home and school settings. In this clear and thorough article the author makes explicit the relationships between theory and practice.

References

Professional Literature

Moffett, James and Wagner, Betty Jane, *Student-Centered Language Arts, K-13*, 2nd ed., Houghton Mifflin, Boston, 1976.

Platt, Nancy G., "Social Context: An Essential for Learning," *Language Arts* 56:620–627, September, 1979.

Rosen, Connie and Rosen, Harold, *The Language of Primary School Children*, Penguin Education, Harmondsworth, England, 1973.

Shuy, Roger W., "A Holistic View of Language," *Research in the Teaching of English* 15:101–111, May, 1981.

Children's Literature

Brady, Irene, *A Mouse Named Mus*, Houghton Mifflin, Boston, 1972.

———, *Wild Mouse*, Scribner, New York, 1976.

Brown, Marcia, *Once A Mouse*, Scribner, New York, 1961.

Coatsworth, Elizabeth, "The Mouse" from *The Mouse Book* compiled and edited by Richard Shaw, Frederick Warne and Co., Inc., New York, 1975.

Conkling, Hilda, "Mouse" from *Poems by a Little Girl*, Stokes, 1920.

Flack, Marjorie, *Walter the Lazy Mouse*, illustrated by Cyndy Szekeres, Doubleday, New York, 1963.

Freschet, Berenice, *Bear Mouse*, illustrated by Donald Carrick, Scribner, New York, 1973.

Fyleman, Rose, "Mice" from *The Mouse Book* compiled and edited by Richard Shaw, Frederick Warne and Co., Inc., New York, 1975.

Hess, Lila, *Mouse and Company*, Scribner, New York, 1972.

Lawson, Robert, *Ben and Me*, Little, Brown, Boston, 1951 (1939).

Lionni, Leo, *Frederick*, Pantheon, New York, 1967.

———, *Alexander and the Windup Mouse*, Pantheon, New York, 1969.

———, *The Greentail Mouse*, Pantheon, New York, 1973.

O'Brien, Robert C., *Mrs. Frisby and the Rats of NIMH*, illustrated by Zene Bernstein, Atheneum, New York, 1971.

Steig, William, *Amos and Boris*, Farrar, Straus and Giroux, New York, 1971.

———, *Abel's Island*, Farrar, Straus and Giroux, New York, 1976.

Stolz, Mary, *Belling the Tiger*, illustrated by Beni Montresor, Harper & Row, New York, 1961.

Titus, Eve, *Anatole*, illustrated by Paul Galdone, McGraw-Hill, New York, 1956.

White, E. B. *Stuart Little*, illustrated by Garth Williams, Harper & Row, New York, 1945.

The Nature of Language
Language Systems

How Oral Language Is Learned
Language Development of Young Children
Language Development of School-Age Children
Summing up the Process

Written Language Development
Scribbling
Message Writing
Writing Explorations
Beginning to Spell
The Developing Writer
Summing up the Process

Implications of Oral and Written Language Development

Language Usage Varies
Functions of Language
Register
Dialect
Second-Language Learners
Implications of Language Variation

Summary

Suggested Learning Experiences

Recommended Readings

References
Professional Literature

Chapter 2

Language Learning: A Powerful Force

The following two conversations between a child and an adult grew out of the same experience—watching the third voyage of the space shuttle *Columbia* on television.

Chris, Age Five

Chris: I don't know anything about the space shuttle, but my dad does.
Adult: Oh?
Chris: He watches the news but I don't watch the news. I hate the news.
Adult: Why?
Chris: It's so boring. But my dad watches the news because he's a policeman. He has to know about the space shuttle.
Adult: So your dad knows a lot.
Chris: He knows all about it. He reads newspapers and magazines about it, too. He works hard, you know.
Adult: About the space shuttle?
Chris: Yeah, you know, he knows all about it but doesn't tell me. I don't watch the news.

It is clear that Chris is a competent conversationalist who can sustain a conversation and keep an adult's attention. Even though his knowledge and his interest in the space shuttle is limited, Chris attempts to relate what he does know to his own background of experience. The space shuttle is news and news appears in newspapers and magazines in addition to the television news programs. He does not watch, read, or like news but his father does, and Chris knows his father. Thus, Chris has shifted the topic of conversation so that it focuses not upon the space shuttle, about which he knows little, but to his father, about whom he knows a great deal. This shift in topic focus reveals that this five-year-old is adept at interaction. The language used is childlike in tone and structure; Chris uses simple words and uncomplicated sentence structures.

Patrick, Age Twelve

Adult: I heard a bit at the end of a news report that said there were some problems with the space shuttle.
Patrick: Yeah. Some of the tiles are coming off the ship.
Adult: The tiles?

Patrick:	The protective covering on the spaceship—like asbestos when it meets fire.
Adult:	That sounds awfully dangerous!
Patrick:	No, it really has no bearing. Below the sear line it would be dangerous.
Adult:	Sear line?
Patrick:	On re-entry, that's where it's very, very hot. When they reenter, they're at an angle so that the tiles on the bottom, below the sear line, are very hot.
Adult:	Uh huh.
Patrick:	And the tiles above it aren't as hot.
Adult:	How did they find out about the tiles?
Patrick:	They have cameras attached all over to record what's happening.
Adult:	I thought I heard the cameras weren't working.
Patrick:	Just some of the cameras are broken. They're not functioning properly on the arm.

These two conversations are juxtaposed to give you a view of the vast strides children make in language during the elementary years. Patrick's conversation is in direct contrast to Chris's in several ways. First, Patrick has a great deal of knowledge about the space shuttle and because of this he can and does focus in directly on the topic. Another interesting difference in this conversation is that it is the adult who is primarily seeking to sustain the communication since the adult is seeking information. Patrick cooperates by responding; this interchange, however, does little for him except allow him to show what he knows and give him the opportunity to interact. Clearly, the interaction is limited by the adult's lack of knowledge.

An analysis of this twelve-year-old's conversation reveals that Patrick's language use closely approximates adult speech. The sentence structures are complex: "When they reenter, they're at an angle so that the tiles on the bottom, below the sear line, are very hot." The vocabulary is precise and diverse: "re-entry, sear line, protective covering, asbestos, functioning." In addition, he has confidence in his knowledge and knows how to disagree with an adult for, when the adult comments, "That sounds awfully dangerous," he replies, "No, it really has no bearing," and offers an explanation.

How did Patrick gain such linguistic knowledge during his elementary school years? And how did Chris come to know so much about language before he entered school? What is the teacher's role in this process? To understand children's developing competence in language, it is important to first recognize the nature of the task; that is, to learn about language itself.

The Nature of Language

Language, more than anything else, sets humankind apart from animals. Although many animals have the ability to communicate, they cannot communicate with the precision and flexibility that human language permits. A dog can wag its tail to tell his returning master, "I'm so glad you've come home," but it cannot also tell him "While you were gone, the telephone rang and woke me up from my nap." Bees can tell other bees where they have found nectar, but they cannot recount the adventures they had while discovering that nectar. Human language is not bound by the immediate physical context. Even young children are able to talk about their dreams or discuss their hopes for what Christmas will bring.

Researchers have taught chimpanzees to communicate through signing (Fleming, 1974). These animals have even shown an ability to use language in creative ways, such as coining new words and putting words together to form sentences they have not been taught. But again, one must note a difference. The chimpanzee must be painstakingly taught while the human infant acquires language simply through interaction with members of a speech community. This almost magical ability of the very young child to learn a complex language system has caused Chukovsky (1963) to refer to the child as a "linguistic genius." The difficulty of the task facing the infant acquiring language becomes even more apparent as the nature of language is examined.

Language is an arbitrary set of symbols. What is called "a house" in English is labeled *una casa* in Spanish, *une maison* in French, and *ein Haus* in German. Nothing is inherent in a dwelling that makes the word "house" especially appropriate. "House" is simply an arbitrary set of sounds that the English-speaking community has agreed to accept as a symbol for that particular building.

Another illustration of this arbitrary quality of language is seen in an examination of the sounds animals make. If one were to ask American children what a dog says, they would probably reply, "bow wow." French dogs, however, say *"ouah ouah"* and Russian dogs say *"vaf vaf."* While roosters in American barnyards greet the dawn with *"cock-a-doodle-doo,"* their French cousins cry *"cocorico"* and their Russian relatives shreik *"kukwika."*

Written language is also made up of arbitrary symbols. While English writing uses the letters A B C D, the Russians use АБВГ , and ك ى ب أ is the way these same letters are written in Arabic. The Chinese do not use letters at all but characters that stand for whole words or ideas. In English, writing begins at the top left-hand corner of the page and moves toward the right while Arabic and Hebrew are written right to left. The Chinese begin at the top right side of the page and move down rather than across and, like the Japanese, begin reading at the back of the book (to us), progressing to the front.

From these examples we can see that language is arbitrary, but it is also systematic. The systematic nature of language makes it predictable and it is this predictability that allows children to learn how to use and to understand language.

By predictability, we mean that language has a structure that can be discovered. If you learned a second language in high school, in all probability you were taught the structure of that language. You learned how tenses are formed, genders are indicated, and verbs are conjugated. On the other hand, when you acquired your native language, you discovered the structure of that language without formal lessons.

As teachers develop better understandings of how language is organized, they will recognize the vast amount of linguistic knowledge that children have acquired before they enter school. Lindfors (1980) points out that such understandings will help teachers to differentiate between teaching children their language and teaching children to read their language, and between assessing children's ability to talk about language and their ability to use language. Such distinctions are vital if teachers are to develop language-arts programs that allow children to increase their range of language uses and to deepen and extend their vocabulary.

Language Systems

Language is comprised of a variety of systems both within language itself and beyond or above language. To begin, we will look at systems within language so that you as teachers will recognize the enormity of the task children assume as they learn to control language.

Phonology. Phonology refers to the study of the sound system in language. As an example, *sard,* though a nonsense syllable, could be an English word, for it follows a pattern heard in other words such as *card, hard,* and *lard.*

However, one would not expect to find *nzr* as a word in an English dictionary because in English one can predict that there will be at least one vowel sound in a word. Further, there are only certain combinations of letters permitted in English. The letter "t" in an initial position in a word may be followed by a vowel or "h," "r," or "w," but by no other consonant. So while "twip" is not an English word, it could be; but "tlap" could not.

Each language has a finite set of sounds and speakers tune in only to those sounds, which make a meaningful difference in that language. Such sounds are called *phonemes* but not all the sounds in a language are phonemes. For instance, the /p/ heard in the word "pin" is an aspirated /p/—pronounced with a puff of air. The /p/ heard in the word "spin" is an unaspirated /p/—pronounced with no accompanying puff of air. You can try this out for yourself if you pronounce both words while holding your hand in front of your mouth. Since there are no English words in which aspiration makes a difference in meaning, English speakers are not aware of this particular change in sound. Think of the problems beginning readers encounter when asked to give the "p" sound in order to decode a word. Which "p" sound? Even further, notice how your mouth moves when you say the phoneme /m/ in "name" versus "mane." Again, which /m/ do you decide to use? Notice how the phoneme /k/ must be articulated differently in "*k*ick" versus "*c*ool." These variations found within a phoneme cluster are called *allophones*. Allophones are deviations within a phoneme that remain unrecognized by native speakers but may pose problems to second-language learners.

Other small variations do change meaning, and so one is aware of them. The only difference in the two sounds /s/ and /z/ is the element of voicing. Both sounds are articulated in exactly the same way—by forcing a stream of air through the teeth. When /z/ is pronounced, however, the vocal cords are vibrated; a small addition, but in this case it makes a great difference, as can be heard in such pairs of words as:

sip/zip
sink/zinc
Sue/zoo

Linguists call such pairs of words "minimal pairs" because one single sound changes meaning. Sometimes dialect variations are the result of the use of different sets of minimal pairs. "Are" and "our" may be pronounced the same by one group, while "hour" and "our" form the homophone pair for another. Teachers may see the influence of minimal-pair dialectal influences in spelling as well as oral language use. Think how children with dialects other than the teacher's may become confused if phonics lessons are given!

Morphology. Morphology deals with the study of the smallest meaningful unit of language. To understand this system, take the following test. Fill in the blanks.

1. I zib today. Yesterday I did the same thing. Yesterday I _____.
2. I had one prin. Someone gave me another. Now I have two _____.

All of us who are English speakers will respond, "Yesterday I zibbed" and "Now I have two prins." We know that when /d/ is added to certain verbs those verbs acquire a past tense, and that when /z/ is added to some nouns those nouns become plural. The /d/ and /z/ phonemes are examples of inflectional morphemes. Other inflectional morphemes in English mark possession, person, and the comparative. In each case their addition focuses the meaning of the original morpheme in a specific way. Derivational morphemes, however, can change a word by moving it from one word class to another. For example, the verb "break" can become a noun when the morpheme "age" is added as a suffix. Just as a phoneme is the smallest unit of sound that changes meaning, a *morpheme* is the smallest part of expression that carries meaning. Some units are called free morphemes, for they stand alone. "Turn" is a free morpheme, but its meaning can be changed when other morphemes are added, as seen in such words as:

turned	returnable
turns	turnpike
turning	turntable
return	turnstile

Morphemes such as "re," "ed," and "ing" are called bound morphemes because they cannot stand alone. Free morphemes may sometimes be joined together to change meaning as in the case of "turntable," "turnpike," and "turnstile."

Morpheme study can be a powerful way to extend vocabulary. For example, when you know that the prefix *anti* means "opposite" or "against," then you can recognize the general sense of a word beginning with "anti-." The same principle works with free morphemes that serve as root words or cognates. *Graph* means "something that writes or describes"; when it is combined with bound morphemes, however—resulting in words such as "graphic," "telegraph," and "phonograph"—the morpheme "graph" gains new meanings.

Syntax. The order in which words are put together to express meaning is the syntax of a language. A nonsense sentence can demonstrate the importance of word order.

The sniggle mipped the darp.

Many times test questions can be answered on the basis of syntax alone; for example, any speaker of English will be able to tell the sniggle did the mipping and that the darp was mipped, for in English one very common sentence pattern follows the order of subject/verb/direct object. Clay (1968) reports that beginning readers correct their own reading errors mainly on the basis of syntactic changes. Children are very sensitive to and aware of the syntax of language.

Semantics. Finally, there is the semantic system of language, based on meaning. Here, too, speakers are able to make predictions. For example, the sentence "John ate the cookie" follows the pattern noun/verb/noun. But not just any noun will fit into the subject slot. While one would not be surprised to hear:

John ate the cookie.
The boy ate the cookie.
He ate the cookie.
The dog ate the cookie.

one would not expect to hear:

The book ate the cookie.
The chair ate the cookie.
The tree ate the cookie.

Obviously, the verb "to eat" requires not only a subject but an animate one as well, alive and able to digest cookies.

Children's growth in both the amount of vocabulary and the depth of meaning attached to that vocabulary was seen in the two conversations that began this chapter. Five-year-old Chris had only the vaguest notion of the term *space shuttle*. Twelve-year-old Patrick had a clear concept of this craft, as well as the precise and technological vocabulary that enabled him to share his knowledge. Clark (1973) suggests that one aspect of children's growth in this area of language may occur as they add semantic features to the categories they are developing. For example, for some very young children, "car" may be the label attached to any four-wheeled vehicle. Later they will add further features that will help them differentiate cars from trucks and buses. Eventually the category of cars will be broken down still further as the children learn to distinguish a Volkswagen from a Rolls Royce or a

Honda from a Ford. The categories may also go the opposite direction, that is, grouping by larger categories, i.e., racing versus family cars.

Semantic knowledge grows throughout our life, as old words acquire new layers of meaning and as new experiences require new terminology. Lindfors (1980) states that it is in the semantic domain that children's growth is most vigorous during the elementary school years. Teachers who provide an environment that allows children to explore the new, to work with the concrete, and to hear and read rich language will provide the base for such language growth. Opportunities to talk with others about what they are observing and learning and to write about experiences and ideas will help children develop greater control over this aspect of language.

This brief discussion of the systems of language illustrates that even though the symbols that make up language are arbitrary, they are used in systematic ways. Learners of a language, therefore, are able to predict how their language will work and to generate sentences they have never heard before. Even though we have treated the systems separately, language in use combines them at all times.

How Oral Language Is Learned

Language Development of Young Children

Not only do children create sentences they have never before heard, the structures of those sentences may differ from the structures found in adult speech. Menyuk (1963) studied the language of preschool children and found when she analyzed the language model these children were using that it differed from that of adults. Children were generating their own grammatical model of language. Slobin and Welsh (1973) examined the grammar use of young children by asking them to repeat sentences. They found that the children they observed could repeat a sentence if it fit in with their own construct of grammar, but if the sentence were structured in a way different from the children's grammar, the youngsters would alter their responses in order to make them fit their own grammatical model. The main point about these two studies is that children generate their own interim grammars to govern language. Even though they understand utterances in other forms, their speech conforms to their own grammar system. Over time their model will approximate more and more closely the adult language that surrounds them.

Why does the child search out the regularities of language? Halliday (1975) contends that children are trying to make sense of the world about them. They are learning "to mean." The way children manage the world is to understand the language that surrounds them and use that language to relate to others. The child tackles this enormous task very early in life. Even in the babbling stages of language, before saying words infants have begun to acquire the intonation patterns of their own language. A trained linguist, focusing on intonation patterns, can listen to tapes of the babbling of babies of different nationalities and identify which baby will eventually speak French, which English, and which Swahili. Even at this very early stage in life, babies have begun to identify some of the patterns of their language. The search for regularities in language truly begins in the crib.

For three months Weir (1962) tape-recorded her two-and-a-half-year-old son as he talked to himself before dropping off to sleep. She found that he practiced language in ways surprisingly like the techniques used by foreign language teachers to drill their students. He did "expansion drills" as in this monologue:

Block
Yellow block
Look at the yellow block

He substituted words within a pattern sentence:

What color
What color blanket
Go get some coffee
What color map
What color glasses
Go buy some coffee (Dale, 1972).

It is easy to see why Chukovsky (1963) said, "In truth, the young child is the hardest mental toiler on our planet" (p. 10).

As the child approaches his or her first birthday, one-word utterances appear. "Mama" and "Dada" are words that will catch the attention of the persons who matter most. Other words soon follow, such as "milk," "doggie," "cookie," "car," and "bye-bye." These words, or others like them, mark objects, activities, or events that are important in the child's life. One-word utterances are, however, much more than a simple labeling. When a child holds up an empty mug and says, "Milk," it may mean, "May I have some more milk?" The same utterance made when the mug has been overturned and the child points to the white puddle on the floor might mean "Hey, look where my milk is now!" The meaning of the word alters with the occasion.

Bloom (1970) found that in order to study the beginning speech of children, it is vital to study the context of the language as well, for she found that the grammatical function changes according to the meaning the child intends.

As children become a little older, eighteen months or so, words are combined in order to focus the communication more sharply. Utterances such as the following are typical:

Daddy go car.
Cookie all gone.
My boat.
More milk.

This type of language is called telegraphic speech because the child uses only the most important words and lets the listener supply the rest. Even this shortened form of language shows that children know how words are related.

Quite early children discover the morphological system of language; they come to understand it so well that they overgeneralize. The child who says "I put the socks on my foots" uses "foots" not because that child has heard others use that word, but because it follows a pattern found in such words as "cats," "books," and "cups" (Cazden, 1972). This tendency to act in rule-governed behavior is so strong that children will drop adult forms such as "went" for the past tense of "go" and use "goed" in its place for a period of time. Gradually, the youngsters learn to accept irregular forms, thus more closely approximating adult speech (Berko, 1967).

Berko (1958) studied children's acquisition of inflectional endings by devising a test that used nonsense words. As one item in the test she would show the child a picture of a strange-looking creature and tell the child that it was a "wug." Then she would hold up a picture of two of the same creatures and ask the child what was in the picture. Children would usually say that they saw "two wugs." While this test may sound quite simple, few adults would be able to state correctly the rule for the formation of plurals in English. Most people would quickly state that one simply adds the letter "s" to the singular, for they would be thinking of the written form; however, the phonological rules are much more complex. One adds /əz/ to a word that ends with a sibilant sound ("boxes"), /z/ to a word that ends in a voiced consonant or a vowel sound ("dogs"), and /s/ to a word that ends in an unvoiced consonant ("coats"). Berko found that by age six most children are able to handle all the complex rules for inflections—a sizable accomplishment.

The attention of child language researchers has shifted from rate and stages of acquisition to variations of language in use. This change has focused upon interactional language and the social settings in which it takes place.

While studying infants three to eighteen months, Snow (1977) found that mothers talk most to their children while in a face-to-face position. They use a conversational model and adjust their speech as the child becomes more able to function as a conversational partner. Interestingly, the mothers in this study talked least to their offspring while feeding them, thus recognizing that interchange is impaired when eating takes place.

A mother's language is influenced by a child's response quite early, according to Lindfors (1980). Adults adjust their language to fit the age of the respondent and to their visible reactions, whether they be sounds or actions. Shorter, simpler sentences appear and contextual support, that is, the events in the here and now, are used heavily. Repetitions occur and the intonational pattern is exaggerated. The language is *not* "baby talk," but an adjusted version of conversation, where the goal is an exchange and a continuance of meaning. One of the initial conversational concepts infants learn is "turn-taking." Thus, language acquisition consists of more than linguistic structures; it embodies developing "communicative competence," a term coined by Hymes (1972), which means the ability to interact verbally according to principles of the social appropriateness of language use.

Shugar (1978) points out that texts (including conversation) are constructed jointly and that with very young children the burden of interaction rests upon the adult, who must identify the child's meaning and establish it as a shared focus for building a text. Amazingly, before the child can put two words together, the interchange of conversation already appears. Shugar suggests that more than knowledge of linguistic structure is occurring; there is also a transmittal of socialization, and thus acculturation is taking place. Cook-Gumperz (1979) states that such talk provides a framework for understanding and presenting social information to others. "Therefore, conversation provides not only the context in which linguistic skills are learned, but also the actual experience of constituting relationships" (p. 212).

Wells (1979) emphasizes the interactive nature of children learning to control the systems of language and sees language as but one part of the context. He points out that meaning is negotiated, representing a compromise between the intentions of the two participants. The parent serves as a coach in the communicative act (Cook-Gumperz) assisting children to converse with others. Wells reports a relationship between the extent to which parents accept and extend children's verbal initiations to children's level of linguistic development upon school entrance and to eventual reading achievement.

All of this research supports the thesis that the contexts in which language occurs shape not only the language that appears, but also what is learned from the experience. Teachers need to be concerned with "tuning in" on their students' meaning when talking *with* rather than talking *to* their students.

Language Development of School-Age Children

The most apparent change one notes while talking and listening to school-age children is how the sheer volume of language produced increases. Descriptions contain greater detail; narratives become more complex; and explanations are more complete.

Youngsters become clearer in their articulation of speech sounds. Some phonemes appear to be more difficult to produce, such as /l/, /r/, /th/, and /s/. It is not unusual to find a kindergartner who says, while pointing to a picture of a red wagon, "wittle wed wagon." Almost all of these approximations of phonemes fade naturally as children mature. There is no speech problem; this is merely a developmental pattern.

When children lose their "baby teeth," especially the two in front, certain phonemes can create problems. A lisp may occur because /s/ and /th/, for example, require the front teeth for articulation. This passing phonological stage has been the source of many humorous stories and jokes. It is an expected event and only a problem if treated as one. Some particularly shy children may not wish to speak to large groups at this time but most are not bothered by their new sounds. They enjoy the effect.

Children also develop in their ability to distinguish among phonemes. Wepman (1960) found that most youngsters could not differentiate among all the consonant sounds until they were seven years of age. Yet most children learn to read before this age, which demonstrates that reading is not a sounding-out process but a meaning-gaining procedure. Reading programs that require children to learn the sounds of language before reading words do not follow the research.

Production and reception of phonemes are important distinctions. Whereas children may produce "little" as "wittle," they often can hear the difference. The change in how children produce the sound may be developmental, as discussed earlier, or a temporary physical phenomenon, such as missing teeth.

School-age youngsters have learned to apply all the basic rules of inflectional endings but overgeneralization appears quite commonly among five-, six-, and seven-year-olds. Several fish may still be "fishes" and "sheeps" may be grazing in the pasture. Later, morphological development occurs in writing when children overgeneralize and learn to refine spelling patterns.

Another aspect of morphological development is children's exploration of how the function of a word may be changed. Can this noun be made a modifier by the addition of an "ish"? The answer is yes for "boy," "child," or "woman" but not for "garden," "table," or "fish." Does the adjective acceptably become an adverb with "ly"? "Happy" may become "happily" and "sad" "sadly," but "red" cannot become "redly" nor "big" "bigly."

Besides changing the function of words, additional meanings may be attached. School-age children develop a greater awareness of bound morphenes such as "pre-," "dis-," and "demi-" and use them both to understand and create new words. Some words in their vocabularies gain generalized use, whereas others become more limited and specific in scope. For example, some children may understand "teacher" to mean only the person in charge in a school classroom and not comprehend the larger meaning of teacher as a role any person may assume in a given situation. Other youngsters may label all broad-winged insects "butterflies" and not differentiate them from moths. In the same vein, "worms" are commonly used for all footless, crawling creatures, including the caterpillar. Another source of vocabulary growth is simply new words. A child's repertoire of words is his or her *lexicon* and an individual word in the lexicon is a *lexical entry*.

Semantic development is closely related to the study of a child's expanding lexicon because of its focus on meaning. The appropriate meaning for a word is selected on the basis of the words surrounding it; that is, the syntactic structure and combined semantic input. Thus, "box" is understood as a verb when it occurs in the sentence "The winner of the Golden Gloves bout will *box* in our city next week" and as a noun in the sentence "Put the shoes in this *box*."

Children learn to organize information in order to participate in a conversation, give directions, debate an issue, and tell a story. These larger units of meaning are complex structures at the discourse level and may be analyzed as a whole rather than word by word or within a sentence. Children learn to construct and reconstruct the meaning by developing a set of discourse structures. For example, to hold a conversation successfully, the speakers must know how to begin, agree on a topic, be able to request further information, know when topics may be shifted, and sense the interest of their audience. This structure of a conversation is determined by the meaning within the discourse and, as such, the conversation is part of a set of structures above the sentence level that guide and direct the language used in the speech or writing act.

School-age children become adept at conversing and are said to be growing in their "social skills." They learn to give precise sequential directions and follow unstated but clear rules in composing a variety of story types such as folk tales, survival adventures, and mystery capers. But school interaction that involves teachers contrasts with earlier parent/child interaction. Whereas early language exchanges have the adult focus in on the child's meaning and build the discourse on that basis, DeStefano, Pepinsky, and Sanders (1982) found the teacher in their study to demand, command, question, and exhort with the result of single-word responses rather than meaningful dialogues. It should be noted that these researchers focused their investigation on language that occurred in reading-instruction lessons. The point remains, however, that typical school language does not provide the reciprocal language situations between adult and child that is available for child language learning in the home.

In looking at the syntax of school-age children, Strickland (1962) found that by the time children enter school, they are able to produce all the basic sentence structures. This does not mean children do not continue to grow in their control of syntax. The developmental difference appears in the usage pattern of these structures.

Another change occurs in syntactic complexity. As children mature, their clauses often become longer and greater use of subordinate clauses occurs. The meaningful syntactic unit expands. Hunt (1965) termed this the T-unit measurement, the main clause plus all subordinate clauses. Instead of linking main clauses together with coordinators, such as "and," children increasingly embed ideas within clauses and form clauses subordinate to a main clause. For example, "The student read his book. The book was *Call It Courage*."

> Coordination: The student read his book and the book was *Call It Courage*.
>
> Embedding by a subordinate clause: The student read his book, which was *Call It Courage*.
>
> Embedding within a clause: The student read his book, *Call It Courage*.

O'Donnell, Griffin, and Norris (1967) found an increase in the number of subordinating connectors such as "while," "as," and "although" in older youngsters' narratives, which made their syntax more complex. By applying the T-unit measurement to children's narrative language in kindergarten, first, second, third, fifth, and seventh grades, they found a chronological increase in the average number of words per T-unit. They also reported that syntactic growth is significantly higher between kindergarten and first grade and between fifth and seventh grades. The T-unit as a measure of language growth will be discussed in greater detail within the language assessment section.

New syntactic structures, more subtle and complex than basic sentence

44 *Foundations of the Language Arts*

structures, enter school-age children's language. One example, although questioned by some (see Lindfors, 1980, p. 151, for references), is an exception to the minimal-distance principle. In most cases the noun preceding an infinitive is its subject. Thus in the sentence "The cat caused the mouse to hide" the animal that hid was the mouse. In a few instances, however, the preceeding noun is not the infinitive's subject. For example, "Marcia promised Jim to sing." Who's going to sing? Marcia, not Jim. Chomsky (1969) found that young elementary school children overgeneralized the minimal-distance principle, consistently choosing the noun preceding the infinitive as its subject. Middle-grade youngsters were more flexible with this rule, recognizing that the verbs "promise" and "tell" alter the position of the infinitive's subject.

Other later-acquired forms which often include not only syntactic but also semantic constraints, are passive constructions, negation, and comparatives. Although children learn important and basic syntactic structures before school age, growth in syntax continues.

In this situation, a non-native speaker is interacting with a teacher and a native English speaker. The conversational exchange allows both to assess their own attempts at communicating. If the environment is positive, the feedback may not indicate a failure but show that further attempts are necessary. (Mrs. Jackson's classroom, Cranbrook School, Columbus, Ohio)

Summing up the Process

The process of initial language acquisition and language development is simple in principle but complex in occurrence. Children learn language through an active search for meaning within their language environment. Appropriate uses and the functions of language within a social context are discovered. Youngsters process this linguistic data to formulate rules or hypotheses about the systems that comprise the ways in which language works. These hypotheses are tested in real-life situations and the rules are often practiced in language play. Feedback on the rules developed and hypotheses formed occurs in a variety of contexts. Children seemingly ask themselves, do others understand what I am saying? Would this particular character in the current play situation speak in this way? Is my language accepted by others?

This process of language acquisition is the same for all children in sequence even though the rate of learning these rules varies. In fact, the trait is universal. All children, whether their native speech be English, French, or Polish, acquire knowledge about their language in the same rule-generating process.

Written Language Development

Written language differs from oral language in many significant ways. Syntax becomes more complex, some different kinds of vocabulary appear, and the suprasegmental system—stress, pitch, juncture—found only in oral language changes most often to punctuation. Educators who define writing as "talk written down" are challenged by their peers and linguists. The differences make that statement too simple to be true for even children recognize that the forms are not the same. This is evidenced by the change that occurs when they dictate stories to be written down. Vocabulary and syntax are altered; they speak more slowly, enunciating each word clearly.

Even though the two modes, oral and written, differ, there exist similarities in the way in which children acquire them. Just as in oral language development, children process the written language about them, make hypotheses about the systems within, test and practice their hypotheses, and finally revise on the basis of the feedback they receive.

This section contains samples of children's writing from the early scribbling to the beginnings of middle school, that is, from ages two to eleven years of age. You may wish to refer back to this section as you read through the text.

Scribbling

The initial stage, scribbling, begins with gestures that are writings in the air and written signs that may be but fixed gestures (Vygotsky, 1978). Early writing is more than random marks for it represents "children's intentions to create visual constructs and messages" (King, 1980, p. 164). Eventually the scribbling takes form and for native English-writing children, the marks move from left to right in connected circles and loops as can be seen in cursive. However, just as in oral language development, the differences among language systems show up quite early, before words are formed.

This scribbling was performed by an Israeli child whose parents speak and write Hebrew. The marks make no sense but this child has noted many details about his native written language. Instead of from left to right, he writes from right to left, as Hebrew is read. The characters are not connected; each one is drawn separately. Dots, an essential part of Hebrew characters, appear judiciously within the work. Just as in the babbling of infants, scribbling shows linguistic differences.

Message Writing

As children gain control over form and gain greater awareness of letter shapes, they begin to realize that letters carry messages. Not always encum-

Language Learning: A Powerful Force 47

bered by their own inability to read, children will "write" forms and ask, "What does this say?" Sometimes, when asked, youngsters will tell you what they have written. These writings often accompany a drawing, as seen in the writing produced by five-year-old Susie.

Susie has moved far beyond scribbling for in both instances she has made her "letters" with up-and-down lines and circles. This line/circle practice will help her when she begins manuscript. Susie is a good example of how children enjoy learning on their own. Her mother "translated" the work into traditional orthography.

Betsy, five years eleven months, reveals her superior control over form and knowledge in the following two captioned pictures. Greater detail appears in her pictures and in the writing. A large variety of recognizable letters are used to convey the message, and in the faces drawing she has shown knowl-

48 *Foundations of the Language Arts*

edge of numerals by including an appropriate "3." No spaces appear between groups of letters; that distinction is yet to come.

This is three happy faces.

OCRARBANDBHCB 3

This is a whole set of dishes.

XNARPBRPUNMROUF

Writing Explorations

Having observed written forms, children practice their knowledge just as Weir (1962) found in her son's oral soliloquies. The next example illustrates this similarity. The youngster copied part of the alphabet, grew tired of that exercise, and decided to fill the page with "A's." He worked arduously at this task and found the page to be long. This problem was solved by enlarging the size to finish. Interesting spaces were left, so this child decided to break the rule of "A" forming and make some upside down, a new exploration. Clay

(1975) labels this practice as inventory, one of the concepts of print she discovered while observing children's explorations. Other principles she found were use of space, directionality, and recurrence.

Some children begin to write on their own with little or no teacher guidance. Don, a kindergartner, produced the captioned picture on page 50 in the early spring.

Don, having discovered the period, knows that it goes at the end, so the dot is placed after each word. This is a clear example of an overgeneralization. Don is beginning to be aware of traditional spelling rules; look at the overgeneralization in his use of silent "e's" at the end of words: "helwe" and "ESTRe." In fact, children's spelling often reveals their search for systems in language, overgeneralizations, and refinements that move toward adult spelling.

Hello, I'm the Easter Bunny. I brung you some eggs.

Beginning to Spell

Read (1975) studied young children's beginning attempts to write. He found that a significant portion of youngsters select vowels on the basis of how they are formed, tense jaw (forward) or lax jaw (back), rather than how they sound. Thus, long "e" and short "i" are both written as "e" (bit = bet); short and long "a" plus short "e" become "a" (red = rad). When letters represent the same sound as a syllable, the young speller uses that letter to write it, e.g., "bcuz." This Read called "letter name." Certain letters such as "r," "l," "m," and "n" often represent syllables (usually with the schwa sound, an unaccented vowel). Examples might be "batr = batter, tabl = table, gardn = garden." Read also reported that formation of the "tr" and "dr" consonant blends influenced young children's spelling. "Train" appears as "chran" or "hran"; "dragon" appears as "chrgn." The nasal consonants "m" and "n" are commonly omitted; for example, "went" may be written as "wat." The important finding of this research is that children are not making random spelling errors but rather forming their own rules to guide them in spelling. These rules differ from adult logic; thus, superimposed "traditional" spelling rules may confuse rather than assist beginning writers.

As children become more sensitive to traditional orthography or spelling, they often overgeneralize a rule, as Don did when he generously added final "e's." Long vowel sounds may be created when two vowels are placed together; thus the previous form "tabl" becomes "taibel" or "teibel." The addition of an "e" with the "i," although misplaced, reveals that the child recognizes the need for a vowel in each syllable and knows that one way of spelling the /əl/ sound is "el"; "le" has yet to be learned.

Dee John's writing includes some examples of Read's findings. How many instances are you able to discover?

> Dc eJohn
> The magic mouse tak's The chrash out siad and he pat·s The chrash in The can so The chrash man can take it an take it to The dupe.
> The magic mouse takes the trash outside He puts the trash in the can so the trashman can take it and take it to the dump.

This young speller is obviously in a transitional stage. He has observed the apostrophe and overgeneralized its use. "Chrash" follows Read's finding for the "tr," as does the omission of the nasal "m" in "dupe" with its generous addition of a final silent "e." Dividing the compound word "outside" is reasonable, as is "siad" for "side," if one considers the possibility of overstressing sounds for spelling purposes. The "an" for "and" may be a careless error or Dee John may be spelling "and" as he pronounces it, omitting the final "d" sound.

The Developing Writer

Evidence of children's development in writing may be seen in their selection of vocabulary, syntactic construction, and use of punctuation. The third-grade youngster who wrote the adventure for Anatole on page 52 clearly knows a great deal about written forms.

She recognizes that written language differs from the oral mode. Sentences are constructed to fit a written story style—for example, "Pierre the Paris Pigeon he saw" and "Just then they're came a roar of wing-flapping." She has moved beyond the staple opening of "Once upon a time . . ." and has the main character define the plot in his opening statements. Use of dialogue reveals growth, for less mature youngsters often avoid writing dialogue. This

title: Aatoles Birthday

"Oh how I wish I wasn't so-so popular." said Anatole. "Today is my Birthday and I Myself has no idea where I am. Just then they're came a roar of wing-flapping. Anatole looked up, and up, and up, until.......... Pierre the Paris pigeon he saw. But instead of looking at Pierre..... he was looking at the wonderful sight he was holding in his beak! .... it was a gigantic "A." Pierre swooped down to wish Anatole a happy Birthday. Then he said where on earth did you get that "A?" Pierre nodded. Anatole knew just what he ment. He ment his six charming children had kept it a secret all week long! The end

young author has a clear sense of audience. Punctuation in the form of a series of dots tells the reader where to pause for effect, taking the place of juncture in the oral suprasegmental system. The story has a clear beginning, middle, and end. It is neatly tied together, although further elaboration would have avoided the rather startling closing.

Further development in writing may be seen in Susan's story, below. This fifth grader is quite sophisticated in her use of dialogue. She demonstrates the ability to convey to her reader who the speaker is without a referent stem such as "said Martha." Susan also shows her control of registers in language. She uses the more formal construction "To whom am I speaking?" to the unknown telephone caller. The informal construction "Oh, yea I'll be ready

> Is it only a Dream.
> One day Martha White was looking through the mail when she saw a lottery ticket form.
> "Well why not if Mr Kirk can win ten thousand dollars then I can and mabey will win more."
> Martha sat down and filled out the form and put a stamp on it and then mailed it. The next week she got a card with a number on it and under that it said the drawing would be on tuesday the sixth and that the winner would be phoned. Martha could hardly wait and then when Tuesday came she sat by the phone. When all of the sudden rings.
> "Hello this is Martha White to whom am I speaking?"
> "This is..."
> "I'm sorry mam but your number has been cut off."
> "Thats all right."
> Martha still waited for a call when again the

> *phone rang.*
> "Hello, this is Mr King from the lottery is Miss White there?"
> "This is she."
> "Well you have just one one million dollars 100 dollars each week till you have gotten one million dollars."
> "You mean I really won?"
> "Yes you did."
> "Oh thank you so very much goodbye."
> "Hello Martha."
> "John what are you doing here?"
> "We have a date tonight remember."
> "Oh yes all be ready in a minute minute." "John you know what just happened?"
> "No"
> "I just dremot something that never happened."
> "Well maybe it will happen."
> "I doubt it I really do."

in a minute" is used in responding to a friend. The dialogue also reveals her ability to write reproducing the sounds of oral speech patterns.

Summing up the Process

Although written and oral modes of language differ, children's process of acquisition of these skills is similar. Youngsters search for meaning in the print around them, form rules and hypotheses about the systems they see, test and take inventory of their knowledge, and receive feedback for making refinements on their rules and hypotheses. These actions may be studied in young children's scribbling, first attempts at letter construction, spelling efforts, and storywriting. Progress in writing may be seen as students gain control over story forms and register switching. An awareness of audience becomes a function of each writing act, and the young author responds by manipulating the language to reach these readers.

Implications of Oral and Written Language Development

A natural language environment contains opportunities for input, practice and testing, and feedback for revising and refining the rules children have generated about oral and written language systems. The context of language learning is most important, for in it children attach meaning to the language used. Youngsters' homes and family activities provide the initial context; a functional language outlet must later be available in school.

This writing center encourages children to produce books, pages, and captions that meet their unique purposes. An opportunity to interact while writing is evident. Children's booklets serve as examplars of what might be done and to show that student writing is valued. (Mrs. Slinger's informal classroom, Barrington School, Upper Arlington, Ohio)

The teacher's role is to structure an environment that will produce an opportunity for students to speak and write naturally. Desks in rows preclude natural speech since looking at the back of peers' heads does not stimulate interaction. Filling in blanks in workbooks does not allow children the freedom to test and practice writing. The acts of talking and writing are ways of learning language, part of language processing.

Young children learn through play. Play offers them the opportunity to try on a variety of adult roles and to use specific language to fit that role and play situation. Teachers can foster play in their classes by arranging space, providing a puppet theater, and accumulating a prop box. Freedom to use areas flexibly, such as the block corner or reading space, encourages diverse play. Valuing play, that is, taking this activity seriously, will enhance children's skill in play and in language. Writing can become an integral part of play. Blank books to be filled, tablets for messages, signs as props, magazines, phone books, and catalogues for wish lists require written language.

Just as parents responded to the meaning of their child's first utterances, the teacher can respond to meaning also. This includes both oral and written modes. Initially, the goal is fluency. Fluency develops from wide experiences and an encouraging, interested audience. Written language comes under scrutiny much earlier than oral language. No one expects adult speech from young children but writing elicits immediate correction. Few youngsters have the opportunity to develop fluency in writing. Correction is not limited to writing, for many primary teachers, including those at the kindergarten level, require their students to respond in complete sentences. Conversations build up a context so that verbal sentence fragments can be meaningful. Forcing complete sentences not only creates stilted talk but it may also inhibit verbal fluency in a school setting. Early restrictions curtail oral and written expression.

Teachers' comments can encourage and focus rather than evaluate. By responding to the idea expressed or the language principle explored and practiced, teachers draw further expressive efforts from their students.

Parents will need to be alerted to signs of language growth so that they may be asked to help accumulate examples of their children's development. When lines between home and school connect, continuity in learning occurs, thus eliminating mismatched goals. Parents have a right and responsibility to know what their children are learning and where growth may be seen. For this to be achieved, teachers will need to educate parents so that they will know what to observe. In addition, files of children's work should be kept so that parents, teachers, and children themselves may see development and receive feedback.

Feedback is different from correction; it is more sensitive and, at times, can tell the speakers and writers how close they are to achieving their goal. If the message becomes understood to the extent that the receiver may respond if he or she wishes, feedback is given to the producer. Although right and wrong responses do occur in natural language, these responses are rare. Most parents relate to the meaning; teachers can also. When the message is impaired, that is, not getting across, teachers more often than parents help the student compose or reconstruct the message. This give-and-take is essential to language learning.

Sources for language feedback in the classroom are basically twofold: the teacher and the other children. These two sources have the greatest opportunity for feedback and input, and of course, they become the most significant. Too often outside sources such as a visiting speaker or a writer's workshop are stressed, but their contribution is necessarily limited. Rather, the advantage of the "home" group should be exploited.

The two classroom sources differ in kinds and ways in which they give feedback. The teacher can extend language more than children by reading more sophisticated language and speaking more richly. Children, on the other hand, can provide better reasons for speaking. They can ask questions and ask for elaborations and explanations that a teacher realistically or honestly cannot. Class peers also provide a chance for practicing, such as explaining first to one group and then another. Children are able to join in and respond at a similar reinforcing level, thus encouraging the activity and not disrupting it.

In writing, children can help edit each other's work, thus becoming more aware of conventions for their own compositions. Youngsters can ask each other for elaboration and explanation of reports that teachers obviously already know. Fellow students give a real reason for sharing. They can also write together, reinforcing writing and making the task easier.

Specific ways to work with children on developing their oral and written language will be discussed more fully in later chapters. The bases for the ideas, however, are derived from what is known about child language learning.

Language Usage Varies

All systems of language exhibit a broad spectrum of variation. These variations may come from the purpose of language use, the context in which it occurs, the region where language is learned, whether it is the first or second language learned, or a reflection of social and educational background.

Functions of Language

One reason that language varies is because it is used for different purposes. In the following dialogue between Debbie and Tammy, language is used to meet a variety of needs. These two fifth-grade youngsters had written about their experiences on a walk to a stream in a wooded area by the school. They are arranging a display made up of their writings and the flowers and plants they collected.

Tammy: First, we have to frame this in a different color and then put it on there. (She holds her writing and works with a large poster board on the table in front of her.)

Debbie: I'm going to put the flower in the corner.

Tammy: Cut that out. It looks stupid there.

Debbie: I'm going to curve it here. (She cuts the corners off her piece of writing.)

Tammy: Here, wait. You like mine? (She holds up a piece of writing framed in colored paper.)

Debbie: No.

Tammy: You like this one? How about this one with it? Or this one? Or this one? (She rapidly switches background papers.) This pink looks like the color of my bedroom.

Mark: (He stops by the table with John where the girls are working.) What are you making? Are these plastic flowers? (He feels the flowers.) I'd press them.

Tammy: What do you mean?

John: You put a book on them.

Mark: You know, you put them between paper and then put them in a book—a big book, you know.

John: You pile books up on top.

Tammy: Yeah. (Boys watch a moment more and then wander off.)

Debbie: Take more off. (Tammy is cutting the corners on her writing.) Do it right.

Stephanie: (Stephanie and Valerie come to the table.) These are pretty. (She picks up a branch with several flowers.)

Valerie: Let me have a teeny, tiny little bit of flower.

Language Learning: A Powerful Force 59

Tammy: Go get your own.

Valerie: Where?

Debbie: Go down the hill. Down, down, down the hill.

Valerie: Where?

Tammy: Climb up a big cliff and then you might fall into the river. (She giggles and takes back the flowers and places them on the poster board. She stands back to look at the effect. Tries a different arrangement. She works like this for a minute or so.) Is this good? (Without waiting for a response, she picks up construction paper to be used for framing the writing.) So you want yellow or green? (Puts green paper behind the writing.)

Debbie: I don't think that looks right.

Tammy: Yeah, it looks sort of dull. (She tries the yellow and holds it up for Debbie to inspect.)

Debbie: (Busy arranging flowers) It doesn't matter.

Tammy: What else did we get? (Not waiting for an answer she goes to another table where they have put flowers, plants, and grasses.)

Debbie: OK. Get everything off it. (They remove everything from the poster board.) Now turn it over.

Tammy: (They reposition their writing and begin placing the flowers.) That ain't in the middle. It's more by yours.

Debbie: Put yours facing this.

Tammy: Oh, neat! Where did you get that?

Debbie: Where do you want to put these?

Stephanie: I'd like these here.

Debbie: Put these in the corners. No, that don't look right. The stick's too high. (Placing a small branch of flowers.)

Tammy: (Holding a spraylike twig of buds.) Look at the shower curtain! See, look! (She parts the flowers.)

Stephanie: I'd put it there.

Tammy: Know how you can get them really curly? (She is watching Debbie arrange some long ribbon like strands of dried grass.)

Debbie: Yeah, use the scissors on them.

Stephanie: What?

60 *Foundations of the Language Arts*

Debbie: Like this. (She demonstrates.)
Tammy: We're going to put on the title, "Spring." Go get the glue.
Debbie: First, go show Miss Charles.

An experienced teacher will recognize this dialogue as a typical exchange among children but a casual observer might consider Debbie and Tammy to be wasting time. However, these children explained, directed, described, asserted, questioned, and had friendly exchanges through the language they used—language used purposefully, that is, functionally. Tough (1977) defines *function* as "the means by which a purpose is achieved." The way to determine how language functions and which function is being applied lies in the examination of the context in which the language occurs. For Debbie and Tammy the context was the classroom, its social history, materials at hand, their task of display, and the growing web of their conversation. Contexts give rise to varying types of language; thus context consideration comes first, for it defines the need and appropriateness of the verbal utterance. Hymes (1972) states "The key to understanding language in context is to start, not with language, but with context" (p. xix). To determine the function of a particular statement, therefore, one must know the speaking context. And for teachers, an awareness of the context allows them to assess their own language-arts program.

The children in the foregoing conversation were adept at using language. Which functions did they employ? By using Halliday's (1976) system of seven categories, the group used all of them. The children's utterances illustrate those categories:

Instrumental: language used to satisfy the child's needs
"Let me have a teeny, tiny little bit of flower."

Regulatory: language for controlling others
"OK. Get everything off it. Now turn it over."

Interactional: language used by the child to interact with others around him or her
"What are you making? Are these plastic flowers? I'd press them."

Personal: language used to express the child's feelings and uniqueness
"This pink looks like the color of my bedroom."

Heuristic: language used to explore the environment
(In response to child saying, "I'd press them [flowers].")
"What do you mean?"

Imaginative: language used by the child to create his or her own world

	(Holding a spraylike twig of buds.) "Look at the shower curtain! See, look!" (She parts the buds.)
Informative:	language used by humans to convey information to those around them
	"You know, you put them between paper and then put them in a book—a big book, you know."

There are other ways to categorize functions of language. Tough (1977) has described four. *Directive* language can be used to direct others or oneself. *Interpretative* language (including reporting use and reasoning use) is concerned with communicating to others the meaning of events in a person's world. It is connected with daily experiences and memories. *Projective* language draws upon the imagination to project situations of which one is not a part. The fourth function is *relational* language, which is used to establish and maintain relationships that exist between humans.

Britton (1975) designates two roles that people take in a language setting: participant and spectator. The participant operates directly upon the represented world, while the spectator focuses on events not now taking place. He defines three functions with subdivisions within. The *transactional* is a participant role, which includes the language of giving and seeking information in addition to the language of persuasion. In the *poetic* function, the spectator is free of the need for action and can attend to such formal features of language as the pattern of events in a narrative or sounds in alliterative forms. The *expressive*, which lies between the other two functions, is that language close to a person. Points of view are given and the self becomes known by others.

Whichever of the systems is studied, the important factor is to understand the role context plays in determining which function of language will be used. Everyone needs the opportunity to use language functionally in authentic settings. Teachers who establish with their students a learning community based upon shared interests and concerns and who give class members the freedom to interact naturally support this use of diverse functions.

Pinnell (1975) analyzed primary children's classroom oral language by applying Halliday's categories. She found patterns of language among differing activities, but one function was within practically all activities. Almost half of the language fell into the "interactional" category, for children were developing and practicing cooperation skills. Other social areas were being explored and extended.

Regulatory language frequently occurred within competitive game situations. If you watch children at play, they become quite directive; they appear

These youngsters are working on a project dealing with medieval times. Their language includes not only accuracy of facts but also the representation of the information they have found—the materials to use in art, the topic, and the details to be included. (Mrs. Monaghan's informal classroom, Barrington School, Upper Arlington, Ohio)

to focus on the rules rather than the content of the game, and winning rather than playing often seems to become the goal. The house corner contained much of the imaginative language but other centers such as block, sand, and water also drew out make-believe talk. Little heuristic language appeared, but when it was used, children were in the act of "discovering" in sand and water play. Possibly heuristic thought occurred at other times but this language function was not applied. Children used language to inform their peers as well as their teachers. When students have the opportunity to devise projects or work out problems themselves or in small groups, they have information to share.

Teachers received many instructional statements and questions from children in addition to informative language but almost no personal language. It should be noted that teachers also used no personal language. Pinnell indicated that both teachers and children did not appear to consider personal language to be a part of their classroom exchanges. Among themselves, however, children did use some personal language.

Adults apply all of these functions; however, Pinnell states, "Educators tend to emphasize informative language, and the imaginative, personal and heuristic functions of language are devalued or ignored" (p. 319). Children need the opportunity to apply language in a variety of ways in order to reach greater language sophistication. This goal may be reached in a classroom community where youngsters share goals and projects and interact in a constructive manner. Together the teacher and children can plan class activities based on common and individual interests, needs, and concerns. To determine which language functions are present, a teacher could make observations to see which ones are in use and where they occur.

Register

Speakers vary language to meet their purposes and modify language as they change audiences. For example, the principal presiding at a P.T.A. meeting who settles a chattering group of parents with "Ladies and gentlemen, may I have your attention, please?" may later that evening settle her own children with "Hush up and listen to me!" The teacher who tells her colleagues, "Johnny is one kid who just can't ever seem to keep his mouth shut" will tell Johnny's parents that "John has difficulty in attending to the task at hand because he seems much more interested in socializing."

Register is bound by situation. There are acceptable ways to talk in specific situations and to certain people. Native speakers of a language are sensitive to them. While it is appropriate to greet a friend with "Hi there. How are things?" it would be inappropriate to greet the President of the United States in the same breezy manner.

A specific kind of language occurs in the classroom, which DeStefano (1978) labels "school register." When teachers say, "Would you like to take out your books now, please?" they are not really asking a question. They are issuing commands, but doing so in school register. Downing (1977) suggests that one special aspect of school register is a reading register. He tested young children by asking them to listen to a variety of auditory stimuli such as a bell, a voice saying the short sound of "e," a voice saying "milk," and a voice saying, "She's a funny girl!" (Downing, 1969). None of the five-year-olds were able to identify the word "milk" as the only sound that should be called a word. When first-grade teachers talk about "words," "sentences," and the "first letter" of a word, they are therefore applying labels to concepts that many children do not yet have.

Some children have had experiences in nursery school, Sunday school, or with older brothers and sisters that lead them to expect school language.

Other children with different experiences may not arrive at school with the same expectations. A teacher's sensitivity to the possible differences between school language and home language will help children as they add this new register to their repertoire.

Register cannot really be taught. A person who is acquiring a second language may become very fluent in that language and still have difficulty with register. One graduate student from Germany, whose English was almost without accent, startled some university deans whom she had just met. When they asked her where she was living, she identified the city as "the armpit of the nation." Obviously this student had spent much time talking with fellow graduate students in informal situations and had as yet spent little time talking with university administrators in more formal situations.

Even though one cannot and should not give lessons in register, teachers can provide the kinds of contexts that will offer children the opportunity to speak to a variety of audiences in a variety of situations. A child might be asked to discuss a book with an adult, or visit another classroom to explain a project or issue an invitation. Sociodramatic play permits children to try on many different roles. Listen to children playing school if you wish to learn how a teacher sounds! These opportunities to shift register as children take on new roles help them develop a greater sensitivity to language and how it is shaped for various purposes and audiences.

Dialect

Some dialects are peculiar to a region. British English does not sound the same as American English and the English that is spoken in Australia has yet a different sound. But an Australian, an American, and a Briton can talk together with mutual understanding. Within the boundaries of the United States it is easy to tell whether a speaker is from Georgia, Massachusetts, New Jersey, or Texas. When President Kennedy spoke to the nation about the crisis in "Cuber," everyone could identify what he meant. When Jimmy Carter became President, *Time* magazine published a brief and amusing handbook for those wishing to understand Georgian. Yet even without this assistance, all Americans were able to understand his inaugural address.

These regional variations in language are largely phonological. Vowels are lengthened, "r's" are softened, dropped, or added. There are few lexical changes. The cooking utensil called a "skillet" in one part of the country may be called a "spider" in another area. The "pop" one drinks in the Midwest becomes "tonic" in New England. While Clevelanders play softball, Pittsburghers play mush ball. These vocabulary differences may amuse, enchant, or annoy, but they cause little difficulty in comprehension because they are so few in number.

Certain social groups can also have their own dialect. Whereas regional dialects vary from so-called standard speech, mostly in the phonological system, social dialects are marked by many more grammatical differences, such as "I ain't," "He don't," or "They don't have none." Differences in vocabulary choice are also distinctive.

Dialects such as Black English or Appalachian are seen by some people as marking the education or income levels of the speaker. This is a dangerous attitude. While it is not bad to be labeled as a person who comes from a certain region of the country, it is often seen as "bad" to be poor or unschooled. Not many years ago children who arrived at school speaking a dialect that deviated from the standard speech of the educated people in the community were labeled as "culturally disadvantaged" or "linguistically deprived." The teacher's task was to stamp out the language the child spoke at home and to train the child to speak standard speech. Programs were developed to teach standard English as though it were a foreign language. The basis of these efforts was the firm belief that one dialect was better than another.

Attitude toward language differences may become a basic problem. Teachers who see children who speak a certain dialect as less intelligent and less able are likely to treat those children in ways that will lead them to fulfill those expectations. Legal action in Ann Arbor resulted in the school board providing instruction to the teachers on Black English. This study project was designed not to make teachers into fluent speakers of Black English but to lead them to new understandings about the dialect and how it works. Such knowledge, it was felt, would help teachers to treat dialect speakers with more sensitivity and to work with them in more beneficial ways. For example, if teachers are using a phonics approach to reading, they need to be aware that in some dialects there is no distinction made between the pronunciation of "pin" and "pen." For such speakers there is little value in lengthy exercises devoted to marking which words contain short "e" and which words contain short "i." Some Easterners make a distinction between the words "Mary," "merry," and "marry;" most Midwesterners do not. These differences in speech may cause problems with spelling. Children who hear "wear" and "where" as homophones may display these understandings in their writing as well as in their speech. A teacher who listens to the message the child is sending, rather than focusing on the grammatical form in which that message is cast, will do more to foster growth in language than the teacher who expects all language in the classroom to match his or her standard forms.

Second-Language Learners

Within the borders of the United States there are large groups of people whose first language is not English. In New England and Louisiana, communities exist where French is spoken and in the Southwest many native American languages, such as Navaho, are the first languages spoken in the home. The Spanish speakers found in Florida, New York, California, and the Southwest qualify the United States as the country with the fifth largest population of Spanish speakers in the world.

School systems that enroll numbers of children who do not speak English generally have programs to meet the special needs of these children. In the Lau Decision of 1974, the court ruled that children must be given instruction in a language or languages that will allow them to participate in the total instructional program of the school. The Bilingual Education Act of 1968 had already led to the development of a variety of curricula designed to help children acquire English as a second language while using their first language to learn in the content areas. Teachers who can teach in the child's home language as well as in English and who have knowledge of both cultures can build a bridge between the home and the school. Learning can move ahead in the child's dominant language at the same time that child is receiving the linguistic input that will help in the acquisition of English as a second language.

While teachers in cities such as Miami, New York City, and San Francisco should expect to work with children who speak a language other than English, other teachers are also likely to receive such children in their classrooms as well. Migrant workers may appear at certain seasons of the year to help with the harvesting of crops. Vietnamese and Cuban refugees have appeared in large numbers. Schools near universities often enroll the children of foreign students; as an example, in one elementary school near a large Midwestern university the kindergarten teacher had twelve children in her class who did not speak English. Among them they spoke seven different languages, including Icelandic.

The first concern of any teacher in such a situation is simply that of communication. How does one work with a child with whom one does not share a language? How does one make a child feel part of a group when he or she is yet unable to communicate effectively with that group? There are other concerns, however, that are just as vital as the linguistic ones; there are the cultural ones. How is a Navaho child, raised in a noncompetitive culture, going to handle life in a classroom where learning is viewed as a competitive sport? How do black children who have been told to lower their eyes when speaking to an adult fare when they talk to a white teacher who has been raised in a culture that sees averting the eyes from a speaker as evasive or defiant behavior? How is the Japanese child reared in a culture where touching is minimal going to feel when the new kindergarten teacher affectionately welcomes her with a hug?

While teachers cannot begin to learn the language systems or the cultural mores for all the children who might possibly arrive in their classrooms, it should be possible to develop the kinds of knowledge that will help them to work with children whose language they do not share. Teachers can, for example, see that language and culture cannot be separated. Language often reflects the values of the culture. The Japanese use many forms to express various levels of politeness. These fine shadings are essential in their particular culture, but not for our own.

Because a child cannot express an idea, it does not always follow that that child is unable to comprehend the idea. One nine-year-old Vietnamese girl who had a very limited knowledge of English was placed in a second-grade classroom where the principal felt she would best be able to "catch up." The child was set to work in a second-grade arithmetic workbook, though she actually had computation skills that surpassed those of most twelve-year-olds. The fact that she could not yet discuss what she knew in English placed the girl in a situation where no real learning was taking place.

Implications of Language Variation

The foregoing discussion has focused upon some of the kinds of language differences a teacher might easily find in any classroom—children who speak a dialect or even a second language, as well as children who handle a variety of registers with ease. These wide differences are to be expected since our American society is broad and diverse. The language one hears in the classroom will reflect this rich diversity. As teachers accept children's language they will be able to work with those children in ways that will help them expand their linguistic repertoire. A classroom can provide situations where children have a need to speak to each other. Drama, working together on projects, explaining to others what one has learned, and playing together provide children with opportunities for purposeful oral language. Further, such activities will permit children to speak with others whose language may differ in some way from their own and in so doing help them learn to become accepting and appreciative of cultural differences.

Verbal responses such as discussion and written composition are stressed in the classroom. Yet there are many ways to express oneself. Children's pictures can clearly show their careful observations on a field trip. Children's responses in movement to a poem may convey more deeply than words the feelings that the sound and rhythm of that poem evoked.

A teacher's knowledge of the nature of language can help in making curricular decisions. An understanding of the phonological differences found in many dialects can help teachers avoid the kind of strict phonic approaches to reading that might create problems for certain dialect speakers. It might develop an awareness of the difficulties some children face in trying to match sound and symbol in spelling. A teacher who is sensitive to such differences will feel that what the child is saying is more important than how it is being said. The form in which the message is given may be shaped and polished after fluency is achieved.

Summary

Language occurs within a context. Context and language are inseparable, for each contributes to the message being communicated. Children acquire language in order to mean. They learn to expect that language appears as a function of some purpose, of someone's intent.

Language is predictable because it is systematic. This single principle, which can be so simply stated, has broad implications. It means that children can acquire language because they are able to make assumptions and then test those assumptions. Children, then, are active learners, not just passive receivers of knowledge. They process information about the systems of language and then form their own rules. Sometimes children's rules differ from those of adults, as can be seen in children's early attempts at spelling. Second-language learners go through much the same process. However, the environment for second-language learning may not be as rich, nor the motivation for acquiring that language as strong as it was for the first language.

Teachers' knowledge about language acquisition and development has sharp implications for classroom practices. Teachers need not focus attention on language analysis. Children are adept at categorizing language in systematic ways; for example, they all have well-developed tacit grammars in their native language. The role of the teacher is to provide the kind of environment that encourages language growth—a classroom community where there are many opportunities to listen, speak, read, and write for a wide variety of purposes.

Suggested Learning Experiences

1. Hold a conversation with a young child and then with a child at an upper-grade level. Let the child take the lead in the conversation. What differences do you find in your role as a participant? In which exchange did you need to be most alert and sensitive to the focus of the child's speech? How did the children's vocabulary differ? their syntax?

2. With members of your class, collect a sampling of children's writing from preschool through grade six. Select average students. Giving no indication of grade level, pool the writing samples and examine them. As a group, decide upon the chronological order of the students' products. Discuss the basis on which you made these determinations.

3. Reread the conversation between Tammy and Debbie found in this chapter and the discussion of language functions that follows. Visit a classroom, taking with you a list of language functions. Observe two different activities in which children are allowed to interact. Make a tally mark beside each language function you identify. At the end of a ten-minute period, develop a percentage graph to show the language patterns that occurred. Why do you think these patterns appeared? How do the language patterns found in the two activities compare?

4. In this chapter we have discussed both Downing's and DeStefano's ideas on the language registers found in classrooms. Visit a kindergarten classroom and a classroom at one other grade level. Listen to the language used by each teacher for instruction. Make note of language you would identify as belonging to the school register. In groups, compare your findings. What similarities did you find? what differences?

5. Engage in a conversation with someone who speaks a dialect other than your own. Tape this conversation. Make a list of all words that are different either in pronunciation or selection. Do the words fall into any kind of categories? What kind of adjustment would you, as a teacher, have to make if this person were your student?

Recommended Readings

Britton, James, "Words and a World," in Anthony Jones and Jeremy Mulford (eds.), *Children Using Language,* pp. 27–40, Oxford University Press, London, 1971.

Britton not only discusses the stages of language acquisition but also the effect that acquiring the ability to utter thoughts aloud has upon the child. The author points out that the acquisition of language gives us a new and powerful way to "represent the world to ourselves and ourselves to other people." He stresses the social factors that affect language growth.

Fox, Sharon E. and Zidonis, Frank, "Protocols of Children's Language," *Theory Into Practice* 14: 312–317, December, 1975.

The Oral Language Protocol Project, which consists of a series of films on concepts of language acquisition, is described within the article. As a class extension, your instructor may wish to order one or more of these protocols to enrich the group's knowledge of this topic. Additionally, in a major portion of this article, the authors discuss myths or common misconceptions of language acquisition—for example, the idea that "children learn language by imitation" is refuted.

Genishi, Celia, "Young Children Communicating in the Classroom: Selected Research," *Theory Into Practice* 18: 244–250, October, 1979.

Genishi provides a most useful service by surveying the recent research literature dealing with a sociolinguistic perspective of classroom interaction. The focus is on young children but the application to older students can be made easily. Genishi goes beyond mere reporting of the studies; she discusses the possible implications for classroom organization and teacher instructional decisions.

King, Martha L., "Learning How to Mean in Written Language," *Theory Into Practice* 19: 163–169, Summer, 1980.

In this article, King uses a chart comparing children's development in oral and written language to point up the rich resources that children bring to the writing task. You may wish to use this chart as a basis for your own observations and examinations of children's language. The discussion of how teachers can most fruitfully support children's growth in writing can help you as you plan experiences for and with children.

Read, Charles, "What Children Know about Language: Three Examples," *Language Arts* 57: 144–148, February, 1980.

Read points out that children come to school knowing a great deal about language. Oral language knowledge is quite apparent but knowledge of written language may be hidden from the teacher unless that teacher provides many opportunities for children to use and share this understanding. He gives examples of three types of language knowledge the young child has developed: speech sounds and spelling, sentence parts, and vocabulary. In the conclusion Read discusses the relationships among these aspects of language and the ways in which children extend their linguistic knowledge.

References

Professional Literature

Berko, J., "The Child's Learning of English Morphology," *Word* 14: 150–177, 1958.

Berko (Gleason), Jean, "Do Children Imitate?" Paper read at International Conference on Oral Education of the Deaf, Lexington School for the Deaf, New York City, June, 1967.

Bloom, L. M., *Language Development: Form and Function in Emerging Grammars,* M.I.T. Press, Cambridge, Mass., 1970.

Britton, J., "What's the Use? A Schematic Account of Language Functions," *Educational Review* 23 (3): 205–219, 1971.

Britton, James; Burgess, Tony; Martin, Nancy; McLeod, Alex; and Rosen, Harold, *The Development of Writing Abilities* (11–18), Macmillan Education, London, 1975.

Cazden, Courtney B., *Child Language and Education,* Holt, Rinehart and Winston, New York, 1972.

Chomsky, C., *The Acquisition of Syntax in Children from 5 to 10,* M.I.T. Press, Cambridge, Mass., 1969.

Chukovsky, K., *From Two to Five,* University of California Press, Berkeley, 1963.

Clark, Eve V., "What's in a Word: On the Child's Acquisition of Semantics in His First Language," pp. 65–110, in *Cognitive Development and the Acquisition of Language,* ed. T. Moore, Academic Press, New York, 1973.

Clay, M., *What Did I Write?* Heinemann, Exeter, New Hampshire, 1975.

Clay, Marie M., "A Syntactic Analysis of Reading Errors," *Journal of Verbal Learning Behavior* 7:434–438, 1968.

Cook-Gumperz, Jenny, "Communicating with Young Children in the Home," *Theory Into Practice* 18: 207–212, October, 1979.

Dale, P.S., *Language Development: Structure and Function,* Dryden, Hinsdale, Ill., 1972.

DeStefano, Johanna S., *Language, the Learner and the School,* Wiley, New York, 1978.

DeStefano, Johanna S.; Pepinsky, Harold B.; and Sanders, Tobie S., "Discourse Rules for Literacy Learning in a Classroom," in *Communicating in the Classroom,* L. C. Wilkinson (ed.), Academic Press, New York, 1982.

Downing, J., "How Children Think about Reading," *Reading Teacher* 23: 217–230, December, 1969.

Downing, J., "Words, Words, Words," *Theory Into Practice* 16: 325–333, December, 1977.

Fleming, J. D., "Field Report: The State of the Apes," *Psychology Today* 7: 31–46, January, 1974.

Halliday, M. A. K., *Explorations in the Functions of Language,* Edward Arnold, London, 1976.

Halliday, M. A. K., *Learning How to Mean,* Edward Arnold, London, 1975.

Hunt, K. W., *Grammatical Structures Written at Three Grade Levels,* NCTE Research Report No. 3, National Council of Teachers of English, Champaign, Ill., 1965.

Hymes, Dell, "Introduction," in *Functions of Language in the Classroom,* Courtney Cazden, Vera John and Dell Hymes (eds.), Teachers College Press, Columbia University, New York, 1972.

King, Martha L., "Learning How to Mean in Written Language," *Theory Into Practice* 19: 163–169, Summer, 1980.

Lindfors, Judith Wells, *Children's Language and Learning,* Prentice-Hall, Englewood Cliffs, N.J., 1980.

Menyuk, Paula, "Syntactic Structures in the Language of Children" *Child Development* 34: 407–422, June, 1963.

O'Donnell, R. C.; Griffin, W. J.; and Norris, R. C., Syntax of Kindergarten and Elementary School Children: A Transformational Analysis, *NCTE Research Report No. 8,* National Council of Teachers of English, Champaign, Ill., 1967.

Pinnell, Gay S., "Language in Primary Classrooms," *Theory Into Practice* 14: 318–327, December, 1975.

Read, Charles, Children's Categorization of Speech Sounds in English, *NCTE Research Report No. 17,* ERIC/NCTE, Urbana, Ill., October, 1975.

Shugar, G. W., "Text Analysis as an Approach to the Study of Early Linguistic Operations," pp. 227–251 in *The Development of Communication,* C. Snow and N. Waterson (eds.), John Wiley, Chichester, England, 1978.

Slobin, Dan I., and Welsh, Charles A., "Elicited Imitation as a Research Tool in Developmental Psycholinguistics," pp. 485–497 in *Studies of Child Language Development,* C. A. Ferguson and D. I. Slobin (eds.), Holt, Rinehart and Winston, New York, 1973.

Snow, Catherine E., "The Development of Conversation between Mothers and Babies," *Journal of Child Language* 4: 1–22, February, 1977.

Strickland, R. G., The Language of Elementary School Children: Its Relationship to the Language of Reading Textbooks and the Quality of Reading of Selected Children. *Bulletin of the School of Education,* 38: 4, Indiana University, Bloomington, Ind., July, 1962.

Teitelbaum, Herbert and Hiller, Richard J., "Bilingual Education: The Legal Mandate," pp. 20–53 in *Bilingual Multicultural Education and the Professional,* Henry T. Trueba and Carol Barnett-Mizrahi (eds.), Newbury House Publishers, Inc., Rowley, Mass., 1979.

Tough, J., *The Development of Meaning,* George Allen & Unwin, London, 1977.

Vygotsky, Lev, *Mind in Society: Development of Higher Psychological Pro-*

cesses, Michael Cole, editor, Harvard University Press, Cambridge, Mass., 1978.

Weir, R. H., *Language in the Crib,* Mouton, The Hague, 1962.

Wells, Gordon, "Describing Children's Linguistic Development at Home and at School," *British Educational Research Journal* 5: 75–98, 1979.

Wepman, J. M., "Auditory Discrimination, Speech and Reading," *The Elementary School Journal* 60: 325–333, March, 1960.

Cognitive Development
One Child's Representation of Her World
Major Principles of Piaget's Theory
Piaget's Stages of Development
Cognitive Development and the Language-Arts Teacher

Moral Development
Some Children's Ideas about Justice
Moral Development and the Language Arts
Cognitive Theories of Moral Development
Emotional Theories of Moral Development

Social Development
Interaction among a Group of First-Grade Children
Knowledge of the Social Situation and Language Development
Social Development and Personality
Stages of Social Development
Role of the Teacher in Grouping Children

Summary

Suggested Learning Experiences

Recommended Readings

References
Professional Literature
Children's Literature

Chapter 3

Child Development: One Basis for Instructional Decisions

While children develop in language, they also grow in their ability to think, make judgments, and interact with others. Each of these areas—cognition, moral development, and socialization—affects and is affected by language use. The purpose of this chapter is to reveal the relationship between teaching that encourages growth in language and teaching that encourages growth in areas of child development. Understanding this relationship assists the teacher planning a language-arts program to make curricular decisions that harmonize with children's patterns of growth and development.

Understanding the child provides a basis for positive interaction between teachers and the children with whom they work. Such an understanding also helps you as a teacher to plan activities and experiences for your students as well as to organize groups in ways that will enhance and support learning. The literature pertaining to aspects of child development that is reviewed in this chapter is meant to assist your interpretation of children's behaviors. Teachers who understand why children are behaving as they do will be able to develop greater rapport with those children. Statements drawn from research and theory on children's cognitive, moral, and social development are generalizations that apply to many, perhaps most, children—but *importantly*, not to *all* of them. Differences occur because youngsters are individuals who grow according to their own unique internal clocks and adapt to the environments in which they live. Language input differs; experiences are varied; and relationships develop along singular lines. We ask that you keep this fact in mind: each child deserves a fresh look that does not place that child into one category. Categorizing children results in labeling, which limits a teacher's perspective and children's opportunities to grow and change. Knowledge of principles of child development may help you to better understand and note behaviors that might not have been otherwise observed as you work to help children learn.

Cognitive Development

One Child's Representation of Her World

April, a five-year-old preschooler, carefully drew her first name and began on the last. She started on the final letter, then hesitated. "How do you make a 'G'?"

Child Development: One Basis for Instructional Decisions 77

[child's drawing and handwritten text: "APRIL LONB", figure of a person, "MOM", "STOP POP"]

The adult sitting by her responded, "Do you remember?"

April said, "Now, let's see, a circle. No, a half circle. Is it a half circle? Yes, a half circle and a line. Is that a 'G'?"

Nodding, the adult asked, "Can you write anything else?"

"Yes," replied April, "a face and teeth! I can make his legs, his toes . . . Oh, he needs arms! Now, a dress." April drew busily.

"Can you write anything else?" inquired the adult.

"Here, it's a swing," said April.

"Can you write anything else?" the adult asked again.

"'Mom.' I can write 'mom.' I can write 'pop.' I can write 'stop.'"

April's work and responses to an adult's questioning reveal that she has learned a great deal about the world around her. Knowing how to make letters and spell her own name shows that she has become aware of print and its very personal relationship to her, although she has not yet developed fluency in letter-making. April recognizes that there are such things as words but she has not yet made the clear distinction between the symbolic representation of an object in a drawing and its symbolic representation as a word formed of individual letters. One act runs into the other, for she drew pictures as responses to the request for words as often as she wrote words.

Her drawing of a person is relatively detailed. The figure has fingers and toes but the number of appendages does not accurately reflect the human figure. The face has two eyes and ears, a nose, hair, and mouth with teeth, but the neck and shoulders are not clearly delineated. "His" dress is transparent, a less mature sign than opaque clothes.

April's journey to literacy and adult reasoning has begun. She will need to explore the world further, drawing conclusions to organize her experiences. Part of this growth includes learning about herself in relation to others, a knowledge reflected in her drawing of a person, perhaps a rendition of April herself. This process of organization is what cognitive growth is about.

Major Principles of Piaget's Theory

Jean Piaget, the Swiss psychologist, has postulated what is probably the most widely studied theory of children's cognitive development. Much time is spent delineating his theory; unfortunately, less attention is given to its implications for instruction, perhaps because it does not provide a one-to-one correspondence between children's behavior and teachers' responses—if a child does this, the teacher should respond accordingly. Rather, the educational implications are broader and more concerned with the learning environment and teacher expectations. Elkind (1973) explains that Piaget considers the child to be a creative artist, not a "mechanical contrivance." Artists do not copy reality nor do they draw solely on an inner vision. Their artwork, an act of learning, evolves from the interaction of the experiences of reality as they perceive it and their inner vision. In Piaget's terms, this is an *adaptation*.

All individuals project their own mental constructions onto the external world. Piaget calls this *externalization*. Adults have such difficulty understanding children's logic because adults expect *their* "realities" to be copied. However, children still have the task of creating their own reality. Reality is not and cannot be a "given" because an individual must create his or her own world.

A parallel can be drawn between this activity of cognitive growth and language acquisition. In each, the child is an active learner. The initiation begins when the child begins to originate rather than imitate language. Children create their own organization of the world about them and this includes language. As cited in the previous chapter, Menyuk (1963) found that a child's grammar model differs from an adult's, an outcome of this mental construction.

The fact that adult logic differs from children's in language learning may be verified by Read's (1975) work in spelling acquisition. Children group some sets of sounds (phonemes) together for several reasons; for example, they may group phonemes as they are formed in the mouth rather than as they are heard, thus producing a different set of letters (graphemes). The spelled outcome appears illogical to an adult unaware of the child's mental framework, but is logical and consistent to the young child.

In describing Piaget's theory, Duckworth (1972) calls this work of creating reality "the having of wonderful ideas." Children have to reach out to the world with their mental tools, grasp it, and assimilate it. If the teacher provides diverse, interesting materials and experiences, applies extending questions, and accepts children's ideas, then innovative thinking will occur. Children need to be supported and encouraged in their quest to create reality. Different ideas will occur to different children from what is seemingly the same experience. The mental constructs each child brings to the activity individualize the response.

Can learning be accelerated? Duckworth (1979) believes this to be the wrong question. She writes that the better question is not how fast but how far can learning be advanced. Children learn from conflicts in their own thinking. At times, however, children see no conflict; for example, moving things are alive; nonmoving things are not alive. A tree is alive when its boughs are moving; on a still day, the tree is not alive. When conflicting ideas are left separated, there is no need to reconcile them. In our example, such dissonance in ideas may occur because the child is preoperational at that stage of thinking or may not be aware of the dissonance because the problem has yet to be met. It is in the latter instance that teachers can intervene by developing the environment in which the problem occurs and by asking appropriately probing questions to reveal that problem. For example, a child exploring things that sink and things that float might quickly come to the conclusion that any metal object will sink if the only objects tested are ball bearings, nails, and paper clips. The teacher might help to extend the youngster's exploration and thinking by adding an aluminum pie plate to the pile.

What of the language arts specifically? How does language learning mesh with Piaget's cognitive theory? As some of the major concepts of this theory are described, implications for language-arts instruction will be pointed out.

In Piaget's theory, *schemata* serve as the framework for incoming data. These structural units are malleable, continually changing their shapes to fit the received information. They are "built" by children's assimilation of world experiences and are their mental representations of the world. This schema concept is reflected in the ideas presented by some of the newer theorists in psychology and reading: Rummelhart and Ortony (1977); Spiro (1977); and Collins, Brown, and Larkin (1980). According to these theorists, schemata are structures for broad concepts stored in a person's memory. Each schema contains a network of "slots," the organization of which reflects the interrelationships of these components to the overarching concept. The reader's task is to assess the organization of the text (that is, its schema) and match it through revision and refinement to the schema that has been developed in the reader's memory. It should be noted that the reader's schema may be altered by the text. The job is a fluid one of adjusting, selecting, and filling in.

Teachers' roles in regard to schema are twofold. First, teachers can help children establish schema by providing new experiences to act upon. Secondly, they can extend existing schema by assisting youngsters to fill them out through the development of additional categories and relationships.

Sometimes adults overestimate the depth of children's understanding. One teacher was surprised to learn of her second-grader's concept of "hard" and "soft." She asked a child who had brought in her rock collection to select the hardest and the softest rock. The little girl carefully felt each stone rather than rubbing them against each other to see which made grooves and which were left without indentations. Holding up a smooth rock, the girl called it the softest. A rough rock she labeled the hardest. The child's schema of "hard" and "soft" consisted of a limited aspect of touch. She needed to explore further, comparing items in a variety of ways to determine their density.

This deepening of understanding, or building of schema, may be developed through activities. Categorizing leaves, for example, particularly in groups where observations of edges, shapes, and veination patterns may be shared, will extend already established schema. Writing about the activity helps children clarify their thinking, thus expanding their schema.

Every act is organized, that is, fit into a schema. The movement of *organization* is *adaptation*. Piaget considers these to be the two basic functions (Phillips, 1969). Adaptation is divided into two types: assimilation and accommodation.

Assimilation occurs when a child takes data from the environment and changes the data to fit an existing schema. Another way of describing this process would be that children make the experience their own. They form it to meet their prior constructs. This is something youngsters must do for themselves; a teacher may not perform the act for them. For example, after a field trip, far more assimilation will occur if teachers do not summarize the trip themselves, but rather assist the students to draw their own conclusions, making their own decisions on the most important and interesting events. This activity is more time-consuming, for it is a difficult process, but in the long run it is more efficient, for real learning will occur.

To assimilate an experience children could write about it, drawing upon their own schema as the framework for the composition. Displaying the work, including art products that may occur, truly sets up a learning environment that encourages assimilation. Art is a channel through which children can express their understanding of the experience.

Talking about an activity facilitates assimilation. Artwork can serve as the focus for such talk, thus allowing the children to think through their interpretation of the experience before speaking. Study trips serve as but one stimulus; experiments, observations, projects, and books heard and read may become the source for other assimilating activities.

The value of sharing—particularly sharing school experiences—becomes quite clear. Children have to decide the sequence of the presentation, the relationship of one event to another, and which aspects are the most important to include. They learn to take their own version, organized within their personal schema, and share it with their peers. Here, an opportunity exists to learn another's point of view, thus developing a sense of audience.

Accommodation occurs when the child's schemata are changed to meet the incoming data. New constructs may be added, old ones dropped or altered. Thus, accommodation consists of reshaping—looking at the known in a different way and adding new concepts to old ones. The activities described in the discussion of assimilation also provide opportunities for accommodation.

The teacher can assist this accommodation function by providing opportunities that will permit conflict in old schemata to occur. Extending activities that build upon prior experiences can help a child to see a situation in a new way. For example, role-playing may place the student within a context not faced before. A known character in a book could be confronted with a decision that was not in the original story. How might Mrs. Rabbit have behaved if Peter had been hurt while fleeing Mr. MacGregor's field? Different schemata may become related. Book discussions offer children an opportunity to accommodate the views of their peers as they look at the characters and their actions from a different point of view.

Choral reading forces youngsters to attend to facets of literature they may not have considered before. To read together, the group must consider each word and its contribution to the meaning, thus extending their original schema. Main ideas and subordinate ideas are discussed as the children decide upon performance procedures of intonation, pauses, and volume.

Since this is a group project, once again the views of others must be accommodated.

Teacher questioning becomes focused. If the child's present understanding of a concept is found through observation in play, work, or verbal interaction, a teacher can decide upon questions that will create a problem to solve or a conflict not seen before. Perhaps a child has been drawing horses that are always standing still. The teacher might ask how the horses would look if they were jumping a fence, if one stallion were fighting with another, or if the horses were fleeing cowboys trying to catch them.

Getting at a child's thinking can be difficult, for the child's answers may be deceptive. A logical response from the child may be confusing to an adult, and a supposedly logical question from an adult may be illogical to the child. Alfred was participating in a Piagetian conservation task of volume. Before him were two tumblers of water. The examiner asked if each glass held the same volume. Alfred carefully eyed the levels of the water and agreed that each held the same. One tumbler of water was then poured into a taller but narrower glass, causing the liquid level to rise higher than it did before. If Alfred conserved volume, he would realize that each container, one of the original tumblers and the taller, narrower glass, held the same volume. If he were not yet conserving volume, Alfred would select the taller glass as having more liquid, based upon his perception. When the examiner asked which container he would *prefer,* Alfred immediately pointed to the tumbler. This answer did not fit the conservation test. Incredulously, the examiner queried, "Why did you choose that glass?" Alfred quickly responded, "Oh, that glass (the tall one) has finger marks on it. The other one is cleaner." Realizing the clear logic, the examiner asked which glass had more water. "Oh, they're the same," said Alfred, probably wondering why such a self-evident question was posed.

Obviously no expectation of right or wrong "answers" or behaviors should occur. Teachers can use their discussions with children to find out how they perceive their experiences and to see whether the students are willing and able to change their schemata to accommodate new data.

Equilibration refers to the process by which structures change while resulting in equilibrium. Piaget believes this process to be basic to human adaptation. "The mind always works ... to find a 'balance' between assimilation and accommodation, to eliminate inconsistencies or gaps between reality and the mind's picture of reality" (Craig, 1979, p. 33). An interesting phenomenon occurs: the very state of equilibrium brings about inconsistencies. For, when equilibrium happens, the structure becomes sharper, more focused than before, and inconsistencies and gaps are delineated that were not previously noticed. Hence, equilibrium is always in a state of flux although series of assimilation and accommodation conclusions will bring periodic stability.

This process of equilibration appears clearly within the language arts. Children read and reread books. They ask for stories to be reread and told in a search for a stabilization of ideas in order to grasp them all equally well. By going over and over the literature, children find things they had not noticed before. Rereading books develops fluency and an ease with language and the story within the text. For beginning readers, going over and over a story allows them to approximate the text more closely. They are seeking an equilibrium between the printed words and their reading of them.

The search continues in writing and oral language. In the prior chapter, a page of "A's" was reproduced. Here, the youngster was practicing his knowledge of "A-making." After he had achieved equilibrium, that is, was able to control the production of this letter, he saw a new problem. What would happen if the letter were turned upside down? So, he tried it. A great deal of practice in oral language is similar to this practice in written language. A child's soliloquies of verb forms, a baby's babbling, and invention of rhymes are all evidences of equilibration, the search for a balance.

Some teachers may misinterpret these practice sessions and believe that no progress is being made; there is a danger, however, in moving on before fluency is developed. An example might be moving to cursive writing before manuscript is fully mastered. Children need time on a plateau of learning for it frees them to explore, to see the task more clearly, which in turn creates possibilities for further learning. This practice time allows youngsters to become comfortable with their concepts and skills. If permitted, children will practice on their own. They do not need drills in the traditional sense. Teachers, however, must permit opportunities to perform an activity over and again.

Piaget's Stages of Development

Possibly one of the best-known aspects of Piaget's theory is the child's stages of development. He states that children do not skip stages; they go through them invariably, although their rate of development varies. The stages begin at the age of zero, but knowledge within each level is important, for all skills developed in one level remain in the following stages.

The initial stage is the *sensorimotor,* which runs from birth until approximately two years. Babies respond on a reflexive level. They suck, grasp, and cry, and their actions on the physical world influence their growth. A combination of maturation and interaction with the environment modify sensorimotor reflexes, and behaviors not present at birth begin to emerge. At the end of this stage thinking occurs. This means children can manipulate objects and events mentally; they become more efficient. "Development proceeds from reflex activity to representation and sensorimotor solutions to problems" (Wadsworth, 1978, p. 15). The development of internal representation allows children to use symbols to represent objects, an essential aspect of language acquisition.

The *preoperational* period extends from about two to seven years of age. During this period language grows rapidly. Children's thinking is based upon what they perceive. In the preoperational stage the ability to conserve, learning to rely on logic rather than perception, begins to emerge. An interesting fact is that conservations develop across two stages, preoperational and concrete operational. Once again the sequence is invariable, although the rate varies. Conservation of length and number appears first at about ages six to seven. Area, mass, and liquid are next, developing near ages seven to eight. Weight comes later, ages nine to ten, with volume arriving last, ages eleven to twelve (Wadsworth, 1978).

Preoperational youngsters believe in animism—trees make the breezes. These children are highly egocentric, for they believe that all others think as they do. It is impossible for them to see another viewpoint. Conflicts with other children occur often, end easily by separation, and are quickly forgotten. Even though group projects prove difficult, interaction with others develops conflict from which children learn that there are views other than their own. These youngsters have difficulty establishing group procedures and goals; therefore, interest centers rather than group projects might be a better classroom arrangement.

Discovery, concrete materials, and authentic experiences form the key to this stage. These children can think but they rely on what they perceive as the basis for their thought. They need the freedom to explore without the restrictions of adult logic. The beginning of the preoperational period may be typified by rapid oral language acquisition; in the middle to latter portion of the stage, most children acquire concepts of writing and print.

When the *concrete operations* state is reached (seven to eleven years of age), children no longer subordinate their logic to perception. This logic, however, appears in concrete problems. These youngsters have difficulty with complex verbal problems, hypothetical situations, and problems of the future. Thought is tied to the concrete and to perception, although not dominated by perception (Wadsworth, 1978).

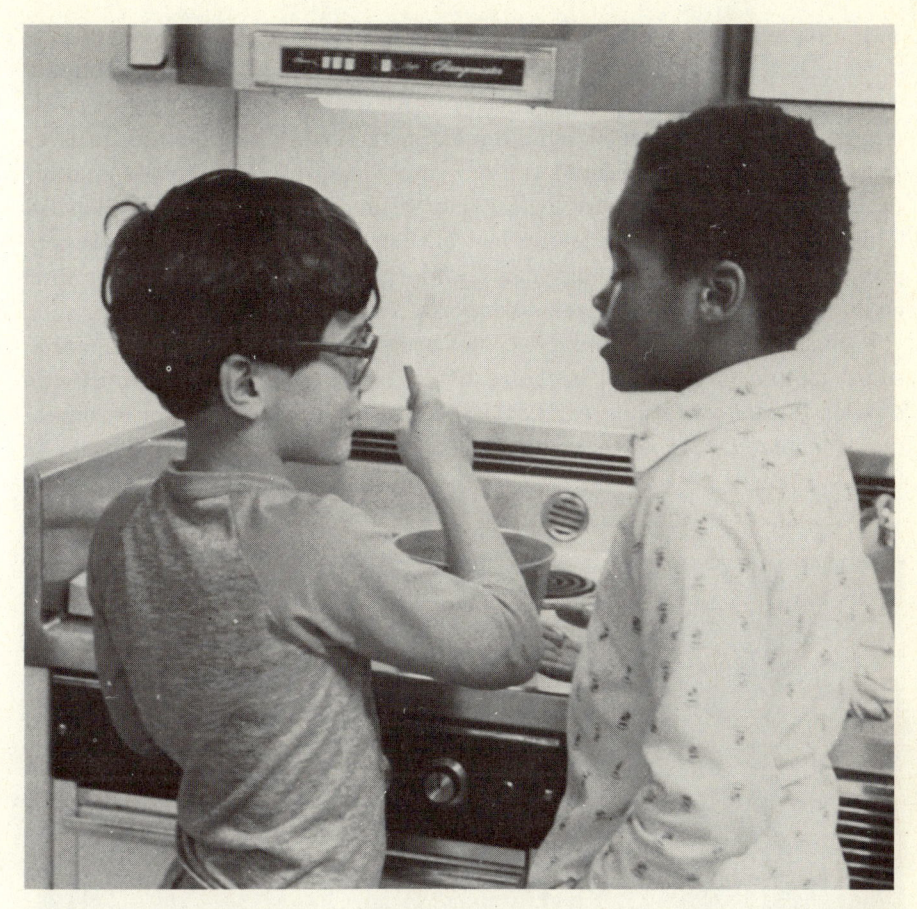

Cooking offers many opportunities for concrete experiences leading toward hypothesizing, comparing, and determining cause and effect. The language that flows from such experiences is rich in diversity and exploration. (Ms. Harrison's classroom, Douglas Alternative School, Columbus, Ohio)

These youngsters are better able to work with cause and effect (animism is over), they can see relationships, and they are able to develop alternative endings to stories. They still need concrete materials and experiences. Writing assignments and the choice of writing as an activity should begin with a concrete experience, e.g., describing what is seen, felt, heard, or touched. Comparing items such as plants or rocks in the classroom or specimens collected on a study trip might be another example. Sharing becomes easier when a concrete object is discussed.

Drama, puppetry, and role-playing are a step away from the concrete but still offer youngsters concrete experiences to work through and eventually write about. These actions serve as mediators for thought and as planning activities for writing.

Eleven- to fifteen-year-old children enter the final developmental stage of *formal operations*. Youngsters can now apply logical thought to any kind of problem; their structures for logical thought are becoming fully developed. This means that the *capacity* for logical thought is present. Logic does not grow but individuals do acquire new knowledge of the various disciplines and elaborate their old knowledge (Wadsworth, 1978).

Formal operational thinking does not necessarily occur in all areas. Since some specific (concrete) knowledge has to serve as a basis on which to develop formal operations, early selection of a major or career aim becomes questionable if a broad educational background is eclipsed. High-school

This child truly has discovered the excitement of having wonderful ideas. She feels free to interact with others, discovering new concepts about the world around her. (Mrs. Beaver's informal classroom, Barrington School, Upper Arlington, Ohio)

vocational and career centers that do not include strong science and humanities coursework could limit students to the development of formal operational thinking in but a few areas. Duckworth (1972) writes:

> In an area you know well, you can think of many possibilities, and working them through often makes demands of a formal nature. If there is no area in which you are familiar enough with the phenomena to have to make sense of complex relationships, then you are not likely to have to develop formal operations. Knowing enough about things is one prerequisite for wonderful ideas (p. 231).

Children's initial use of logical operations may appear immature for it is egocentric. They use their own logic as the sole criterion for what is "right" and "moral." These youngsters fail to take the real world into account, for what happens in reality is not always logical. Decisions need to be seasoned with experience. Pure logic does not always apply (à la *Star Trek*'s Dr. Spock!). Crusades, calls for fairness, and disillusionment with adult behavior become common.

The most important point for language-arts teachers to keep in mind about this final stage is that although the top level of cognitive thinking has become possible, such logical thought does not appear automatically. The student has to have a concrete grounding as the basis for thinking. Writing is still easier when it comes from an experience rather than when it is based on an abstract topic. For example, it is easier for students to explain what happened on the first day of school than to explain how they think others would describe them or to discuss "honesty." When the children become fluent at composing in a variety of forms, they can try more abstract topics and innovate freely with style.

Cognitive Development and the Language-Arts Teacher

Parallels can be drawn between actions that foster cognitive growth and language development. For teachers, the child's present level or stage of development is not as significant as the process of development itself. A rich environment in which children may explore freely with an opportunity to interact with others supports both cognitive and language growth. Knowledge builds upon knowledge. Duckworth (1979) claims the idea of "diagnosing" children to design individual instruction to be impractical, considering the variety of notions and levels that must be considered. For her, teaching should concentrate on broadening and deepening the children's use of the notions they already have:

> Certainly we would want each child to have the occasion to work at his or her own level. The solution for the teacher, however, is not to tailor narrow exercises for individual children, but rather to offer situations in which children at various levels, whatever their intellectual structures, can come to know parts of the world in new ways (p. 311).

Nor do narrow exercises in language skills expand language growth. The focus of our methodology chapters is to provide alternatives to filling-in blanks, diagramming sentences, and copying paragraphs in which to place punctuation marks. A rich input of language that can be used in a natural setting promotes language development.

Even though the process of learning is the most important consideration, the teacher must remember that seven-year-old youngsters do behave differently from those ten years of age. An awareness of such differences makes planning for teaching easier. In his book *A Sympathetic Understanding of the Child: Birth to Sixteen,* Elkind (1974) has described some of the general characteristics of children in profile form from year one through age sixteen. The seriousness and quietness of seven-year-olds in comparison to their behavior just a year before is explained as a result of a newly developing "digestion" of new experiences. Seven-year-old children reflect on old information, sorting and categorizing it to make sense of their world. They become sensitive, even moody at times, and wish to have their work in perfect form. This is the period when teachers find so many erasures on the paper that often holes are worn through!

Ten-year-olds enjoy organized group activities and being with their family. Schedules in school are appreciated. Girls begin their physical advancement and many may be taller and heavier than the boys. With girls' physical maturity comes an interest in sexual matters, not yet a concern for boys, whose onset of puberty comes later. Reading interests divide by sex.

Elkind's descriptions are far more thorough than those given here. He includes a broad-ranging discussion of physical, social, and cognitive development across age groups. Anyone interested in one particular age level must remember that a class of children will contain a range of behaviors, both younger and older in nature.

Moral Development

Some Children's Ideas about Justice

McKenzie (1972) studied the moral development of children by asking them questions revealing the way they felt about the book *Crow Boy* (Yoshima). This is the story of Chibi, a shy, lonely child who hides beneath the schoolhouse on the first day of school to avoid the other children. He is teased by them but the schoolmaster draws him out, not only from under the building but also, eventually, from himself. Chibi's talent for imitating crows is recognized and appreciated. "Crow Boy" grows in self-confidence. The story closes six years later with Chibi's award for perfect school attendance.

When McKenzie asked the children what they would do if they were the teacher and found Chibi hiding, one youngster, Ruth, responded that she would keep him after school. Ruth was then asked why Chibi was hiding. "He was shy and he was afraid the other children would bully him and be unkind to him," Ruth answered.

"Would punishing make him feel better about that?"

"No," said Ruth.

"So would punishing him be any use?"

Ruth answered quickly, "Not really, but he was naughty so he has to be punished."

Ruth revealed an understanding of Chibi's feelings but she believed in a strict balance of right and wrong. "Wrong," hiding under the building rather than attending school, must be punished. Ashley, an eight-year-old, agreed: "He hid under the school because the other children didn't like him. It was careless to hide under the school in case the building was on fire. He should have been punished." The adult role is an authority figure who metes out discipline for "bad" behavior.

In contrast, Emma stated "The teacher should have taken Chibi out and talked to him and explained to him that wasn't what you did at school. After all, it was only his first day and he was frightened." Emma is on her way to developing a more sophisticated understanding of human problems.

Moral Development and the Language Arts

We should note that while many educators and psychologists agree that there are stages of moral development, some have doubts about its existence and still others consider stages of this development to be culturally induced. We have decided to include a description of this body of work because many language-arts activities stem from moral origins such as agreeing about what is fair, deciding class rules, and accepting those different from ourselves. Too often such topics are seen in contexts of social studies or health, but, in reality, language can serve as a way to understand the thoughts and feelings of others and to accept the fact that differences of opinion will occur. Using language in these ways will assist the development of communicative competence, which includes the social context and setting. A discussion of moral development gives us, the authors, a forum to make a connection between classroom experiences in making judgments and the language arts.

Moral development has a direct impact on the language arts, for values are included in the curriculum. Judgments of fairness, of what is right and wrong, occur daily and become an integral part of classroom discussions. Teachers need to recognize where opportunities to make value judgments exist in their classes. In this way they will be able to make sure children have open-ended learning activities to develop their own moral system. Language arts is the logical avenue in which such development may grow and mature.

How do children learn to make decisions on what is right and what is wrong? Why do children make the judgments they do? Psychologists have studied the moral development of children by centering on this development's components—cognitive, behavioral and emotional—and the relationships among these components. The cognitive facet refers to judgments of good or bad and knowledge of ethical rules. The behavioral component has been investigated by observing how youngsters react in specific situations. The emotional aspect may be viewed through such focuses as guilt and anxiety (Hetherington and Parke, 1979B).

Cognitive Theories of Moral Development

Beginning with the cognitive stage of "moral realism," Piaget (1965) believes that youngsters progress to the more mature stage of "moral reciprocity." Very young children begin with little or no awareness or concern for rules. Preschoolers may be playing a game together such as ring toss but each will be using his or her own rules, not caring what the other player is doing. No discussion of combining or changing the rules will take place.

By school age, around five, rules become far more important. They are devised by outside authority, usually adults, and are not to be questioned. In Piaget's terms, "moral absolutism" is in place for there exists but one set of rules. A game may not be played using a variety of procedures. Adults provide the authority for such rigid rules, and punishment will occur if the rules are not followed. Thus any discussion of altering rules for these children becomes impossible but for different reasons than in the earlier stage.

Breaking a rule results in "immanent justice." A child may reason that her toy broke because she disobeyed her mother, a pattern found in many folk and fairy tales. Children understand the reasoning for the boy turning into a deer when he drank from the brook, for he was warned not to do so. The degree of wrongness is determined by the consequences of the act. Intent has no place in this level of moral thinking.

Piaget (1965) believes that two factors influence the development of moral realism: egocentrism and realistic thinking. Egocentrism prevents children from subordinating their own experiences so that they may see situations as others would. The development of realistic thinking at first creates a confusion of external reality and children's own experiences.

Morality of reciprocity emerges at about nine to eleven years of age. Rules may be questioned and changed because children become aware of their arbitrary nature. Adults may be wrong, even parents. Violation of rules is not necessarily wrong and punishment may not follow. Intention of the doer becomes important and should be considered in the punishment situation. Everyone should be treated fairly and for these children that simply means everyone should receive exactly the same treatment.

Piaget stresses the significance of peers in moral development. Through interaction with others, children learn to compare and question their own viewpoints. Group projects help sensitize students to members' beliefs, positions, and experiences. This is a good period for small-group work where participants establish their own goals, procedures, and assignments. Concern and respect for others grow when equals share the work. Such sharing not only supports moral development but also development of language skills.

Building on Piaget's early theory, Kohlberg (Kohlberg and Hersh, 1977) has evolved a series of moral stages, which are sequential, indicative of hierarchical integrations (the inclusion of prior-level accomplishments), and cognitive in nature. Kohlberg states that because children may show that they are able and can comprehend the reasoning at a higher stage it does not mean they will perform at that level. However, if children have not cognitively reached a higher order stage, they will not be able to perform at that level. Thus, the attainment of a specific stage in moral development only *allows* certain types of moral judgments; it does not necessarily *predict* their occurrence.

Kohlberg's six stages are divided into three broad levels. The first is the *preconventional* stage, where the child responds to labels of "bad" and "good" in terms of the physical repercussions of punishments or rewards. Stage one is grounded in punishment and obedience, when power lies with those who dole out the punishment or reward. The system, such as parenthood, is not respected in and of itself; respect for parental control, however, is acknowledged. Such a book as Potter's *Peter Rabbit* is appreciated, for it reenforces what will happen if you do not obey your mother. The farmer just may catch you and you will be sent to your bed without your supper! A reverse theme appears in Mitchell's *Where Did My Mother Go?* The young kitten looks all over the animal town for his mother, who is not there. Finally, he goes home, where she has just returned after a series of errands for her son's benefit. He scolds her anyway for not letting him know where she was just as a worried mother would scold her child. This play on roles is amusing to children and lets them imagine what their reactions would be if they were the parent.

Careful observation of a child's dramatic play will reveal youngsters' understanding of parental practice. "Bad" children are spanked or punished in some fearful manner, often harsher than their parents' true actions. Children are sent to bed without their dinners just as Max was in Sendak's *Where the Wild Things Are.*

Stage two, the *instrumental–relativist orientation,* consists of satisfying current needs and possibly those of others. Conformity occurs to manipulate others, to gain something wanted, while sharing may be viewed as a bartering process, trading one favor for another. Childish spats are common for this age and level group. Udry's *Let's Be Enemies,* which tells of a fight between two youngsters who become enemies and finally return to be friends at the conclusion, is a fine example. One day's events have little effect on the following day's actions. Even one hour's argument may evaporate during the next hour's cooperative venture. Trading activities flourish as the language of bartering evolves. Children will set up their own rules of what constitutes a fair trade and proper procedures for this act. Time for private, personal conversations assist children in developing the functional language of interaction.

The second level, *conventional,* contains stages three and four. Within this level youngsters have a concern and loyalty for social order. They value their family, social group, and nation and are willing to support and justify these systems regardless of immediate consequences. In stage three, *"good boy–nice girl" orientation,* children still base judgments on the reactions of others but the decision is made according to approval or disapproval rather than physical force. The intention becomes important; "he meant well" is now taken into account. These youngsters are able to discuss books, dramatize scenes, and role-play where they assume and interpret a character's actions that may differ from their own. Through these activities students can enhance their understanding of others' actions and motivations.

"Law-and-order" orientation, stage four, reveals a fixed view toward rules. Authority should be obeyed and a "good" person performs his or her duty showing the appropriate respect. "My country, right or wrong" would be an example of a belief that might be held at this stage. Stories that involve conflict among "good" rules provide challenging discussions here. *Across Five Aprils* by Hunt reveals the conflict between family loyalty and allegiance to a belief. Greene's *Summer of My German Soldier* is another novel that centers on the conflict between a kind, bookish prisoner of war seeking freedom and a young girl's search for friendship. On an easier reading level, *Sam, Bangs, and Moonshine* by Ness serves as a focal point for the dilemma What is truth? Small-group discussions allow youngsters to enter according to their own reading level and level of moral development. A wide variety of such groups assists a teacher in individualizing a language-arts program. A cautionary note in use of literature should be assumed here for, as McKenzie (1972) states, "The primary purpose of literature is aesthetic, not to educate morally. The situation in literature provides insights into the human condition, and that children exposed to worthwhile literature are put in a position to make moral judgments and to develop moral concepts" (p. 27).

The third, final, and most controversial level, *postconventional,* deals with students' efforts to define moral values apart from social groups and their identification with them; rather, moral decisions are made on self-established standards. Stage five, the *social-contract, legalistic orientation* accepts flexibility within moral beliefs. The individual acknowledges the fact that social norms are necessary and must be established but these morals may be modified when members of the group agree to the need for modification. Kohlberg and Hersh (1977) state that there is a legislative point of view that allows one to examine the changes that are brought about by a rational consideration of society's needs. Individuals seeing their roles and responsibilities as members of a society will form contracts and agreements, which carry obligations. At this stage discussions may focus both on the appropriateness of legislating morality such as the Prohibition Amendment and on the morality of specific pieces of legislation such as state aid to private schools. Classroom discussion can become quite lively at this stage of moral development, for not only can world problems be debated, but also personal and interpersonal aspects of morality previously considered can be reexamined with deeper understanding.

The final stage, *universal–ethical–principle orientation,* refers to moral decisions made on the basis of self-selected ethical principles such as the Golden Rule. Rules applied are broad and abstract, with universal application. Individuals will use their own criteria even if it does not agree with the decision of the majority. An example would be those who worked to save the Jewish population in Germany during World War II even though it was against the law and contrary to the behavior of most of the populace. Such books as Hautzig's *The Endless Steppe* and *Anne Frank: The Diary of a Young Girl* could serve as springboards for discussions of what children think they would have done as youngsters in those times.

Researchers have explored Kohlberg's stages to determine whether they are sequential and do exist. The findings, particularly on the first four stages, have been positive and some investigators found they could influence movement from one stage to another. A common result was that movement appeared more easily when the individuals had nearly passed through their current stage and were "ready" to shift to the next one. In her survey of the research literature, Paolitto (1977) reports that classroom experiences can stimulate students' moral development. Such experiences include the idea of the teacher serving as a catalyst for creating moral cognitive conflict within oneself and stimulating students to see problems through the eyes of others. Teaching strategies were role-playing, peer counseling, cross-age teaching, discussion of real or hypothetical moral dilemmas, learning about moral philosophy, and the planning and implementing of institutional change.

All of these teaching activities are part of the language arts. A teacher must keep in mind that students will be at different levels in their moral development. At times the same activity will assist all. Drama and role-playing a moral dilemma offers the same opportunity for each child to grow and interpret at his or her own level. Even though the youngsters' discussion may seem to be at cross purposes, their interaction may serve as a basis to see and understand the view of others. Small groups offer greater opportunity for participation. Classroom problems such as roughhousing on the playground or crowded lines in the school cafeteria provide very real purposes for moral-development activities.

Emotional Theories of Moral Development

In contrast to the cognitive component, Chukovsky (1968) and Bettelheim (1976) deal with the emotional, seeing folk and fairy tales as avenues for children's moral development. Each considers the learning of values to come from an identification with the hero or heroine rather than learning from any "preaching" within the tale of what is good and evil. Chukovsky, a noted Russian author, observed that children have an active sympathy for characters who struggle and they participate with them in imaginary quests for justice, goodness, and freedom. At the time of his writing, Chukovsky believed he needed to defend the fiction of the folk and fairy tale from those in the Soviet Union who thought only realistic fiction should be given to children. He noted that youngsters kept away from fairy tales would assert their rights and make up their own to fill this void. He stated that tales are normal for children, for they regard the world in fantastic ways, a statement reminiscent of Piaget's animistic stage. Stories, especially fairy tales, are important for child growth. Chukovsky wrote:

> The goal of storytellers ... consists of fostering in the child, at whatever cost, compassion and humaneness—this miraculous ability of man to be disturbed by another being's misfortunes, to feel joy about another being's happiness, to experience another's fate as one's own (p. 138).

Bettelheim sees the child as identifying not only with those representing good but also at times with those representing evil in the tales. For "evil is as omnipresent as virtue ... [and] propensities for both are present in every man. It is this duality which poses the moral problem, and requires the struggle to solve it" (pp. 8–9). Punishment does not serve as the deterrent to crime but the fact that crime does not pay in these stories produces the moral teaching for children. All wish to be winners, to identify with the hero or heroine of the story, and triumph "as virtue is victorious." By listening to and reading fairy and folk tales children work through the "monsters" of evil within themselves, choosing the virtuous path not because it is "right" but because the character who epitomizes goodness arouses the child's sympathy. The choice is simple, for good and evil are polarized in these tales. Bettelheim writes that children need

> ... a moral education which subtly, and by implication only, conveys to him the advantages of moral behavior, not through abstract ethical concepts but through that which seems tangibly right and therefore meaningful to him (p. 5).

Morality is not found in all tales; for example "Puss in Boots" and "Jack and the Beanstalk" really deal with the weak in life. "The Three Little Pigs" is illustrative of several values. First, there is the value of planning as displayed by the third pig, who delays playing in order to build a strong house and saves his own life. In retributive justice, the wolf who ate the two other pigs and wished to eat the third ends up as food for the survivor because of his cleverness in descending the chimney. The wolf is a bad character because he wished to destroy. It is all right to eat but not to devour as the wolf did.

In his justification of fairy tales, Bettelheim strongly states:

> ... more can be learned from them [fairy tales] about the inner problems of human beings, and of the right solutions to their predicaments in any society, than from any other type of story within a child's comprehension (p. 5).

The value of this kind of literature is that it is a springboard for drama, role-playing, puppetry, and inclusion in general play. Children will naturally select fairy tales in their language-arts activities. The stories are accessible, clearly drawn, and without too many miscellaneous details to confuse young learners.

As youngsters mature, other books will evoke questions of a moral nature. How should an individual support family honor? Is it fair to harm some people for others' benefit? How do these problems affect daily decisions in youngsters' lives? Moral development is a strand that runs through many language activities in the elementary and middle-school years.

Social Development

Interaction among a Group of First-Grade Children

Four first-grade girls sat in a row at the table working on their mural. Each had her own set of crayons and appeared to know exactly what she wanted to do. The conversation ranged in topics. One youngster, Susie, said, "I'm going to put pink flowers in mine." No response came from the others; probably the two at the end could not hear her. Suddenly a pink flower appeared in Mary's section next to Susie's. Ellen, seated by Mary, cast a casual eye on Mary's drawing and a flower eventually entered her segment. The child on the end drew her portion without flowers. The work continued.

These girls worked together on a group project, the mural, but their level of socialization deterred rather than enhanced a truly joint venture. Young children do interact with each other and are influenced by their peers; the main source of influence, however, is still the family and significant adults in their lives. These girls will do much growing in the area of socialization. Importance of peers will increase rapidly and with this increase will come the development of social skills that result in cooperation, ability to develop shared goals, and group responsibility. Language is one of the most important resources in which this socialization process may grow.

Knowledge of the Social Situation and Language Development

Communication is a social act and for normal children, communication and social skills develop together. The pragmatics of language, that is, language in use, takes the social context into account. A speech act is what one is doing with an utterance: asserting, questioning, or commanding, among other functions. The elocutionary force is the intent behind the act. A speaker and listener have to learn the force of what is said. For example, a question may not be merely a question. "Do you have any pencils?" may mean "Give me a pencil." Or, "It's cold, don't you think?" may mean "Close the window."

Subtleties of language use are learned within a social context. Children quickly learn that a mother's "please" may actually be a command rather than a situation of choice. Success in language use corresponds with success in social settings since social development is an integral part of language development.

Social Development and Personality

Social development is also closely tied to the development of personality since children's behavior reflects their self-esteem and since their behavior determines how they are accepted by others. Children who have a high overall self-concept and approach not only tasks but also other people with the expectation of success will probably be successful. With this self-confidence children will not be afraid to follow their own judgments, express their own convictions, and consider novel ideas (Mussen, Conger, and Kagan, 1979B). Such willingness to explore is an essential component of learning, for those who would learn must dare to risk failure. Children with a low self-concept fear failure; they test their environment more gingerly, thereby having less data to adapt to their organization of the world about them.

Children's self-concept is mainly based upon experiences at home and parental influences, but other people and experiences such as day-care enrollment, extended family in the home, and siblings do play key roles. Later on children's views of themselves are derived from the views their peers have of them; that is, children see themselves as defined by their social group. If other children perceived them as being good in sports, they will consider themselves athletes. If they are among the last chosen for teams, they will not try a variety of sport activities.

Social skills are learned. Hurlock (1978) writes, "[There is] ... little evidence that people are born social, unsocial, or antisocial, and much evidence that they are made that way by learning" (p. 228). She cites four essentials of socialization: 1) many opportunities for socialization with children their own age and with a variety of adults; 2) skills to communicate clearly on topics of interest to others; 3) motivation for social activities based upon satisfaction from social experiences; 4) learning social skills with the guidance of others through role-modeling an admired adult or sibling.

Hurlock (1978) believes that a variety of factors contribute to the influence a group has on its members. These factors include:

1. *Acceptability to the Group.* Popular children and those who are successful in receiving the group's acceptance rely less on family for self-esteem. Those who do not find success in the group often turn to their families.

2. *Security of Status.* Youngsters secure in their status within the group feel free to disagree. Less secure youngsters are apt to conform, following the group's consensus of opinion.

3. *Type of Group.* The type of group itself asserts varying degrees or influence. The strongest is a primary group, such as the family or peer group. The second in influence is a secondary group, such as organized play (Little League, Girl Scouts) and social groups. The least influential is a tertiary group, those encountered briefly or by chance, such as patients in a doctor's waiting room.

4. *Different Members of the Group.* A leader has the greatest influence on members; the least popular has the least influence.

5. *Personality.* Members who feel inferior conform more closely to the group. Interestingly, children with an authoritarian personality also conform to group standards closely because they fear rejection.

6. *Affiliation Motive.* The stronger a child's desire to be a member of the group, the greater the influence of that group on the child.

The traditional view that has been supported by research but is now being questioned is that children tend to choose their like sex for friends, an action that begins in the preschool years. Boys generally have a broader range of friends than girls. Towards puberty, those boys who mature later are rated by their peers as being more childish, less relaxed, bossy, talkative, and attention-seeking. The early-maturing boys, on the other hand, have greater peer acceptance, thus becoming more popular (Hetherington and Parke, 1979C). Girls are inclined to have a narrow group of friends, often a single best friend. They play in small groups and behave in closer conformity to the group than boys. Later-maturing girls have a social advantage, at least during the early onset of puberty. They are considered to be more sociable (Hetherington and Parke, 1979C). These sex differences may disappear as newer views toward sex roles become more evident in society.

Popular children have a good adjustment to social situations, are seen as friendly with a responsiveness to others, show low anxiety and a reasonable level of self-esteem. These children possess the social skills of reinforcing others and communicating well. They initiate interactions effectively (Hetherington and Parke, 1979C). It seems the more a child has, the more social expectations that are fulfilled.

Stages of Social Development

Social development may be viewed in three stages: early childhood, middle childhood, and puberty. Children learn to behave in socially approved ways with increasingly sophisticated skills.

Early Childhood. During these formative years, the home serves as the basis for social attitudes and behaviors. The presence of brothers and sisters, grandparents, and father and mother provide socializing experiences. Positive ones make the child seek more such experiences; negative ones can turn the child against them. Hurlock (1979) believes that social attitudes and behavior established in early years usually persist with little change.

Children who attend preschool have the advantage of making many social contacts early in their lives. Group participation supports social adjustment. Since this stage extends until age six or seven, most children have group experiences before entering middle childhood.

Foundations of the Language Arts

The role of the family is central even during beginning school years as can be seen in the writing of two first-graders:

> My mom and Dab
> Love me so much I
> can't take a break
> and they call my
> name,,
> "Snuggy Buggy"

> My Baby Brother has
> hazel eyes   My Mom
> Breast Feed hmi and
> Chainss hsi Daiprs and
> she take Kreae hmi and
> I halp hre take Kreae
> of hmi   we take
> Kreae of hmi by
> Chainssing hsi C los and
> I halp hri by hiteing The Food

Both of these youngsters appear to have begun the process of socialization successfully. "Snuggy Buggy" obviously has strong ties of which she is proud. Family matters often become the subject of compositions and casual conversations. The second child tells about the new addition in her home and how she is a vital part of this event. She began with some help in spelling but pursued her message without the limitations of spelling constraints. This child was fortunate in having a teacher who was more interested in the message than the form of the composition.

> My baby brother has hazel eyes. My mom breast feed him and changes his diapers and she take care of him. We take care of him by changing his clothes and I help her by heating the food.

The speech during early childhood is egocentric. This self-centered talk restricts the amount and kinds of socialization that may occur. Youngsters need shared projects on which to work so that the focus of their talk becomes an object and what can be done with it, rather than themselves and what they are doing. For example, two kindergarten children built a space station out of blocks and other materials they found in the classroom. When visitors arrived one day, these children described the function of each section, told how spacecraft landed, and then had a demonstration battle in the air. It was obvious that these children had discussed in detail the intricacies of their project, for their explanation was most lucid.

Egocentric speech gradually fades as children approach middle childhood; however, it never entirely leaves. Many of us as adults, perhaps all of us, have a favorite topic—ourselves!

Middle Childhood. This stage ranges from age seven until puberty and has been named the "gang age." Children in this stage enter gangs with glee, forming their own organization with a name (often from comics or where they live); develop secret codes and signals; create an insignia, such as caps or badges; hold initiation ceremonies; meet in a special place away from adults; and perform activities, some of which may be forbidden, such as smoking (Hurlock, 1978). If one thinks about all the decisions and plans that are being made, the realization of the amount of language that is going on is overwhelming.

Many positive social skills may be learned from gangs. Hurlock (1978) lists: independence from adults, loyalty to the group, playing of games and sports, taking the part of those mistreated, being a good sport, accepting and carrying out responsibility, competing with others, displaying socially acceptable behavior, and being cooperative.

Middle childhood is the time when the influence of peers becomes greater and the influence of parents and teachers begins to diminish. The point should be made that significant adults, parents, and teachers still exert socializing pressures; however, the *greatest* conforming pressure emanates from the peer group. Children held back from peer-group participation fail to develop mature social skills.

Cooperative projects with little adult supervision become most fruitful. Interest clubs may be developed, such as the "Mysterious Capers" for youngsters devoted to reading mysteries. Probing space may collect yet another group of children. Here, both fiction and nonfiction materials could be explored. Each group could be given class time for meetings and a schedule might be established where they could share with others what they had accomplished. Social skills expand and with them language competencies grow.

Puberty. Sometimes called a "negative phase" or "period of disequilibrium," the puberty stage marks a decline in group activities. These children have a tendency to prefer being alone. Antisocial attitudes and behaviors may appear, for children will intentionally do the opposite of what is expected (Hurlock, 1979). Reasonably calm family units may disrupt because the child in puberty will taunt and tease his brothers and sisters, interrupt their games, and create disciplinary problems for parents.

The worst evidences of antisocial behavior occur in the six- to twelve-month period preceding sexual maturity. Approximately one year's difference lies between girls' and boys' development. Most girls become sexually mature at twelve to thirteen; most boys, at thirteen to fourteen. The strongest negative or antisocial behavior occurs with girls (Hurlock, 1978). Perhaps the physical change is more frightening or the fact that girls are more conforming makes their nonconforming actions more vivid, thus noticeable. This period of antisocial behavior ebbs. The period may be unpleasant for those around teenagers but few permanent scars are left. Puberty may be thought of as an interruption in social development.

The upheaval comes not only from physical factors but also from the environment. Adults can do much to alleviate the tension aroused in this period. One problem is that these youngsters look like adults, so adult expectations are placed upon them. They are given new duties and responsibilities. Children often develop a sense of martyrdom. They are "touchy" anyway and further demands only increase their unhappiness.

Flexibility in grouping and in teacher expectations is the key to this age.

The degree of antisocial behavior varies with each individual child. Not all wish to avoid group interaction. Not all feel depressed and unsatisfied with themselves. In addition, the onset of puberty covers a wide age range. Some girls begin menstruation at nine, others start as late as fourteen. Boys vary as widely as girls.

Out of this time of intense sensitivity and introspection can come perceptive book discussions. The feelings and reactions of characters are better understood, for these youngsters come to realize that others share their feelings and emotions. *Bridge to Terabithia* by Paterson is a good example of a book that contains a range of emotions on friendship and death for the reader to interpret and share.

Sometimes groups of children who form bonds of friendship like to talk together about their day, plans, or feelings. In a free-flowing classroom there is time for all types of interaction—interaction that leads toward advanced social skills. (Douglas Alternative School, Columbus, Ohio)

Role of the Teacher in Grouping Children

Teachers have a limited but significant role in socialization. If a classroom is rigidly structured with the teacher as the center of whole-class activities, there is little room for social interaction; thus, social development must occur only outside the classroom. If, on the other hand, teachers include a variety of group activities and opportunities to work with and meet different people, they will be supporting extending social experiences.

Some of the teacher-established groups may center on book discussions, not just on one book read but on a group of books pertaining to a theme such as survival, books written by the same author, or books with the same illustrator. Favorite poems could be shared and discussed, each student using his or her own preference as a basis for sharing. Projects that are rich in socializing opportunities are those where decisions must be made, such as dictating results or procedures, proofreading each other's work, and reading one to another.

Interest groups need not be restricted to classroom membership but cross-class participation could be encouraged; this would extend children's social contacts and create new situations in which the need for socializing language might occur. Even the sharing of projects from one class to another evokes the use of social language. By relaxing the formality of presentation, individuals or small groups of youngsters could share their projects with groups from another class. In addition, a diversity of classroom aides, including not only parents but also retirees and people from other cultures, offers new social and extending language experiences.

Although competition strengthens group solidarity, it also increases hostility, rivalry, and conflict. Whether between groups or individuals, competition encourages aggression. Working together to achieve meaningful goals, on the other hand, can override group tensions.

> The more free and egalitarian relationship with peers permits a new kind of interpersonal experimentation and exploration, and most particularly a new kind of sensitivity, which will serve as one of the cornerstones for the development of social competence and the capacity to love (Hetherington and Parke, 1979C, p. 476).

With a warm, relaxed teacher, children are more interested and involved in classroom activities. They express their feelings freely and volunteer for more tasks (Mussen, Conger, and Kagan, 1979A). Independence increases and active decision-making takes place, while talk leading toward greater social skills abounds.

Teacher expectation affects children's productivity. A self-fulfilling prophecy appears. Hetherington and Parke (1979C) claim that when teachers believe children to be capable, they establish a warmer social-emotional climate, provide greater feedback and input to those children, and demand better performance from them. If only all children would be considered capable!

Summary

Flexibility in a classroom is needed because all children are in movement as they grow in cognitive abilities, develop greater sophistication in making moral judgments, and become socially adept in their interactions. Small groups foster growth in all areas and support necessary interaction among children. Concrete experiences provide a focal point around which diverse activities may evolve. The growth is not a smooth continuum. A child may behave quite maturely one day and regress the next. Leaps of insight may appear and depths of understanding reveal themselves unexpectedly.

Lack of flexibility within the classroom results in the teacher's inability to deal with individual differences. Discipline problems occur from the too-tightly structured environment. Requiring a slower developing child to summarize may cause frustration, for not all youngsters learn to generalize at the same time. The child's reaction may be to poke an available classmate.

Knowledge of child development helps a teacher to understand students' actions better. Children may "talk back" to the teacher in order to please their peers. They are seeking social acceptance; the teacher is beside the point. At specific stages of moral development there exists a strict sense of fairness, a concern that everyone should be treated the same. A teacher may be considered unfair by some children if the teacher takes a variety of factors into account when decisions are made.

Language development and use appear throughout the various components of child development. All are closely related, each supporting the other as they grow. A knowledgeable language-arts teacher can build on these interrelationships.

Suggested Learning Experiences

1. Observe a child on the playground and in the classroom. Are there any relationships between the child's role in the play group and the child's

performance in the classroom? Does this relationship hold true for other children you observe?

2. Ask a child to tell you about a favorite hero or heroine (Wonder Woman, Spiderman, etc.). Which traits are most admired? How much of the child's discussion is on the outcome of the hero or heroine's actions? What can you surmise about the development of values in relation to Chukovsky's and Bettelheim's hypotheses?

3. Collect an assortment of young children's artwork, asking the young artist to tell you about the picture. In a small group, discuss how each youngster may be viewing the world which he or she encounters. How does the language the child used to explain the picture illuminate the objects or scene drawn? Would the child's language alone be as revealing as the picture itself? What advantages are there to both sources of data?

4. Listen in on a group of youngsters discussing a problem that concerns their own actions, such as rules for behavior in the cafeteria. Note each child's contributions. Which levels of moral thinking have been reached? Are all at the same level of development?

5. Observe one day in a classroom noting the topics of all the talk that appear within the whole class and small groups that you can. How many of these topics concern judgments or interpretations based upon one's own value systems?

Recommended Readings

Bettelheim, Bruno, *The Uses of Enchantment,* Knopf, New York, 1976.
    In this chapter we discussed Bettelheim's views on fairy tales and their relationship to child development. In his book Bettelheim includes separate chapters in which he discusses such fairy tales as "Cinderella," "Sleeping Beauty," "Hansel and Gretel," and "The Three Bears." You will enjoy reading selections from this book. It will not only help you see aspects of fairy tales in a new light, but will also show you how fairy tales meet some special needs of children.

Duckworth, Eleanor, "The Having of Wonderful Ideas," *Harvard Educational Review* 42: 217–231, May, 1972.
    Duckworth challenges "the teaching of Piaget," that is, instructing children to learn Piagetian tasks. Her view is that the teacher's role is to help children test out ideas that they find significant; this she calls "the having of wonderful ideas." She recommends that teachers should accept the child's point of view and allow that to serve as the framework for generating ideas.

Elkind, David, *The Hurried Child: Growing Up Too Fast Too Soon,* Addison-Wesley Publications Co., Reading, Mass., 1981.

The pressure on children to achieve, to win, to be popular, to hurry into adulthood is a syndrome of our time. We read about teacher "burnout" but we are unaware of the stress placed upon children. This book, brief and very readable, will heighten your awareness of the problems of these hurried children of the eighties. As you read this book, try to think of ways a teacher could create an environment that would ease the pressure on children.

"Moral Development," *Theory Into Practice,* Volume 16, April, 1977.

For those of you who are interested in this rather controversial area of moral development, TIP has devoted an entire issue to the topic. Articles that explain the theory, survey the research, and suggest applications are included.

References

Professional Literature

Bettelheim, Bruno, *The Uses of Enchantment,* Knopf, New York, 1976.

Chukovsky, Kornei, *From Two to Five,* Miriam Morton, trans. and ed., University of California Press, Berkeley, 1968.

Collins, Allan; Brown, John Seely; and Larkin, Kathy M., "Inference in Text Understanding," in *Theoretical Issues in Reading Comprehension,* Rand J. Spiro, Bertram C. Bruce, and William F. Brewer, eds., Lawrence Erlbaum, Hillsdale, New Jersey, 1980.

Craig, Grace J.; "Theories of Human Development: An Introduction," chapter 2, pp. 23–46, in *Child Development,* Prentice-Hall, Englewood Cliffs, New Jersey, 1979.

Duckworth, Eleanor, "Either We're Too Early and They Can't Learn It or We're Too Late and They Know It Already: The Dilemma of 'Applying Piaget,'" *Harvard Educational Review* 49:297–312, August, 1979.

Duckworth, Eleanor, "The Having of Wonderful Ideas," *Harvard Educational Review* 42:217–231, May, 1972.

Elkind, David, "The Educational Implications of Piaget's Work," pp. 182–203, in *The Open Classroom Reader,* Charles E. Silberman, ed., Vintage, New York, 1973.

Elkind, David, *A Sympathetic Understanding of the Child: Birth to Sixteen,* Allyn and Bacon, Boston, 1974.

Hetherington, E. Mavis, and Parke, Ross D., "Cognitive Development: A Structural-Functional Approach," chapter 9, pp. 304–343, in *Child Psychology: A Contemporary Viewpoint,* 2nd ed., McGraw-Hill, New York, 1979A.

Hetherington, E. Mavis, and Parke, Ross D., "The Development of Morality and

Self-Control," chapter 16, pp. 604–640, in *Child Psychology: A Contemporary Viewpoint*, 2nd ed., McGraw-Hill, New York, 1979B.

Hetherington, E. Mavis, and Parke, Ross D., "The Peer Group As a Socialization Agency," chapter 13, pp. 475–520, in *Child Psychology: A Contemporary Viewpoint*, 2nd ed., McGraw-Hill, New York, 1979C.

Hurlock, Elizabeth, "Social Development," chapter 9, pp. 227–256, in *Child Development*, 6th ed., McGraw-Hill, New York, 1978.

Kohlberg, Lawrence, and Hersh, Richard H., "Moral Development: A Review of the Theory," *Theory Into Practice* 16:53–59, April, 1977.

McKenzie, Moria G., "A Study of Children's Moral Development as Revealed in Their Responses to a Selection of Literature," dissertation, Froebel Institute of Education, London, England, May, 1972.

Menyuk, Paula, "Syntactic Structures in the Language of Children," *Child Development* 34:407–422, June, 1963.

Mussen, Paul H.; Conger, John J.; and Kagan, Jerome, "Extrafamilial Influences on Socialization," chapter 9, pp. 385–421, in *Child Development and Personality*, Harper & Row, New York, 1979A.

Mussen, Paul H.; Conger, John J.; and Kagan, Jerome, "Personality and Social Development: Socialization in the Family," chapter 8, pp. 325–384, in *Child Development and Personality*, Harper & Row, New York, 1979B.

Paolitto, Diana Pritchard, "The Role of the Teacher in Moral Education," *Theory Into Practice* 16:73–80, April, 1977.

Phillips, John L., Jr., *The Origins of Intellect: Piaget's Theory*, Freeman, San Francisco, 1969.

Piaget, Jean, *The Moral Judgment of the Child*, Free Press, New York, 1965.

Read, Charles, Children's Categorization of Speech Sounds in English, *NCTE Research Report No. 17*, ERIC/NCTE, Urbana, Illinois, October, 1975.

Rummelhart, David E., and Ortony, A., "Representation of Knowledge," in *Schooling and the Acquisition of Knowledge*, pp. 99–135, Richard C. Anderson, Rand J. Spiro, and William E. Montague, eds., Lawrence Erlbaum, Hillsdale, New Jersey, 1977.

Spiro, Rand J., "Remembering Information from Text: The 'State of Scheme' Approach," pp. 137–165, in *Schooling and the Acquisition of Knowledge*, Richard D. Anderson, Rand J. Spiro, and William E. Montague, eds., Lawrence Erlbaum, Hillsdale, New Jersey, 1977.

Wadsworth, Barry J., *Piaget for the Classroom Teacher*, Longman, New York, 1978.

Children's Literature

Frank, Anne, *Anne Frank: The Diary of a Young Girl*, rev. ed., translated by B. M. Moozart, Doubleday, New York, 1967.

Greene, Bette, *The Summer of My German Soldier*, Dial, New York, 1973.

Hautzig, Esther, *The Endless Steppe,* Crowell, New York, 1968.

Hunt, Irene, *Across Five Aprils,* Follett, Chicago, 1964.

Mitchell, Edna Preston, *Where Did My Mother Go?,* illustrated by Chris Conover, Scholastic, New York, 1978.

Ness, Evaline, *Sam, Bangs, and Moonshine,* Holt, Rinehart and Winston, New York, 1966.

Paterson, Katherine, *Bridge to Terabithia,* Crowell, New York, 1977.

Potter, Beatrix, *The Tale of Peter Rabbit,* Warne, New York, 1902.

Sendak, Maurice, *Where the Wild Things Are,* Harper & Row, New York, 1963.

Udry, Janice M., *Let's Be Enemies,* illustrated by Maurice Sendak, Harper & Row, New York, 1961.

Yoshima, Taro, *Crow Boy,* Viking, New York, 1955.

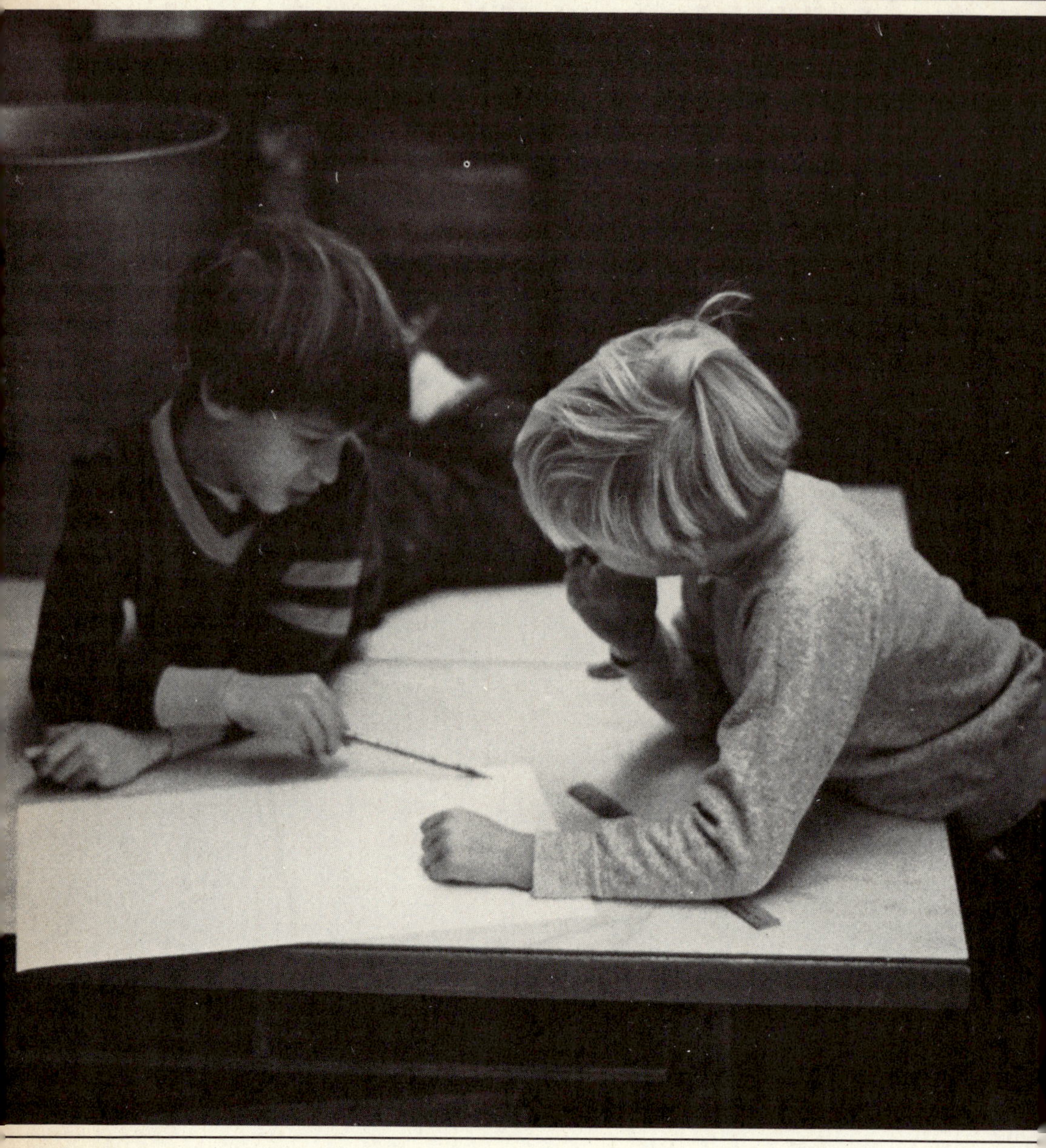

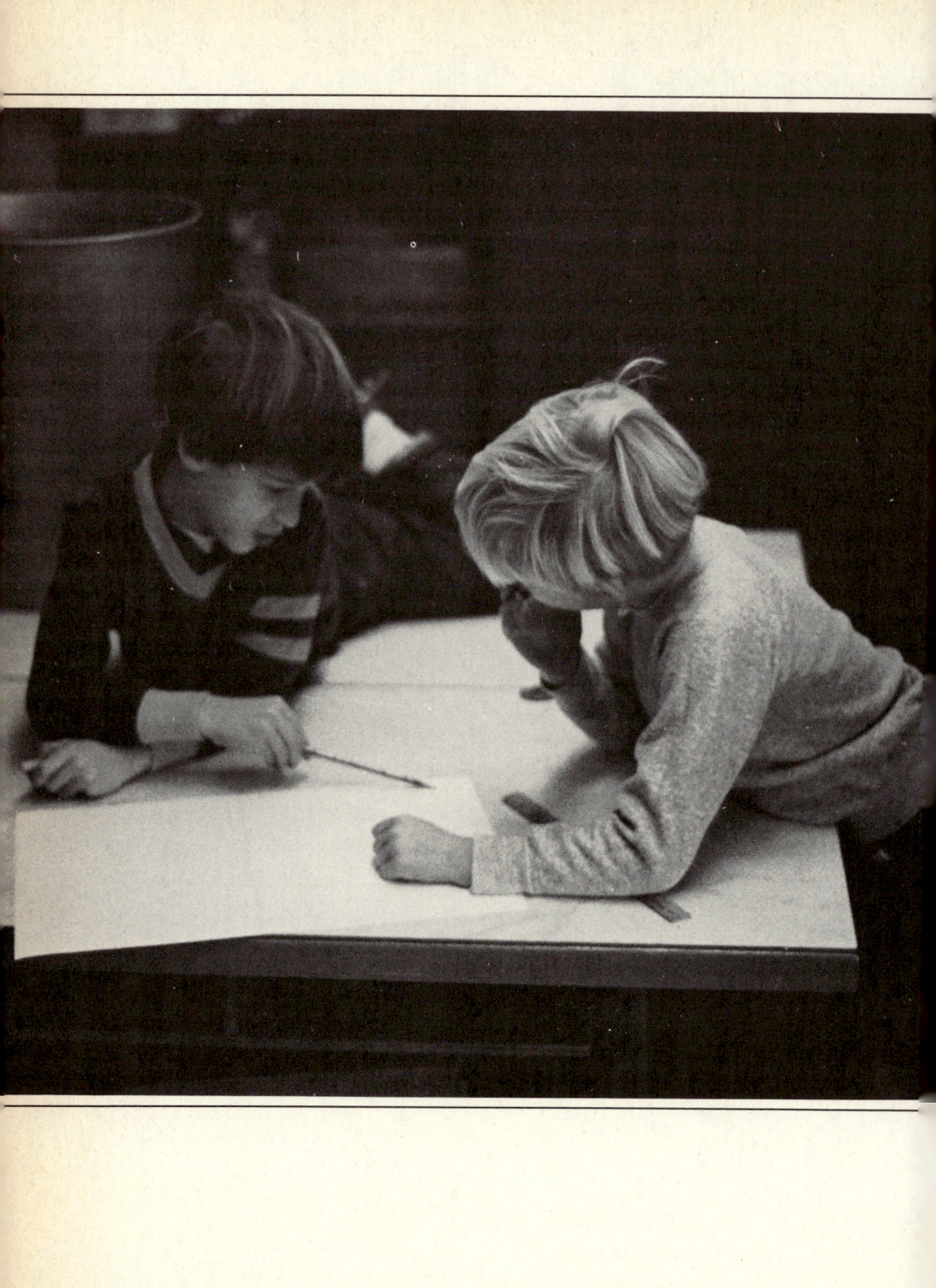

PART 2 Integration of the Language Arts

A Book Discussion: An Act of Discourse

Early Studies in Listening and Speaking
Research on Listening
Research on Speaking

Discourse
Discourse, a Contribution to Learning
Basic Competencies in Discourse
Social Conventions of Speaking
Listening Aspects of Social Conventions
Summary and Chart of Basic Competencies in Discourse

Planning for Growth in Student Discourse
The Teacher's Role
Organizing into Groups for Discussion
Activities that Encourage Discourse
The Classroom Environment

Assessment
Spontaneous Language Observations
Story Retelling

Summary

Suggested Learning Experiences

Recommended Readings

References
Professional Literature
Children's Literature

Chapter 4
Listening and Speaking

With this chapter, the first in a series on teaching methodology, our emphasis changes. The initial section of this text examined children and language; this section examines children, language, and teaching. We will look at a variety of ways teachers can work with children as they develop programs, arrange classrooms, and provide experiences that will allow those children to continue to master increasingly sophisticated aspects of language, just as they did in their preschool years. The discussions in the preceding chapters illustrated the fact that children are active learners who search out and test systems. They do not segment their learning, but from the very beginning use whole language for very real purposes. This kind of learning can and should continue through their school years.

We do not see listening and speaking as two sets of discrete skills to be taught, but as aspects of discourse, an act that is far more complex than sentence production or sentence comprehension. To appreciate the complexity of even a simple discussion, we will ask you to "listen in" on a classroom book discussion. As you read the following transcription, ask yourself these questions about the children. How do they

- reveal their knowledge of the book?
- begin and end the discussion?
- focus on their topic?
- build upon the comments made by others?
- each contribute differently?

A Book Discussion: An Act of Discourse

Several students in a fifth-grade class were asked to tape-record a discussion of *The Cay* (Taylor), a book all had read. It was the first time they had formally discussed a book without their teacher's assistance. To understand the following exchange, a brief summary of *The Cay* is necessary.

> In 1942 Philip, a young boy from Virginia, sails from Curaçao to the United States. His ship is torpedoed by a German submarine and he is thrown up upon a small Caribbean island with an elderly black man named Timothy. An injury causes Philip to become blind. He is forced to rely upon Timothy's wisdom and support in order to survive. Philip has all the prejudices that are attributed to Southerners of his era. *The Cay* is a survival story. It is also the story of prejudice overcome by trust, respect, and friendship.

When the seven students were all gathered around the table, Michelle started the tape recorder and began the discussion.

Michelle: This is a discussion about *The Cay*. Okay, now, this story is about a kid. His family lived on this island and they were getting attacked and so his mother was getting real frantic and everything. And so they left and everything. And their ship got wrecked and this boy lands on this island. Now this is what we are going to be talking about.

Rodney: Yeah, it was neat when the one ship exploded.

Tracy: That was neat?

Rodney: Yeah, cause you could picture it in your mind. You could picture the flames.

Tracy: You could picture the whole thing in your mind, the book.

Rodney: Yeah, it was like a book that didn't have words but had words. You had words in your mind but not on the page.

Anne: I think it would be neat if you could live on an island, you know, by yourself with another person, like, say you were prejudiced against an Indian and you had to live on the island with that Indian.

Michelle: I'd get homesick. I would get so home....

Janet: I would, too.

Tracy: That's a problem. That's the problem he had on there. His family didn't think black people could be nice.

Michelle: And another thing, wouldn't that be terrible if like you're with this person that you know your mom and dad was prejudiced against? And, you know, you were told, "Oh, no, stay away from there." And "Oh, no! They're creeps."

Tracy: When you've never been around them.

Michelle: Yeah, and then you get blind and you have to have them help you. And then they are real nice to you.

Anne: But and then some of the time he thought Timothy was going to be mean to him or something.

Michelle: Yeah, that was funny when he said, "Are you still black?" That was so funny.

Gerry: My favorite part, well, it wasn't one of my favorite parts, exciting part it was, when he fell in and Timothy went in to get him and the sharks could of ate up Timothy, too.

116 *Integration of the Language Arts*

Janet:	My part was when a ... What was that part where I was reading real fast, Tracy?
Tracy:	When Timothy died.
Janet:	Oh yeah, when that storm—I was whipping through the pages—I finally got to it. I was sitting there going....
Tracy:	Janet, they can't see what you're doing!
Janet:	I know! I know! And then it was exciting, well, I wasn't sure what he was going to do with that cat. What's his name, the little boy, couldn't find the cat and Timothy thought that the cat brought bad luck or something. And so he couldn't find the cat, so he thought Timothy killed the cat until they finally found him.
Gerry:	I thought he may have like put him on a raft and sent him off.
Anne:	Let's let everybody talk.
Tracy:	Yeah.
Janet:	What?
Michelle:	Those three haven't talked much.
John:	Tracy's the one talking. I was getting ready to say something. When it was my turn, Tracy started talking.
Todd:	I don't know anything else.
John:	I know. Tracy, I can not think of nothing.
Janet:	Okay, guys, Todd, it's your turn.
Tracy:	Rodney, you've talked before, let Todd.
Todd:	I told you, I can't think of anything right now.
Anne:	I, I ... it would be really weird. I don't think I've ever seen anybody in their sixties or seventies that couldn't spell "help."
Rodney:	I know.
John:	WELL, that was in the old times.
Gerry:	I know, and not only that, he probably never went to school or anything else he didn't have to.
Tracy:	Yeah, because in the old days, black people didn't have the rights they do now.
Gerry:	Blacks weren't even allowed to learn in the old times.
John:	They had to hide their books.

Tracy: Yeah, and I saw this one story about when these white people came to these black people. They said, "Give us your education books." And they said, "We don't have any." And they searched the house and they found some and they shot the whole family. They went around and shot almost the whole town. It was really sad.

Anne: Oh, see, he kept asking Timothy "How are you" and Timothy kept lying. And so he knew sometime Timothy was going to die and he figured that was the reason why Timothy was teaching him all that stuff was that Timothy knew he was going to die while they were on the island.

Tracy: Timothy knew he was going to die.

Anne: I like when after he just died and he tried to go fishing by himself. And he fell in that hole. He was going to go deeper and a fish got a hold of his hand like and he tried to get it off. And finally it came off.

Michelle: That book was kind of like *Call It Courage*.

Todd: It was good.

Janet: Yeah.

Anne: That boy had to survive on the island by himself even though the other one, he didn't have to survive by himself for that long.

Tracy: It was like, um, I don't know, *Island of the Blue Dolphins*.

Rodney: Oh, yeah, cause she had to survive by herself.

Tracy: Well, I think the boy had it worse than her 'cause he was blind and couldn't see. She could see.

Anne: The boy had a partner.

Tracy: Not for all that time; she had a partner, too.

Anne: Well, for one minute, my gosh!

Tracy: Not for one minute!

Anne: My lordy be!

Todd: For a couple of days.

Tracy: Rodney, do you want to say something?

Rodney: Um, yeah, not all of it was like *Call It Courage* 'cause they didn't have eaters of men and if you were to rate it, what would you rate it from one to ten?

Tracy: I'd rate it a four.
Janet: Two.
Anne: Four.
Michelle: Two.
Todd: Four.
Rodney: Why did you rate it "four"?
Todd: Because it wasn't the best book I've ever read. I've read better books.
Rodney: Why did you rate it "two"?
Janet: It was not exactly one of the best books but it was one of them.
Rodney: And why did you rate it "two"?
Michelle: Same reason. I've read better books, but I did like it though.
Rodney: Same excuse for everybody.

If one had sat down with these fifth-graders and asked them to talk about the what and the why of book discussions, they might well have said:

> A book discussion is a good way to share a book. You can tell about your favorite part or compare it to other books you've read.

> You can discuss what the book is about. *The Cay* is about surviving. We've read some other books that are about survival like *Call It Courage* and *The Island of the Blue Dolphins*. *The Cay* is also about prejudice.

> When you have a discussion, everyone should get a chance to talk. If people are quiet, you should try to bring them into the discussion.

> Someone has to start the discussion off and say when the discussion is over.

> Taping a discussion is different. You can't show things or use your hands when you want to describe something.

The teacher, as he listened to the tape, could learn a great deal. Compare his assessment to your own assessment. The teacher noted:

> All the children have indeed read *The Cay*. They are able to relate it to books with similar themes and to point out some contrasts with those books.

> They were able to conduct a book discussion without adult guidance. They began the discussion, stuck to the task in a purposeful manner, and brought the discussion to a close.

During the discussion they listened to each other, verbally supported the comments of others, and were at times able to extend points made by other children. The discussion had a flow but did show abrupt shifts.

The children did not question each other frequently. Some parts of the discussion were less fruitful than others, such as the ranking of the books.

Individual students displayed some interesting abilities. Michelle, Anne, and Tracy were the leaders during most of the discussion but Rodney took the leadership role at the end. Gerry moved the group into discussing their favorite part of the book. Tracy and Rodney had a nice exchange on the visual imagery in the book. Tracy was able to get out of an argument by shifting the focus of the discussion. Todd and John had very little to say in this particular book discussion.

Some important aspects of *The Cay* were not discussed at all, or were handled superficially, such as the character development of Philip and the theme of prejudice. Little was done to explore the significance of specific acts of the characters. For example, what did finding the fishing poles show Philip about Timothy? Why was the term "boss" used and accepted?

The seven children in the preceding discussion were actively involved in speaking and listening. While each child was expressing his or her own feelings and thoughts, that child was also listening to other children expressing their opinions. Together they were attempting to weave a cohesive commentary on a book they had all read. The teacher in listening to the tape found out some things the children had learned from their reading. More importantly, he was able to see how well the children could speak and listen in a small-group situation without adult supervision.

In planning for further instruction, the teacher could decide the kinds of experiences these students needed next. Obviously, the children know a lot about discussions but need to build upon each other's contributions more. Maybe listening or reading the transcript of a tape of this discussion would help them to reflect on each others' contributions. They could start talking with one another about what each meant and develop an appreciation for the value of each remark to the discussion's flow. Another child could be chosen to be the leader and the group encouraged to discuss another story to see who the new initiator might be. Perhaps Todd and John need to be drawn into more book discussions with the teacher to learn more about how to talk about books. Since Todd and John may have felt overwhelmed by the loquaciousness of the rest of the group, another tactic would be to form a new group with quieter members of the class. And finally, in an assessment of the literature program, although books on survival were mentioned, none on prejudice were cited. The teacher might decide to bring in *Edge of Two*

Worlds (Jones) and *Journey to Topaz* (Uchida), which deal with prejudice toward Indians and the Japanese.

Early Studies in Listening and Speaking

Historically, researchers have examined listening and speaking separately. While some of these research studies are older, they still give insights that help teachers think about their own teaching practices.

Research on Listening

For many years listening was largely neglected in the classroom. One of the very early research studies to demonstrate the importance of listening was done in 1926 by Rankin, who found that of all the time people spend using language (reading, writing, speaking, and listening), 42 percent of that time is spent listening. When Wilt (1950), almost 30 years later, asked teachers to list the amount of time that children spent in each area of language arts during the school day, she found that teachers thought children spent the largest part of their day reading. Wilt found, however, that children were spending 57.5 percent of their class time listening. The figure rose to 90 percent by high school. Lundsteen (1976) summed up the findings in a dramatic way when she wrote, "It might be said that we listen a book a day; speak a book a week; read a book a month; and write a book a year" (p. 75). Children who are "talked at" for so much of the day will have little time left to use language themselves in interactive ways.

Research on Speaking

Even though listening takes precedence in most classrooms, children arrive at school with the ability to produce all the basic sentence structures (Strickland, 1962) and a vocabulary of several thousand words (McCarthy, 1950). For many years researchers such as Smith (1926), McCarthy (1930), Day (1932), Davis (1937), and Templin (1957) looked at length of sentences students produced for growth, sex differences, and effect of socioeconomic level. The findings were that sentence length and number of words uttered increases with age. It was initially found that girls tend to have longer utterances than boys; however, Templin found this not to be true. This contrary finding was explained by possible shifts in child-rearing practices, since Templin's study was conducted at least 20 years later than McCarthy's.

Socioeconomic level did influence language production with high socioeconomic status correlating with greater length and volume of words. Davis (1937) reported interesting findings on twins, single (that is, children born one at a time), and only children. Only children demonstrated more advanced language skill than did single children; single children ranked higher than twins.

Strickland (1962) and Loban (1963) investigated the language development of elementary-school children. Loban conducted a longitudinal study of youngsters beginning in the kindergarten year. Among his significant findings was that the most advanced speakers could be identified by their use of "flexibles" in a sentence: a portion of a sentence that can occur in several places without changing the sentence's meaning. For example, "The leaves fell *on the lawn.*" "*On the lawn* the leaves fell." or "The cat moved *gracefully* across the room." "*Gracefully,* the cat moved across the room." "The cat *gracefully* moved across the room." Thus, control and the ability to manipulate language signify linguistic maturity.

Strickland found that youngsters were more sophisticated in language use than had previously been thought. When comparing textbook sentence structures to children's actual production, she reported that the least used sentence pattern of children was the most applied pattern in basal readers. Her study resulted in greater diversity in sentence patterns and vocabularies in basal texts.

More recent studies have questioned some of the earlier findings. Although O'Donnell, Griffin, and Norris (1967) reported that boys produce longer utterances, as measured by the T-unit, thus supporting Templin's (1957) findings, current opinion usually holds that sex differences in language production may be context-oriented. This focus on context denotes present research interests.

In this chapter, rather than looking at listening and speaking as separate skills to be taught, we will deal with them as acts of discourse, for this is how listening and speaking function. Each feeds into the other. Even in monologues there is at least one listener, oneself.

Discourse

Discourse, a Contribution to Learning

Looking at listening and speaking within the totality of the discourse act is important for several reasons. It allows the examination of language as it occurs naturally. Furthermore, it permits the exploration of the interaction that occurs. This interaction not only leads to communication but also to learning. When children are encouraged to talk to each other about a topic of mutual concern or interest, their competence in conversation and discussion is a base upon which their knowledge can be extended in a very special way. Discussion permits the members of a group to compose, arrange, and form priorities of their ideas with the assistance of others. Together children can test and try out ideas in a safe environment. Suggestions by one child can be enlarged by another because a proposal can be altered or a meager idea can be fleshed out by other group members. An important point is that one does not fail alone. Dialogues or discussions may be considered externalized compositions. "Soloing rises out of collective effort. Monologue, the basic act of writing, is born of dialogue" (Moffett and Wagner, 1976, p. 30).

Speech is a way to learn, a precursor to writing. Barnes (1976) describes talk as a way to control thinking. He distinguishes between speech as communication and speech as reflection. Moffett and Wagner (1976) reveal how group interaction develops the thinking of youngsters.

> The *cooperation* of groups becomes internalized as the mental *operation* of individuals. Thus, in keeping with the emphasis on the oral base, talking provides far more exercise in trying to formulate thought than actual writing does and permits speaker and listener to identify and work out communication problems together. Eventually individuals internalize the reader's needs and amend thought and speech without external aid (pp. 32–33).

Reflective speech and composing speech are possible in the classroom only if the teacher has helped to construct a social context that encourages and supports such talk. In fact, the point of control for the teacher is the context, both specific to the situation and to the general learning environment. In the book discussion that began this chapter, the teacher had set up the specific activity, had multiple copies of the book, and had allowed the time for discussion. The children brought to this activity their security in the discussion environment and willingness to take leadership roles. They had learned to value each others' contributions and knew their talk was going to be valued by the teacher.

Establishing both a current and long-term learning context includes not only the teacher, space, and materials but also the students' own contributions. The Rosens (1973) write

> When a school creates this kind of living context a delicate web of relationships is established.... Activities which are different in quality, which lure the children to think and behave in new ways, also prompt them to reach out in language and take hold of more of the resources available to them (p. 32).

It may be seen, then, that certain kinds of experiences extend, vary, and provide a basis for talk. Some experiences spring from an interaction with others, such as a student's family, classmates, or teacher. Others grow from exchanges with adults in their work roles or from talks with younger children. These interactions encourage language to be used for interviews, surveys, direction-giving, explanations, or descriptions, besides the reflective learning talk already discussed.

Another set of experiences comes through modeling, such as hearing stories read aloud, listening to adult career resource people, or linking into an oral library of tapes and records. The third set is composed of concrete experiences, and provides the opportunity for students to use all their senses for exploration and examination: for example, an artifact might be examined in class, something might be constructed by the students, or objects collected on a field trip might be explored and discussed. The richness of the experience blends into the language produced.

In all three types of experiences—interactional, modeling, and concrete—students are given something to share and to attach labels to for vocabulary development, and provided with opportunities to extend their knowledge. In addition, they may reorganize the known and develop new structures for forming and receiving information. The chapters that follow describe specific ways in which discourse can become a part of the curriculum. Note especially suggestions in Chapter 7, "Language Arts in the Content Areas" and Chapter 8, "Literature-Based Language Extensions."

Basic Competencies in Discourse

There are basic competencies in acts of discourse needed both by the speaker and the listener. These competencies can be divided into three major areas: identifying and using the context, directing listening and speaking for specific purposes, and the social conventions.

Identifying and Using the Context. Language is shaped by the context from which it springs. This context is established not only by the speaker's message but also by the listener's focus and the social circumstances of that moment. The speaker needs to have a sense of audience; that is, an understanding of what the listener will have to know in order to receive the message. That message might include information, argument, persuasion, humor, or have an emotional impact. To convey a message, then, the speaker needs a sense of the experiential background of an audience and its expectations, and an understanding of the social context.

Consider the case of a person who has witnessed a traffic accident. She would describe what she saw one way in talking to the police officer at the scene and in another way when telling a close friend about the same occasion. To the police officer she would recite the specific details that officer would be most interested in knowing: the speed of the cars, the direction of the skid, the color of the traffic light at the moment of impact. The friend, on the other hand, might hear more of her feelings when she saw the accident: the quick rush of panic, the sound of crunching metal, the sight of blood, and the way she trembled when it was all over. The selection of specific details that is shared and the wording that is used is varied by the speaker because she is aware of the focus of each listener. The police officer is interested in making an accurate report, while the friend is concerned about the speaker's well-being. The speaker needs the competency to use language within changing social contexts, both in formal and informal situations. This ability to shift language to function in a variety of social contexts is one aspect of register.

The listener, on the other hand, needs an understanding of the speaker's context. In order to receive the real and total message that the speaker is sending, the listener must be aware of the speaker's biases, background of experience, and intent. The listener must understand the speaker's literal meaning and also be able to extract inferences and comprehend symbolic uses of language. For example, one second-grade class took a trip to the zoo as a culmination of its study of birds. Each child selected a different bird to observe and sketch. The students wrote about their birds. Later they elaborated their drawings using a variety of media.

When the children shared their projects, there was no need for any child to discuss the trip to the zoo for all had shared that same experience. Rather, as children read their writings and displayed their artwork, other children were listening to the language used to describe the sounds, the movements, the plumage of particular birds. The teacher's preparation for the trip brought about this sharply focused listening behavior. In addition, since this writing and sharing practice was common in this classroom, all the children were aware of the speaker's prior performances. They could compare this new writing with previous writing and thus see how the child had grown, both in ability to use language effectively and to observe fine detail. In contrast to the situation just described, when a youngster discusses a hobby or shares a collection such as coins, stamps, or model cars, the student listener must use the current social context and the context of the message to comprehend the new ideas and vocabulary presented.

Directing Speaking and Listening for Specific Purposes. Speech is used for a myriad of purposes. Sometimes one only wishes to socialize, to share experiences in a way that says "I'm interested in getting to know you better." Other occasions call for an ability to sway opinion, provide direction, or explain results. Sometimes speech is used to learn. Barnes (1976) calls this "groping toward meaning 'exploratory talk'" (p. 28).

In order to meet these different purposes, speakers must be able to sequence ideas, focus the listener's attention, use their voices for dramatic effect, and deliver remarks with appropriate timing. Further, they need to select words with precision in order to convey their intent. Giving directions calls for short, unambiguous sentences with little elaboration. Describing the best meal one has ever had may call for comparisons, more complex syntax, and metaphorical language. Directing speech for specific purposes is often categorized into the functions of language. Children learn to use the func-

One valuable opportunity for listening that occurs each day is to share both ongoing and completed projects. Such sharing allows children to learn from each other. The atmosphere for listening is established by the teacher, who models attentive behavior. (Mr. Embry's classroom, Douglas Alternative School, Columbus, Ohio)

tions of language by being involved in situations that call for a variety of language uses.

Just as speaking may be directed for different purposes, so may listening. Competence in listening includes flexible listening behaviors, for it is inefficient to listen to everything at the same level of intensity. There are times we listen marginally, as when we half-listen to a news report in order to catch the weather forecast. At other times, we listen intently, as when we get complicated directions on how to get to a friend's home.

An effective listener is a purposeful one, able to listen for the speaker's underlying organization and adjust to the speaker's rate of speech. Included in the array of listening competencies is the ability to listen critically; that is, to apply what is known about the speaker and the context in order to analyze the message. Critical listening skills can be developed at all age levels. A beginning stage would be the ability of young children to listen to a story and then to judge whether the story were fact or fantasy. Older students may deal with propaganda techniques and the art of persuasion, a vital competence in a democratic society.

Social Conventions of Speaking

An unwritten rule book exists that tells speakers of a language how that language is to be used in socially appropriate ways. These rules are social conventions of language. There are acceptable ways to interrupt, to begin a conversation, to add to a conversation without seeming to dominate, and to close a conversation. Children enter school with a degree of conversational competence. It is from this base that teachers can hope to extend children's tacit knowledge of social conventions.

Many adults would say that there are rules that must be obeyed at all times, such as "Don't ever interrupt!" Yet in actual practice, the real rule is "Children do not interrupt adults with impunity," for adults do interrupt each other often and children interrupt their peers. This interaction with peers is the most powerful source of youngsters' growth in knowledge of the social conventions.

These social conventions go beyond the mere niceties of behavior, for they may affect the very fabric of the message itself. There are, for example, a number of socially appropriate ways to interrupt:

Pardon me for interrupting, but there is a phone call for you.

Pardon me, but I would like you to meet Karen. She's been to Greece, too, and would love to hear about your stay in Athens.

That reminds me of....

Have you talked to Mark about buying that kind of car? Just let me tell you what happened to him!

I quite agree with your last point, but I think you should also consider....

From even this brief sampling, one can see that there is a variety of acceptable ways to interrupt a conversation. In general, a bridge must be built between the ongoing statement and the comments of the person who is breaking in. In other words, the person who interrupts has to acknowledge the topic of conversation and create a tie from that topic to what he would like to say. The only time this is not necessary is when one interrupts in order to give a message of some urgency, such as the phone call in the first example. However, even in this case an apology or an excuse is expected. Secondly, one must wait for a natural break in the conversation. The person who wants to put in a comment will signal an intent to do so through eye contact, a gesture, or body movement. This complex act of interruption is typical of many of the social conventions.

Usage. The totality of the message goes beyond *what* is said to include *how* it is said: the tone of voice, whether the manner of speech is tentative or firm, the pause for effect, the emphasis given to certain parts of the sentence, gestures, and facial expression. Beyond this metalinguistic system, the use of words can play an important part in the social conventions. Certain expressions such as "ain't," "he don't," and the use of double negatives can affect the acceptability of the message. Many individuals judge others by the way they use language. These language variations are called social dialects. Certain forms of usage may be appropriate in one social setting, but not in another. Most language-arts textbooks contain exercises to practice using the standard forms of language but such practice is generally to no avail. Shuy (1981), in discussing a project that was set up to teach speakers of vernacular English to produce standard English, reports that "... standard language can be learned but ... it is unlikely to be taught very effectively, if at all. Learning standard speech seems to happen if and only when the learner wants to do so. Drills do not appear to help" (p. 173).

There are ways to assist youngsters to acquire standard forms. Strickland (1979) found that when children used the language of books in drama, book discussions, choral readings, puppetry, and role-playing, they gained competence in using standard forms of English without losing competence in their own social dialect. Acquisition of standard forms is similar to the process of initial-language learning. Children need a rich input of language and the opportunity to practice and use language in purposeful situations.

Listening Aspects of Social Conventions

The social conventions of speech cover not only the words selected and the way they are put together, but also the quality of voice, types of extralinguistic behavior, and sets of complex rules for use. Social conventions are learned gradually. An awareness of the complexity of this task can assist teachers in their goal of helping children develop greater ability to communicate with competence.

Listening is the other aspect of the ability to communicate with competence. Signals sent by speakers let listeners know when they can interject, respond, shift the topic of conversation, or when they should assist in bringing the conversation to a close. One cannot be a capable conversationalist without being a capable listener. This goes beyond mere listening courtesy, for the listener must think about what the speaker is saying.

Traditional description of listening courtesy remains important, but it is so superficial that it rarely helps a youngster to become a good listener. A good listener needs to be aware of the cues, not only in conversation but also in more formal discourse, that signify shifts of topic, a request for some kind of response, or closure. Part of the listener's responsibility is to respond to the speaker's comments without breaking the flow of the discourse, which goes beyond the fact of paying attention. It may require nodding, laughing, grimacing, or questioning. In the English-speaking culture such behaviors are important, for they support the speakers in their efforts to communicate.

The foregoing discussion points out why listening and speaking cannot effectively be taught as separate skills and why it is more fruitful to approach them as aspects of the total act of discourse. Telling children to pay attention and to speak clearly only focuses their attention on the superficialities of language. The discourse act represents far more complex behaviors than simplistic rules would suggest. The only way to discover these rules is the same way the child acquires language: that is, by many varied opportunities to engage in purposeful experiences that require the child to speak and to listen.

The following table may help to clarify the relationships of speaking and listening within the act of discourse.

Table 4.1. Basic Competencies in Discourse

Speaking	*Listening*

1. *Identifying and Using Context in Speaking*
Developing a sense of audience
  What the listener will need to know to understand you
  Effect created on an audience
Being able to use language flexibly in the social context
  Register
  Formal and informal language
	1. *Identifying and Using Context in Listening*
	Developing an understanding of the speaker's context
	  Layers of meaning
	  Background of experience
	  Bias
	  Intent
	Building a meaningful context for new ideas and vocabulary

2. *Directing Speaking for Specific Purposes*
Being able to use language for a variety of intents
Sequencing presentation of ideas
  Time
  Purpose
  Attention
  Dramatic effect
Choosing vocabulary and syntax
	2. *Directing Listening for Specific Purposes*
	Listening
	  Flexibly, intently, and marginally
	Being able to follow the speaker's rate and organization
	Listening critically
	  Applying what is known about the context to analyze the message

3. *Social Conventions of Speaking*
Exhibiting socially appropriate speech, e.g.,
  how to interrupt;
  how to add to a conversation
Using the voice flexibly:
  to create a mood;
  to speak persuasively;
  to vary tone quality
Choosing appropriate vocabulary and syntax
	3. *Social Conventions of Listening*
	Listening for signals sent by the speaker
	Demonstrating appropriate listening behaviors
	Using listening as part of the thought process

Planning for Growth in Student Discourse

The Teacher's Role

As part of the communicative circle within a classroom, the teacher has responsibility for both speaking and listening. Sometimes the teacher will be a model of language, extending children's experience through selection of vocabulary, types of experiences shared, reading aloud, and modulating the tones of language. In addition, the way in which others are listened to and the displaying of appropriate social conventions of speech will model sophisticated, communicative, competent behavior for children.

Marland (1977) has described the range of teacher behaviors one could expect to find in a class. These kinds of talk all make contributions to classrooms and move from a more formal input, which has little child input, to informal situations with much child/teacher interaction.

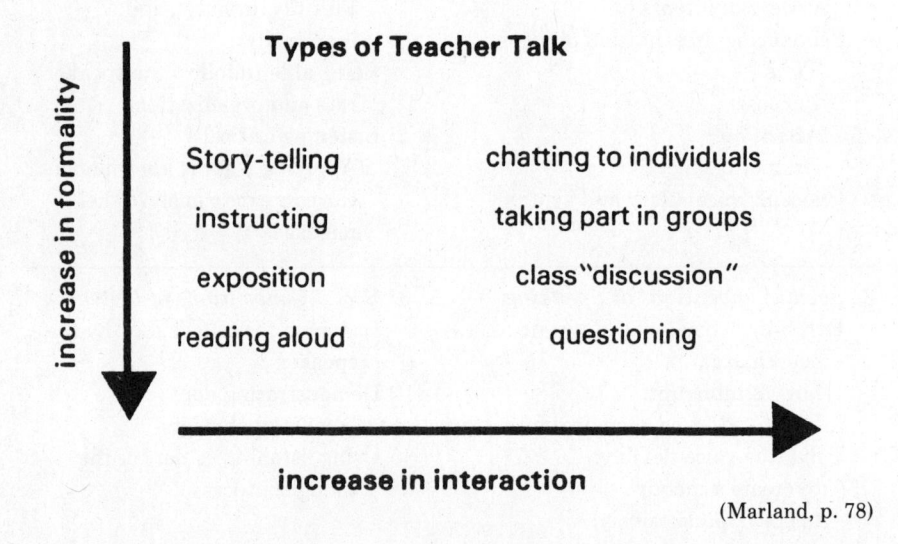

Types of Teacher Talk

increase in formality ↓

Story-telling	chatting to individuals
instructing	taking part in groups
exposition	class "discussion"
reading aloud	questioning

increase in interaction →

(Marland, p. 78)

Listening to children is an art that takes much practice and thought. Sometimes adults do not realize how they are reacting toward children and sometimes children become quite adept at controlling adult behavior. In one first-grade classroom the teacher was timed according to how long a wait existed between her questions and either an answer or her moving on to another child. The low reading group was given an average of 1.7 seconds wait-time. The high group received an average of 2.5 seconds, over 50 percent more time. One possible significant difference was that most members of the high reading group made some type of sound, not necessarily a word, after the question was asked. The teacher would then wait. These youngsters were obviously highly sophisticated in their knowledge of the social conventions of speech. They knew that some acknowledgment of the question would give them more time to consider their responses.

How does a teacher talk with children? Tough (1973) described an "invitation to talk" in which the teacher encourages youngsters to use language to express their experiences and perhaps to find a new meaning for the incidents being discussed. These significant conversations can become an important part of the oral language curriculum. Mrs. Kerstetter, a kindergarten/first-grade teacher spoke with Billy, age six:

Billy: See my new sports shoes, Teacher?

Mrs. K.: Wow, Billy!

Billy: You take them off like this. They just slide off your feet. Aren't they great?

Mrs. K.: I love the color.

Billy: It's a pretty blue. Do you like the white stripes?

Mrs. K.: (nods and smiles)

Billy: I got them at Rink's. (Taking off shoe) See here? It says "Sport" inside. That's because they're sport shoes.

Mrs. K.: For what sports?

Billy: Well, when we have movement (done in barefeet) I can just slide my shoes on and off. I don't have to tie.

Mrs. K.: What a good idea!

Billy: I like them to wear. They're pretty nice.

Mrs. K.: (smiles and nods)

Billy: I can jump high up and down in them. (He jumps up and down.) These are sports shoes.

Whereas it is not uncommon for a child to have a new pair of shoes, it is less common for teachers to take the time to talk with children about them. Billy was obviously excited about his shoes and had many things to say—the color, design, where he bought them, and what he can do in them and with them. Mrs. Kerstetter allowed Billy to take the lead in this conversation, joining in his joy and encouraging his continued talk. She "invited" his talking by saying very little, twice only nodding and smiling. Her responses stayed in the realm of Billy's previous statements. Often teachers think the way to extend a conversation is through questioning, which instead creates a testing situation. In the above conversation, the teacher asks but one question, taking it from the child's prior statement.

Adults are accustomed to conversing at length. Youngsters need to learn this skill not only with their peers but also with adults. It requires effort and concentration for the adult to step back and let a child take the conversational lead. A significant conversation with a child is a skilled act, an important event in the school day for both teacher and child.

Barnes (1976) writes that "speech is not only a tool which each of us can use in making sense of the world, but also a means of imposing our version of the world on others" (p. 116). Too often teachers do not allow youngsters to apply what they know to the episode being discussed. When children personalize experiences, they are bringing their lives into matching positions with the new. Some teachers treat such responses as being "off the subject" and attempt to force students into using a given framework. In effect, they are telling students that their knowledge is irrelevant, not important to the

Small-group interaction with children encourages talk from both the teacher and the children. This adult contact fosters an interactional exchange where meanings are negotiated rather than told. (Miss Enciso's informal classroom, Barrington School, Upper Arlington, Ohio)

topic at hand. Children need to shape the new information into a form that melds with their sense of the world. Careful listening and tuning in by the teacher into the child's framework is needed.

How does a teacher respond? Barnes (1976) discusses two ways, the reply and the assessing response (p. 111). When a teacher replies, that teacher is taking the student's contribution seriously in a collaborative relationship, as equal partner in the discussion. The assessing response, on the other hand, takes what the student has said and matches it to some standard of measurement. Both the reply and the assessing response are important aspects of the teaching act. Too often, assessing predominates, thus pushing students toward predetermined performance levels rather than allowing them to make sense of their experiences in the light of their own understanding of the world. Whereas reply indicates a sharing situation, assessing indicates a presentation, a performance. To state the difference in another way, the reply situation encourages exploratory language, a "rehearsal of knowledge" in Barnes's terms (p. 113). Assessment is the final draft for the distant unknown audience.

The ways in which a teacher talks in general and talks with students specifically can extend and enrich children's growth in language competence. If a teacher understands that conversations may be invitations to talk rather than question-and-answer situations, that students need to blend what they know with what is new, and that replies facilitate growth more than assessment of performances, then that teacher is truly encouraging rich discourse for learning in the classroom.

Organizing into Groups for Discussion

Traditionally, classroom discussion has been dominated by the teacher. Teachers controlled the talk by asking the questions, calling upon children to respond, and then evaluating their responses. Children, in order to talk, needed to compete for the teacher's attention. Small groups, most often a part of the reading program, were again teacher dominated. The teacher would talk with one small group while the rest of the class worked at quiet tasks. Small groups, however, can be one of the strongest ways of providing numerous oral language opportunities if the teacher is not always required to take on the role of discussion leader.

Permitting children to work together in small groups to plan a project, discuss a book, share information, or solve a problem has many values. Small-group discussion seems to stimulate ideas. Further, it permits much more response to each person's ideas than can possibly occur in the large-group situation. One person's idea may be enlarged by another, or it may inspire the development of a new parallel. Such talk provides the opportunity to develop what May (1967) calls a listening attitude—that is, an attitude in which one is open to the ideas of others. One does not tune out the speaker who puts forth ideas that differ from one's own.

Talking in small groups encourages every person to participate because one can take risks in a small group that one would not take in a large group. These small-group discussions provide an arena for what Barnes (1976) calls "exploratory language" as opposed to "formal presentation." Barnes sees a difference in the kind of language that occurs with an "intimate audience" and language that is presented to a "distant audience." In a small group, children are working with others whom they know and trust. Language becomes less guarded and ideas are expressed freely. Suggestions can be made before they are completely thought through. When speaking to a "distant audience," the language and tone become more formal and the presentation, polished and shaped. Barnes has charted these differences thus:

	Intimate Audience	*Distant Audience*
Size	Small group	Full class
Source of authority	The group	The teacher
Relationships	Intimate	Public
Ordering of thought	Inexplicit	Explicit
Speech planning	Improvised	Preplanned
Speech function	Exploratory	Final Draft

(p. 109)

Group size may range from two to six but five is often proposed as an ideal number. A group of five promotes a variety and a large number of ideas and yet is not large enough to intimidate shy members or to be cumbersome. On the other hand, Moffett and Wagner (1976) suggest that some writing and drama tasks are best done in pairs or trios.

Frequently membership in a group has been decided by achievement level. The better readers are placed in one group and slower readers in another. Many now see that such heterogeneous grouping practices can create a poor self-concept, since they label children. A second problem is that they can limit language growth. Moffett and Wagner point out the need for children to talk and work with other children who are not exactly as they. These variations may be differences in dialect, socioeconomic level, sex, intelligence, or verbal ability. "Youngsters exposed to peers of other cultures and languages simply know more than youngsters restricted to their own kind ... it is *dif-*

ference that teaches, not similarity.... Having to talk across language differences, to accommodate differences in thought and speech, is excellent education" (p. 37).

Group talk can grow from a variety of topics. Sometimes a small group of children share a common interest or concern and meet to plan or share: for example, the discussion of *The Cay* at the beginning of this chapter. Moffett (1968) suggests that the teacher can help frame the discussion in ways that call for increasingly higher levels of thinking. He suggests three such topics: topics inviting enumeration, topics inviting comparison, and topics inviting chronology. An example of the first might be having children list ways in which time is measured. This type of discussion is simple in that it is merely a listing and may be done by even young children. The second topic, which invites comparison, is more sophisticated. After gathering leaves, children might compare their similarities and differences. All the leaves have a stem; all come from a plant; but there are differences in veination, size, shape, and color. The third topic, that of chronology, is one that is often done by children. Discussions such as how to plant seed in the school garden require an ordering of activities. Upper-graders may explore the chronology of events that ended in a specific situation, such as the events leading up to the firing upon Fort Sumter.

Sometimes groups may be convened for a short time period. The group that discussed *The Cay,* for example, met for about 20 minutes and did not reconvene. Other groups may last for much longer periods of time. A group working on the leaf comparisons might extend its discussion of similarities and differences through developing leaf prints and writing in order to share its findings with others. Such a group could work together for several weeks. The short-term groups have the advantage of affording each child in a class the opportunity to interact with many kinds of people for a wide range of purposes. The groups of longer duration allow children to work together in order to solve a problem in ways that call upon them to experiment, plan, explore, and finally to produce a product.

As children work together to solve a problem such as how to share all they have learned through their comparison of leaves, they learn to function within the group. They begin to see that in a discussion people can play a variety of roles. A person can support the ideas of others, can help reduce friction, can clarify ideas, can oppose, can ask questions, and can summarize (May, 1967).

While children have begun to acquire sensitivity to the rules of conversation, they need many opportunities to acquire the skills needed for discussion. Children need to learn, for example, how to step into the discussion when there is a break, without the necessity of raising one's hand. Marland

(1977) proposes that children keep in mind the following discussion techniques:

1. Remember you are taking part in a discussion
   (a) to learn
   (b) to help other people learn.
2. Always have a paper and pencil handy during discussions.
3. Ask for anything you do not understand to be explained.
4. If two people have misunderstood each other, help them out.
5. If someone has said something that you think is important, remind the group about it.
6. Always let other people "have their say" even if you are bursting to say something.
7. Be prepared to change your mind if you have been proved wrong.
8. Do not shout people down just because you don't agree with them.
9. Do not show off in a discussion.
10. You must take part in a discussion even if you feel shy.
11. Listen carefully to what everyone else in the groups says.
12. Always have one member of the group writing down the most important points discussed and any decisions that the group has made.

(pp. 133–136)

The kinds of discussion we have explored are informal. There are other kinds of discussion that are more formal, such as panel discussions and debates done by older children. These kinds of discussions build upon all the skills acquired in informal discussion, such as listening with an open mind, supporting the ideas of others, questioning, and summarizing. But these more formal types of discussion require preparation, research, and planning before the panel or debate takes place.

The teacher's role is not only to provide opportunities for a wide variety of types of discussion, but by quiet and light-handed intervention at carefully selected moments, to assist the discussion. The teacher does this by helping children to participate, focusing their discussion, moving their talk along, and by guiding them into summarization.

Activities that Encourage Discourse

Sharing. "Show and Tell" has long had an established place in primary classrooms. In the past it was too frequently confined to one particular time during the week when every child was expected to bring in something to share. These sessions have been the source of humor and complaints. For example, some colleagues have dubbed it "Bring and Brag," while parents have moaned about ransacking the house at 8 A.M. in a frantic search for something—anything—for their child to take to school.

Sharing, on the other hand, can provide a strong base for language growth. Telling friends about things and events that have a special meaning is one way adults get to know each other better, and children have these same social needs. While adults may share the finding of a new restaurant or the details of the latest happenings at the office, children may choose to share the old bird's nest they found on the way to school or the papier-mâché dragon they created.

The best sharing grows naturally from the ongoing work of the classroom and from the child's experiences away from school. A classroom, where not all children are engaged in working on the same task, calls for sharing. Children can talk about a book they have read with others who would be interested. A science project with electric magnets can be demonstrated and explained. An idea for a future activity can be proposed. Special and unique experiences such as a new baby in the family or an airplane trip can be narrated.

Sometimes children may choose to talk to the whole class. Everyone may be anxious to hear about Judy's trip to the hospital to have her broken arm set. Sometimes sharing is best done in a small group; for instance, if Brian, a fifth-grader, is showing how he built a crystal radio set, a small group of children clustered around the table would be able to see and touch and try out his radio. Such small-group sharing encourages the children to ask questions and allows the speaker to clarify and sharpen his or her explanation.

Sharing need not be confined to the child's own classroom. Brian, for example, might share his radio with an interested class of third-graders and also with his principal. Each audience would require a different kind of explanation and would ask Brian different kinds of questions. Not only is the size of the audience being varied, but also the level of sophistication.

Sharing allows children to extend and develop their utterances. The child has to capture and hold the attention of the audience. The child needs to make decisions about how to sequence what is told. The teacher's attention and questions will help the children in the audience to see their role as an active rather than a passive one.

Projects and Field Trips. When youngsters work on projects, a great deal of talking and listening evolves out of deciding the project focus, planning what will be done, assigning members to specific tasks, and determining how to share the work with others. The actual topic of study might be one that occurs in science, such as finding out about the birds that come to the class bird feeder. In social studies, the group may wish to work individually on a common inquiry, which might be their own family's history and the development of a personal timeline of events. Math could be part of either project just described or serve as a focus, such as finding out how to tell time by the sun's rays.

While making decisions about materials and using them, children's discourse takes place naturally. Not only do discussions occur in which participants learn from each other and about the topic at hand, but also conversations evolve in which participants learn about each other and the social conventions of speech. Pinnell (1975) reported that approximately 50 percent of the talk in small-group discussions of children was in the interactional function. The art center, block corner for younger children, reading center, and all-purpose work areas provide the space and opportunity to talk.

Some projects require students to interview or survey others for a data base. They may question themselves, other class members, or go beyond the classroom to different groups of people. A fourth-grade class visited a college campus to study architecture. One group of youngsters decided to find out what college students thought of the two buildings on campus being studied. They developed a set of questions to answer their query and then interviewed college students entering the structures. The fourth-grade group compiled their interview data into a chart, which they displayed and shared within their own classroom.

Field or study trips are especially good activities for extending language, for the diverse experiences included provide opportunities for a wide range of language uses. It begins with the language of planning for the trip, such as deciding which observations to make, what materials should be taken along, who will join the agreed-upon activity groups, and how individual projects may be carried out. The trip establishes the basis for a shared class experience. Less background information needs to be shared among class members for all have attended, thus establishing an opportunity for "reflective, exploratory language" in the Barnes sense. This common experience becomes the basis for future relationships and the building of metaphors, describing one item or experience in terms of another.

Projects—whether they are isolated topics of interest or developed out of either a class theme-study, or from a shared field trip—can extend and enrich the discourse in a classroom. They form the foundation of authentic experience in which natural speaking and listening situations occur.

Choral Reading. Choral reading was popular in the 1950s. It seemed ideal for those P.T.A. programs where teachers needed to make sure that every child had a chance to participate. Booklets were published with poems for choral reading in which each line of every poem was marked for reading aloud in parts. Notations would include such items as: solo 1, solo 2, whole group, row 1, girls, etc. The teacher assigned parts and the group read following hand signals; however, such poetry readings structured and directed by teachers had a rather limited value for children. Choral reading can, however, provide rich opportunities for speaking and listening. Poetry is meant to be heard. The sound of a poem is a vital part of the poet's message. One of the joys of poetry is saying it or helping to create a poem in its spoken form.

Teachers who read a great deal of poetry will find that children will naturally begin to chorus the refrain of poems they have heard often and that they love. Some brief poems may be heard so often that children will learn them by heart, as they memorized nursery rhymes. Other poems have inviting refrains, such as Vachel Lindsay's "Proud Mysterious Cat," with its repetitive phrases and the "mew, mew, mews" that end each stanza.

The teacher's selection of poetry and the way the voice is used when sharing poetry can help children focus on the sounds, the rhythms, and the imagery that set poetry apart from prose. Children will enjoy the rhythmic beats of poems like "The Pickety Fence" (McCord) and delight in the way that de la Mare used soft sibilant sounds in "Silver." Hearing such poetry entices children to want to say it aloud themselves.

A teacher might begin a choral reading experience with a poem such as Rossetti's "What Is Pink?" The question-answer format of this poem lends itself to reading aloud with one group asking and another group answering. As they try out ways of saying the lines, the children learn to use the voice to achieve specific effects as they modify tone, pitch, and pause in order to change or add depth to the meaning of the printed words. A teacher could extend the reading of the Rossetti poem by asking children to find other poems that use this same question-answer format. When they have found a number of such poems, they might wish to select a few to share with others in the class.

One group of children liked the poem "Questions" by Ridlon. These children decided to prepare a group reading. The preparation involved much discussion about who was asking the questions and why they wanted to know the answers. Everyone was able to relate it to a similar experience he or she had had. The children decided which words to stress and how to handle the pauses marked by the ellipses in the fifth stanza. They decided to write in the parts, underline the stressed words, and tap their feet ten times when they came to the ellipses. The tapping, they concluded, would show the irritation of the speaker, create the needed pause, and intensify the word "ten" all at the same time. The poem with their notations follows.

QUESTIONS

<u>What</u> did you do?
<u>Where</u> did you go?
<u>Why</u> weren't you back
An <u>hour</u> ago?

Group I
Father grumpy

How come your shirt's
<u>Ripped</u> on the sleeve?
Why are you <u>wet</u>?
<u>When</u> did you leave?

Group II
Baby Brother whiney

What scratched your <u>face</u>?
<u>When</u> did you eat?
Where are your <u>socks</u>?
Look at your <u>feet</u>!

Group III
Big Sister bossy

How did you get
<u>Paint</u> in your hair?
<u>Where</u> have you been?
<u>Don't</u> kick the chair!

Group IV
Mother worried and anxious

<u>Say</u> something now.
I'll give you till <u>ten</u>.
. . .
"See if I <u>ever</u>
Come home again."

Group I
Father
Tap feet ten times
Solo, disgusted

A great deal of language went into the preparation of the poem, as children explained, questioned, and tried out phrasing. Choral reading provides good opportunities for a variety of language uses.

Drama. Drama provides a unique opportunity for children to listen and speak. It is necessary to separate drama from theater. Theater requires an audience, and is focused upon producing a finished performance that can be repeated; drama, however, is more fluid. It does not require an audience, but does require improvisation on the part of the participants. The focus of drama is process rather than product. Because of this, drama has far greater value in the elementary classroom than does theater.

As young children dramatize a tale they have heard and loved such as "The Three Billy Goats Gruff," they will need to listen to each other intently in order to take turns without breaking the natural flow of the story. They will need to be able to respond appropriately and react to the points the speaker is making. By their voices they will need to show the timidity of the smallest goat, or the fierceness of the troll.

As an activity, drama may be considered beyond the play setting—that is, a group of youngsters assuming roles within a story. Other kinds of drama might include enacting radio or TV programs, which could include the news, complete with weather reports. Another media event might be author interviews: a child becomes Madeleine L'Engle and responds to questions about her recent book, *A Ring of Endless Light*. Political interviews and campaigns can also be staged.

Role-playing need not be limited to radio and TV activities but could also become a source for book sharing. By assuming another's role, a child has the opportunity to practice using language to create different effects for an interpretation of the character.

Puppetry is another way of assuming roles. This activity has the advantage of focusing attention on the puppet itself instead of a shy or inhibited child. Just as in other drama, decisions about sequencing events, character choice and interpretation, and story selection involve speaking and listening to others.

A final type of drama is the act of storytelling. Although a solo effort, storytelling does encourage practice and does include listening by others. In addition, a child could retell a story told or read by the teacher. The child may have listened to a story in the listening center or an older youngster could have read to him or her. When retelling it, the child may tape the story and listen for self-evaluation and improvement. Storytelling allows a child to practice the language of books, using that specific kind of vocabulary and order of words. The child learns to speak to an audience, gaining and holding its attention.

All types of drama are chances to practice using language before others. But beyond this formal aspect, drama is also a chance for children to speak and listen to each other as they make decisions about their participation. We have also discussed the uses of drama in chapter 6, "Reading and Writing," and in chapter 8, "Literature-Based Language Extensions."

The Classroom Environment

Classrooms where growth in speaking and listening is an important goal are rooms where social interaction is encouraged. Desks arranged in rows do not promote child-to-child talk. Small tables, learning centers, and interest areas *do* invite children to speak and listen to each other in order to get a task done, solve a problem, or share information.

Whereas some talk will be about the job at hand, some will be purely social. The latter is as important as the former. Desegregation has provided opportunities for children from various socioeconomic and ethnic groups to get to know each other. However, if the only real chance for children to talk together about social matters occurs on the bus or in the lunch room, where "bus friends" tend to sit together, then children will probably find most of their friendships with those from their own neighborhood.

A classroom that encourages talk need not be noisy or chaotic. The teacher can arrange the room so that there are noisy areas and quiet places. The game shelf, the art corner, and the drama area are going to be "noisy spots." Children also need areas where they can be by themselves to work quietly. Other areas where quiet is important are the book corner, where books are read aloud, and the listening center, where children can listen to tapes and records. The room arrangement must be planned so that children can move easily from one area to another without disturbing their classmates. Such fluidity of space will encourage a sharing across areas. The poetry heard in the listening corner may be extended when the child moves over to the art area. The book read aloud in the reading corner may become a part of the language going on in the drama area. An important part of becoming an independent learner is to be able to direct one's own learning by making good choices in how to share what one has learned and extend one's knowledge by talking with and listening to others.

When considering the talk environment, teachers need not be limited solely to their own class. Visitors to the schoolroom, such as parents, other teachers, the principal, resource people, and tutorial aid from other classrooms enrich discourse. They provide diversity in language input and constitute new audiences. The sharing of one room with another not only at similar age levels but also with older and younger age groups requires students to shift their language use to meet these new audiences.

The classroom environment which encourages purposeful talking and listening will extend children's abilities in discourse. This discourse may be assessed by the teacher to see whether the classroom environment is supportive of language growth.

Only when children are free to interact with each other about a task at hand will natural language flow. Who knows the topic of conversation for these two children? Is it time? Does it really matter? (Mrs. Weisent's classroom, Cranbrook School, Columbus, Ohio)

Assessment

Spontaneous Language Observations

Standardized tests for listening and speaking are available for use in the classroom. Recent investigators have questioned the validity and reliability of these tests. Cazden (1972) found that children acquired morphological control earlier than Berko's studies would have suggested. Cazden attributes this to the fact that her data came from spontaneous language, whereas Berko's was collected in a testing situation. Both Labov (1972) and Black (1979) found that the testing situation resulted in hypercorrection of language forms: for example, the pluralization of an already plural form such as "feets." In a more informal environment children were found to use more mature speech. All of these researchers recommend that language be assessed in a natural setting in order to get a clear view of what language children are truly able to produce and understand.

Two ways to maintain informal records are through anecdotal notations or with a checklist. In an anecdotal record be sure to note:

The child's name
Date
Time of day
Current activity
Setting
Others in group
Either quote actual words or paraphrase the language in a way that will convey effect
Child's gestures, behavior, body language
Child's intent and the interpretation of that intent by others
Your own interpretation of this event

It is often difficult to keep records. One way to simplify this task is to keep a stack of note cards handy. When observational opportunities occur, notes can be made and then slipped into the child's folder. The file can be evaluated later in order to get a more complete picture. At certain times the teacher will want to focus upon specific children, perhaps making several notations a day; at other times once or twice a week may suffice. It is vital to include a child's language strengths as well as problem areas. Anecdotal records are particularly helpful when there is concern about usage. If time is taken to note *exactly* what the youngster does say, the results often show that nonstandard usage is in reality but a few words, not the child's total speech pattern.

Black (1979) has developed an Interactional Competency Checklist, which is helpful to consider when assessing children's language. Although the checklist was developed from Black's observation of children in a sociodramatic play area, it could be adjusted to meet the needs of teachers in a variety of classroom settings.

INTERACTIONAL COMPETENCY CHECKLIST

I. *Ability to Adapt to Changes in the Setting*

This category is based on Cicourel's second and fourth properties of interactional competence and attempts to assess whether young children can "behave as if they share the same social setting and are receiving and processing the same information," and "can normalize discrepancies to sustain social interaction" (Cicourel 1972, pp. 217–18). These properties were adapted to the sociodramatic environment under the following subcategories.

A. Adjusts to the various themes of play .... ☐
B. Extends the organization of the plot .... ☐
C. Extends character development .... ☐

II. *Nonverbal Appropriateness*

This category is based on Cicourel's fourth property of interactional competence, and attempts to assess whether young children possess "'normal form repertoires' of possible appearances, behaviors, and utterances that can be understood when emergent in contextually organized settings" (Cicourel 1972, pp. 217–18). This property was adapted to the sociodramatic environment under the subcategories of gestures, facial expressions and body movements. In addition, two other subcategories of nonverbal behavior, vocal intonation and stress, were included based upon Mishler's (1976) research which indicated first graders' use of appropriate stress and intonation.

A. Uses appropriate
   gestures .... ☐
B. Uses appropriate facial
   expression .... ☐
C. Uses appropriate body
   movement .... ☐
D. Uses appropriate vocal
   intonation .... ☐
E. Uses appropriate stress ☐

III. *Familiarity with Normal Constraints and Conditions*

This category is based upon Cicourel's third property of interactional competence which concerns such items as a knowledge of who can speak first or next, what topics are considered socially relevant, how to terminate an exchange, repair, recycling, and repeating (Cicourel 1972, pp. 217–18). ...

A. Knows when to speak
   first or next .... ☐
B. Discusses topics
   socially relevant to the
   situation .... ☐
C. Knows how to terminate a conversation ... ☐

D. Repairs (corrects) oral
   language .... ☐
E. Recycles (rephrases)
   oral language .... ☐
F. Repeats oral language . ☐

IV. *Sequencing*

This category is based upon Cicourel's first and sixth properties of interactional competence and attempts to assess whether young children demonstrate the ability to think back or reflect upon previous experiences with present and possible future informational events, objects, and resources within the communicative setting (Cicourel 1972, pp. 217–18).

A. Links past experience
   with present information events .... ☐
B. Links past experience
   with possible future
   informational events .. ☐
   (pp. 532–533)

There are two ways to gather information for assessing discourse: direct observation and taping. Both types of data collection need to exist because each provides different types of input. Personal observation allows the teacher to see the metalinguistic behavior and to gain a more sensitive awareness of the "feel" of the interaction among participants. Usually note-taking for records, however, comes as an afterthought, a remembrance of what went on.

Listening to a tape has the advantage of allowing a teacher to stop midway to take notes and thus allows more careful observation and notation of student behavior. Reflective analysis can occur and taped portions can be replayed for further information. While some students may feel restrained by the tape-recorder's presence, others could focus on the recorder as the audience, thus concentrating on performance rather than interaction. Time and repeated exposures could alleviate this type of response, but it should always be taken into account. Taped language should be compared with its spontaneous observed counterpart. Taped sessions also allow for students to listen to themselves for self-assessment, and for teacher colleagues to listen so that their perceptions may be included. Often others can identify aspects of discourse one person alone cannot.

To prepare to analyze a taped discourse, record a group of adults and listen to the tape. Teachers in the lounge room would be a good protocol because of the natural language You will find that sentence fragments and heavy reliance on context makes the taped discourse almost nonsensical at first. Practice makes a listener able to disregard extraneous dialogue; in fact, for ease of reading, garbled language was deleted from the book discussion on *The Cay* that began this chapter.

What should you look for? The context determines the functions of the language produced. Barnes (1977) suggests that if teachers are evaluating themselves, the primary question is if they are instructing in the way they intend to instruct. The following set of questions is influenced by Barnes's (1977) writings. A teacher might ask:

Student/Teacher Discourse Observation Guide

Are student experiences included in the discussion?

Do I make "replying," not just "assessing" responses?

Are extended responses encouraged with few "yes/no" options?

Can students ask each other for elaborations and information?

Are different types of thinking and relationships among ideas involved in the discussion?

Do students feel free to question my statements?

Can students sometimes discover for themselves or are they always told?

Do a range of topics and kinds of language occur over a period across discussions?

148 *Integration of the Language Arts*

When listening to students discussing among themselves, the teacher could question:

Student/Student Discourse Observation Guide

Is each student assuming responsibility within the discussion to further the group's progress?

Are all participants respectful of the others' contributions?

Does the language reveal that perceptive and diverse thinking has occurred?

Can the students deal with differences of opinion without degenerating into disruptive argument?

Are the participants able to formulate problems and develop hypotheses to test and arrive at conclusions?

Do the students not only recognize that each group member is different, but also adjust their expectations and interpretations in this light?

Story Retelling

Another way to analyze children's language is to listen to their story retellings. Story retellings are limited in view of context and of responsive language, but there are inherent properties of storytelling that are not easily revealed elsewhere. Such properties include the special vocabulary and syntax of stories—for example, "scoundrel," "there was a long time ago," "said he"; the use of a sequence of events to introduce relevant detail; and the interpretation of characters through intonation and word choice. David, a second-grader, retold a Norwegian folktale, "The Man Who Was Going to Mind the House." Observe how much he knows about language and the language of stories.

THE MAN WHO WAS GOING TO MIND THE HOUSE
A Second-Grader's Retelling

Once there was a tired old grumbly old man that that um was very unpatient and ... he went ... one day when he came home from working in the fields he was extra grumbly. "I'm very thirsty and hungry and I work hard and is all you do is sit around here in the house." So his wife said, "Well ne... tomorrow YOU can stay at the house." And and so the next day ... mm Fredericks or whatever his name ... Frederick um wife went out out to tend the fields and he stayed home to mind the house. And first he finished his breakfast. And started to ... and he decided to stir the ... uh butter make the butter. And and he stirred and stirred and stirred and got very hot and thirsty so he went down the basement and got a glassful of beer. And he heard something upstairs just before it was full. And he ran upstairs and the pig had knocked over the butter and he ... (Laugh) ... he ran ... and then he was out of time. And he was licking up the milk. Then he just remembered the beer sitting down the basement! And he RAN downstairs again ... and he was too late! And and um the beer was flooding the basement. And and then he ... cleaned that up ... and he he decided to go upstairs and make dinner. First make butter but then make dinner. And he had the butter all made except for stirred and he went upstairs and started to make dinner. But then he just remembered that he had forgot to bring the cow to the field. But the field was a long way off. And they had a turf roof. So he decided to go up the hill and lay down a board, walk over the board with the cow, and put him on the roof. So he did. And then he said, "You know that's partly good, but I guess I guess I should ... um get some water." So he ... um ... went down to the well and get some water. But before he went out he had put the butter thing on his mouth on his back and so he and wen... so the baby wouldn't knock it over again. So when he leaned over to get the bucket, the butter spilled into ... (dramatic pause) ... the well. (Laugh) And then he walked into the house and forgot all about dinner. So he started to fix dinner. And the cow was up up on the roof. And he decided if he walked it would have fell off and broke its leg. So he went up there, tied a string around his neck, and tied it to his foot. But while he was making dinner ... and he brought it down the chimney and tied it to his foot ... while he was making dinner the cow moved and fell off. And he went up the chimney and he stopped, he got stuck and so he ... and they were hanging there. When his wife came back she slashed the rope from the ... uh ... from the from the cow and the cow fell down. Meanwhile, why Frederick fell into the pot upside down. The end.

David knows how to begin stories: "Once there was." He uses descriptive language: "a tired, old, grumbly, old man" (a neat way of stressing age!). He can make the listener feel the fatigue of the old man's work by repeating, "and he stirred and stirred and stirred"; no wonder he "got very hot and thirsty!" David can clearly relate the sequence of events and even include the old man's thinking, "But then he just remembered that he had forgot to bring the cow to the field. But the field was a long way off and they had a turf roof." Use of the dramatic pause to show what happened to the butter reveals his adeptness with language style. David is able to construct complex utterances: "One day when he came home from working in the fields, he was extra grumbly" and "But then he just remembered that he had forgot to bring the cow to the field."

Although David is highly sophisticated in his storytelling abilities for a second-grade child, he needs to retell simpler stories where he can have a clearer grasp of the plot, sequence, and characters in order to develop and gain fluency in language skills. Since this story was selected and read to David, perhaps he should have the opportunity to select stories himself to tell that would conform to his abilities. In addition, the teacher might try telling a story to David using a flannel board and then encourage him to retell the tale to others. David has a strong beginning; he just needs more practice.

Further discussion of story retelling as a teaching tool and assessment technique will follow in chapter 8, "Literature-Based Language Extensions," where a retelling of a five-year-old is compared with a retelling of an intermediate-grade-level youngster so that developmental differences can be seen. For now, it is sufficient to note the many aspects of language available for study in story retelling.

Summary

Listening and speaking take place in acts of discourse. Each language arts area interacts with the others, influencing the meaning of the total discourse. The context in which the discourse occurs shapes the function, the intent of that act, in which the message itself becomes part of the context. Basic competencies in discourse include identifying and using the context, directing speaking and listening for specific purposes, and knowledge of appropriate social conventions.

Teachers can do much to promote growth in children's discourse abilities. They can become models of the social conventions, hold significant conversations with children, and assist youngsters to extend their language uses and thus influence knowledge gained from an experience. Groups may be organized for shared interests, diversity of views, or a mixture of abilities. In group situations children will have the opportunity to use language to reach a variety of goals set among themselves at times, and with the teacher at other times. Activities such as drama, choral reading, sharing time, projects, and field trips encourage wide language use as well as natural in-class interaction. The environment, both physical and social, sets the language context, for language is learned through the doing, the making, and the exploring that children need to work through at home and at school.

Suggested Learning Experiences

1. Place a tape-recorder with a group that is working without an adult. Be sure to tell the children to speak up so that their voices will record well. Analyze the tape. Who are the group leaders? Who contributes little? How would you compare this group to the group that discussed *The Cay?* Were they aware of an audience? What kinds of experiences does this group need?

2. Select one student in order to observe her listening behavior. How does she listen to a story? How does she listen to other members of the class? Do her contributions to a discussion reflect what she has heard? What situations seem to cause her to listen more intently? How might you extend this child's listening skills?

3. Invite a child to talk with you. Let the child choose the topic of conversation. Can you respond to him without questioning? Does he need questions to encourage a response? Are you able to let the child lead the conversation? Does he need help in talking, or is he able to sustain a conversation?

4. Select a folktale at the appropriate level to read to a child. Ask that child to retell the story to another youngster in the classroom. Tape-record the storytelling. Analyze the similarities in the vocabulary used and the vocabulary found in the story, the story language used, and the sequence of events included. How sophisticated are the language structures the child uses in comparison with the language structures of others in the class? Ask another child to retell the same story. What are the similarities and differences between the two children? Who needs to listen to more literature? Who needs more experiences in storytelling?

Recommended Readings

Barnes, Douglas, *From Communication to Curriculum,* Penguin, Harmondsworth, Middlesex, England, 1975.

 In chapter 1, Barnes sets out the role of language in the classroom and includes a discussion of his model of communication and learning. His stress on the significance of context in language learning and use supports the position we have taken. In the following chapter Barnes has included student dialogues stemming from such sources as air pressure in science to the discussion of a poem. His analyses of these language samples reveal how children use language to learn.

Dillon, David, and Searle, Dennis, "The Role of Language in One First-Grade Classroom," *Research in the Teaching of English* 15:311–328, December, 1981.
   Although the sampling was narrow to allow depth of analysis, the description seems applicable to many classrooms we have visited. Child language use was restricted and teacher language focused upon the transmission of knowledge. Compare the dialogues in this article with the dialogues included in the present chapter. How do they differ in language use and role of the participants?

Pinnell, Gay Su, ed., *Discovering Language with Children,* National Council of Teachers of English, Urbana, Illinois, 1980.
   This small book contains a collection of articles written by linguists and educators on child language acquisition, language variation, and ways to promote and evaluate language growth. The entries are brief and readable, geared to classroom teachers.

Tough, Joan, "The Invitation to Talk," chapter 7, pp. 66–73 in *Focus on Meaning: Talking to Some Purpose with Young Children,* George Allen and Unwin, London, England, 1973.
   Using several transcripts of conversations between a teacher and a child, Tough illustrates ways an adult may interact with a child without overpowering the language that occurs. She discusses each dialogue, analyzing the child's language use and the kind of appropriate teacher response. Talking with young children can be especially difficult for a beginning teacher since much of the adult role lies in supporting and encouraging rather than acting as an equal partner.

References

Professional Literature

Barnes, Douglas, *From Communication to Curriculum,* Penguin, Harmondsworth, Middlesex, England, 1976.

Barnes, Douglas, "Monitoring Communication for Learning," pp. 171–178 in *Language Across the Curriculum,* Michael Marland, Heinemann, London, 1977.

Black, Janet K., "There's More to Language Than Meets the Ear: Implications for Evaluation," *Language Arts* 56:526–533, May, 1979.

Cazden, Courtney, *Child Language in Education,* Holt, Rinehart and Winston, New York, 1972.

Cazden, Courtney, "Hypercorrection in Test Responses," *Theory Into Practice* 14:343–346, Dec., 1975.

Cicourel, Aaron V., "Cross Modal Communication: Representational Context of Sociolinguistic Information Processing," in *Monograph Series on Language and Linguistics, Twenty-third Annual Round Table,* edited by R. Shuy, Georgetown University Press, Washington, 1972.

Davis, E. A., *The Development of Linguistic Skill in Twins, Singletons with Siblings, and Only Children from Age Five to Ten Years,* Institute of Child Welfare Monograph Series, 1937, No. 14.

Day, E. J., "The Development of Language in Twins, A Comparison of Twins and Single Children," *Child Development* 3:179–199, 1932.

Labov, William, *Sociolinguistic Patterns,* University of Pennsylvania Press, Philadelphia, 1972.

Loban, W. D., The Language of Elementary School Children, *National Council of Teachers of English Research Reports,* No. 1, Champaign, Ill., 1963.

Lundsteen, Sara W., *Children Learn to Communicate,* Prentice-Hall, Englewood Cliffs, N.J., 1976.

Marland, Michael, *Language Across the Curriculum,* Heinemann, London, 1977.

May, Frank B., *Teaching Language as Communication to Children,* Merrill, Columbus, Ohio, 1967.

McCarthy, D. A., *The Language Development of the Preschool Child,* Institute of Child Welfare Monograph Series, No. 4, University of Minnesota, 1930.

McCarthy, D. A., "Child Development—VIII. Language," in W. S. Monroe, ed., *Encyclopedia of Educational Research,* rev. ed., Macmillan, New York, 1950.

Mishler, E. G., "Conversational Competence Among First Graders," Paper presented at the Conference on Language, Children, and Society, Ohio State University, May, 1976.

Moffett, James, *A Student-Centered Language Arts Curriculum, Grades K-6: A Handbook for Teachers,* Houghton Mifflin, Boston, 1968.

Moffett, James, and Wagner, Betty Jane, *Student-Centered Language Arts, K-13,* 2nd ed., Houghton Mifflin, Boston, 1976.

O'Donnell, R. C.; Griffin, W. J.; and Norris, R. C., Syntax of Kindergarten and Elementary School Children: A Transformational Analysis, *National Council of Teachers of English Research Reports,* No. 8, Champaign, Ill., 1967.

Pinnell, Gay S., "Language in Primary Classrooms," *Theory Into Practice* 14:318–327, December, 1975.

Rankin, Paul T., "The Measurement of the Ability to Understand Spoken Language," Ph.D. dissertation, University of Michigan, 1920: *Dissertation Abstracts* 12 (1952); p. 848.

Rosen, Harold, and Rosen, Connie, *The Language of Primary School Children*, Penguin, Harmondsworth, Middlesex, England, 1973.

Shuy, Roger W., "Learning to Talk like Teachers," *Language Arts* 58: 168–174, Feb., 1981.

Smith, M. E., An Investigation of the Development of the Sentence and the Extent of Vocabulary in Young Children, *University of Iowa Studies in Child Welfare*, 1926, 3(5), 5–92.

Strickland, Dorothy S., "A Program for Linguistically Different Black Children," *Research in the Teaching of English* 7, 79–86, Spring 1973.

Strickland, R. G., The Language of Elementary School Children: Its Relationship to the Language of Reading Textbooks and the Quality of Reading of Selected Children, *Bulletin of the School of Education* 38, No. 4, Indiana University, July, 1962.

Templin, M. C. *Certain Language Skills in Children: Their Development and Interrelationships*, Institute of Child Welfare Monograph Series, No. 26, 1957.

Tough, Joan, "The Invitation to Talk," Chapter 7, pp. 66–73, in *Focus on Meaning: Talking to Some Purpose with Young Children*, George Allen & Unwin Ltd., London, 1973.

Wilt, Miriam E., "A Study of Teacher Awareness of Listening as a Factor in Elementary Education," *Journal of Educational Research* 43:626–636, Apr., 1950.

Children's Literature

de la Mare, Walter, "Silver" in Arbuthnot, May Hill, and Shelton L. Root, Jr., eds., *Time for Poetry*, 3rd General Edition, Scott Foresman, Glenview, Ill.; 1968.

Jones, Weyman, *The Edge of Two Worlds*, illustrated by J. C. Kocsis, Dial, New York, 1968.

L'Engle, Madeleine, *A Ring of Endless Light*, Farrar, Straus, Giroux, New York, 1980.

Lindsay, Vachel, "Proud Mysterious Cat," in Arbuthnot, May Hill, and Shelton L. Root, Jr., eds., *Time for Poetry*, 3rd General Edition, Scott Foresman, Glenview, Ill.; 1968.

McCord, David, "The Pickety Fence," in *Far and Few, Rhymes of Never Was and Always Is*, Little, Brown, Boston, 1952.

O'Dell, Scott, *Island of the Blue Dolphins*, Houghton Mifflin, Boston, 1960.

Ridlon, Marci, "Questions," in *That Was Summer*, Follett, New York, 1969.

Rosetti, Christina, "What Is Pink?," in *Sing-Song,* illustrated by Margarite Davis, Macmillan, New York, 1924.

Sperry, Armstrong, *Call It Courage,* Macmillan, New York, 1940.

Taylor, Theodore, *The Cay,* Doubleday, New York, 1969.

Uchida, Yoshika, *Journey to Topaz,* illustrated by Donald Carrick, Scribner, New York, 1971.

Literacy Begins in the Home

Ways in Which Children Begin to Organize Print
Beginning Writing
The Role of the Teacher
Signs of Reading Knowledge in the Classroom

Beginning Writing and Reading, Teacher-Initiated
Accepting Dictation
Ways of Using Children's Dictation
Word Banks
Learning from Children's Attempts to Read

Conventions of Print
Handwriting
Spelling

Building a Literacy Context

Summary

Suggested Learning Experiences

Recommended Readings

References
Professional Literature
Children's Literature

Chapter 5
Writing and Reading: The Beginnings

In a kindergarten class, five-year-old Cristi enthusiastically drew this picture of herself.

It is a picture typical of many drawn by children of this age. The subject is a sticklike figure beneath the sun, which is surrounded by sharp little rays. The details are sparse. As Cristi matures, her drawings will begin to show much greater detail but, for now, her flowers have no leaves, her hands no fingers, and the body is drawn as a simple rectangle.

We often make the assumption that when first-graders start off for school in September, they take their first steps toward literacy. Is their first school experience, however, also their initial contact with written language? By looking at what Cristi already knows, there is evidence that she has often met print before entering school. She knows how to write her name, which is not surprising for a kindergartner, since at this egocentric stage children are deeply concerned with themselves. While many five-year-olds label their work with their first names, Cristi has moved a bit beyond. Her interest in print has led her to include her middle and last name as well. At first glance, one might dismiss Cristi's writing as a little lopsided and even messy. But careful examination shows that she is beginning to handle the intricacies of print very well.

Cristi already knows that when you write, you move from left to right and from the top to the bottom of the page. She considers space in a flexible way; when she runs out of room for completing her middle name, she simply lists the letters that follow beneath the "l." All the letters are drawn accurately and though most appear in capitals, two are in lower case—the "i" and "t." Perhaps she selected these forms because of their distinguishing features, the dot and a crossed line. Although most children of this age write in block or upper-case letters, many mix these with the lower case.

Luckily, Cristi is in a classroom where she will have many opportunities to explore written language. Her school environment contains books, labels for supplies and displays, and the writings of the other students in her class. Cristi's development in her knowledge of print will be shown later in this chapter. But first, how did she come to know so much about writing before she entered school as a kindergartner? What kinds of experiences with literacy did she have at home?

Literacy Begins in the Home

Close observations of young children show us that their experiences with reading occur long before they enter the classroom. Typically, reading begins on a parent's lap. It is here that a child can begin to see books as a source of pleasure. Children enjoy the sounds and rhythms of nursery rhymes and the warm contact with the person who reads them aloud. Favorite stories will be requested again and again and when a weary parent deviates from the text or skips a page he or she will quickly be called to task. Children like to join in and chant the refrains that are a part of many books; for example, they love to help the Gingerbread Man each time he reiterates, "I ran away from a little old woman and a little old man,/ And I can run away from you, I can, I can."

We are all aware of how young children shape their actions to imitate the adult behavior they see. Children dress up like Mommy and Daddy and act out adult roles—cooking, driving, using tools to fix things, and mothering their dolls. They also may begin to initiate reading behavior if they see adults who are frequently absorbed in books. Many children will spend long quiet times poring over books that have been read to them, or looking through new books and magazines. You may see children who "read" to their dolls or stuffed animals, using the illustrations in the book as a stimulus to their retelling. If you eavesdrop, you will often hear children begin their stories with "Once upon a time" and close with "And they lived happily ever after," for their experiences with books have led them to expect to find literary language between the covers of a book, rather than the ordinary spoken language of everyday life.

However, books are not the only source of print for the child. We live in a world of print. Soup cans, cereal boxes, and toothpaste tubes are all labeled. Streets are marked with traffic signs that tell us to stop and billboards that invite us to buy. Even television commercials are overlaid with print.

As children acquire their language by sorting and categorizing sounds they have heard in meaningful situations, so, too, they begin to process the print they see. Almost universally, children will recognize the golden arches of McDonald's restaurants. These arches, seen as they stop in to get a favorite meal, pointed out by Daddy as they drive down the highway, and shown on television commercials, form a strong association. Meeting these arches in meaningful contexts will enable many children to recognize these symbols out of context. Upon seeing the logo printed above the word "McDonald's", children say "hamburger" because they are reading the meaning the symbol has for them. Similarly, the word "Crest" may be read as "toothpaste" or the word "Oreo" as "cookie." Harste, Burke, and Woodward (1982), who performed the preceding study of young children's developing understanding of print, believe it to be more helpful to use the term "print settings" rather than "encountering print." When the term "print settings" is used, the significance and contribution of the context in which print occurs is taken into account. Children use information from all system sources—mathematical, linguistic, artistic, and behavioral—as a means to differentiate and refine their understanding of the world about them.

The child's reading has grown out of print in a meaningful context. It is through such experiences that children begin to develop a sense of print not simply as patterns on a page, but as purposeful communication. As they realize this, children will attempt to use print for their own purposes, such as labeling drawings or writing notes to Grandmother. Sometimes a child will cover a sheet of paper with letters or scribbles and then ask an adult to tell what it says. One three-year-old sat beside his mother as she made out her grocery list and worked busily at a list of his own. "There," he said as he carefully pointed at each squiggle in turn, "it says ice cream, cookies, and lollipops." Though he could not yet write, he had already begun to see print as a tool for communicating needs and directing the behavior of others.

Learning to read and write do seem to go together, for in studies of young children's early development of literacy, the findings overlap. One generality appears to be that children behave as they see others, especially adults, behave. In their study of early writers, Hall, Moretz, and Staton (1976) found that writing occurs in the home as a part of everyday life. Youngsters see writing as a functional activity that adults choose to do. In addition, these researchers reported that the children are read to not only by their parents but often by brothers and sisters. Durkin (1966), who investigated children who read early, and Clark (1976), who looked at young, fluent readers stated similar findings. Durkin called early readers "scribblers," for these children write or behave as writers while learning to read. In all three studies parents of children who were becoming literate established homes where print was found in a purposeful setting, where writing materials were available, and where the parents used print to meet their own and their children's needs.

When teachers are aware of all that each child brings to the literacy task, they can build upon those prior learnings with new, extending experiences. Teacher observations are vital if they are to help students continue to develop their understandings about print.

Ways in Which Children Begin to Organize Print

Some believe that, if left to their own devices, children would write first and then read later (Chomsky, 1971). We have observed that while writing sometimes precedes reading, it most often does not. We do not know how much of this is a function of classroom instruction and organization, but within the very same classroom, some youngsters will begin writing and then reading their own writing before going to outside sources as books or teacher-accepted dictation. Others begin by showing an interest in what words and letters say but do not attempt to write; for these children, the teacher must initiate writing by transcribing the child's statements. A third way that often occurs with the other two learning styles is text approximation. Some children try to "read back" stories they have heard. They remember the story and the pictures help lead them through the book. Gradually as they hear the story read to them again and again, their attempts more closely approximate the text. They are learning to associate print forms and meanings, developing a set of sight words (McKenzie, 1977).

Beginning Writing

Vygotsky (1978) believes the first scribbles grow out of gestures the young child makes; these gestures represent meaning. Infant scribbling can seem formless to adults but as these youngsters mature, a person observing their

162 *Integration of the Language Arts*

efforts might see the children's ability to move from left to right and from top to bottom. Often these messages conclude or begin with the child's name, his or her first legible word. Some children show their scribbling to an adult and ask, "What does this say?" indicating their awareness of the message function of writing.

For those children who initiate writing themselves, the early signs may be hidden. Beginning writers often mix their artistic endeavors with letter play. If you look carefully at the turtle below you can find the letters "o," "c," "r," "p," and "e" and the numerals "6" and "8." The child who drew this turtle delighted in using letters and numerals as decorations.

"Lynn," found within the drawing at the top of the next page, is the name of the young artist/writer's sister. Besides the face, he decided to draw the upper-case letters "A" and "B." Children often choose to write the names of their sisters and brothers and mother and father. This practice assists them in their initial compositions, which usually deal with family experiences.

Rachel enjoys writing her name and when the space runs out, she simply proceeds to complete her last name on a following line.

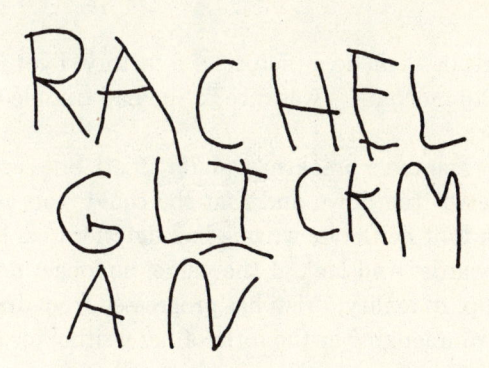

Judging the space needed for writing is an advanced skill. Some children might have placed the last letters vertically under the "m" as Cristi did in our beginning sample of writing. Either method of solving the space problem illustrates additional knowledge of the directional conventions of print—left to right and top to bottom.

164 *Integration of the Language Arts*

The Development of Writing Skills. Progression in the development of writing skills is not a consistent sequence. However, there do exist aspects to look for, advancements that may be overlooked if you are not attuned to particular writing attributes. Perhaps the best way to discuss the development of writing is by studying one child's progress.

Cristi began her kindergarten year writing her full name, as we saw earlier. In January she proudly brought her first "message" writing to her teacher.

[handwritten: BV ɔʀ I SʜTMADAPAPHRƆFAFARDD A]

She read, "I made a picture of a factory." Cristi's teacher suggested that she rewrite her message so that it could be displayed.

[handwritten: I MADAPHR DR APKDEAIGLL tFORIZMIZZ tWBUt FRA VANDIH V AN B iWIt]

This time Cristi read, "I made a picture of a factory. I got it for Christmas. It was brand new to me and . . . was nice?" She had trouble reading the final portion of her work.

The writing represented a breakthrough for Cristi. She recognized that her thoughts could be written down and that she could read and reread them. Some might think that her letter writing had deteriorated; both the "s" and "c" are now backwards. And look at the name, no longer an art project but a sign of authorship! In reality, Cristi has progressed from drawing her letters to writing them, from looking at the form of her writing for accuracy to concentrating on meaning, the function of writing. She has developed a sound-symbol system that she can use to convey meaning. "Made" is spelled "mad," a typical generalization for inventing spellers. The /h/ sound in "picture" is recorded and the "r" serves as the /er/ sound. No spaces between words appear; this is a common act of beginning writers. The second writing, in which she elaborated her statement, became overburdening. Her letters

Writing and Reading: The Beginnings 165

grew in size and decreased in legibility. She had trouble reading her own work. Perhaps the task was too much for her; sheer verbal encouragement may have been enough.

A few weeks later Cristi produced the following writing. Some people might think she was taking a step backward. Instead of neatly formed letters, we have what at first appears like scribbling. When asked to read her work, she said, "I made a picture. I made a picture of a monster. The rest I wrote in cursive and I don't know how to read that."

Cristi is extending her writing by trying out a new form, cursive. This "scribbling" is quite different from infant scribbling in several ways. Can you find the letters "e," "t," "r," and "w"? Her strong self-confidence is seen by a willingness to explore the new and recognize her own inability to read cursive. She is not afraid to test, to practice as a way to learn. Her teacher, recognizing that cursive was beyond Cristi's immature grasp, merely showed an interest (which was real!) in what the child was doing and agreed that cursive was difficult.

Three months later Cristi drew this picture and wrote and rewrote but two words, "the girl."

Her concentration is on form, the spelling of "girl." She knows that "grilly" is not accurate and is determined to have the word look "right" and be in her own handwriting. You can see where Cristi crossed out the teacher's "girl" so she could do it herself. Another interesting aspect is that in rewriting "the," there is a different combination of upper- and lower-case letters each time it is written. In this instance the teacher made a note of Cristi's new interest in spelling but did not reinforce this focus. Writing fluency had yet to be developed.

The next year, in first grade, Cristi is an established writer. Her ability to sustain an interest in a project has expanded as has her knowledge about the writing task. How does the following sample illustrate her growth?

> BxCristI
> OncS A Pon A Tam Tar lavd
> A Mother and a father They
> had one kid and his Name was
> ChriSChrgel and he grewup to be
> SantaClaus he aet Jllee to mack
>
> his Stamck Rumlbl lock thanoan
> he lokt fane wan he laft
> hohoho Mare crastmas
> he is love

Once upon a time there lived a mother and a father. They had one kid and his name was Kris Kringle and he grew up to be Santa Claus. He ate jelly to make him fat. His stomach rumbled like thunder. He looked funny when he laughed. "Ho, ho, ho, Merry Christmas!" He is love.

In form, Cristi has developed a concept of word as denoted by the spacing. There is some knowledge about the use of capital letters, although inconsistant and overapplied. She capitalizes names—"Santa Claus," "Chris Chrgel," "Mother," and even "Name" itself, but not "father." "Merry" is also capitalized. Cristi's writing illustrates that she understands what a sentence is, for she capitalizes the first word of each of her sentences. Her name is still a mixture of upper- and lower-case letters with an attempt at a cursive "y," but no reversals appear.

This composition reflects Cristi's sense of story. She knows the literary "once-upon-a-time" formula and she combines events in a logical sequence. Obviously Cristi has been exposed to other stories of Santa Claus and Clement Clark Moore's famous "A Visit from St. Nicholas." She has garnered this information and incorporated it in a story of her own.

Many of the words are spelled conventionally, even words that are irregular in sound-symbol relationships, such as "mother," "father," "grew," and "they." Other words, when analyzed, reveal a growing knowledge of spelling from experiences with print. "Once" is spelled not as it sounds, except for the concluding "s," but mostly as it looks when read. The spelling "Chris Chrgel" shows an awareness of the /ch/ in Christmas and the sophisticated information that the sound /gəl/ may be spelled "gel." And "Jllee" demonstrates the logic and creativity that Cristi brings to her writing.

What factors aided Cristi in her writing development? How did her teacher assist her as she explored the variety of systems within written language?

The Role of the Teacher. Cristi's classroom was a kindergarten-first grade combination. From the time that she entered the room, she saw writing being produced by other children. There existed an atmosphere of expectation that all would eventually write and that this task was pleasurable and worthwhile. During sharing time each day children would proudly read their compositions and be praised. Cristi's teacher said that some kindergarten children would hold up pictures they had produced and proceed to "read" about them—much to the consternation of the sophisticated first-graders, who would call out, "You can't do that! There are no words!" But these young kindergartners would continue, knowing the appropriate thing to do.

Writing was an important task. Most children in the class chose to read their efforts to the teacher first or would do so as she visited with them while moving around the room. This enabled her to extend and praise, suggest and appraise. In this classroom, when a child completed his or her *first* written composition, it was the procedure to stop everything so that the work could be immediately shared. Since this would occur not more than ten to fifteen times a year, the event was quite special.

Work was displayed around the room. Usually writing was preceded by some type of art project such as drawing or painting, sculpture or construction. Youngsters took pride in their work for they knew others would view it. Recopying did not occur very often because at this developmental level the physical task is too arduous. However, when placed on construction paper matting or superimposed on cut-out shapes, the writing combined with the art work looked impressive and valuable.

The room was arranged in centers so that all children would not be doing the same thing. They could choose activities for their daily work and select the medium in which they wished to produce their thoughts. Some children elected to do all their work in oil pastels; others used felt pens; many chose to mix their media in collages, using pencil and crayon for the writing. As in play, these youngsters might be together doing a similar task but in parallel fashion. Some children are able to plan and work together on projects but others move independently at all times, not ready to leave their egocentric world to view problems with their peers.

Since Cristi directed her own progress, the role of the teacher is that of facilitator and extender. In this case the teacher needs to determine which aspect of writing Cristi is exploring and practicing. If Cristi is centering on the *form* of writing, as in her labeled drawing of a girl (page 166), this is not the time to ask her to write more about the picture. Rather, the teacher might ask Cristi how she knew there was another way to spell "girl." And, since form was the topic of the study, the teacher could observe and instruct on the basis of the way in which Cristi made her letters. Does she begin the lines from the top? Are features of the letters unnecessarily traced in their formations rather than using an economy of effort? How does Cristi hold her pencil?

Cristi's Santa Claus story is a clear example of centering on the *function* of writing, the meaning. In this instance the teacher might say, "I knew you were writing a story as soon as I read 'Once upon a time.'" and "No wonder Kris Kringle shakes like a bowl of jelly when he ate it to become fat!" A discussion of which ideas came from stories Cristi had heard and which were new ones might occur.

Writing is a difficult task because there are so many things to remember besides the physical coordination problems. Those children who self-initiate their writing need to have the opportunity to be relieved at times from producing all their own written products. Perhaps a teacher could assist by accepting their dictation for the beginning or ending of their compositions. In some instances the entire writing might be performed by the teacher. This not only frees the child to elaborate upon his or her thoughts but also provides an opportunity for the teacher to show how letters are formed most easily and how capitalization and more difficult punctuation are used. If appropriate, spelling relationships could be discussed.

In making observations about children's beginning writing, the following set of questions can help direct your assessments.

> *Observation Guide: Children and Beginning Writing*
> 1. What is new in the writing that has not appeared before?
> 2. Is the child centering on the form—the shape, spelling, or sounds—or on the function—the message in the composition?
> 3. How often does the child choose to write?
> 4. Can he read his own writing? Is he able to reread it the following day?
> 5. Are the compositions becoming longer as she gains control over letter formations and develops a sound-symbol relationship?
> 6. Does the spelling indicate a growing awareness of the conventions in print, such as doubling vowels or adding a final "e" for a long sound? Is there a movement toward the meaning of a word as its spelling basis rather than pure sound?
> 7. Is the language heard in stories and poetry and possibly read appearing in his or her writings?

Signs of Reading Knowledge in the Classroom

Sharing books with small groups of children provides an opportunity to discover much about the child's budding literacy. A teacher reading Keats's *The Snowy Day* to five-year-olds can focus on the attention given by the group. Some children will listen with rapt attention, eyes never wavering from book and teacher; others may appear less attentive, stirring frequently and letting their eyes wander about the room. However, these children also may be attending to the story. It is the children's response to the story that permits the teacher to discover both the quality of attention that has been given to the reading and the background of experience that each child has brought to the book.

Some children may be able to recall other books about Peter that were written by Keats, such as *Whistle for Willie* and *Peter's Chair*. Others may relate their own feelings to those of Peter when he awakened to the wonder of a snowy world. Children may become intrigued with Keats's illustrations and develop their own collage. They may respond with movement and show how Peter lifted his feet as he walked through the deep snow and how he moved his arms and legs to make snow angels. A flannel board with figures might encourage some children to retell the story. One can then note a child's ability to relate the story in sequence. Frequently a young child will begin by recounting the last part of the story, but another child may be able to recall each event in the story in order.

As children are permitted to move about the room and make choices, the teacher can learn a great deal about their interest in reading. One group of children may curl up and look through books quietly by themselves; another cluster may be sharing books with each other. A child may choose to "read" a book over and over again, focusing upon the print and coming closer and closer to approximating the text.

Observations in a wide variety of situations can help the teacher discover the child's understanding of and involvement with print. The teacher can focus observations by posing these questions:

Observation Guide: Children and Books

1. What kind of attention does the child give to books, both in quiet times when permitted to explore books and during story time when listening to books being read aloud?

2. How does she participate when books are discussed? Is he able to retell the story? Does she raise questions about the book? Can he compare one book with another?

3. Which kinds of books does he seem to enjoy most? What books does she select to look at by herself?

4. What kind of response is the child able to make to books? Can he or she use art, drama, or movement to convey an understanding of a story?

5. When given a choice of activity, does the child most often choose to explore books, use writing materials, use art materials, play with other children, or use manipulative materials?

Decisions Based upon Observations. A child does not need to exhibit each of these behaviors to demonstrate the fact that he or she is entering the world of print. Some youngsters do not "play" at reading; others have little interest in telling stories themselves. However, most children, when beginning to create order out of the print about them, do act in several of the ways described.

Teachers have a critical role at this time. If they are sensitive to the child's focus of interest and concepts about print, they can safely extend the progress. If not, an early reader, accomplished in scouring print for meaning independently, may not only be held back but also become bored with reading.

For example, in some classrooms all children are "run through" the same "prereading program." There are no opportunities for early readers to apply their skills. On the other hand, a child who still finds print unmeaningful or who has had little opportunity to explore print might become frustrated if teacher expectations are inappropriately high. Along this continuum between frustration and boredom lie a variety of experiences and activities that assist children in their writing/reading progress. A teacher need not "wait for readiness"; instead, the teacher can plan the curriculum to encourage each child in his or her individual growth toward literacy. But, how does one begin?

Beginning Writing and Reading, Teacher-Initiated

Accepting Dictation

Leslie showed her teacher a picture she had drawn. "This is my sister," she said as she pointed, "and this is me." The teacher asked, "What are you saying in the picture, Leslie?" Leslie replied, "I'm saying, 'This is my sister.'" Above the picture Leslie had drawn of herself, the teacher drew a balloon. In the balloon she printed the words "This is my sister" and read them to Leslie, who beamed and repeated them. All day long Leslie exhibited her picture to friends and read them the words in the balloon.

The teacher's writing the words Leslie had dictated is one very good way of helping children move into writing and reading. As the teacher wrote, he was helping Leslie discover that her thoughts can be recorded, preserved, and shared with others.

Dictation may be the outgrowth of a wide variety of activities. The simplest form may be the captioning of the child's drawing with a descriptive sentence, such as "We are playing in our fort" or "This is my house." Storytelling and book sharing encourage many children to retell a story such as *The Three Little Pigs*. Literary language will often appear. Children may begin their story with "Once there was" and close with "and they lived happily ever after." Repetitious phrases, such as the pig's insistent response, "Not by the hair of my chinny, chin, chin, I won't let you in," are often included in the retelling. After a walk in the newly fallen snow, children may use narration as they dictate what they did, such as making snow angels or building a snowman. They may use descriptive language as they tell how the arrival of the snow changed their familiar world, putting little white caps on fence posts, painting tree branches, and turning cars into soft, white monsters. A science experiment to see which materials will sink and which will float can develop writing skills as children make a chart of materials used, report their procedures, and explain their findings.

Some dictation can be a group effort. The children will suggest sentences, which the teacher writes on the board. Together the group reads the sentences as they are recorded and rereads as new sentences are added. The use of chalk permits the group to add words, rearrange phrases, and sharpen their writing. The following story was dictated by a kindergarten class who had visited a zoo. The words inserted show changes the children made as the text was written, read, and reread. Of course, in the actual version changes were not made by insertions but by erasing and rewriting.

A Visit to the Goats
~~The Goats~~
~~Our Trip to the Zoo~~

We went to the ∧ zoo.   (petting)

We fed ∧ crackers ∧ to the goats.   (special) (and peanuts)

A baby goat drank milk from a bottle.

He sucked so hard that the nipple ~~came~~ off.   (popped)

A big goat ∧ tried to eat the buttons on Danny's coat.   (with curly horns)

The teacher helped the class reread each sentence they wrote by moving her hand under the print as the words were read. This helped the children follow along in the left-to-right direction. The teacher's question "How did the nipple come off the bottle?" prompted the change from "came" to "popped." When the children were asked if anyone could remember how the goat looked, the words "with curly horns" were added.

Much dictation is taken from individual children as they describe their artwork, share information they have collected, label displays, and compose stories. In taking dictation the teacher is modeling writing. The child stands beside the teacher as the writing takes place to see how the pencil is held and the letters are formed. In this way children can see print appear, beginning at the top left-hand side of the page, moving to the right-hand margin, and then moving back to the left again. They see spaces used to mark boundaries between words and observe how punctuation marks are put in to show intonation and meaning. Such examples will lead many children to want to explore writing.

Billy drew this picture of a boy standing in the rain, with the sun and a rainbow above his head. He talked with the teacher about his picture and dictated a story to be displayed with it. Then with a pencil he carefully traced over the teacher's writing (top of next page). By tracing, Billy had made the writing his own and also was learning how letters are made. The teacher could help him by showing the direction in which letters are formed and remind him of the words he is writing—the first step toward independence in literacy.

Another child, after dictating a story about a houseboat, was asked to copy the text below the words that the teacher had written. Copying is a step beyond tracing, for the child is more on his or her own. The close proximity of the print to be copied and the child's own version makes the handwriting act easier. Even so, the task may be a difficult one.

It is sprinkling and the sun is still out. He is playing in the rain And it turned into a rainbow. by Billy

This is my houseboat. My bed is in the houseboat. My houseboat has windows. The outside of my houseboat is painted red.

Jason had dictated many stories to the teacher. After hearing *One Fine Day* (Hogrogian), Jason used an illustration in the book to guide him as he designed a collage. Then he copied the text from the book onto his picture.

> The fox ran to the stream and begged for some water and the stream answered, "Bring me a jug."
>
> — Jason J

Jason's choice of copying a script not his own shows that he is able to transfer print from a distance. It would be a good idea to check and see whether he can read the passage. Quite possibly he will know a number of the words!

Ways of Using Children's Dictation

Teachers can use dictated stories to help children begin to focus their attention on specific aspects of reading. Here Tommy has been asked to reread his own story and underline a word he knows, "the," each time it appears. In this way he begins to attend to patterns of words and to build a sight vocabulary.

(17)
The houses are under t̲h̲e̲ water and the boat is on top of t̲h̲e̲ water. T̲h̲e̲ wife is scared of the mice. Noah is sending t̲h̲e̲ bird to see if there is land.

Laura looked for each occurrence of the letter "e" she could find and copied the letter beneath it. She was not only sorting out letter differences but focusing on details needed to reproduce the letter.

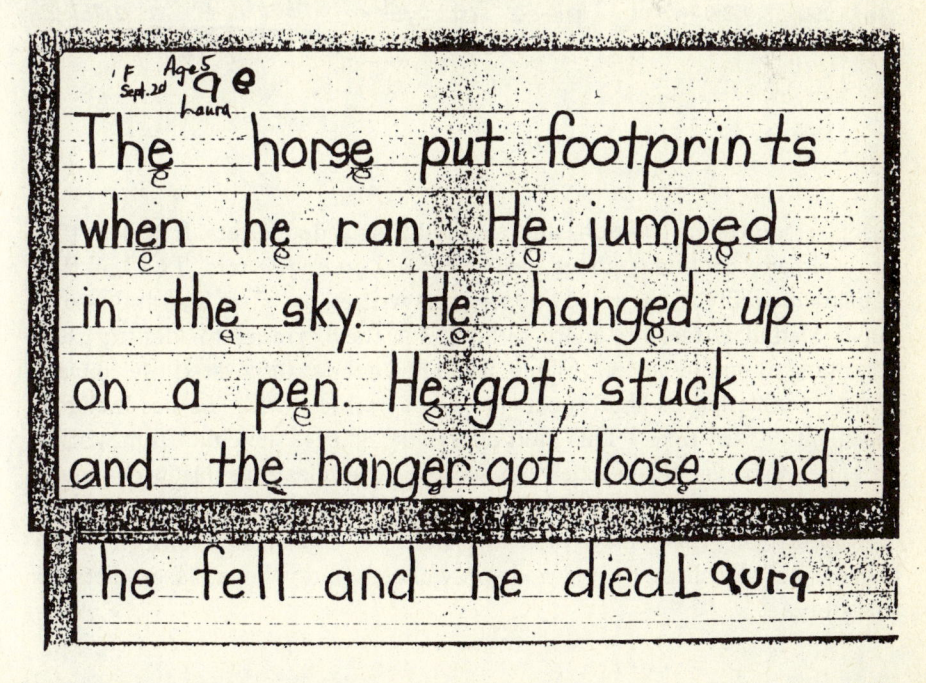

F
Sept. 20 Age 5
        Laura   q e

The horse put footprints when he ran. He jumped in the sky. He hanged up on a pen. He got stuck and the hanger got loose and he fell and he died Laura

178   *Integration of the Language Arts*

The teacher recopied instructions on how to make a collage similar to Jason's. This time she left out certain beginning, ending, and medial letters.

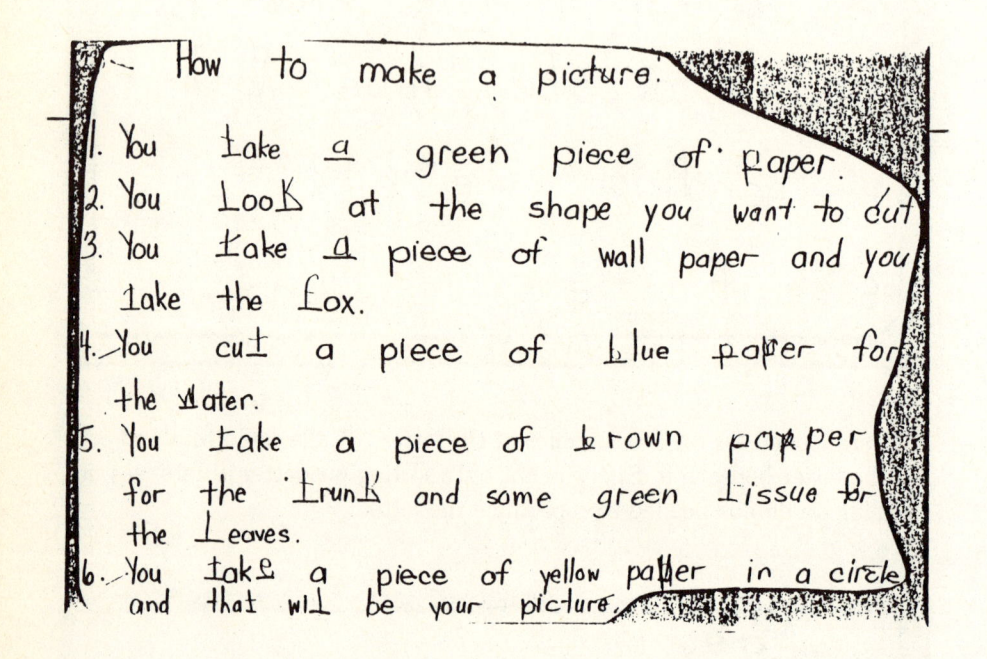

```
How to make a picture.
1. You take a green piece of paper.
2. You look at the shape you want to cut
3. You take a piece of wall paper and you
   take the fox.
4. You cut a piece of blue paper for
   the water.
5. You take a piece of brown papper
   for the trunk and some green tissue for
   the leaves.
6. You take a piece of yellow paper in a circle
   and that will be your picture.
```

Jason reread the instructions and inserted the needed letters. It is clear that he is already confident about beginning and ending letters. The "p" that appears medially in the word "paper" was written as "r" at first and also as "pp." Medial letters are more difficult for the beginner to identify than beginning or ending letters. While Jason has not yet discovered the convention of double letters that appear in words such as "will," he has included the silent "e" in "take." This kind of activity relieves the child from writing an entire text, yet the teacher can see the generalizations Jason has made about words.

After drawing this picture of shaded hills stretching to the horizon with a backdrop of sky sliced by a jagged spray of reds and yellows, Jason dictated this story.

Writing and Reading: The Beginnings   179

> The mountains are high. There is a cave down at the bottom of the mountain. The sun is shining. The fox got bombed up because there was a bomb under the fox and it exploded.

After it had been read many times, shared, and displayed, the teacher copied it, leaving blanks where the words "the" and "a" appeared. Jason filled in all the blanks showing his control over letter and word form. He even added blanks of his own at the top of the page and wrote in an entire sentence.

Once again the burden of writing is removed but Jason has the responsibility of inserting meaningful words. The task stresses that reading is a meaning-gaining activity.

Word Banks

Dictation will encourage children to produce their own writing. Eventually, they will begin to compose stories independently. John, a first-grader, was engrossed in telling his story about a pirate battle.

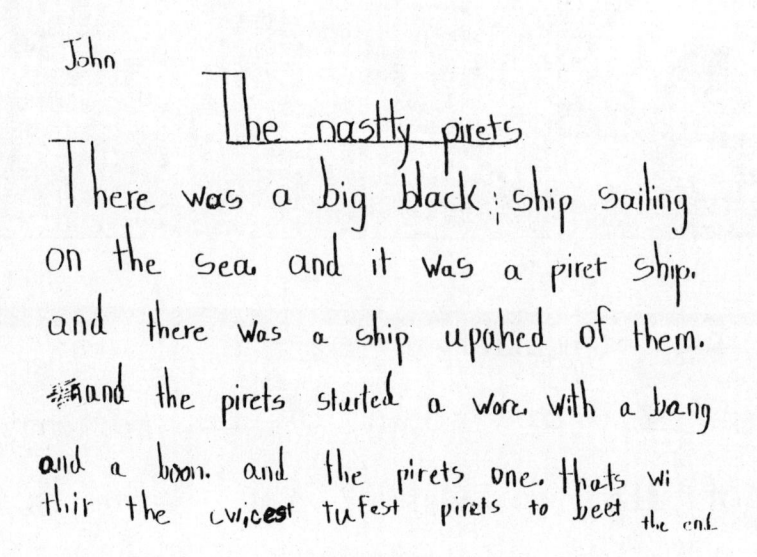

John

The nastty pirets

There was a big black ship sailing on the sea and it was a piret ship. and there was a ship upahed of them. and the pirets sturted a wore with a bang and a boom. and the pirets one. thats wi thir the cwicest tufest pirets to beet the end.

The Nasty Pirates

    There was a big black ship sailing on the sea and it was a pirate ship. And there was a ship up ahead of them. And the pirates started a war with a bang and a boom. And the pirates won. That's why they're the quickest, toughest pirates to beat.

The End.

John has a good writing vocabulary. He knows how to spell many high-frequency words and can spell accurately such words as "sailing" and "sea." Since he hears "up ahead" as one word, he spelled it "upahed." His rendition of "quickest," "toughest," and "why" as "cwicest," "tufest," and "wi" demonstrate a well-developed understanding of letter and sound relationships.

In writing "beat" as "beet" and "won" as "one" he has selected the homonym, since he is familiar with that form.

At this point, a word bank becomes a valuable source of help. The teacher prints words the child will use. They may be words that are needed for a particular purpose, such as "astronaut" or "spaceship," or words that are important because of their high frequency, such as "is," "was," "then," "came," and "saw." There are a number of ways word banks can be organized. Words may be printed on individual cards and arranged in a shoe box. They may be organized in a pocket chart, which is displayed in the writing corner. They may be written in a tabbed notebook and used much as a dictionary is used. A word of caution must be expressed. Many children will be attending to form and anxious to know how to spell some words. However, they should also be permitted and encouraged, as John was, to use their own invented spellings in order to free their writing from the constraints that might be placed upon it by a too-early attention to correctness.

Learning from Children's Attempts to Read

Dictation is only one way the teacher can help children move into reading. Equally important are storytelling, book sharing, easy-to-read books, and a display of purposeful print in the classroom. Teachers frequently share books with groups of children. They share a book with an individual child much less frequently. However, reading a book while seated beside a child permits the teacher to help that child focus on directionality and some aspects of print.

The need for this individualized attention can be seen in observing one teacher who has a quiet time for her kindergarten children to "read" books. As she moved about the room, she was making careful mental notes. John was sitting crosslegged, holding the book in front of his chest with the text facing his imaginary audience. He turned the pages just as he had watched his teacher do. Monica, lying on her stomach, began to look at her book by letting it flop open to the middle and was looking at the pictures one by one, moving toward the front of the book. Karen was reading her much loved *Goodnight, Moon* (Brown). As she went through the book from beginning to end, she was saying the words softly to herself rhythmically and with evident enjoyment. Kelly was holding a closed book in her hand as she stared out the window, watching snowflakes swirl among the tree branches.

This view of children's reading behavior can offer the teacher certain insights. She can see that John has focused intently on the way she has shared books with groups of children. Monica is engrossed in the book illustrations, but does not yet show an awareness that in reading one moves from the front of the book to the back. When the teacher picked up *Goodnight, Moon* and asked Karen to show her where it said "Goodnight, mouse," Karen pointed to the picture of the mouse. Karen had memorized the words, but as yet, she has no concept that the meaning lies in the print rather than the illustration. Even after the teacher helped Kelly open her book and talked with her for a few minutes about it, her eyes drifted about the room. She fidgeted and appeared anxious to move about. Kelly, the teacher noticed, had little interest in exploring books, but she was much more interested, at this point, with the social aspects of school. Each child exhibits different kinds and levels of knowledge about books.

Clay (1972) has found that close observation of young children as they work with books can help teachers discover what concepts about print children have already internalized. For example, a kindergarten teacher read the book *Mr. Gumpy's Outing* (Burningham) to Kevin. She asked him to hand her the book so that they could begin to read it. Kevin opened the book to the first page, showing her that he knows where one must start reading in a book. When she asked, "Where must I begin?" Kevin was able to point to the first word on the page. Clay has found that by asking such questions as

Where do I go now?
Can you show me a letter?
Can you show me a word?
Can you find an *m*?
Do you know another word that begins like this one?

the teacher can learn a great deal about the child's readiness to work with books and print.

As children begin to read their own dictated stories and easy-to-read books, Clay suggests that the teacher should be aware of the self-correction behavior of children. For example, in a small book entitled *Doctors and Nurses,* from the Breakthrough to Literacy Series, the text said:

The doctor looks at my doll next.
He gives her a shot.

Megan, whose father is a doctor, read the text in the following way:

The doctor looks at my doll next.
He gives her an injection.

Then looking at the page again, she said, "Oh no! It's not a big word, it's a little word—shot—yes, it's shot. He gives her a shot." Megan corrected herself unnecessarily which, if a persistent behavior, may slow her reading development. She did show an awareness of word length. Children who are able to use cues that tell them that they have deviated from the meaning of the text and then self-correct their reading are on the road to becoming efficient readers (Clay, 1969).

The reading act requires attention to directionality, the similarities and differences of letter forms, patterns in words and phrases, and a sense of story. At the beginning stages of reading the child may need to focus more closely on one particular aspect of reading and thus neglect another. Biemiller (1970) studied beginning readers and found that in their first attempts at reading, children tend to give their attention largely to meaning. A text that reads "John went to the store" may be read as "John went to the grocery store" or even as "John went to Kroger's." Children later become more aware of the correspondence of sound to symbol. At this stage, they are likely to hesitate more in their reading, as they attempt to attend to the way the letters are used to represent the sound of our language. Eventually, they will become fluent readers, able to attend to both meaning and graphic display.

What, then, is the teacher's role in helping children develop into persons who will be able to use print for their own purposes with both pleasure and efficiency? Teachers can:

> read aloud every day from fine children's books, to the whole class, to small groups, and to individuals;

> bring into their rooms a wide variety of books and arrange them so that children will have the time and the space to explore them;

> provide the kinds of experiences that will bring forth the rich discussion that leads to writing;

> model writing behavior that will demonstrate to children the mechanics of the writing process;

> help children see the value of their writing through the way it is displayed and shared;

> record children's own language to help them predict what is written;

> observe with care and attention the behavior of children as they write and read, in order to support their efforts in the most effective way.

Conventions of Print

Handwriting

As we have stated before, children's explorations of print may be self-initiated. Cristi, whose work began this chapter, is a child who had already begun to do some writing before she entered school. In her class there were but two other children who were such explorers. The majority of children wrote little but their names in their kindergarten year and did not begin writing until their teachers helped them. We have found this to be common. A few students will begin to write on their own if given time, opportunity, and encouragement, but most need assistance from their teacher.

In order to write children need not only an awareness of the different shapes of letters but also the small motor skills required to recreate those letter shapes. Having a large amount of print available in the room such as labels on supplies, displays of children's writing, and a multitude of books supports the child who is developing a growing awareness of print.

Plastic or wooden letters, which children can handle and move about, aid the exploration of print. These materials permit them to group letters in a variety of ways without writing, which, for beginners, is a fatiguing task. Some children might sort according to stem letters such as "b," "p," "l," "h," "q"; round letters such as "o," "c," "a," "b," "d," "g." Upper-case letters may be matched with lower-case counterparts. Some children may form words or create messages. A teacher, through observation and questioning, could discover the direction and kind of thinking children are doing as they manipulate the words and letters. Often children apply surprising logic to their work. For example, Susan's arrangement of "H, P, O, S" might appear illogical until one heard her explanation that she was matching the first letter of words she saw around the room—"*H*elpers, *P*aint, *O*ctober, *S*cissors."

A wide variety of experiences will help children to focus upon those aspects of letters that are constant and those that change. For example, upper-case "A" may be written with a fine-line pen or carved from a wooden block, written to look long and narrow or short and squat; but it will usually have two slant lines that meet at the top with the center space divided by a cross bar. That same letter in lower case is quite different (A, a). The name is the same, but the shapes vary markedly. The lower-case letter also has a range of representations (а а а).

Children need opportunities not only to see and observe letter shapes but also to manipulate them. Linc, age 5 years, 9 months, is exploring a variety of ways to write his name. He has changed standard forms by adding to them, modifying, and decorating them. He is working on what Clay (1972) calls the flexibility principle. Such explorations help children gain control of letter forms.

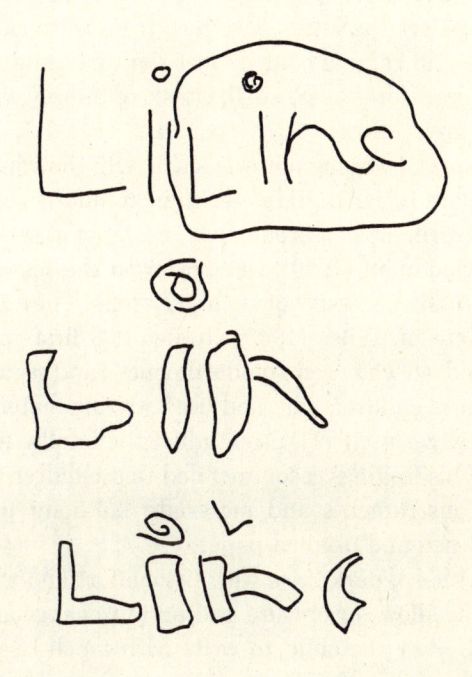

As can be seen from Linc's work, art experiences are closely related to writing. Children who paint, cut, draw, and model clay are developing control over the small muscles they need to use in writing. Further, they are learning to control space. Graves (1978) has pointed out that facing a blank piece of paper requires children to work in a new space dimension. Many opportunities to use art materials can help children relate the space of their bodies to the space of the paper. What is the distance of the head from the paper? How does one move the hand across the page? Where is the axis of the body in relation to the paper? Art frees children to explore this new space dimension and builds a strong base for writing.

Freedom to explore print and a rich print environment to encourage such explorations are vital, but they are not enough. Writing is a difficult and complex task. One writes to communicate, but communicating with pencil and paper requires not only that one encode the message into symbols and use a writing instrument to record those symbols but also that one do so with a sense of spacing, directionality, and form. Beginning writers find that task demanding indeed, for they must give attention to the many aspects of writing all at the same time. Nothing is automatic yet. Children must hold in mind the message they want to send and also remember where to begin on the page, where to start the letter, and how to execute each letter in turn. These children are still gaining control over the small muscles that are used to control thumb and forefinger, so the task of simply putting letters on paper will require great effort.

Many feel that special writing materials will help the young writer. Beginner pencils, which are larger in diameter than standard pencils, are used in a great number of primary classrooms, as are large sheets of widely ruled paper. Coles and Goodman (1980), who reviewed the research, report little evidence to support the necessity of such materials. They cite work done by both Wiles and Krzesni. Wiles (1940) studied 800 first-graders and found that first-grade children who used standard pencils and regularly ruled paper wrote as well as those children who had used writing materials designed for primary children. Krzesni (1971) also studied the handwriting of beginners and on the basis of his findings recommended that children be offered a wide variety of writing instruments and materials: ballpoint pens, colored felt pens and pencils, lined and unlined paper.

Felt pens create sharp, dark lines with little effort and therefore ease the writing task. Pencils allow for erasure and permit change and editing. Soft-leaded pencils will allow the child to write with much less effort than will pencils with hard lead. Lined paper adds to the complexity of the writing task for beginners. They must not only form the letters legibly and accurately, but must also match letter features above and below a physical line. Unlined space relaxes this constraint and allows the child to consider meaning and legibility prior to alignment.

Writing space is as important as writing material. Typically children will write anywhere: lying on the floor, hunched over the corner of a table, or kneeling before a chair seat. However, to write well, it is best to have a smooth and cleared writing surface. Children need to have enough space so that they can have their forearms supported, a place for their papers, and enough elbow room so they do not bump arms with neighbors. Chairs and desks that are at the right height for the child are also required.

As teachers observe children writing, they can help them develop, from the start, the kinds of habits that will make it easier for them to write both legibly and efficiently. As the teacher moves about, assistance can be offered as the child needs it, before poor habits are formed. One child may hold the pencil so tightly and press so hard that the act of writing causes her to tire quickly. The teacher can help the child learn to relax her grip by showing her that the pencil should be held in such a way that someone could slip the pencil from her fingers as she is writing. Small triangular plastic pencil grips are available commercially and are sometimes helpful if this tenseness in grip should continue.

The teacher might find that some children have not found the most efficient way to make a letter. For example, a child who writes **a** as **a** is making the letter more difficult than it needs to be, for the retracing is unnecessary. That child could be shown how to make the letter with an economy of motion and effort (next page).

This child is recopying her writing for display. A teacher can observe the techniques she has developed in the mechanics of writing to see if she is efficient in her strategies. Awkward manipulations can decrease writing production. (Cranbrook Elementary School, Columbus, Ohio)

c c a

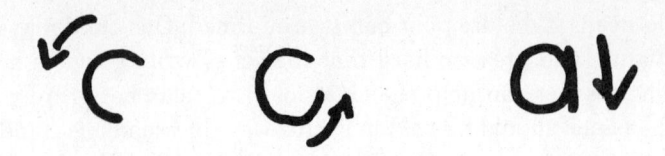

Grouping letters that are formed in a similar fashion could help the child control a family of letters such as the following:

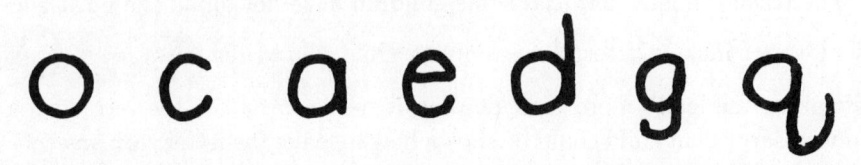

o c a e d g q

All of the above letters are started in the same place and are made with a counterclockwise movement. Mackay and Simo (1976) point out that while "b" and "p" look like they should belong to this group, they do not, for they are made with a clockwise movement. Other letters in this "clockwise group" would include:

n m h r

Still another group of letters would be those made of straight lines and slanted lines:

v w x l i t

Commercial materials are available that will help teachers by describing how letters are formed and suggesting how to group letters for instruction and practice. Charts such as the one on the next page by the Zaner-Bloser Company showing the letters are very useful.

Alphabet charts are often placed above the chalkboard, but a better practice is making smaller charts available so that children can have them beside them as they write. This would eliminate the need for children to shift their eyes from paper to board, a movement that is tiring and that causes them to focus and refocus for different distances. For these same reasons, children should not be required to do a great deal of copying from the chalkboard.

Commercially prepared materials can provide models for writing, but since their smooth, machinelike perfection could seem unattainable, these

Writing and Reading: The Beginnings 189

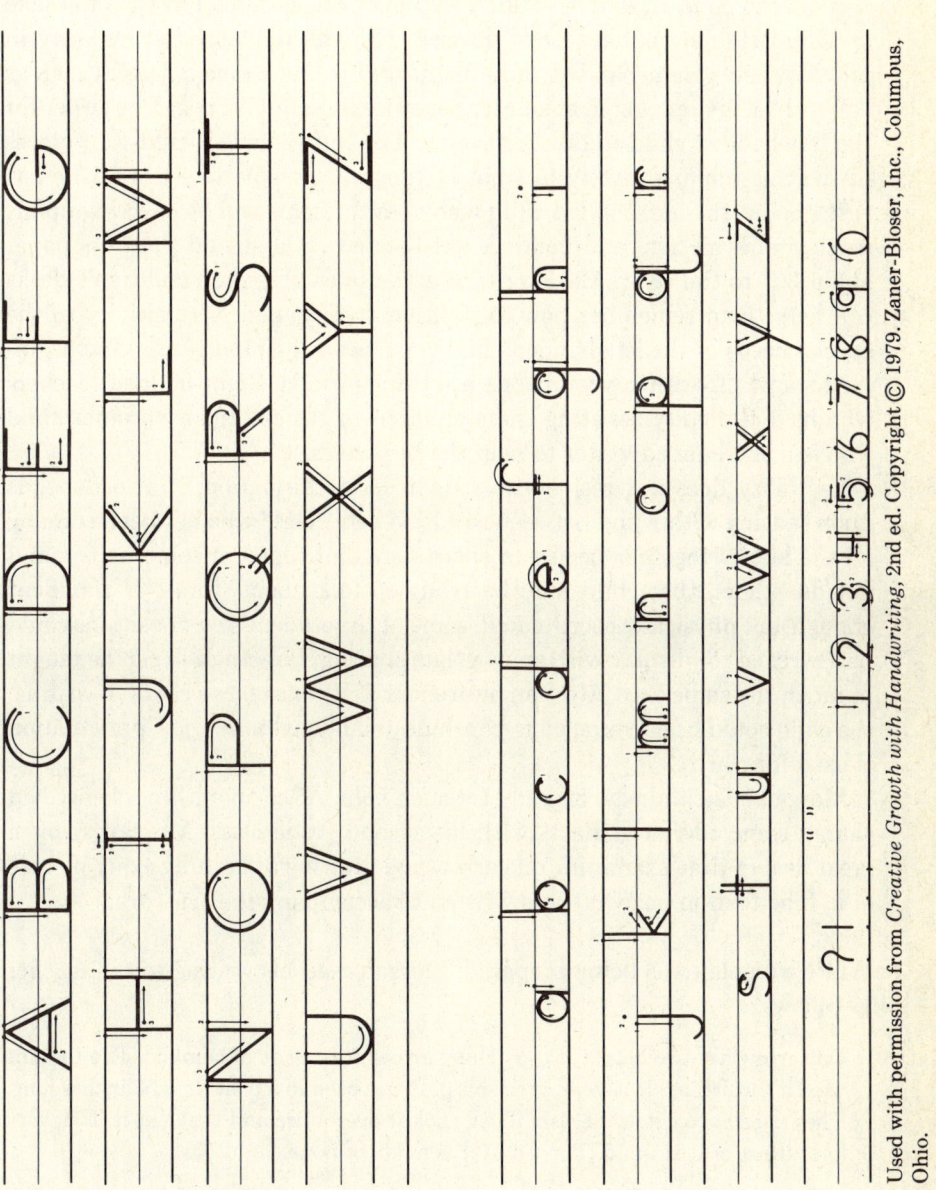

Used with permission from *Creative Growth with Handwriting*, 2nd ed. Copyright © 1979. Zaner-Bloser, Inc., Columbus, Ohio.

materials should not be the only models. Teachers and other children are also sources for good writing samples.

A special concern is the left-handed child. Suggestions for ways to make specific letter forms have been devised with the right-handed majority in mind. While a right-handed child might find it best to make letters such as "c" and "o" by moving in a counterclockwise direction, it might be easier for the left-handed child to do the reverse. The right-handed child who places his writing paper squarely in front of him will be able to see what he has written, but the left-handed child who does the same will be covering up his writing with his arm and hand. A left-handed child should slant his paper about 30° to the right. Masking-tape guide lines placed on children's desks can help them remember how to position their paper. A sensitivity to the special needs of the left-handed child is particularly important at the beginning stages of writing when habits are being formed. Right-handed teachers who have difficulty assisting these children might call upon an older child who is a left-handed writer to help the beginners.

Legibility does not rest entirely upon letter formation; it also depends upon spacing within and between words. When a child who has been running all the letters together begins to space here and there on some papers and not on others, that child may be ready to talk about words. If confident enough and physically coordinated, some of the student's compositions could be rewritten for display with appropriate spacing. Punctuation can be taught in much the same way. After an awareness of its existence occurs in writing, the child could be encouraged to continue and helped to see how punctuation is used for clarity.

Morgan is a child who is ready for such help. After an anthropologist had shared some Indian artifacts with his second-grade class, Morgan spent a great deal of time examining one arrow and drawing a carefully exact picture of it. The text on page 191 was written to accompany the art work.

While a display was being prepared, Morgan read his writing to the teacher as follows:

> One arrow has two heads. It is a fishing arrow. It is made of bamboo. The Indians used it for fishing. It is very, very sharp. It was used in a boat. It is 58 inches long. They used it to catch the fish. They cook it over a fire and they eat it. It is very light. Part of it is wood. The tip of it is made of bone.

As can be seen, he left out some words in the written version that he included when he read. After the child had read the paper, he and the teacher talked about how spacing and some punctuation could make it easier for others to

Morgan Lewis

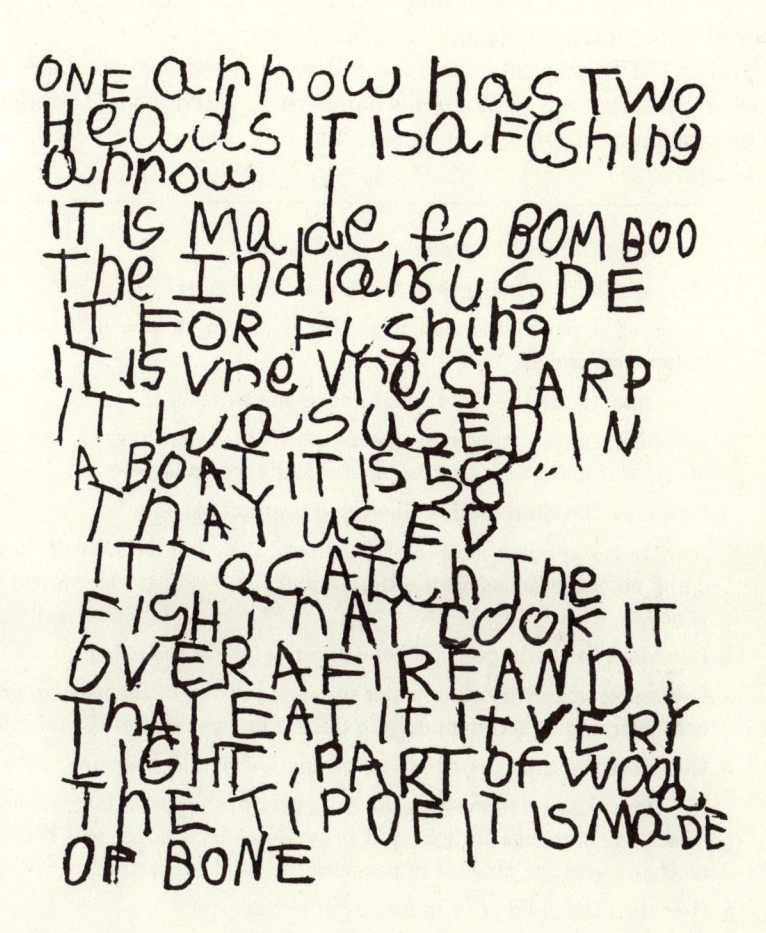

One arrow has two heads it is a fishing arrow
it is made fo bomboo
the Indians use
it for fishing
it is vne vne sharp
it was used in
a boat it is so
thay used
it to catch the
fish thay cook it
over a fire and
tha eat it it very
light part of wood
the tip of it is made
of bone

read what he had written. Morgan and his teacher examined other papers and some books. Morgan reread his paper and the teacher copied it as he read, showing him where spaces were needed and how punctuation marked pauses. The story was then recopied and displayed on a bulletin board beside his drawing. This recopying was not viewed as a chore, but simply as a part of publication. This is an example of the best kind of writing practice: both purposeful and meaningful. Morgan wanted others to read what he had written; furthermore, the practice focused upon what the child needed at a particular moment. Most of the other children in the class did not need this kind of assistance. Whole-class lessons are often dull because they are not related to the real needs or purposes of many of the children. Individualized instruction lets children progress at their own rate and gradually develop the skills needed to become capable and efficient writers.

Graves (1978) suggests that the following questions can help sharpen teachers' observations of children's handwriting activity, and thus help them to provide instruction at the moment that it is needed.

Observation Guide: Children and Handwriting

1. How are children using their thumb and forefinger?

   Gripping a pencil too tightly is tiring; holding a pencil too loosely reduces control.

2. How smooth are the child's motions as she writes?

   Stopping and starting may mean the child is pausing to formulate ideas, or it may mean that her motor skills are an issue.

3. How does the child use his elbow and position his body?

   If there is too much motion of the elbow, it may interfere with developing efficiency in using the thumb and the forefinger to control the pencil.

4. How does the child position herself in relation to the paper?

   Beginning writers position paper squarely in front of themselves, gradually learning to accommodate to the left or right side of the middle.

5. How does the child distribute his strength when he is writing?

   In order to use small muscles the child needs to suppress large muscles. Observing a change in light and heavy lines on a paper will help the teacher assess the amount of pressure the child is exerting.

6. How does the child grow in his use of writing space?

   Beginning writers use space flexibly. It is only later, as they develop concepts about words and sentences, that they begin to use space in more conventional ways.

Spelling

Too often children attend to their spelling so carefully that they base their selection of words solely on ones they are sure they know how to spell. When they focus on spelling too early in writing ventures, the content and length become limited. This pressure for accuracy can come from both home and school, for it seems the initial adult response to writing is to its form; however, when children learn to speak, the response is to the content. The same kind of response is needed in writing to encourage further compositions. Children learn the conventions of print, including spelling, while they function as writers. The search for systems in written language is an active process, which is best performed in a purposeful context rather than in isolated drill. At some time, however, it is appropriate to attend to orthographic, that is spelling, systems.

When do children profit most from studying spelling? Since the main goal of early writing is to develop fluency, the timing of the focus on spelling is exceedingly important. Our recommendation is that it is better to delay instruction longer than necessary than to begin it too soon. One first-grade teacher told about her experience in using individual spelling dictionaries, that is, booklets in which the teacher writes those words that children wish to use in their writing. Each page is used for words beginning with a different letter. Most years she started personal dictionaries for most of the children in the spring but this year she began during the fall term when many of the children were beginning to write. Her writing program changed considerably. The children became inhibited in their compositions, writing briefly and selecting only the words they knew how to spell. The teacher said that after this experience she would never begin a spelling focus so early.

Teachers will know when to step in and help children in their attempts at spelling by observing children as they write and noting the questions that arise:

Can they write their own names?

Are they able to copy accurately written material?

Is there a flow to the child's compositions, that is, has the child developed fluency?

Does the student show an awareness of regularities in spelling?

Is the child searching for systems in spelling by asking questions or systematically spelling similar sounding or meaning-related words?

Can the student generalize, seeing similarities across words?

Does the student care about spelling accurately?

Relying upon Henderson's research and his own findings, Read (1978) developed a table (page 194) showing children's development in spelling. A

Table 5.1 *Some Stages of Spelling Development*
(Adapted from E. H. Henderson, IRA, 1978)

Standard	Preliterate	Initial Literate	Letter–Name	Transition
table	*scribble*	T or TL	TABL	TEBEL, TAIBLE, TEIBLE
candy	*scribble*	K or KD	KADE	CANDY
went	*scribble*	Y or YT	WAT	WENT
seed	*scribble*	S or SD	SED	SID, SEAD
bit	*scribble*	B or BT	BET	BIT
Cinderella	*scribble*	S	SEDRLU	SINDARELA

Reproduced with the permission of Charles Reed and Edmund H. Henderson.

review of Read's study discussed in chapter 2 may help you to better understand the chart.

The "preliterate" stage may involve recognizable letters in many directions or a scribble mark. In the "initial literate" stage, the first letter of the word, syllable, or consonants may appear. At the "letter-name" stage, vowels appear but a letter may stand as the entire syllable, for example, "l" for "le" and "r" for "er." The "transition" stage reveals the child's growing understanding of the systematic regularities of print. Thus, "table" may be written as "taibel" since two vowels occurring together often form a long vowel sound and "el" can make the /əl/ sound. When children reach and are comfortable in the transition stage, spelling instruction is appropriate.

One way to begin is with individual spelling dictionaries where children and their teachers can select words to enter into a booklet. Two types of words need to be noted at this time: high-frequency words, which must be learned by sight, such as "want" and "come," and words that fit into spelling patterns, such as consonant-vowel-consonant (cvc), short-vowel sounds ("bit," "fan," "cut"), consonant-vowel-consonant-silent "e" (cvce), and long-vowel sounds as a result of a silent "e" at the end ("bike," "flake," "note"). Words of interest and of high frequency belong in the personal dictionary. Words that fit into patterns need to be grouped together so that children may see relationships. An extended discussion of spelling generalizations and an organized way to look at children's spelling is discussed in the following chapter.

Building a Literacy Context

Structuring the environment goes beyond the physical setting. It includes social interaction, value creation, and attitudes toward writing. Freedom of choice influences compositions. Graves (1975) found that unassigned writings were longer and, especially for boys, classrooms in which students selected their own mode of expression produced more writing. Even acquisition of the conventions of writing such as punctuation is influenced by the context in which it occurs. Calkins (1979) reported that third-graders who learned punctuation marks as they came across the need for them in their writing could define or explain many more marks than those students who had direct lessons on punctuation. The interest of the audience appears to relate to success in writing. Based upon her research, Birnbaum (1980) recommends that children have authentic purposes for writing, just as they do for talking. Audiences need to be real rather than contrived, with composition topics emerging from children's own interests.

Literacy learning does not differ greatly from learning to speak, for in each instance the child's goal is to communicate with others. Thus, all attempts at language learning have social meaning. Florio (1978) stresses children's need to have their attempts at producing language noted by others. These attempts have meaning because the child is a member of a community that provides a supportive meaning context. Fragments and phrases stand as communication because of the physical and social context in which they occur; contexts build from membership in a community—at first the home and then the classroom. Just as oral language resides in context, so does writ-

The reading center can resemble a living room where members can exchange their reading experiences together or sit by themselves to read a book. The area is especially active with young children, a good sign of a developing learning community. (Mrs. Hodges' informal classroom, Greensview School, Upper Arlington, Ohio)

ten language. Teachers, therefore, need to develop a social world in their classrooms "where meanings are shared and values held, and they individually constitute small communities with cumulative histories, shared beliefs, and rights and responsibilities of members" (Florio, 1978, p. 3).

School experiences should not contrast greatly with many of the children's early home experiences in which print played an important part. Of course, a school's function and purpose differ from the home, but including a playhouse, a kitchen corner, and a workbench in the classroom allows the child to replicate in play everyday living experiences. Many of these activities will call for writing and reading. The telephone table invites a phonebook and pad and pencil for telephone messages. The reading center could serve as a living room, where magazines, newspapers, and shelves of books can be found. Although books and other reading materials are not limited to just one area, a reading corner can provide a special focal point within the classroom. Cushions and soft rugs can make it an ideal place for settling down with a book. Stuffed chairs and a sofa are good for sharing stories and discussing books. The shelf in the kitchen corner may display recipe books and a file containing blank cards to fill with favorite recipes, while other shelves may contain commercial boxes and bottles of foodstuffs and cleansing agents. These labels provide a reading source and may be used by children as they prepare their grocery list; thus, paper and pencil become a functional part of the kitchen. A workbench needs supplies that are labeled for storage; for example, each tool could have a labeled hook. "How-to" books, home repair information, and catalogues are references from which the children might learn vocabulary, write down information needed to order further supplies, and tacitly discover that reading and writing are a part of every work experience, including construction.

Summary

In this chapter we have described and illustrated children's growth in literacy. As children explore the world about them, they develop concepts of print. Early indications of their discoveries can be found in scribblings and artwork. Later, some, but not all, begin to write messages. Other children are guided by their teacher to explore print through the written transcriptions of their own language. Here they may trace, copy, and complete compositions. Reading and rereading become an integral part of the process.

Sets of questions for teacher observations and suggestions for the classroom environment and experiences are provided. Greater emphasis has been placed on writing rather than reading since our purpose in this text is to show how reading may be integrated within the language-arts curriculum. Further information on the beginnings of reading instruction may be found in the annotated bibliography.

Suggested Learning Experiences

1. Collect samples of young children's writing from parents and nursery-school or kindergarten teachers. In small groups share and discuss your collections. See if you can categorize the samples. Try to identify emerging signs of literacy. What kinds of details do you see in their artwork?

2. Visit a classroom and observe the children's use of incidental opportunities for writing. How many children choose to use writing materials? Which kinds of writing materials did you see? Where were such materials located?

3. Accept dictation from a child or a small group of children. Describe the experiences that stimulated the language. What kinds of activities would you select to extend these children's knowledge of print? Will they trace, recopy, choose words they know, or add words to a word bank?

4. Look at one child's writing over a period of several months. What different kinds of explorations in print and growth in writing do you see? Which kinds of experiences do you feel would be important to give this child now?

5. Choose a first-grade child and do some selected in-depth observations. Find out what the child knows about print through your analysis of his or her writing. Determine the child's familiarity with books and interest in reading. How does the child feel about his or her own ability to read and write?

6. Select one child. Without talking to the child, spend one day observing him or her in the classroom. Sum up all you have learned about the child's knowledge of and attitude toward reading and writing. What are the important questions you must now explore?

7. Several ways of organizing words that children use for reading and writing were described in this chapter. As you work with a child, help him or her to organize some of the words chosen. You might choose a personal dictionary, a file box, or a pocket chart.

Recommended Readings

Clay, Marie M., *The Early Detection of Reading Difficulties: A Diagnostic Survey.* Heinemann Educational Books, 1975. International Publications Service, 114 E. 32nd Street, New York, New York 10016.

    In this booklet, Clay examines some of the simple but vitally important understandings young children need to acquire about books and how they work; for example, where the front of the book is. Included is a diagnostic survey Clay has developed that guides the teacher's observations as she shares a book with a child. Full details are given for the administration of the *Concepts About Print Test.*

Clay, Marie M., *What Did I Write?* Heinemann Educational Books, 1972. International Publications Service, 114 E. 32nd Street, New York, New York 10016.

    In this monograph Clay describes children's early explorations of print. Many examples are provided that illustrate the concepts and principles she found in analyzing children's work.

Hall, Mary Anne, *Teaching Reading as a Language Experience,* 3rd ed., Chapters 1, 3, 4, and 5. Merrill, Columbus, Ohio, 1981.

    Experience stories, their elicitation from small groups or individuals, and follow-up activities are described. Hall includes a clear, helpful discussion of the beginning of writing in school and "prereading" experiences.

McKenzie, Moira, "The Beginnings of Literacy," *Theory Into Practice* 56:315–324, December, 1977.

    In this readable article, McKenzie identifies three stages the child goes through in becoming literate, and suggests a variety of ways that teachers can assist the child at each stage. For example, one way to monitor the very earliest attempts at reading is to read a story aloud to a child and invite him or her to read it back. She includes a chart showing one child's growing ability to approximate the language of the text.

Smith, Frank, "Learning to Read by Reading," *Language Arts* 53:297–299, 322, March, 1976.

    Through sharing his experiences with one three-year-old, Smith describes how children begin to read using the physical and pictorial context in which print occurs. He points out that formal reading instruction may hinder a child's search for meaning in print.

References

Professional Literature

Biemiller, Andrew, "The Development of the Use of Graphic and Contextual Information as Children Learn to Read," *Reading Research Quarterly* 6:75–96, Fall, 1970.

Birnbaum, June Cannell, "Why Should I Write? Environmental Influences on Children's Views of Writing," *Theory Into Practice* 19:202–210, Summer, 1980.

Calkins, Lucy McCormick, "When Children Want to Punctuate: Basic Skills Belong in Context," unpublished paper, University of New Hampshire, 1979.

Chomsky, Carol, "Write First, Read Later," *Childhood Education* 47:296–299, March, 1971.

Clark, Margaret M., *Young Fluent Readers*, Heinemann, London, 1976.

Clay, Marie M., "Reading Errors and Self-Correction Behavior," *British Journal of Educational Psychology* 39:47–56, February, 1969.

Durkin, Dolores, *Children Who Read Early*, Columbia Teachers College Press, New York, 1966.

Florio, Susan, "The Problem of Dead Litters: Social Perspectives on the Teaching of Writing," Research Series No. 34, Michigan State University, East Lansing, Institute for Research on Teaching, DHEW #400-76-0073, June, 1978.

Goodman, Yetta, and Coles, Richard E., "Do We Really Need Those Oversized Pencils?," *Theory Into Practice* 19:194–196, Summer, 1980.

Graves, Donald, "An Examination of the Writing Processes of Seven-Year-Old Children," *Research in the Teaching of English* 9:227–241, Winter, 1975.

Graves, Donald H., "Research Update: Handwriting Is for Writing," *Language Arts* 55:393–399, March, 1978.

Hall, Mary Anne; Moretz, Sara A.; and Staton, Jodellano, "Writing Before Grade One: A Study of Early Writers," *Language Arts* 53:582–585, May, 1976.

Harste, Jerome C.; Burke, Carolyn L.; and Woodward, Virginia A., "Children's Language and World: Initial Encounters with Print" in *Bridging the Gap: Reader Meets Author*, Judith A. Langer and M. Smith-Burke, eds., International Reading Association, Newark, Delaware, 1982.

Krzesni, J. S., "Effect of Different Writing Tools and Paper on Performance of the Third Grade," *Elementary English* 48:821–824, November, 1971.

Mackay, David, and Simo, Joseph, *Help Your Child to Read and Write and More*, Penguin Books Ltd., Harmondsworth, Middlesex, England, 1976.

McKenzie, Moira, "The Beginnings of Literacy," *Theory Into Practice* 16:315–324, December, 1977.

Read, Charles, Children's Categorization of Speech Sounds in English, *National Council of Teachers of English Research Report No. 17*, ERIC/NCTE, Urbana, Illinois, October, 1975.

Read, Charles, "Some Stages of Spelling Development," Early and Middle Childhood Education Mini-course, The Ohio State University, July, 1978.

Vygotsky, Lev, *Mind in Society: The Development of Higher Psychological Processes*, Michael Cole, ed., Harvard University Press, Cambridge, Mass., 1978.

Wiles, M. E., The Effects of Different Sizes of Tools Upon the Handwriting of Beginners, Unpublished doctoral dissertation, Harvard University, 1940.

Children's Literature

Brown, Margaret Wise, *Goodnight, Moon,* Harper & Row, New York, 1947.

Burningham, John, *Mr. Gumpy's Outing,* Holt, Rinehart and Winston, New York, 1971.

Doctors and Nurses, Breakthrough to Literacy Series, Bowmar; Noble Publishers, Inc., Los Angeles, 1973.

Hogrogian, Nonny, *One Fine Day,* Macmillan, New York, 1971.

Keats, Ezra Jack, *Peter's Chair,* Harper & Row, New York, 1967.

Keats, Ezra Jack, *The Snowy Day,* Viking, New York, 1962.

Keats, Ezra Jack, *Whistle for Willie,* Viking, New York, 1964.

An Example of Self-initiated Writing

The Relationship Between Reading and Writing

The Writing Process

Sources of Writing
- *Concrete Experiences*
- *Drama*
- *Literature*
- *Peer Influence*

Writing Conferences
- *Purposes*
- *Types of Conferences*

Looking at the Writing Product
- *The Role of Revision*
- *Responding to Writing*
- *Evaluating Writing*
- *Recordkeeping and Evaluation Forms*
- *Student Self-evaluating of Writing*

Writing Context

Skills of Writing
- *Handwriting*
- *Spelling*
- *Report Writing*

Summary

Suggested Learning Experiences

Recommended Readings

References
- *Professional Literature*
- *Children's Literature*

Chapter 6
Reading and Writing: On the Way

An Example of Self-initiated Writing

What makes writing happen in a classroom? Miss Charles reported the following incident, which tells how a writing experience began for one of the children in her classroom:

> We had just received a Christmas tree in our classroom, a gift of a child's parent. Since the Christmas "spirit" began overflowing, I decided to web Christmas language-arts ideas with the class for those who might choose to express their responses to the season. After that Jody, a fourth-grader, came to me to discuss her idea.

J: I want to do a "point-of-view" writing.

Miss C: What point of view do you want to take?

J: I want to do a "point of view" of a stocking but I've never done a point of view about anything before.

Miss C: Tell me about the stocking.

J: Well, I decided I'd have the stocking hanging from my dad's chair and he [the stocking] doesn't like it. (She went on to tell me about her stocking, which actually hangs on the back of her father's chair.)

Miss C: Why doesn't he like it?

J: It gets anxious for Christmas morning to have all the toys taken out of it because it hurts it but I don't know how to start it. Should I say, "Hi! I'm a stocking?" (Jody made a face that indicated that she wasn't terribly pleased with that beginning.)

Miss C: You could start that way; how else could you start it?

J: It could say, "I really don't like hanging around here." Then I could write something like, "I would much rather be in my box."

Miss C: Give me a word to describe the box.

J: The *cozy* box.

Miss C: I like that description. Why does it like to be in the box? (She started writing and I helped her sketch her stocking.)

J: "There's nothing in me to scrunch me around—no scrunch me to death. And my lace might rip."—No, I said it's a boy. "The colors that are on me are red and green and, boy, do I hate those colors!"

Miss C: Why?

J: (Giggle) Because they are Christmas colors and I don't like Christmas!

Miss C: What a Scrooge stocking! Go ahead and work on your writing and show it to me later.

This one short episode tells the reader a great deal about how Jody and her teacher approached writing. Jody's writing was not assigned; it was self-initiated. Jody not only decided that she wanted to write, but she even set herself an assignment—"a point-of-view writing." The child displayed both an interest in form and a developing knowledge of the author's task. She began her writing not by setting pencil to paper but by talking with her teacher. Jody knew what she wanted to do, but she did not know how to begin. The teacher did not give her any directions or explanations. Instead, she asked questions based upon what the child had said, taking her lead from the child and then listening thoughtfully to the child's replies:

"What point of view do you want to take?"
"Tell me about the stocking."
"Why doesn't he like it?"
"Why does it like to be in the box?"

This kind of prewriting talk helped Jody get at her own thinking and to make it explicit. As the girl talked, her enthusiasm for and her involvement in the project increased. She moved from a reluctance to share what she felt was a weak idea to happy delight when she came up with the thought of a Christmas stocking who dislikes Christmas—"a Scrooge stocking." Jody's discussion with the teacher did more than let her try out ideas. It let her try out the language that would later appear in her writing. Even as she talked, she began to edit her ideas and her language:

"There's nothing in me to scrunch around—no scrunch me to death. And my lace might rip."—No, I said it's a boy.

The Relationship Between Reading and Writing

The preceding incident illustrates the influence of reading on writing. Jody's interest in writing from a specific and original point of view grew from several sources. The teacher had read Gasztold's *Prayers from the Ark* to the class, a book that contains a series of prayers from the point of view of different animals. Several children tried writing from a different point of view after hearing these poems and then shared and displayed their writings. All of these experiences had motivated Jody to try writing using this particular form. Writing and reading, then, are closely related. The language children use in writing is unlikely to be more sophisticated in either vocabulary or syntax than the language they read or have had someone else read to them.

Any classroom that is to produce children who write is a classroom where a variety of books are made available and are read aloud. Children who love to write are usually children who love to read. What they read will greatly influence what they write. This point is well illustrated by examples of children's writing taken from a study by DeFord (1981). She observed three first-grade classrooms for seven months in order to explore the impact of various language environments upon reading and writing. One first-grade teacher used a phonics approach to reading; a second followed the skills approach of a basal reading series. The third teacher taught what DeFord labeled "a whole-language approach." In this class teacher and children shared stories, poetry, and information books rather than basal texts. Writing was an important focus in the children's learning experiences.

The following is representative of the writing children produced in the class where phonics was the main approach:

> I had a gag.
> I had a dad.
> I had a cat.

The children from the classrooms where basal readers were central were likely to turn out writing that followed the patterns found in their reading texts:

> Bill can run.
> Jill can run.
> Jeff can run.
> I can run.

Whole-language classrooms produced writers whose use of language was much more sophisticated:

> Iran is fighting us. 19 bombers went down. 14 fighters. We only have 3 bombers down 6 fighters. we have dropped 9 bombs over iran the hostages have been ther to long. Now we head twards them It's like a game of checers. . . . (p. 657)

Just as children's reading will influence and extend their writing, children's writing will deepen their understanding of reading. As children write, they become authors and learn the author's task. Their own writing makes them aware of how authors sequence their writing, make transitions, develop a plot, and use dialogue. Children who have had opportunities to write descriptions of things they have observed closely or moments they have felt deeply can appreciate more acutely the art of the poet.

Children who have been keeping a journal will find pleasure in reading journals written by others, such as *A Gathering of Days* (Blos) and *Anne Frank: The Diary of a Young Girl*. Children who have worked together to write a class newspaper will be more likely to explore the pages of their local daily newspaper.

Reading and writing are intertwined. Reading, even minimally, requires a consideration of the author. The simplest writing requires a consideration of the prospective reader. While this chapter will not focus upon how to teach reading, it will examine those aspects of reading that mesh with the writing program.

The Writing Process

Even though this chapter is titled "Reading and Writing," showing the influence of children's reading upon their written compositions, a study of the writing process reveals a link between speaking and writing. According to Vygotsky (1962), writing grows out of oral language development. Simply put, Vygotsky saw children's language development, including writing, as evolving from social speech, which is global and multifunctional in nature. Later, two major divisions appear: communicative speech and egocentric speech. Communicative speech is used for social contact whereas egocentric speech accompanies children's ongoing activities and is used for planning and organizing actions. Egocentric speech may help youngsters overcome difficulties, for it is speech for oneself, in contrast to the role of communicative speech. Vygotsky believed egocentric speech to be a transition stage from vocal to inner speech. Inner speech is thinking in pure meanings, a condensed, abbreviated speech that is a prerequisite to written speech. Writing implies a translation from inner speech because inner speech is too abbreviated to be understood. This growth process from social speech to inner speech can be diagrammed in the following way:

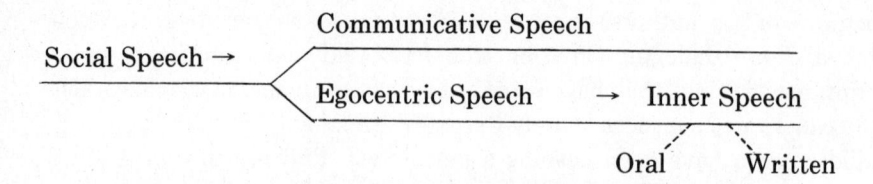

```
                      Communicative Speech
Social Speech →  ⟨
                      Egocentric Speech    →   Inner Speech
                                              Oral    Written
```

As the diagram reveals, inner speech need not be translated into the written mode alone; oral speech may occur. The product may be practice for a talk or may result in "reflective" speech using Barnes's (1976) term. Such speech is used to "talk through" an idea or plan. It is language used to learn, and writing is often referred to as a way to learn a subject.

One of the roles of oral language in writing becomes evident. Children learning to write need to use speech to plan their composition, to think aloud. Such egocentric talk can be expected as one aspect of the child's development. Even adult writers, when they become "stuck", will mutter to themselves or talk with a colleague about their writing problem. The importance of conferencing is clear. Talking before, during, and after the writing act supports thinking.

In chapter 4, "Listening and Speaking," the relationship between oral and written language was discussed. Writing may be thought of as a monologue. The contribution of dialogue to the growth of monologue becomes evident when one recognizes that group cooperation in dialogue leads to the development of an individual's sense of audience (Moffett and Wagner, 1976). Conversation or discussion provides practice in thinking of others and anticipating and identifying their needs. Monologues, that is, sustained speech, precede writing. Britton (1970) recommends that teachers help children sustain their speech since this is the most productive source for writing. Retelling stories, explaining, and describing are all activities that require sustained speech.

Writing and speaking do have similarities, particularly if each mode serves the same function; however, important differences do exist. The physical acts differ. Writing a sentence takes more time than speaking a sentence. The memory load for the conventions of writing is far greater than that needed in common speaking situations. Such formalities as capitalization, punctuation, spacing, placement, and spelling place greater demands for decisions on the writer. In addition, the time needed to perform these acts weighs upon the memory system.

On the other hand, certain aspects of writing make sending the message easier. Since words may be reread rather than remembered, one may go back to correct. Coherence can be checked more easily. A wider vocabulary may be selected since pauses to think of a word inherent in the writing process do not appear in the text; nor do the pauses required to organize one's thoughts or to reorder events become evident. Revisions need not be visible to the reader. Only recorded oral speech may enjoy such manipulations.

Britton et al. (1975) have divided the writing process into three stages. The initial stage, *conception,* is the way a writer describes to him- or herself what the task will be. Understanding this task may be the most difficult portion of the process. Some children become overwhelmed and may recall only prior failures. The teacher may wish to simplify the work by making detailed suggestions at the beginning of the writing program and gradually lessen such directions as children gain confidence. For example, in the writing task of describing a plant, numerous questions may be asked about its color, texture, shape, and leaf patterns. Later such detailed prodding will not be necessary in descriptive tasks.

The second stage, *incubation,* is time-consuming by its very nature. Children plan their writings in different ways. Some jot down word associations; others let thoughts "marinate" in their minds, drawing relationships and organizing their thoughts gradually. Teachers can be less directive in this stage, for each child incubates his or her writing ideas uniquely.

The final stage, *production,* is the actual writing. Pen, paper, and author's thoughts merge. Getting started is a difficult task. Children may begin and then rewrite their starts over and over. While many times teachers would be quite satisfied with the initial writing, students themselves are often picayune about their beginnings, revealing the knowledge of the importance of opening words.

Graves (1975) investigated the writing process of second-grade youngsters by dividing the process into three segments that differed from Britton et al.'s. Graves' first phase is *prewriting,* which includes occurrences and stimuli noted or influencing the writing, such as conversations, artwork, materials, or events in the classroom itself. The second phase, *composing,* consists of the behaviors that occur during the actual writing, such as spelling, rereading, proofreading, erasures, interruptions, peer interaction, and pupil/teacher exchanges. The final phase, *postwriting,* includes all behaviors that follow the writing. These include reading the composition aloud or displaying the work. There could also be an evaluation conference with the teacher.

Graves found the prewriting phase to be very important. Many times youngsters developed ideas for their writing while drawing. They would talk about their work or play with the items they drew and would imitate the sounds the figure would make. This is the time when ideas arise, topics are chosen, and plans are made. Writers, especially young writers, do not initiate the act of writing with pencil and paper; rather, they select and plan with prior actions. Children may use egocentric speech during these activities to compose, that is, to think through, what they will write.

Sources of Writing

In looking at children's writing it is necessary to consider not only the process of the writing act but also the context from which the writing grows. A child's writing may spring from a variety of classroom experiences.

Concrete Experiences

Initial writing begins with children's description of concrete experiences that serve as a basis of something to say. Such a concrete experience helps to extend the writing beyond a cursory description. The presence of an actual object encourages further elaboration, for the writer can look again and again for greater detail, but this type of writing too often ceases as the students continue in school. Continued use of concrete sources of writing has real value especially when students are taught to look carefully. This position is supported by Hillocks (1979), who investigated the effects of observational activities on student writing. He found that specificity in writing increased significantly and that such student compositions were judged as being more creative. Organization and supportive detail were also evaluated as being significantly higher in those compositions than in compositions written by students who studied the structure of paragraphs.

Opportunities for careful observations may be very simple. This primary youngster looked carefully at a violet. We suggest that you read the composition aloud so that you may hear the child's play with the sounds of language.

> the pedals are shaped like a gleeming star, look inside one and it's a medow so far. It's colors are a silent purple, a yellow that's so slick, and theres a snowy, crystally white swany colored and thick. the insides of the pedals feel like dried up milk, the outsides of the pedals feel like woven silk. the violet smells like a pretty day, just about in the middle of may. the texture of the violet is very smooth, it makes a flicky sound when it moves. I found my violet were theres a hard ground with violets growing all around. the inside is not the same as the

outside as any one would know, If they were the inside would grow grow grow. The violet is 5 cm. and 5 mill. tall, and it's two inches and 1 cm. tall, if it were any taller it would Fall! Fall! Fall! The violet weighs 20 millagrams, thats very little to hold in your hands.

Obviously this child had heard much rich, descriptive language, probably in literature as well as in class discussions. The sensory language used enables a reader not only to visualize the flower but also to feel the texture of its petals and to smell its scent. The object, a violet, gives the child a point on which to focus, use, and test descriptive language skills. An analysis of the writing reveals that this youngster is combining poetic and reportive language, making no differentiation between the two functions. It is part of the charm of this composition. The child's teacher should probably encourage further writing from concrete experiences and provide books that include descriptive writing to serve as expanding models.

Comparing concrete items promotes the use of metaphor—talking about one thing in terms of another. Careful observation is an integral part of the formation of metaphors. In Eric's description of a swan, his developing skill of observation and subsequent use of metaphor is evident. He has heard many poems and much rich, descriptive prose and has used metaphors before in his writing. As you read Eric's writing, see how many metaphors you can find.

> I see a snowy, crystally swan floating gracefully along the pond fluffing up her feathers. There is a female dull gray goose picking up peices of straw around her with her beak to make a nest like a crane picking up logs to make a log cabin. Pip pip pip pip pip the swan is drinking water like a leaky faucet leaking slowly, After the swan dranks, it always wags it's tail like it was faning some thing. Plop plop plop plop plop goes the water and all is silent like a butterfly talking.

How would a teacher expand the writing ability of this precocious second-grader? One way would be to make available descriptive literature and to share poetry, which uses the metaphor so well. Eric does not need direct instruction; encouragement and appreciation of the writing currently being produced should suffice at present.

In addition to the careful observation of a specimen, children can relate their experiences. This fourth-grade girl went to a perception laboratory on a study trip as part of a class theme on architectural shapes. Aware that others in her class had the same experience, she selected a different aspect of the visit to report. Jackie wanted to grab her audience's attention and to sustain it. This dual task of reporting and being sensitive to an audience requires skill. As you read this account, try to discover the kind of rationale Jackie used to select her topic.

The Spiral and Devil

Mr Dale Rice showed us optical illusions and how our eyes and mind play tricks on us. of the many things he told and showed us one of the most interesting was the spiral and the devil. I was going to write about the lobsided room but since most of the people will tell about that I wont. I decided insead to write about the spiral and the devil. By now if you don't already know what the spiral and the devil is you are probably pretty curious. So I'll tell you what it is. Well the spiral and the devil goes like this: first Mr. Rice twirled a big black and white spiral it looked like we were going into a turning tunnel. Then he said "ok look at the devil and when we did the devil went away from us. Then he turned the spiral the other way. It looked like we were walking backwards through the tunnel then when he said "look at the devil it popped out at us! Im not *sure* why it did this but my guess is that we got so used to going forwards and backwards through the tunnel that we thought the same about the devil.

Jackie has written in an oral speech form; a style of writing many find difficult to use. To extend this child's writing abilities, the teacher might bring in books that contain good models of oral speech style in written language. These would provide input to support her continuing growth. Eventually she may be able to move to an imagined eyewitness account of an event. Richardson (1964) labels compositions based upon concrete experiences "thought writings." "What we have called *thought writing* and others have called *associative writing* seems to fit naturally many children's way of thinking. It is the expression of their streams of consciousness, but it enhances these by making the children more aware of their own observations and thoughts" (p. 101). Richardson's idea of thought writings has become popular in the United States as "thought ramblings." Teachers take their youngsters out of doors to some place where they may spread out to write alone. The children are asked to think about how they feel, what they smell, hear, and see. Sometimes teachers ask these questions of their students in a group so they can focus on and talk about their sensory experiences orally before they are sent off to write their thought ramblings. Back in the classroom, children can revise their work and share it with the class. Such writing experiences steer children away from trite verses that focus on rhyming and into the production of lyrical poetic language.

Drama

Just as concrete experiences provide both a sharp focus and an input of rich detail for children's writing, so too does drama. The term "drama" is used to mean improvisational drama where children work together within the framework of a situation in order to build their own story. This is opposed to theater, where children act out lines of a script that has been written for them. While in drama the focus is upon process, in theater the focus is upon product. Improvisational drama is strongly advocated by Dorothy Heathcote, who sees drama as discovery. She says that it simply means putting yourself into other people's shoes. She points out that by using personal experience to help you to understand the point of view of others, you may discover more than you knew when you started (Wagner, 1976).

We would like to share with you how one teacher used improvisational drama in his classroom. A group of children wanted to dramatize the journey of a family moving west by Connestoga wagon. The teacher worked with them to do what Heathcote calls "building belief." He got the children to think about their wagon. They mapped out the wagon size on the floor with chalk, discussed what they would take with them, and talked about what they would have to leave behind. As they made decisions about food, water, tools, weapons, medicines, clothing, and furniture, the rigors of the journey and the unknown dangers that lay ahead seemed more and more real. Blankets became more important than beds, food more important than china, tools more important than toys. As the children packed their imaginary wagon and roped down the canvas covering, they had to consider the weight and size of the boxes and barrels, the strength needed to stow them in the wagon, and how rope is pulled to make canvas taut.

Just as tasks were explored, so too were emotions. Leaving on a journey to unknown parts, a journey of many months, and a journey from which one is unlikely to return is quite unlike taking a plane trip to see grandparents. Good-byes are difficult since one thinks of things one will not see again. But there is also a sense of excitement, of looking forward to a new life. As the children prepared to leave, saying good-bye to friends and to their old home and to pets that had to be left behind, they discovered more about pioneering than books could tell. Drama offered them the opportunity to "live through" a moment in history.

This kind of drama feeds writing because it slows things down. Children can stop to explore all aspects of an experience. As they think of the way the wagon would move and how they would need to brace their feet, they also keep in mind the rutted roads, the swirls of dust kicked up by the horses' hooves, and the unyielding wooden and iron wheels.

Drama acts both as a magnifying glass and a prism. Just as a magnifying glass can focus upon one small aspect of an object and enlarge, so can drama. In the foregoing example, the original idea of the children was the journey west. Drama enlarged one aspect, the leavetaking. Just as a prism separates a beam of light into fingers of color called the spectrum, so does drama help the child see the many separate facets of a given situation—the physical as well as the emotional.

The kind of thinking and discovery that grow out of drama support writing. A child who has gone through the drama of the leavetaking can then write an entry of a journal for a boy or girl who is in that Connestoga wagon. The child can do this because of the bank of experiences and detail from which the writing can grow.

Drama is a form of composition just as written narrative is, but with some important differences. While written composition is often done alone, drama is a cooperative effort. This group support helps children sustain a narrative sequence and develop characterization in ways which they would not be able to do on their own. There is a fluidity to drama that is not possible with pen and paper. Drama allows for quick shifts and changes. Finally, drama permits immediate feedback. A message stated unclearly or imprecisely calls forth questions from other participants in the drama: "What do you mean? I don't understand," or "Why did you say that?"

Experiences that children have had to work through within the fluid framework of drama are often reflected in their writing. Mrs. Murphy had read the book *Mrs. Frisby and the Rats of NIMH* (O'Brien) to her fifth-grade class. Later the children had done role-playing, taking the parts of Jeremy the crow, Mrs. Frisby the mouse, her son Martin, and others. One of the children, Ben, later wrote a book which he titled *A Visit to the Rats*. Ben's story was a lengthy one. He spent several weeks on the project, writing, revising, recopying, and illustrating. In one part of the story Ben tells how Martin saved his mother from the claws and the jaws of Dragon, the cat. As you read this, notice how the child builds suspense and uses dialogue as a source of differentiation among the characters:

... Martin went everywhere looking for his mom. And then what he saw made him freeze in his footsteps.

There was his mother just like he thought, but she was underneath ... Dragon!

A chill went up Martin's back. He was stiff. He didn't know what to do.

"I could call Jeremy and ... no, no. Yes! I could call Jeremy back and could fly down and scare Dragon and ... scare Dragon? Impossible! Dragon's already biting her nose!"

And before he knew it, Martin himself, was running with all of his might, he took a giant leap behind Dragon and. . . .

"Owwwww!!!" exclaimed Dragon leaping into the air like a rocket taking off from Cape Kennedy.

Martin had bitten 1 inch out of Dragon's tail! Dragon who didn't have too much to say except for a few groans in between screams, left immediately.

"Martin," said Martin's mother, "I don't know whether to be grateful or angry. I risked my life comin' out here alookin' for you! What on earth made you think you can just leave the house anytime ya want without agettin' my consent?! I want you to go straight home! March!"

Because of the drama that had preceded this writing, Ben has a real sense of how each character ought to sound, and that is apparent in his writing. Mrs. Frisby has a bit of a country twang in her speech: "'I risked my life comin' out here alookin' for you!'" Furthermore, Mrs. Frisby is a firm, nononsense mother: "'I want you to go straight home! March!'" Ben uses dialogue to share Martin's thoughts, employing punctuation to mark pauses, hesitations, and shifts in thinking. Beyond dialogue one can see the effect of drama by Ben's use of movement: "'A chill went up Martin's back. He was still.'" And yet again: "'Owwwww!!!' exclaimed Dragon leaping into the air like a rocket taking off from Cape Kennedy." It is also obvious that Ben is taking on the syntax of literature. He is using subordinations: "Dragon who didn't have too much to say except for a few groans in between screams, left immediately." The double input of text and drama provided a strong base for Ben's writing.

Drama not only supports writing; it also strengthens reading. Because drama helps children see beneath the surface of a text, it deepens reading comprehension. As a child attempts to discover how a character would think, react, move, and gesture in a given situation, that child is really working at discovering the subtext or deep structure of a story.

Literature

Reading Aloud. When literature is read aloud, children become exposed to ideas, vocabulary, and complex syntax that they do not meet in their own reading. Selections read aloud are often chosen above the class's current reading level since children's listening comprehension exceeds their own reading comprehension. Besides this opportunity for hearing more sophisticated stories, the act of hearing text read aloud can make the story more memorable for many children. The group experience and group exchange in

216 *Integration of the Language Arts*

discussing the day's reading can influence children greatly. When children choose to write on the basis of a class reading experience, they can seek support from others who have had the same experience. In addition, in the postwriting phase their work may be more highly appreciated since all have shared the book together.

The Dark Is Rising (Cooper), a book of high fantasy, was shared with a fifth-grade class. This is a powerful story of a young boy's battle with the forces of evil and darkness. The teacher chose to read it aloud because although it was a difficult and complex book, it was one that would capture the imaginations of children. Possibly because of its difficulty, Nathan's first form of response was simply to retell the story.

> One day Will came home from school and walked up to his dog to pet it. It started to bark and growl and Will said, "what's wrong with this dumb dog?" while he walked in the house. When Will got in the house he asked his mother if she fed

the dog she said yes. Then she asked Will a question, "did you feed the rabbits?" Will said "no, I'll do that right away." He put on his coat, hat, boots and gloves and went out to the shed where the rabbits lived. He unlached the lock and opened up the door and there were the rabbits all huddled up in a corner.

The writing, competent but not terribly original, was probably one way in which Nathan worked to understand the story. The teacher became aware of the depth of his interest by the fact that he was engrossed in the intricate detailing of a scene from the book (page 216).

While talking with his teacher, Nathan explained he had chosen to draw his picture in black and white to reflect the theme of good and evil in the story.

Sometimes a book read aloud may inspire a child to further reading, which, in turn, generates a written response. Mrs. Marcus had read *A Wrinkle in Time* (L'Engle) to her fourth-grade class. Nicole so enjoyed the book that she read another book in the L'Engle series, *A Swiftly Tilting Planet*. The teacher and the child talked together about the book. As you read Mrs. Marcus's description of her interaction with Nicole, look for all the experiences that took place before the final composition was completed. How did the teacher manage to extend Nicole yet provide a supportive base?

Nicole read *A Swiftly Tilting Planet* after *A Wrinkle in Time* and it became her favorite book. Often Nicole loves to extend with discussion but rarely in artwork or writing. Since she loved the book so much, I sat down and talked to her about hearing Madeleine L'Engle speak last spring. We discussed both books and she told me why she preferred *Swiftly Tilting Planet*. I told her that if she was interested in making an illustration of the fantasy I had some fluorescent paint she could use. She sketched the unicorn—half in reality, half in fantasy. She began a writing, summarizing the book. When she finished, she read it to me and told me that she didn't like it. I suggested that since it was a fantasy that perhaps she should not confine her writing to sentences, paragraphs, etc. I showed Nicole several examples of concrete poetry. I then asked her to give me movement words and phrases that pertained to the book. We then discussed writing them in a shape, rather than a list. After she wrote the words on scrap paper she asked me to help with spelling. She pointed out words she thought were misspelled and together we came up with the correct spelling. We talked about creating a pause with a slash, comma, period, or space. She then rewrote her writing in a curving shape on white drawing paper. After Nicole framed her work, she seemed very satisfied and was eager to share it with other children in our class.

Kything with Meg—
Traveling though time and space—
Saving the world—
Leaving the star, watching rock going into space—
Changing a might have been—
Meeting Creatures some friends some not—
Going into some one else leaving behind your body,
going in with your soul—
Flying from reality to fantasy—
Saving the world from World War III—
To know what would happen tomorrow—
Fighting the Echthroi.

In both instances it is the artwork that reflects the sophisticated level of interpretation of each book. The writing appears less complex but it, too, is a source for a teacher's understanding of what the children have learned. Together, artwork and writing provide an illumination of children's thinking.

Books as Themes. In a fifth-grade class, several girls had become deeply engrossed in the book *Sing Down the Moon* by O'Dell. The story is based upon the historical fact that in 1863 Kit Carson was ordered to destroy the crops and the livestock of the Navahos in order to chase them from their canyon homes. This was done and the Navahos were taken on a forced journey, the Long Walk to Fort Sumner. During the two years that they were held prisoner there, nearly 1,500 Navahos died.

O'Dell has told this story through the eyes of Bright Morning, a Navaho girl on the brink of womanhood as the story begins. For her the world is full of promise. She loves her home in the beautiful Canyon de Chelly. She dreams of Tall Boy, who is soon to be her husband, and of owning her very own sheep. But events take a cruel turn. Tall Boy is wounded and the bullet shatters not only his arm but his spirit. The Long Walk and the imprisonment break the will of the nation of the Navahos. Bright Morning endures and continues to hope and plan. She urges and prods Tall Boy to action. Eventually, with their baby son, they escape from Fort Sumner and go back to Canyon de Chelly to build a new life on the ashes of the old.

This is a powerful book. It can be both the base for a comparison of cultural values and provide a window opening onto a view of the past. The story

The box was planned to encourage discussion and a wide variety of reading and writing activities. How many different sources of information about Indian life and culture do you see? Could you develop a similar set of materials that focus on another book?

220 *Integration of the Language Arts*

may encourage children to explore the life of Navahos today as well as their cultural heritage. Realizing this, the teacher developed a box of materials that would let children extend their experience with the book *Sing Down the Moon*. The web on page 221 served as a map to the materials in the box.

The box contained a sampling of various kinds of related books. There were some books of Native American poetry, such as *The Trees Stand Shining* (Jones) and *Moonsong Lullaby* (Highwater) besides other books about Native Americans, such as *Bear's Heart* (Supree) and *Annie and the Old One* (Miles). Some paperback editions of other novels by Scott O'Dell were included. Since one of the central themes of *Sing Down the Moon* is the subjugation of one group of people by another, the book *Journey to Topaz* (Uchida) was included. This is the story of a Japanese family interned during the Second World War, a good story to compare with *Sing Down the Moon*. The book *Art from Many Hands* (Schuman) was placed in the box with a marker indicating pages that contained illustrated directions for making a sand painting and for setting up a small loom. Along with the book were samples of such work: a sandpainting and a piece of weaving, both done by sixth-grade Navaho children. There was a folder of maps that showed the path of the Long Walk as well as maps that indicated the changes in the Navahos' land over the years. Children were invited to make their own map of the Long Walk and to include illustrations of events from the story. One reading experience a number of children greatly enjoyed was exploring some beginning readers written in Navaho. Accompanying the readers was a tape of a Navaho child reading the text.

There were also suggestions for possible writing experiences. Those who tried their hand at sandpainting or making a loom were asked to take photographs of each step and then to make a chart or a booklet about their experience. An envelope contained pictures of sixth-grade Navaho children from Naschitti School in New Mexico. On the back of each photo was that child's name and address along with an invitation to write a letter and a promise to respond quickly to any letter received.

Some children responded to the book *Sing Down the Moon* through artwork; one example appears on page 222.

Note how the perspective of the artists, looking down on the marchers, heightens the sense of loneliness. The geometric shapes show the influence of the Indian designs that were used in the illustrations of many of the books in the box. When the drawing was completed, mounted, and displayed, the teacher asked the girls if they might want to do some writing to accompany their illustration. The poignancy of their text shows the degree of empathy

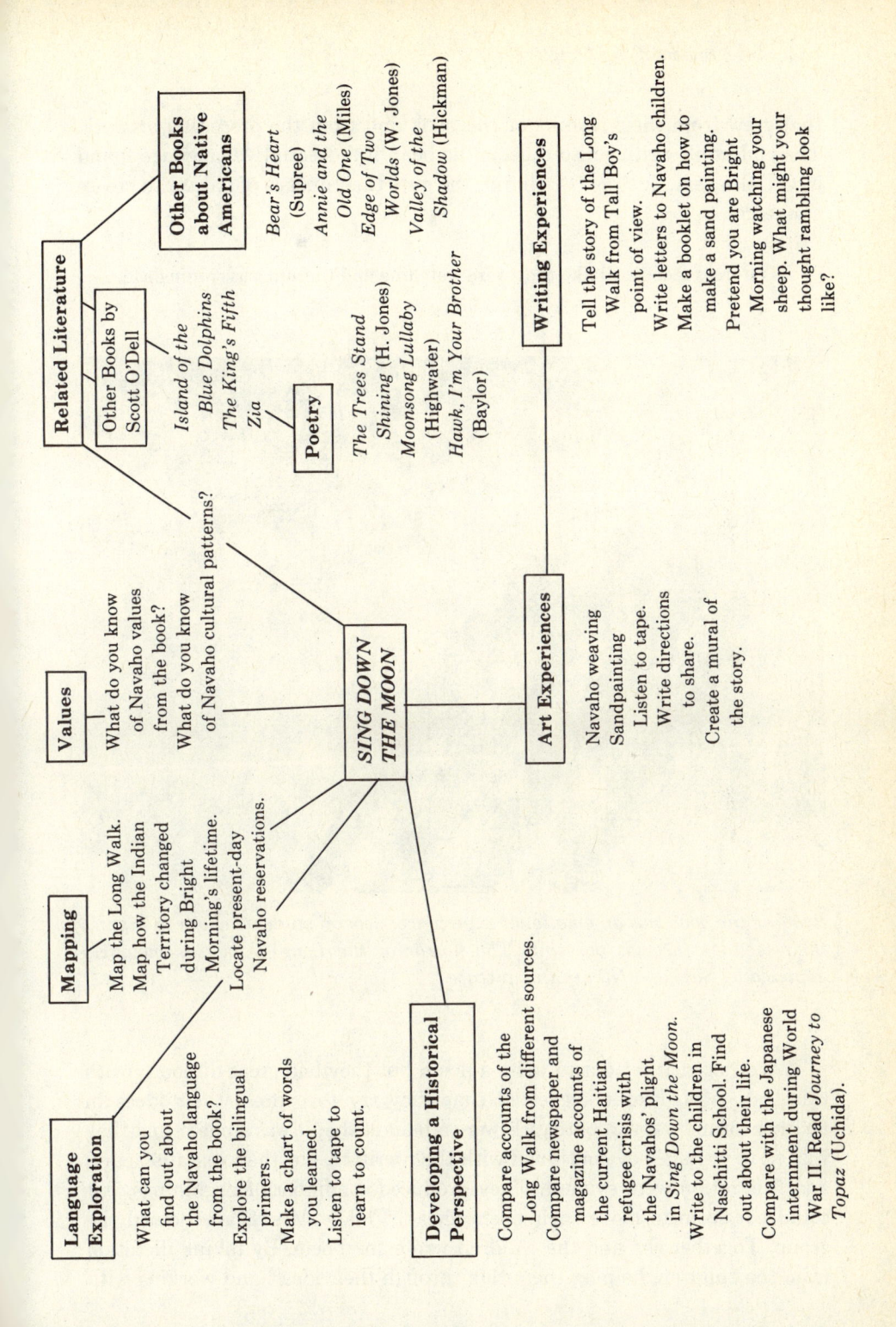

SING DOWN THE MOON

Related Literature

Other Books by Scott O'Dell
Island of the Blue Dolphins
The King's Fifth
Zia

Poetry
The Trees Stand Shining (H. Jones)
Moonsong Lullaby (Highwater)
Hawk, I'm Your Brother (Baylor)

Other Books about Native Americans
Bear's Heart (Supree)
Annie and the Old One (Miles)
Edge of Two Worlds (W. Jones)
Valley of the Shadow (Hickman)

Values
What do you know of Navaho values from the book?
What do you know of Navaho cultural patterns?

Mapping
Map the Long Walk.
Map how the Indian Territory changed during Bright Morning's lifetime.
Locate present-day Navaho reservations.

Language Exploration
What can you find out about the Navaho language from the book?
Explore the bilingual primers.
Make a chart of words you learned.
Listen to tape to learn to count.

Developing a Historical Perspective
Compare accounts of the Long Walk from different sources.
Compare newspaper and magazine accounts of the current Haitian refugee crisis with the Navahos' plight in *Sing Down the Moon*.
Write to the children in Naschitti School. Find out about their life.
Compare with the Japanese internment during World War II. Read *Journey to Topaz* (Uchida).

Art Experiences
Navaho weaving
Sandpainting
Listen to tape.
Write directions to share.
Create a mural of the story.

Writing Experiences
Tell the story of the Long Walk from Tall Boy's point of view.
Write letters to Navaho children.
Make a booklet on how to make a sand painting.
Pretend you are Bright Morning watching your sheep. What might your thought rambling look like?

that grew from their reading of the book and from the preceding artwork. The children's writing also reflects the beautiful descriptive language found in O'Dell's text. Just as O'Dell did, the girls used images of nature to create a mood:

The trees stood still like they were watching and the sun was shining sad.

Reading the book was an emotional experience. Several students chose to express their feelings through painting. The horror of the Long Walk was movingly depicted by Suzi and Niki in this picture.

Two other girls set out to write a poem but they had great difficulty with this task. Mrs. Blazer suggested that they try to express their ideas in another form; however, both girls were adamant that it was a poem that they wished to write. They continued with their writing, but their dissatisfaction and frustration were evident. They produced a number of beginnings, but could not seem to move their poem ahead. Finally Mrs. Blazer joined the group. Together she and the children wrote the poem. By taking dictation from the children, helping them talk through their ideas, and working with them to rearrange some of the writing they had already produced, a poem that was deeply satisfying to the girls was produced:

A Sound from the Trees

Haughty and proud, a leader, Tall Boy
    sought Bright Morning.

A sound from the trees,
In an instant life changed.

The warrior's skill shattered,
With pain came shocking confusion.

Set aside the past. Start a new life.

A different future altered his thinking.
He learned new courage from Bright Morning.
Together they learned to face the future.

This example of a literature theme shows how a wide diversity of writing may come from experiences in reading. Children can take tangents from the same organizing book and follow their own interests, creating writing as well as art work as products of their study. We discuss literature as a source for writing in chapter 8, "Literature-Based Language Extensions."

Books that Children Read Themselves The materials children read influence their writing. When children are allowed to make their own choice of reading materials, this influence becomes greater, for personal interests can be pursued. This, then, is an additional rationale for having a diversity of literature and other reading materials available in the classroom. By including a number of sources on the same subject, children can compare information. They are able to generalize across references and eventually learn to synthesize, going beyond the information presented.

Many children become intrigued with different genres. If journals are read, they often like to try writing their own or writing one for a character in a book. When letters are received, it is fun to write them. Poetry styles can be fascinating. Concrete poetry is especially popular.

One fourth-grade youngster wrote the following. Read the poem aloud, using the spacing and undulating lines as cues for pauses and inflection.

> A water
> spider has six
> legs and a
> very   little
> body.   When
> it   jumps
> it   makes
> a   little
> splash   in
> the   water.
> the splashes make little waves. The spider
> can float on the water without sinking.

This child has caught the notion that word placement can influence how the words will be read and this in turn can reflect the meaning that is represented. Further opportunities to explore what poets have written in a variety of forms will help refine this child's developing sensitivity to word placement.

Tom, a fifth-grader, was drawn to the poetry of Mendoza (1971): "A poem is a pond/for the moon to bloom." He chose to write in Mendoza's style about a tree in a less abstract fashion. Notice how he moves between concrete experiences—"A tree is a place where squirrels run and play"—and abstract images—"A tree has a dress that shimmers like moonlight."

> A tree is a monster reaching for the ground
> A tree is a old man with a thousand arms
> A tree is alive with fun in its veins.
> A tree is a place where coolness comes and goes
> A tree is a man reaching for the sky.

A tree is a giant as tall as a house
A tree is a place where squirrels run and play.
A tree has a dress that shimmers like moonlight.
A tree is a man who rules over the world.
A tree is a magical feature which changes the
    seasons
A tree is a cycle of fun through all its life
A tree is as peaceful as a cool spring breeze

All kinds of materials influence children's writing, not just literary works. Cookbooks have a vocabulary and format of their own. Songbooks and sheet music make fun reading. One youngster wrote "The Twelve Days of Thanksgiving" in early anticipation of the following season. Magazines and newspapers are fun to read and children can develop classroom versions. Advertisements have a style and exaggerated language children love copying.

Peer Influence

Children can influence each other in their writing through sharing. They can share when the class gathers to discuss their day. Children can then read their compositions to the class. Some youngsters may ask questions if portions of the writing are unclear while others may state what they particularly liked about the composition. These actions give feedback to the writer. In addition, class members become exposed to the writing adventures of their peers. Perhaps they have not read the same books or just did not become interested in the topic or style; this presentation by a fellow student reintroduces the opportunity.

A different mode of sharing is through display. By mounting and hanging a piece of writing, students gain a different perspective of their work. They can view it as others see it, perhaps gaining a better sense of audience. The act of display can be considered as publishing because the audience extends beyond intimacy. Writing on display is of interest to others in the class who will be curious to see what their friends have done. No verbal response may be noted, but the effect can be seen in the writing that follows.

The previous discussion has centered on the influence of children's writing products on each other, but youngsters may also be affected by their peers while they are in the act of writing itself. As they talk with each other, ideas are given and questions are asked, which result in elaboration. A child writing with one idea often changes what others at the same table are doing. Spelling questions are asked and writing conventions are queried.

Writing can be a collaborative effort if youngsters are allowed to interact with each other. The two friends are obviously writing their own compositions but conversing for friendly interaction or assistance. (Ms. Harrison's classroom, Douglas Alternative School, Columbus, Ohio)

Writing Conferences

Purposes

The purposes of writing conferences are as varied as are the forms in which they may take place. The word "conference" conjures up a formal image, where the student and teacher in a scheduled period talk about a school-related issue. But formality need not be present. A conference may be a simple informal interaction, such as the casual talk between teacher and child while the student is in the act of writing. The child may come to the teacher when he or she has finished writing and proudly share the composition. Perhaps the youngster is stuck on a point and wishes to read that portion written so far, then get an idea from the teacher for moving on. The purpose of any conference is to support the writer. Conferences may occur before, during, and after the writing.

Teachers need not be the sole responder. Peer conferencing is most helpful. When children assist each other, they learn more about the process of writing itself. Youngsters learn to ask good questions by being asked good questions by their teacher. In addition, the teacher may formally act as a model by holding demonstration conferences with students. The composition could be written on a transparency so the entire class may see it.

Too often conferences occur only after the writing is completed but children also need assistance during the prewriting phase in developing an idea. Many times talking about a subject helps students formulate writing plans. They can see the possibilities of their topic if asked questions that open their thinking or change their current direction of thought. Sometimes no questions are needed. An audience for oral "thoughts" may be just as stimulating.

Types of Conferences

An important aspect of any conference is trying to determine the student's goal. Perhaps the goal is diffuse; if so, a teacher can help a student focus his or her intent. What is the topic? Who is the audience? What is important for them to know? How does a writer go about informing the audience?

Writing conferences can serve many different purposes. Calkins (1981) described six different types of conferences:

1. *Content*—talking about the information written or to be written. Calkins reminds teachers that an active listener "draws" words out of the child. When children retell their story, they frequently tell more than was in the initially written version.

2. *Focusing*—narrowing the focus of the composition. Often a child's writing is vague, covering too broad a topic or more than one topic. A teacher in this situation asks, "What is the writing really about? What is the one most important thing?"

3. *Expanding*—generating energy for the piece. An expanding conference often follows a focusing one. In this instance the child takes the lead as he or she talks about the topic. The written piece itself is pushed aside so the youngster can generate oral language freely.

4. *Process*—teaching the writer, not writing. Questions in this framework center on what the child is thinking about his or her writing. "What new writing problem did you run into?" "Sometimes when you write, you stop and think. What do you think about?" "How do you go about writing a story?" "What are you planning to do next?" "How do you intend to revise?"

5. *Evaluation*—learning to self-evaluate. During these sessions children develop their own criteria for evaluating their own writing. This procedure may begin with the question "What do you like about your story?" Sometimes comparing several pieces of their own writing can elicit evaluations.

6. *Editing*—making noncontent changes. Children need to edit first, to proofread their own work carefully. Sometimes peers may be asked to help in this process, for it is often easier to see errors in other students' work than in one's own. The last editor is the teacher, who at this time can note the child's use of the conventions in writing for future and current lessons.

In all likelihood, several of these conferences may occur within one teacher/pupil exchange. Caution needs to be taken that one gives enough support for the youngster to begin or continue writing, yet does not overload the student with the idea that an overwhelming amount needs to be done. Children respond individually. While some need prodding, others need only a hint of a suggestion.

Looking at the Writing Product

The Role of Revision

If the child shares completed writing, a teacher may feel little can be done to change that particular product and, therefore, suggests ideas for future work. Children, especially at this stage past the beginnings, need to learn about revisions. One helpful, encouraging comment is "That's a good beginning," implying that further work will occur.

Many times children don't know how to go about revising, for the mechanics have not yet been learned. Teachers might consider modeling revision behaviors. On the blackboard or an overhead tranparency a teacher could write a composition. Insertions, crossing out, arrows leading to additional sentences written in the margins, and the sign for beginning a new paragraph could be illustrated. Even the trick of placing a question mark over a word indicating the need to check on spelling might be shown. Ways of signaling to the author how he or she has revised without rewriting the entire composition, make the act of revision easier. Of course, at times the author may simply wish to begin again. Some ideas are not worth keeping.

If teachers were to verbalize what they were thinking while revising, children would be able to consider their own writings in ways different than before. Am I using the same word over and over again? Is this point clear or do I need to add information? Can the reader visualize the experience I am sharing? Is the passage too wordy? Did I leave out an interesting part of the story? Perhaps part of my writing should be left out because it adds little.

Not all work needs to be or should be revised. Sometimes youngsters write chapter after chapter about a story. Their focus is to tell the tale. It would be overwhelming and perhaps ruin the joy of writing if revisions were requested. Even the task of copying it over may be too much. An adult may be needed to type it up or serve as "secretary" for the young author. At other times the writing intent does not call for revision. A note to oneself or a friend, an entry in a diary, or even lack of personal commitment to a particular composition are examples of such occasions.

Responding to Writing

Teachers may respond to writing in a variety of ways but, too often, the only comments children receive are evaluative. Searle and Dillon (1980) looked at the responses teachers wrote on student papers in one school for grades four through six. Rather than reacting to the content of the compositions, almost all of the written remarks focused on their form. Specific types of responses fell into two categories—evaluation and instruction. The evaluative comments were usually broad and general such as "Well done," "Excellent," "Good story," or a letter grade. Instructional comments were usually centered on mechanical errors such as spelling, paragraphing, or capitalization.

But what else might be said? Children expect some kind of response from their teachers. One way to consider response is to think of the remarks as a way to carry on a written conversation. The student has completed a monologue. If it were oral, one would not think of evaluating it or correcting usage; instead, one would respond to the content in order to open a dialogue.

Three ways to respond without evaluating or instructing are to answer with a personal reaction, with a related event in one's experience, or with a similar style of writing. Some examples may help to explain these types of responses. Wendy had heard alliteration and become so intrigued with it that she wanted to try it out for herself. This writing needs to be read aloud in order to appreciate all the work this child has done.

> Pretty Pink Pale Pettels are a Path of a Peddler. There are so many Pretty Pink Pale Pettals that there also a path of a Pretty Pink Pale ribben. Pretty Pink Pale Pettals look like they could Pop because their so Puffy. But there Powerful. There also like a Powder-Puff because it's so Puffy. Pretty Pink Pale Popy Peddler Pettals. They feel like a pretty Puffy Powerful Powder-Puff. They smell like

> Pretty Pink Powerful Puffy Popy rose. Because sometimes roses or Pale Pink Powerful roses insted of red. And they smell Perfect and not like a Pig. So rember the p's to be Perfect Powerful Pretty Pale Pink Popy Puffy and not like a Pig. Pretty Pink Pale Plus Pettals look like Pointsettas. In a bunch they look like Patunyais.

What kind of response could a teacher make? Wendy had "overdone" the alliterative style; yet her venture into a new literary form should be recognized and supported. The teacher responded in kind by writing

> The soft smooth song of sounds sifts through your writing. It's difficult to use similar beginning sounds and have it make sense, isn't it? I'll bet you worked very hard to achieve that effect.

Joetta, an eight-year-old, did not write very much in class. Her efforts had been sparse and very rudimentary in nature. The following composition represents a great step forward for her.

> I woke up one morning I looked out my bedroom window. It was snowing. I was so glad that I jumped up and down. But first I eat my breckfust and went outside and made a snowman. Than I made snow angels in the snow. Than I went inside and took a nap. I had a lot of fun.

In this instance the teacher wanted to make sure the content was noted in the written comment. Joetta needed encouragement. The response was a personal reaction.

> Your excitement about snow really came across in your writing. I could just see you jumping up and down and making snow angels.

Ann, a first-grader, wrote about an experience she had with her mother. This simple narrative is a good example of much first-year writing.

The Wind

> The Wind Blowd at me and my mom it may be that it is mad at me becus I was mad at him but me and my mom ran away then the wind came back but we got away.

The response of Ann's teacher was a related event showing that she understood the writing and had had an experience similar to the child's. This type of response helps to form personal bonds between the child and teacher since each is sharing personal experiences. Notice how the adult selected her language so that Ann will be able to read it herself.

> Ann, I know how you and your mom must have felt when the wind was blowing so hard. One time, I was hiking in the mountains, and the wind blew very hard

at me. It blew so hard that my hat blew off my head and fell over the cliff. I never got my hat back. I was angry at the wind for stealing my hat. I wonder if the wind was mad at me, too.

Written responses should not be feared by children. They can become one mode of conversing between teacher and child. Evaluative remarks will be of the most help in a conference situation where questions may be asked, and teachers have the opportunity to determine more easily the writer's intent. Too often, length, neatness, and the conventions of writing gain the teacher's primary attention.

Evaluating Writing

Teachers do need to evaluate how their students are progressing in order to determine which kinds of learning experiences will be most helpful for them. Here is a set of questions that covers most areas teachers want to think about when assessing a child's writing.

Guide for Evaluating Children's Writing

1. *What is the child's focus?* Is it on the message, the form, or both? Does this represent her first attempt on this focus or has she tried this task before? How successful is she at achieving this goal?

2. *What is the source of the writing?* Does it fit a specific style, such as an advertisement? Are there other examples the child needs to see? Is it from a book or poetry the teacher has read aloud? Could that child be particularly influenced by oral experiences? Does this show a new interest?

3. *How well is the writing organized?* Is it easy to read? Are the events sequentially placed? Does he need to outline his writing? Would telling the episode first help the organization? Does he need help in revising?

4. *Is the writing cohesive?* Does it "hang together" or is it broken apart by different styles of writing? Is there a flow from one event to another? Are relationships made clear and sustained throughout the writing? How is the composition meshed into a whole?

5. *Which words are selected for the composition?* Does the writing reflect the child's actual vocabulary capabilities? Could she have fallen into the trap of using easy-to-spell words? Is there a need for further rich language experiences? Has she tried to be innovative in her word choice?

6. *Is there a diversity of syntax?* Are the sentences constructed so that the writing may be read easily? Does the syntax reflect what the writer wishes to say? Is the same sentence pattern used over and over so that the reader is lulled into not thinking about the material? Can the writer form complex yet easily understood sentences?

7. *Does the author have an audience in mind?* Would that audience understand what has been written? Are referents clearly made? Would the audience be interested in the topic, be stimulated by the style, and feel their questions were answered? Can the author write for more than one kind of audience?

8. *Is the information given supported adequately?* Are relevant details included? Do anecdotes support main ideas? Are explanations available when needed? Did the author include descriptions to provide a sense of place, character, or feeling?

9. *How does the child use form in his writing?* Is he aware of the variety of formats available for his use? Has he selected an appropriate form for his message? Is the form used accurately (i.e., business letter format, tone, vocabulary choice)?

10. *Has the child gained control over the conventions of writing?* How are punctuation, capitalization, paragraphs, and margins used? What words are misspelled? Which conventions are the most important to be worked upon at present?

11. *What has or will happen to the writing during the postwriting period?* Will the composition be shared? In what way? Does the child need to revise her work? How can a teacher help her with this task? How is the child responding to her own work? Is she still interested in her writing? In what ways does she think she can improve the writing? How does she evaluate this piece of work herself?

In looking for growth a teacher can compare the writing children produce throughout the year. A caution is needed. Since types of writing produce differences in the way syntax and vocabulary choices are made, similar types of compositions should be studied when looking for growth. The traditional categories of exposition, argument, description, and narration may not be sufficiently discriminating among compositions. For example, Bret wrote these two pieces of descriptive writing from observations made while on a study trip in the downtown area of a city.

Buildings

The new state office tower is a modern building with modern arts. The tower has 40 stories and the elevator goes 1,000 feet in one minute. The tower is made of granite. Each block weighs 460 pounds and it is the biggest tower made of granite in the state. The color is a dull gray. When it is raining, it looks like purple. It is the tallest building in Columbus. It is tall and thin. Because if it were fat and short, it would take up too much room.

St. Joseph's Cathedral

Click Flickety Flick The old church benches crackle when you sit in them. The windows look so pretty with the pictures and designs on them. They look like wild flowers blooming all over the church on the hottest day of summer. The silence in the church makes you wonder what it was like when Jesus was alive. The lamp above me looks like the golden sun shining on the world below him. The steeple with Jesus in it, somehow it has the shadow of the star of Bethlehem twinkling.

Is one composition better than another? Some might choose the cathedral account as being better because of the inventive way words are used. The difference in tone is evident. By looking closely, one can see that more descriptive words and strong metaphors are used to describe St. Joseph's Cathedral. The State Office Tower appears dull by comparison. Many more counted facts are given. Yet, if an individual were asked to tell a newcomer what a building looked like, the visitor would be taken back if the colorful prose of the cathedral composition were used.

The tower was described in a transactional language function whereas the cathedral was in the poetic language function, to use Britton et al's (1975) terms. Their idea of participant and spectator roles is more helpful when considering types of writing. The participant "constructs a representation of the world as he has experienced it *in order to operate in it*" (p. 79). The spectator "may manipulate the representation *without seeking outcomes in the actual world*" (pp. 79–80). Thus, the participant may write a report to give to someone, whereas the spectator may write a poem to reflect his feelings about the experience. The intent of the author is most important when deciding whether compositions belong in the same category or not.

Recordkeeping and Evaluation Forms

Records of children's writing may be kept in three ways: files containing sample compositions, anecdotal records, and periodic evaluations of writing. Files of work are most helpful for both the child and teacher. The child can learn to self-evaluate his or her work by comparing beginning-of-the-year compositions with more recent ones. Evaluation conferences could focus on selective aspects of the composition. Teachers find such files helpful not only to remind them of their students' prior efforts, but also as resources for parent conferences. When parents can see the growth themselves, they will better understand the school activities designed for their youngsters. Parents also will learn to appreciate the work their children bring home.

A teacher may use anecdotal records to note the child's behavior during the writing process. If only the product is evaluated, the help comes too late to be of assistance. Observations made while the child is conceptualizing the writing task can be helpful in explaining postwriting behaviors. Children's oral explanations and elaborations may be lost if not noted. A record of topics can reveal changing interests or a narrow scope that needs to be enlarged. How much time did the child spend on the writing? Was there a partner? Is there usually a partner? Where does the student like to write?

Evaluations may be noted in several different ways. One way to record teacher evaluations would be to develop a grid of categories that could be applied to a composition. The evaluation questions discussed earlier have been condensed into a grid. To see how it works, an eleven-year-old's composition (pages 235–236) has been evaluated (page 237).

Not all compositions deserve such detailed analysis, but if periodic records are kept, progress becomes apparent. One way to choose the pieces that should be analyzed in detail might be to select writing that represents the student's best efforts. Continuous records reveal the change of student foci, development of control over the conventions of print, and maturation in written language use. These records are helpful in preparing for parent conferences, end-of-year reports, and above all, planning appropriate learning experiences.

Some schools have a unified composition recordkeeping system. In one school teachers select representative samples of children's writing in different modes and place them in a file divided by appropriate categories. This procedure is followed each year so that teachers can look over prior years' writing to assess growth. At the end of each year a card is completed on

Part I

The Egg

January 16

One lazy summer afternoon, John and Jim Smith were walking through a huge field, when all of a sudden Jim spied a big egg. "Hey, John," Jim said pointing to the egg, "Lets go take a look at that."

Jim and John walked up to the spot where the egg was. "Jim, what do you think will hatch from that egg," asked John, "a monster?"

"Naw," said Jim, "probaly an ostrich."

The two boys stood looking at the egg when all of a sudden there was a noise. "What was that," asked John half startled, "What was that Jim?"

"I don't know," answered Jim, "but it sounded like it came from the egg!"

Part II

The Egg

The two boys looked at the egg and saw that Jim was right, there was a great big crack in the egg which made all kinds of strange noises. "Let's get out of here," yelled John, "That noise from the egg gives me the chills."

John started to run when Jim called him. "Hey, John," called Jim, "I bet you'll be so suprised when you see this."

John ran to Jim and stopped in his tracks when he saw what had hatched out of the egg, a boy! "John, are you okay," asked Jim, "You look pleased and suprised but yet so pale!"

"I'm okay," answered John looking at the boy, "Hey kid, do you want to play?"

Jim and John took the kid to their house and told their parents the whole story. Their parents adopted the boy and named him Jim.

Writing Evaluation Grid

Focus/Source	Organization/Cohesiveness	Word Choice/Syntax	Sense of Audience/Supporting Points	Use of Form/Conventions	Revised/Proofread
Focus seems to be on dialogue and narrative form. Used *The Enormous Egg* (Butterworth) theme as a spinoff.	Logically organized but ending abrupt. Used dialogue well—no lost referents.	Book language evident: "One lazy summer afternoon," "asked John," "stopped in his tracks." Wide vocabulary: "spied, half startled." Syntax advanced: "John ran to Tim and stopped in his tracks when he saw what had hatched out of the egg, a boy!" "'Hey, John,' Tim said, pointing to the egg, 'Let's go take a look at that.'"	Has sense of audience in use of cohesion but not in audience interests and questions. There's a let down at the end—probably lost interest in story because tired. Did achieve focus. Needs much more detail—What did egg look like? Color? Size? How standing?	Good grasp of form and conventions. Used quotes and other punctuation forms extremely well. Shows awareness of difference between oral and written language—really well done.	Second draft of story. Did proof her work and caught most but not all errors. Needs to learn more about revising—to change focus to new area when going back.

238 *Integration of the Language Arts*

which teachers rate the child and write evaluative comments. The rating side of the card follows:

Low 1—3 High	*Directional*	*Descriptive*	*Informational*	*Poetry*	*Story*
PREWRITING (quality of ideas)					
WRITING (development of ideas)					
(organization)					
REVISING (changing ideas)					
PROOFREADING (changing mechanics)					
PRODUCT (vocabulary)					
STRUCTURE					
PUNCTUATION					
SPELLING					
HANDWRITING					

Highland Park Elementary School, Southwestern School District, Grove City, Ohio.

Teacher comments are placed on the other side of the card. Here are teacher comments on one child over a three-year period. The child's growth and teacher concerns are evident.

First Grade   C. writes daily and is a fine, thoughtful author. She incorporates new learning styles into her writing and improves daily. Her thoughts can go far and she is capable of a great deal. She needs more work on organizing her thoughts, thinking through writing before committing it to paper, etc. She just began experimenting with poetry at the end of the school year.

Second Grade   C. understands story sequence and her writing usually shows this. She enjoys writing but not proofreading or revising. She needs to be helped in this area.

Third Grade   C. is spending more time thinking through her writing before actually writing. She does not like to proofread, correct, or revise any mistakes. She chooses to write on a regular if not daily basis. Vocabulary is very strong.

Student Self-evaluating of Writing

One goal of any classroom writing program is for the students to learn to evaluate their own compositions. Sager (1973) found that middle-grade youngsters could use a writing scale and that these students' compositions improved as a result.

How can students learn to self-evaluate? Perhaps one way is through in-class sharing and discussion of pupil compositions. Another way is for the child to compare several pieces of his or her own writing. Mrs. Harbert, a primary teacher, interviewed several of her students to see how they evaluated their own work and what they thought about writing. Here is one interview:

John, eight years old

Mrs. H: John, from your three best pieces of thought ramblings, would you choose the one that you like the best? Could you tell me why you chose this one?

John: I like "The Reflecting Stream" because it has more descriptive words than the other two. It's neat because it says "sunrise reflecting in the cool river; colors dazzle in the blue, blue sky; stream flowing softly." The writing tells where you are when you read it. Makes you feel good inside. The title is neat.

Mrs. H: Why did you not choose these pieces of writing? How are they alike?

John: They're really not that bad. Maybe there could be more descriptive writing. Here, I could have said, "glowing, sparkling, shimmering rain" instead of "wet, cool rain." The writing is not quite as neat as the other one I chose. This one about the snow should have more descriptive words, too. Both the writings talk about things that are wet. This one is rain and the other one is about frozen rain, snow.

Mrs. H: What makes a good writer?

John: I think you have to be happy. It makes you happy when you can go someplace and do a thought rambling. You have to have ideas in your head—need to smell, look around, and think about what's around you. Then get it down real fast so you don't lose it in your head. You have to write real good and use descriptive words. You have to practice and write a lot. I think you should write about a lot of things.

Mrs. H: How can you improve your writing?

John: I should use more periods and use lots of descriptive words. It would help sometimes if I sit where no one is talking, at least sometimes. I could work more on neat titles. I should also practice by thinking in my head lots of neat words. I need to write lots, write a little every day.

Mrs. H: How do you feel about your writing?

John: I like it! I feel happy inside when writing and after when I read it, because people say that's "fantastic" and you say that, too!

John obviously is a confident author who knows what to look for in thought ramblings. The feeling of acceptance toward student work helped him gain such confidence. Mrs. Harbert's program of extending and accentuating vocabularies worked for him. He is consciously aware of manipulating words. In addition, Mrs. Harbert can learn a great deal about her own writing program, which may help her evaluate her curriculum.

When other students described what they considered thought ramblings to be, further clues of her program become evident.

> ... when you use descriptive words like "shiny," "flaky," "frosty," and "crunchy." We share other people's thought ramblings.

> ... write what you hear, see, and feel all around you. It's like an adventure—all you need is a notebook and a pencil.

... when you go outside and use your senses. We get in a group and talk about what we hear, see, feel, and think. We talk about colorful words like "pitter-patter of white, cottony snow hitting the ground," and "plink plank—rain is plinking in the puddles." You usually find a cozy place and write all about your thoughts. We call it a thought rambling because you take out your thoughts and put them on your paper and call it a thought rambling because all your thoughts ramble in your head.

... talking about interesting things and think of unforgettable thoughts.

An intermediate-grade teacher interviewed her students about writing. She asked them several questions. Here are a few interesting ones with the children's responses:

Miss C: Why do you like/dislike writing?

Responses: It's like being a director. You can make anything happen that you want.
You can let your imagination go.
I don't like it when you don't know what to write next.

Miss C: Where do you get your ideas for writing?

Responses: Books!
When I do something exciting.

Miss C: How do you know if your writing is good?

Responses: When you work on it a lot.
When you enjoy it.
When it has a lot of detail.
When other people say so.
If it comes to me easily.
When you get a lot of ideas and a lot of writing.

Miss C: What kind of writer are you as compared to the beginning of the year? Why have you changed?

Responses: I use more descriptive words.
My writings are a lot longer.
I'm a much better speller.
I do more research.
I don't have to do it. I do it because I want to.
I've had lots of practice.

Miss C: Why is writing important?

Responses: It helps your imagination grow.
You have to do long reports when you go to high school and college.

These are children who have obviously learned to evaluate not only their own writing but also the writing process. Their teacher has conferences with them often about their work, making the process explicit.

Writing Context

If writing is to grow from classroom experience, there needs to be a context that encourages writing. Time is extremely important—flexible amounts of time that permit the writer who is intensely involved with a piece of writing to continue uninterrupted. Time is needed so that conferences, elaboration, revision, sharing, and display are all seen as accepted parts of the writing program.

Time, however, is not enough. If children are to write often, they need room for a variety of writing activities. A classroom where writing is to occur should have areas where children can be alone with their thoughts and not be disturbed.

Quiet corners can be made in the classroom by using filing cabinets, book cases, or folding screens to block off a writing area from the rest of the room. In one classroom, writers busily at work hung up "Do not disturb" signs to guarantee they would have quiet, uninterrupted moments.

There should also be a place where children can work together on a writing project. A center with accessible writing resources and with space for display is also essential. Such a center should provide the tools of the writer's trade: materials to support, encourage, and stimulate writing efforts. There could be jugs filled with all kinds of writing instruments: soft-leaded pencils, colored pencils, felt-tipped pens in a variety of colors and with a variety of thicknesses, ballpoint pens, and fountain pens. A pencil sharpener and erasers should be close at hand. Paper in several sizes, white, colored, lined, and unlined should be accessible. Writing becomes a more serious venture when the child's work is seen as being important enough to merit carefully arranged tools.

As a choice, a box of blank booklets in which one can write may be inviting. Books may be of different shapes with wallpaper or construction paper covers. Sometimes books may have special shapes, such as houses or mittens or cars. Such books will encourage the children to think about matching the shape of the book to the message they choose to write inside the book.

Some resources can be extremely helpful as the writer forms, shapes, and edits his or her work. A variety of dictionaries can aid the budding writer. Simple dictionaries can help the child in spelling those common words that are often difficult. More complete dictionaries are useful to locate full meanings, examples of word uses, and word origins. A thesaurus is a help when a child wishes to find a fresh word to replace a shopworn one. When it is time to edit, writing guides, which are found in many of the language-arts textbooks, can assist the child to find rules for punctuating, paragraphing, and capitalizing. As children work with different forms, it is good to have available folders of samples of different kinds of writing, such as friendly letters, business letters, forms of various kinds of poetry, reports, advertisements, and news stories.

If there is an ongoing unit of study, such as colors or magnets, a chart of words that children might need to use in writing about that topic could be included. One group of fifth-grade boys were involved in developing a book about football. Together with their teacher, they developed this web of words they thought they would need.

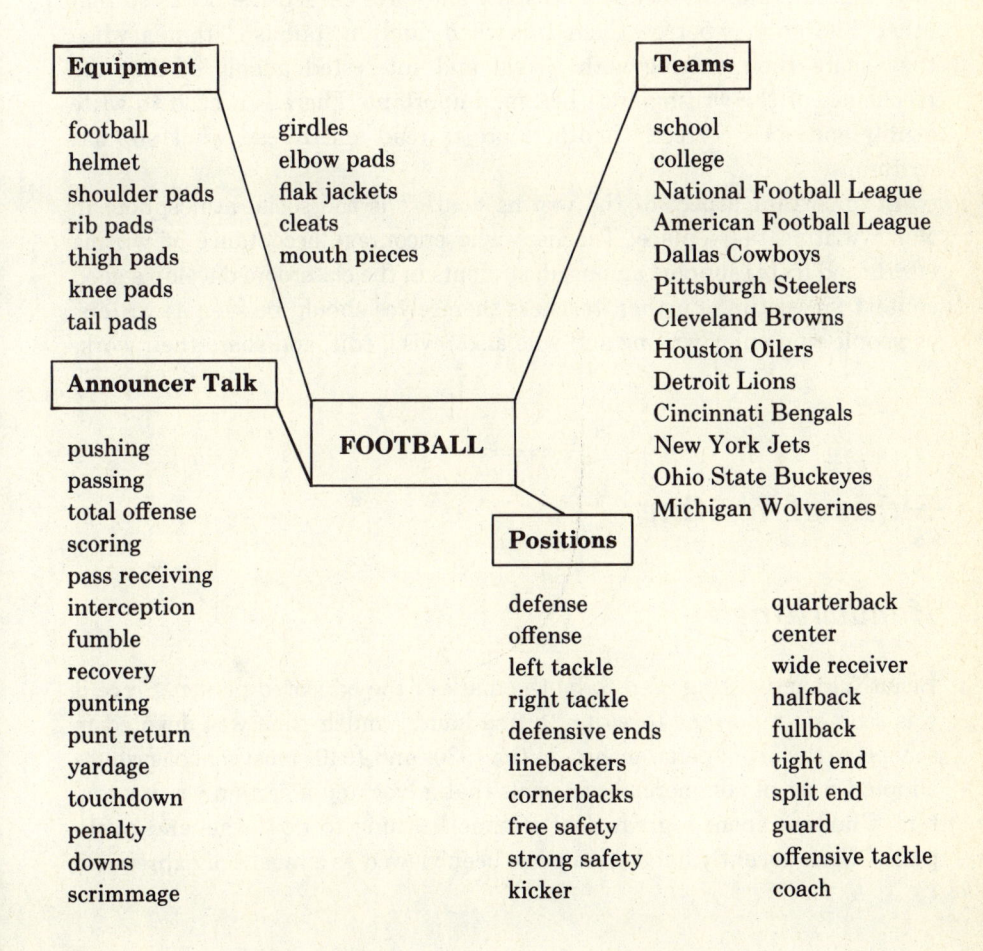

Equipment

football
helmet
shoulder pads
rib pads
thigh pads
knee pads
tail pads

girdles
elbow pads
flak jackets
cleats
mouth pieces

Teams

school
college
National Football League
American Football League
Dallas Cowboys
Pittsburgh Steelers
Cleveland Browns
Houston Oilers
Detroit Lions
Cincinnati Bengals
New York Jets
Ohio State Buckeyes
Michigan Wolverines

Announcer Talk

pushing
passing
total offense
scoring
pass receiving
interception
fumble
recovery
punting
punt return
yardage
touchdown
penalty
downs
scrimmage

FOOTBALL

Positions

defense
offense
left tackle
right tackle
defensive ends
linebackers
cornerbacks
free safety
strong safety
kicker

quarterback
center
wide receiver
halfback
fullback
tight end
split end
guard
offensive tackle
coach

When children have created a piece of writing they are proud of, it should be "published" in some way. "Publishing" can mean carefully mounting the work and displaying it attractively on a bulletin board. Writing can also be written into a book and then bound. At this point children often like to have their writing typed in final form before binding. So a writing center is also a place to have a supply of materials needed for bookmaking: needle and thread to sew pages together, cardboard and remnants of cloth for covers, and pretty papers to serve as endpapers.

One good way to bind books calls for the use of drymount tissue which is available in photography shops. We think that the directions on page 245 are clearly stated, but we recommend that you try binding a book yourself before trying it out with children.

Bound books permit writing to be shared and preserved. Some children include copyright information and blurbs about the author. School librarians have placed children's books on display and have carded the books so that other children may borrow them. It is when children "publish," that is, when they share their writing with a real and interested audience, that the mechanics of the writing craft become important. There is a need to write legibly and spell correctly if others are to read and reread what one has written.

An important aspect of the writing context is the social atmosphere in which writing takes place. Teachers who encourage acceptance of writing efforts and foster support among all students in the classroom develop a good context for writing. Further, teachers themselves should be seen as writers, as people who enjoy writing and who also revise, edit, and share their work.

Skills of Writing

Handwriting

Beautiful handwriting used to be the mark of the educated person. Since it was seen as important to write "a fine hand," much time was devoted in schools to the art of penmanship. In the 1930s and 1940s most school systems adopted a set of commercial materials that advocated a certain writing system. Children spent a great deal of time learning to do "ovals and push-pulls." More recently handwriting has been viewed as a means of expression,

BOOKBINDING TECHNIQUE (WITH DRYMOUNT OR GLUE)

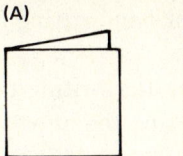

(A)

(B)

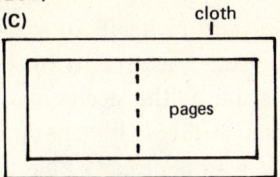

(C) cloth / pages

1. Fold paper in half for pages. Diagram A.

2. Sew along dotted lines with needle and thread (Some teachers are mass-producing all sizes and shapes using their sewing machines to sew paper). Diagram B.

3. Cut cloth, wallpaper, or contact-type paper one inch larger than cardboard (lay pages open and flat to measure). Diagram C.

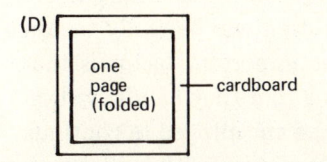

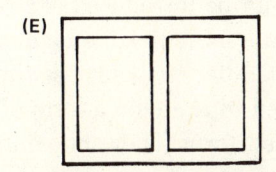

(D) one page (folded) — cardboard

(E)

4. Cut TWO pieces of cardboard each slightly larger than the page when folded. Diagram D.
   OR
5-6. Brush mixture of water and white glue onto cardboard pieces and then adhere to cloth. (instead of using drymount)

5. A piece of drymount is cut to fit each cardboard. Diagram E.

6. Lay cloth flat; place drymount on cloth; then place cardboard on top. Leave space between cardboard pieces to allow book to open and shut. Diagram E.

7. With iron, press a few places to hold cardboard in place (omit if using glue mixture).

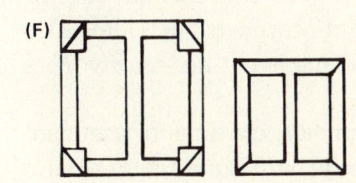

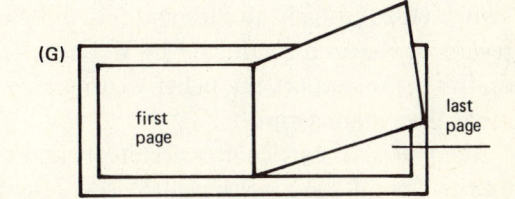

(F)

(G) first page / last page

8. Fold corners in; then fold top down and iron; then fold bottom up and iron. Diagram F.
   OR
Apply glue-water mixture to exposed edges of cloth; then fold edges over cardboard.

CAUTION: NEVER PLACE IRON DIRECTLY ON DRYMOUNT.

9. For endpaper pages: cut two pieces of drymount the size of the page; lay drymount on cardboard and press first page to it. Do the same with the last page. Diagram G.
   OR
Apply glue-water mixture for endpaper pages.

Permission granted by Charlotte S. Huck, The Ohio State University.

not as an end in itself. In some cases this has meant that handwriting has been neglected, especially in the upper grades.

In chapter 5, the needs of the young child approaching the writing task were discussed. In this chapter the focus is upon supporting the efforts of the child who is already able to use writing in a variety of ways. This stage is as important as the first, for it is as children develop more fluency and speed that their handwriting can often begin to deteriorate.

Beginning writers use some form of manuscript; as they get older, children wish to acquire cursive writing as well, for this is the writing of adults. At one time second- or third-grade teachers would move their entire class into cursive writing at the same time. There was much controversy as to when cursive writing should be introduced. The current view is that this subject should be treated in a more flexible manner. Children will be ready to add this writing style at different points in time. The important factor is that children not be asked to abandon a form of writing that they handle well in order to acquire a new form. They should instead be encouraged to continue to use manuscript and to add on another style when they wish to do so. A sudden demand to shift to cursive just as children have developed facility with manuscript could mean that children will write less, for once again they will need to focus sharply on the mechanics of writing rather than the message.

While it is important that all children learn to read cursive writing, it is not vital that all learn to write using this form. Manuscript writing is generally conceded to be more legible than cursive. However, it is frequently stated that cursive permits one to write with more speed, because the pen or pencil does not have to be lifted after each stroke as it does in manuscript. Winch (1926) did six studies and found little evidence that this was so. The results of research conducted by Washburne and Morphett (1937) and Hildreth (1945) support the belief that cursive writing is not necessarily more rapid than manuscript.

Many adults, particularly architects and engineers, continue to use manuscript for all their writing purposes. Manuscript writing is required in a number of places—on application forms, for example. Therefore, even after cursive writing is presented the child should be encouraged to keep up manuscript writing as well.

In helping children to acquire cursive, the teacher can introduce the form by writing short, familiar messages on the board. Brief announcements can be written and then later read aloud. At this point the entire attention is given to reading the message. Later some children will want to try to write in this style. As small groups of children become interested, the teacher can provide instruction for those children. When they start to learn, children will need to be helped to position paper correctly. In manuscript writing the paper is usually squarely in front of the child; the side edges of the paper are perpendicular to the desk. In cursive writing the paper is tilted at about a 30° angle to the left. For the left-handed child the paper should be turned in the opposite direction. Left-handed children may wish to angle their paper even more sharply. It is important that left-handed children feel comfortable and that they not hook their hands in order to write, for that position is very tiring.

To write well children should be comfortable and relaxed. The desks and chairs need to be the proper height, so that children's feet touch the floor and both arms can rest comfortably on the desk top. Desks cluttered with books, or tables with neighbors sitting too close can cause children to be tense and cramped as they write.

There are many commercially prepared writing programs, and most school systems have adopted one set. These materials give the teacher instructions on how to help the child form letters and how to group letters with similar strokes, such as *i*, *u*, *t*, *w*, and *h*. They also make the teacher aware of special difficulties with specific letters, such as making connections between letters like *oc*, *be*.

After children have learned the forms of cursive, the main emphases should be on helping them learn to evaluate their own writing and on providing them with many opportunities for meaningful practice. Writing charts that show all letter forms should be available for children to keep with them as they write. This is more valuable than having the letters above the chalkboard. (See the example on page 248.)

It is more meaningful for children to copy stories they have written into a booklet that can be shared than to copy a maxim from a workbook. As previously discussed, binding books and displaying children's written products elicit good handwriting. Letters written to find out information for a class project, to invite guests to view classwork, or to thank a class speaker will also be written with great attention to handwriting. Some groups have class poetry books, beautifully bound books, in which children can copy poems that are special favorites, so that they can be shared again and again. Good handwriting becomes important when that which is written is seen as being valuable.

Older children who become more at ease with writing will suddenly focus on developing their own style of writing. This is the stage when children will

Used with permission from *Creative Growth with Handwriting*, 2nd ed. Copyright © 1979. Zaner-Bloser, Inc., Columbus, Ohio.

try writing backhand, dotting their "i's" with tiny circles, decorating capital letters, or writing as small as they can. Everyone must develop his or her own writing style, so children should not be discouraged. However, they do need to be aware of those who will be reading their writing, for this requires a concern for legibility. If writing is shared and displayed, children will develop this necessary sense of audience.

To make children more sensitive to those aspects of writing that make it legible, the teacher can have them analyze the handwriting of others. Envelopes can be a good data source for this kind of exploration. The children can work in small groups to categorize the writing on the envelopes in a variety of ways—most attractive/least attractive, most sophisticated/least sophisticated, most legible/least legible. As they categorize, they can try to decide which aspects of the writing helped them decide which category to place the writing in. They will find that spacing, uniformity of slant, and letter formation are all important aspects of legibility.

In order to help children evaluate their own writing, a folder of their writing can be kept, so they can see their progress over time. From time to time children can compare their writing to a model and circle sections that they feel are very well written—their best writing. At other times they can examine their work to find a letter or a group of letters that they would like to work on. They can exchange samples of their writing with other children to discover how easy it is for others to read what they have written.

As they evaluate their own writing, they should develop a sense of how one can adjust writing. At certain times speed of writing is the primary consideration. In taking notes from a speaker, one writes quickly and only well enough so that the notetaker will be able to read what has been written. Writing for sharing with an audience is slower and more careful writing.

Older children who might find the usual kinds of writing practice boring will enjoy other aspects of writing. Finding out about the writing systems used in other cultures can be very interesting to children. The book *Alphabet Art: Thirteen ABCs from Around the World* (Fisher, 1978) is an exquisite presentation of such alphabets as Hebrew, Eskimo, Cyrillic, and Arabic. As children try their hand at writing using another alphabet, they will once again have to focus on form. Many children will also enjoy italic writing. Books and kits are available. Most stationery shops and art stores carry the special pens needed to give the thick and thin strokes that contrast so beautifully in italic calligraphy. The study of writing can be an enjoyable experience if children realize they are developing a repertoire of styles to use in meeting their writing needs. Information about these styles adds to children's interests.

Spelling

Spelling is often seen by children and teachers as requiring dull, repetitious, rote learning. Yet the acquisition of spelling, like the acquisition of language, is a process of discovery. Chapter 5 contained a discussion of how young children approach the spelling task. These children use their vast knowledge of the sound system of language and how those sounds are produced, trying to match it to their developing understandings of the writing system. As children acquire more and more knowledge about written language through reading and writing experiences, their ability to spell grows. The teacher can assist growth by providing the data children need to continue their exploration of spelling patterns, sound–symbol correspondence, and words related by meaning. Beyond this, the teacher can help the children develop a sense of spelling; that is, an understanding of the need for correct spelling, strategies for tackling unknown words, and an ability and desire to proofread their own writing.

In order to provide this kind of assistance and instruction, the teacher needs to know where the child is, what knowledge about spelling has already been acquired, and what that child is in the process of discovering. An examination of one child's writing can serve as an example of what the teacher can learn. Edward, a fourth-grader, had read the book *Amelia Bedelia* (Parrish, 1963) with much delight. He then set his hand to writing his own Amelia Bedelia tale.

Amelia Bedelia

One day Amelia was makeing cream puff's when Mrs. Rogers came down and Mrs. Rogers said I wold like ceral with my coffy and she got a cup and put ceral in it then put coffy on top of the ceral then Mrs. Rogers said Your fired! Amelia packed her bags and left. She walked to a hair dresers. Ther was a sign that said lady wanted. She wet in and the lady hired her. She said you can pin lady's hair up. So she got som pin's and pind hair up with safety pins.

In this short passage Edward misspelled 14 words or about 16 percent of them. From the weight of these numbers, Edward would appear to be a poor speller. Yet one has no difficulty in reading the passage because he is a logical speller. If the teacher analyzes this child's errors, she can discover his spelling strategies and plan an instructional program for him. The following grid provides a framework for this kind of analysis:

Spelling Analysis Worksheet

Developmental	Generalizations	Irregular Forms	Pronunciation	Miscellaneous

Letter Name	Types
	  phonological
	  morphological
	  semantic
		Homophones
		
		Borrowings
			Dialect	Careless Errors

Transition	Generalization
	  not yet
	  learned
		High Frequency	Mispronunciation
			  —from child's
			    oral language
			  —for spelling
			    purposes
				No Pattern

Reversals	Overgeneralization	Silent Letters		

The initial category, *Developmental,* contains those errors that children make as they begin to write, such as using the names of letters to stand for words ("R" for "are") and ignoring vowels ("pls" for "police"). Later children become more aware of traditional orthography and work at approximating adult spelling. At the transitional stage they include more vowels and may use two vowels ("taible" for "table") for any long vowel sound. For a further discussion of initial spelling, see chapters 2 and 5.

If most errors are basically developmental ones, then formal instruction should be delayed. A child at this stage needs to be exposed to a rich variety of print and encouraged to write freely.

The category of *Generalizations* includes errors made because a child has not yet learned a spelling generalization, as well as errors made through overgeneralization. Generalizations may be of three types: phonological, morphological, or semantic. Phonological rules are those that apply to the relationship of sound to symbol; for example, the consonant-vowel-vowel-consonant pattern (cvvc) encountered in such words as "beat," "feed," and "coat." Morphological rules are those that center on how one adds prefixes and suffixes as well as the formation of compound words; for example, doubling the final consonant on words that fit the consonant-vowel-consonant pattern: "cut"—"cutting." Semantic generalizations are those that deal with the relationship of meanings among words that may be apparent in their spelling. For example, in the word "sign" the letter "g" is silent. Yet, that "g" marks the relationship that ties together the words "sign," "signal," and "signature." If children make errors in this category, they need to be assisted to discover predictable spelling patterns.

Irregular Forms are words whose spelling cannot be predicted. Many of the most common words in English do not follow a predictable pattern. Words such as "would," "were," "to," "was," "one," and "come" are derived from the Anglo-Saxon roots of English, and their spelling does not represent present-day pronunciation. Many words in the English language have been borrowed from other languages, words such as "parfait" and "cello," which represent the sound–symbol correspondences of French and Italian languages rather than English. There are other kinds of words that present special problems for the speller—words with silent letters, such as "comb" and "knight" and homophones such as "sun"—"son" and "stationary"—"stationery." If children have many errors in this column, the teacher will have to decide which of the words are important for the child to learn at this particular time. These will simply have to be studied and learned. See the Rinsland list that begins on page 256.

Errors in the category of *Pronunciation* may occur because the child's home dialect is reflected in his or her spelling. "Ask" may be spelled "ax," or "oil" might be spelled as "all." Children may mispronounce words such as "library" ("libary") or "February" ("Febuary") and this might show up in their spelling. Even in their very attempts to pronounce words carefully for spelling, children may "overenunciate," thus misspelling a word. For example, "hungry" might be spelled as "hungery." A child who has errors in this category will need help in recognizing natural pronunciation from the deliberate enunciation commonly used in spelling.

Errors that do not seem to fit into the other categories go into the *Miscellaneous* column. They may be careless errors or errors related to handwriting and punctuation. Here the child will need to be helped to proofread work.

Using these categories it is now easy to analyze Edward's spelling:

Spelling Analysis Worksheet

Developmental	Generalizations	Irregular Forms	Pronunciation	Miscellaneous
	maKeing Puff's Pin's dresers Pind	Wold coffy som your(you're)		ther wet Ceral

    This categorization system for spelling errors, even from this brief sample, provides some valuable information about Edward's spelling. There are two spelling generalizations he is not yet able to use: that of dropping the silent "e" when adding a suffix beginning with a vowel ("make"—"making") and that of doubling the final consonant in a single-syllable word that follows the consonant-vowel-consonant (cvc) pattern ("pin"—"pinned"). Edward overgeneralized the use of the apostrophe and has it before an "s" even when that "s" does not show possession or mark a contraction.

    Several words that Edward has misspelled are irregular ones. "Would" and "some" are very common words that are used with high frequency. *Coffee* is a borrowing from the Arabic. "Your" and "you're" are homophones. The misspellings of the words "there" and "went" were classified by the teacher as careless errors because she said that Edward had spelled these words correctly on other papers.

    In order to help Edward move ahead with his spelling, the teacher must begin by finding out how many of these errors the child can find and correct for him- or herself. People, adults as well as children, often make careless mistakes when writing quickly. Letters can be left out, reversed, or poorly framed. Children should be asked to look over their papers and see if they can find any words that they would like to change. When they find these words, they should try to correct them. They can also mark those words about which they have a question. Children can be asked to work in pairs as proofreaders in order to check each other's work. This step is an extremely important one, for it asks children to look at their own work with a critical eye. Focusing on their own spelling helps children develop that sense of spelling they need if they are to become independent writers.

    At this point, Edward would probably change "ther" to "there" and "wet" to "went." Even though the teacher classified "some" as an irregular word to be learned, the child might very well change "som" to "some." Of the other words in the irregular column, "would" is a basic word that needs to be learned. The child can be given that word on an index card as a "word to be studied." Since "should" and "could" follow the same pattern, they ought to be included as well. The homophones "your" and "you're" can be handled the same way. After the teacher has shown Edward some sentences such as

You are eating.
You are happy.
You are my friend.

she can show him how it is possible to drop the "a" in "are" and substitute an apostrophe. To practice using the homophones she can give the child two cards, one marked "your" and one marked "you're."As she reads sentences, Edward would show which of the two homophones he would use. Later these cards would be placed in the envelope with the other words to be studied. The initial introduction to the apostrophe might be through his reading. He and his teacher could look through a passage for apostrophe use, discussing what is meant in that instance.

The two generalizations that Edward does not know are related and can be presented together. If children are told to learn a rule and then try to apply it, they will be able to recite the rule, but will not have internalized it. If, on the other hand, they are able to discover a pattern for themselves, they will have acquired a concept. In this case the teacher could begin by writing a list of words on cards and ask the child to give the root word. The list could consist of these words:

pinning	hating
smiling	biting
skipping	shutting
hitting	knitting
patting	piling
roping	waving
batting	

As the children give the root words, the teacher writes each root word on a card and places it on the table in front of the children. The children can then examine all the root-word cards and try to find groups of words that are alike. Eventually they should be able to find two large groups of words:

Group I		*Group II*	
pin	pat	wave	file
skip	win	hope	paste
hit	fit	smile	hate
shut	bat	bite	bake
sit	cut	rope	date

Reading and Writing: On the Way   255

They have found the cvc pattern and the cvc silent "e" pattern in which "e" marks a long vowel. The children can then be given the "ing" cards and asked to match them. They will end up in four groups:

Group I	Group II	Group III	Group IV
pin	pinning	wave	waving
skip	skipping	hope	hoping
hit	hitting	smile	smiling
shut	shutting	bite	biting
sit	sitting	rope	roping
pat	patting	file	filing
win	winning	paste	pasting
fit	fitting	hate	hating
bat	batting	poke	poking
cut	cutting	date	dating

After the children have had a chance to see if they can determine how groups II and IV are different, they can try their hand at adding "ing" to words such as the following:

tag	type
set	dine
jog	line
chop	bake
sag	shine
skim	bike
hop	rake

If they are able to do this, they have acquired the generalization and could be asked to tell how they knew what to do. They will give a rule, a rule in their own words and based on their discoveries. On their own, children can do some exploring to see if they can add still other words to these lists. The spelling books in the room can be examined to see if they have groups of words that fit these categories. If there is a rule in the spelling book, it can be compared to the children's rule. These same spelling books will be a valuable source for developing a list of spelling generalizations.

The above groupings were arranged so that children could discover phonological and morphological spelling patterns. Other groupings are also valuable. Chomsky (1970) discussed how the semantic relationships of words can be helpful to the speller. Some silent letters become heard when a suffix is added—"bomb"—"bombard." Phonological spelling clues are given when these relationships are recognized. In addition to silent letter clues, related words assist the student in determining letter choices, such as whether an /s/ sound is indeed represented by the letter "s" or "c": "medicine"—"medicate." Vowels appearing in unstressed syllables provide few cues but other forms of the word may eliminate the problem: "photography"—"photo."

Another way of grouping information about a word is a word web. The following web considers the phonological, morphological, and semantic aspects of one word. Children can work together to develop their own word webs like the one on page 257.

As teachers work with children's spelling, they will need to make decisions. Spelling generalizations taught should be the ones that are most useful. Irregular words assigned to be learned should be words that have a high frequency. There are a number of word lists that can assist the teacher. Horn (1926) compiled a basic writing vocabulary by tabulating words used in adult writing. Later Rinsland (1945) did an extensive study of the writing of elementary-school children, while Fitzgerald (1951) examined the letters written by fourth-, fifth-, and sixth-grade children outside of school. The list that follows is made up of the words that Rinsland found to be used most often by children.

a	because	cold	first	has
about	bed	come	five	have
after	been	coming	for	he
again	before	could	found	heard
all	best	country	four	help
along	better	daddy	friend	her
also	big	day	from	here
always	black	days	fun	him
am	book	dear	gave	his
an	boy	did	get	home
and	boys	didn't	getting	hope
another	bring	do	girl	house
any	brother	dog	girls	how
are	but	doll	give	I
around	by	don't	glad	if
as	called	door	go	I'm
asked	came	down	going	in
at	can	each	good	into
away	car	eat	got	is
baby	cat	every	grade	it
back	children	father	great	its
ball	Christmas	few	had	just
be	close	find	happy	know

Reading and Writing: On the Way 257

Minimal Pairs
- take—tack
- take—quake
- take—tame
- take—teak
- take—shake
- take—rope

Minimal Pair Chain
- take
- rake
- race
- rice
- mice
- mine

Rhyming Words
- take
- break
- quake
- opaque

Affixes
- mistake
- intake
- undertake
- undertaker
- retake
- overtake

Word Associations
- take to school
  - —pencils
  - —books
  - —paper
- take from pocket
  - —keys
  - —coins
  - —pencil
- take to picnic
  - —basket
  - —ham

Inflections
- taken
- takes
- taking
- taker

Different Meanings
- take a magazine (subscribe)
- take advice (follow)
- take a vacation (go on)
- take him for (look upon)
- take one's bearings (ascertain)
- take up time (monopolize)

Linguistic History
- taka—Old Norse
- tacan—Anglo-Saxon
- taken—Middle English

Combinations with Other Words
- take up
- take over
- take in
- out take
- take upon
- take out

Synonyms
- grab
- seize
- snatch
- gather
- collect
- pick up

TAKE

large	never	read	their	water
last	new	red	them	way
let	next	right	then	we
letter	nice	room	there	week
like	night	run	these	well
little	no	said	they	went
live	not	Santa Claus	thing	were
long	now	saw	things	what
look	of	say	think	when
looked	off	school	thought	where
lot	old	see	three	which
lots	on	she	through	while
love	once	should	time	white
made	one	sister	to	who
make	only	snow	today	why
man	or	so	told	will
many	other	some	too	wish
me	our	something	took	with
men	out	soon	town	work
milk	over	started	tree	would
more	people	summer	two	write
morning	place	sure	until	year
most	play	take	up	years
mother	played	teacher	us	you
much	please	tell	very	your
must	pretty	than	want	
my	put	that	wanted	
name	ran	the	was	

Children can develop personal spelling dictionaries in which they enter words they have found they needed to learn how to spell or words that are consistently misspelled. Each child's dictionary will contain different entries but all the youngsters' booklets will be categorized and divided by the alphabet. An additional section might include thematic lists of words such as holiday words, space words, or measuring words.

A spelling program can be developed for both individuals and small groups. Children with similar problems can help each other as they explore words, looking for relationships in the way they are spelled. Pairs of youngsters can test each other on their irregular word lists to learn. Children can proofread each other's papers; therefore, the responsibility for the spelling program need not rely solely on the classroom teacher. A good program develops independent spellers who are aware of traditional spelling patterns.

Report Writing

It used to be that writing was divided into two types—creative writing and practical writing. The first category included stories, poetry, and descriptive compositions. The second was made up of such things as business letters, reports, and research papers. This division is now seen as both arbitrary and useless since all writing is a way of thinking. Therefore, writing of all kinds can be treated creatively. The writing process does not change; only the form changes. When a child has a need to write a letter and has decided upon the message to be sent, it is easy to help that child cast his or her message in the proper letter form.

Learning to write a report, however, is not such a simple matter. Writing a report has many aspects:

> finding a focus
> locating and selecting resources
> gathering information
> taking notes
> organizing what you have learned
> writing the report
> citing sources

The process of doing research is essentially the same, whether one is a kindergartner finding out how many different kinds of trees there are on the school ground or a doctoral student writing a dissertation on photosynthesis. At all levels the purpose of research is to find answers to questions, to learn.

A fourth-grade class was deeply involved in an exploration of folktales. Two boys in the group decided that they wanted to find out how much knowledge other people in the school had about this genre of literature. The boys decided to prepare a test about folktales and since there was much discussion about to whom they would give the test, their teacher shared with them some ideas about sampling. What follows is the cover sheet the boys wrote and one of the four pages of questions that made up their test.

Finding Out What You Know About Fairy Tales

Paul and Jeff are trying to find out what you know about fairy tales. We want to find out if the K, 1, 2, 3, 4, 5, or adults know more about fairy tales. We will take the results and put them on a chart and bring the chart for each class to look at.

The test will be anonymous and we will take a random sample. This means that the way we will choose people to take the test is:

1. We will get a class list from each teacher.
2. We will cut out the names and draw 4 names for each grade from each room out of a hat.
3. If you do not want to take the test another name will be drawn.
4. We are asking you not to put your name on the test because we don't want anybody to have hurt feelings.

We will help the younger children take the test if they need it but if they can read the test they can take it by themselves we won't. The older children and adults will do it on their own.
This is not a timed test.
You need a copy of the test and a pencil. You mark your answers by circling one of the three choices under the questions.
Paul and Jeff will check the tests.

1. In *Vasilisa* did she have
    a) a doll
    b) a dog
    c) a cat
2. In *Beauty and the Beast* was there an enchanted
    a) prince
    b) frog
    c) pig
3. In one version of *Cinderella* her stepsisters cut off a part
    a) of their hand
    b) of their hair
    c) of their foot
4. Thumbelina was supposed to marry a
    a) mole
    b) mouse
    c) fox
5. In the book *Sleeping Beauty* did she sleep for
    a) 100 years
    b) 100 months
    c) 100 days

6. Did the Fool of the World go flying in
   a) a ship
   b) a airplane
   c) a balloon

Jeff and Paul are clearly on their way to understanding and doing research. They posed for themselves a question they wished to answer and then set out to collect the data needed to answer that question. When the boys had given the tests, they gathered a team of four children to help them tabulate the results. When they organized their information, they found that certain folktales such as "Cinderella" and "Sleeping Beauty" were more widely known than "The Fool of the World" and "Vasilisa." They made a large chart to show what they had found, which was shared not only with their class but also with other classes in the school.

Children who have had experiences like those of Jeff and Paul have developed a base that will help them to do library research, for they understand the purpose of research. Frequently children are merely assigned reports: "Write a report on a European country of your choice." A child faced with doing a report on France, for example, has an extremely difficult task. The topic is too vast and too unwieldy. When given this type of assignment, children often resort to copying large chunks from encyclopedias, rephrasing them slightly. Little learning has taken place.

Another way to approach the same topic, France, is to begin by helping children to narrow their focus by finding a question or questions that they would really like to answer. One group of four children decided they wanted to learn which sports were popular in France. They began by looking through the resources they found in the classroom: a set of encyclopedias, several social studies texts, and several information books about France. They identified four sports: soccer, bicycling, skiing, and jai alai as most interesting. Each child took one sport to study.

The teacher took several research groups to the library and showed them how to use library resources to find information. Mark, with the help of the teacher and the rest of the group, thought about how he might look up his topic in the card catalogue. He decided to look under the following subject headings: sports, bicycling, racing, *Tour de France,* France. The children also explored journals and magazines. *The Guide to Periodical Literature* turned up two articles in *Time* and *Sports Illustrated* on the famous race, the Tour de France. Mark also found a journal in the library called *Bicycling* and the librarian helped him use the index of that magazine. The children took time to browse through all the material they had collected. They signed out only those materials that contained a good amount of useful information.

In order to help the children take notes, the teacher asked them to think of questions they wanted to answer. Working with each research group, he helped them devise a chart to organize information and keep track of where they had found that information. Mark's first sheet looked like the chart on page 263.

McKenzie (1979) has termed such charts of information "Data Charts." Developing charts allows students to compare information from several sources, pull together related information, and then synthesize what they have learned from their research. The charts also help children learn to write a report in their own words.

As children put together their report, they can be shown how to use the outline format to plan: marking main topics with Roman numerals, subtopics with capital letters, details with Arabic numerals, specific points about a detail with small letters. A chart of this form can be placed in the writing center. The outline Mark developed began like this:

Sports in France

I. Bicycling: Road Racing
   A. *Tour de France*
      1. Where
         a. map
         b. towns pay for tour to go through
      2. Equipment
         a. frames of bikes
         b. gear system
         c. costumes
      3. Rules
         a. how winner is decided
         b. yellow jersey
         c. stops for food and rest
      4. Stars
         a. Poulidor
         b. Ovion
         c. Merckx

When the students had collected information from a book, they made a bibliography card for that book and put it in a file box for their committee. The teacher showed them where to find the bibliographical information in the book and how to write it on the card. Model cards for books, magazines,

Sport: Bicycling
Topic: Road Racing

Source	Rules	Equipment	Famous Players	Special Events	Interesting Facts
World Book Encyclopedia, 1975, Vol. 2, p. 228	Player with shortest riding time wins	Bikes have special light-weight frames. Gear system has a *derailleur.*		*Tour de France* 100 participants; covers 3000 miles; lasts 21 days	
French magazine *Tour de France,* June, 1977	Map of tour (p. 50)		Raymond Poulidor Regis Ovion Eddy Merckx		
U.S.A. France Culture Capsules	The leader at the end of each day is given a yellow jersey which he wears the next day.				Towns pay to have tour go through.

and newspapers were placed in the writing center. When the report was complete, the children alphabetized their cards to make a bibliography page.

While the children had acquired valuable study skills that they would continue to use into adulthood, they had also acquired many understandings that would help their reading. In making an outline, the children focused their attention on how an author must organize information for a reader. When these children are taught how to write notes in outline form from a written text, they will realize that it is a real discovery process. The notetaker is trying to locate the skeleton that underlies an author's thinking. Their own research has developed skills in using both an index and a card catalogue, in skimming to locate information, in reading maps, and in comparing sources.

Written reports are not meant to be homework. Children need assistance in developing study skills; this assistance is the teacher's responsibility.

This child is using a resource book on period clothing to write her report. She has made her desk a personal writing center by displaying artifacts of importance to her. In the background is a teacher-made chart illustrating the meaning of a suffix, ful. Writing is best pursued in a "homey"—comfortable—atmosphere. (Mrs. Monaghan's informal classroom, Barrington School, Upper Arlington, Ohio)

Some parents are not able to help their children in report-writing, possibly because they do not have the materials needed or the time to go to the library or because they themselves have never developed study skills. As children work together, they question, exchange ideas, share resources, and help teach each other. A teacher, monitoring this ongoing work, can feed in appropriate references and provide specific instruction when needed. The teacher's role is to provide input to the writing and support for the child while the writing is being done. The tasks for both teacher and child are complex and difficult. But in writing, one can rely on oral language and reading to provide frameworks for success.

Summary

Even though we have titled this chapter "Reading and Writing," the importance of oral language to these written language areas can be seen throughout, beginning with the initial teacher/child conference, to the writing process, to the kinds of conferences, to reading aloud, and finally to group report-writing. When reading and writing are "on the way," that is, when children have gained some fluency and control over written language, the two modes can support each other. Reading serves as an input to the writer for vocabulary, style, organization, form, and topic. Writing experiences can serve an introductory purpose of providing a glimpse into a new form to be read and of enhancing an appreciation for another author's skill.

Since our goal is to show how reading is related to the other language arts rather than to describe how reading can be taught, the major portion of this chapter centered on aspects of developing writing competencies. It has been said that writing is a lonely task, but in an elementary classroom it need not be so. The classroom context can support writing by offering opportunities to exchange ideas with friends; to receive a rich input of language, books, and experiences; and to share writing with others. Teachers in such classrooms will respond to children's writing in ways that make those children want to write more and that will help them to see with greater clarity not only what is good about their writing, but also why it is good. This is the kind of knowledge that brings about growth.

Suggested Learning Experiences

1. Go outside to an area where you can be alone. As you use all your senses, write a thought rambling. How did you feel about writing? Self-evaluate

the composition. Do you wish to share it with others? What do you want them to say? If you can, take a small group of youngsters where they can spread out to do a thought rambling. Talk with them first about what they see, smell, feel, and hear. How will you follow up on the children's compositions?

2. Using the evaluation grid that was developed from the questions discussed in the evaluation section, turn to Jackie's composition, "The Spiral and Devil," and examine her writing in small groups. When you have completed this task, decide how you might extend this young author in ways not suggested in the text.

3. Look over a collection of children's writing and select one that intrigues you. Write a response back to the child in which you do not evaluate. Will you select a similar style, personal reaction, or a related event?

4. Examine three current children's language-arts textbooks. See how writing is treated in each. How do these texts' activities compare with the suggestions given in this chapter? In what way could you use these books in a classroom?

5. Collect a sample of unedited compositions from classrooms across the grade levels. In small groups representing writing from different age groups, analyze the spelling error patterns you find according to the spelling grid presented in this chapter. Can you see any developmental differences? What individual spelling program would you recommend for the child whose writing you analyzed?

Recommended Readings

Mearns, Hughes, *Creative Power: The Education of Youth in the Creative Arts*, 2nd rev. ed., Dover Publications, New York, 1958.
    This book, a classic, is an older one, first published in 1929. However, Mearns's belief that every child has a unique quality that can be shared through the expressive arts is as valid as ever. The author shares his own experiences working with children in creative education at the Lincoln School of Teachers College, Columbia University, and tells of the ways that children in these classrooms explored drama, poetry, and writing. How do the ideas Mearns proposes mesh with the suggestions in this chapter?

Richardson, Elwyn S., *In the Early World: Discovering Art Through Crafts*, Random House, New York, 1964.

In this chapter we discussed "thought ramblings," an idea that sprang from the work of Richardson. You will enjoy this account of his eight years as a teacher in a poor rural school in New Zealand. Richardson, a master teacher, creates a strong context for writing by beginning with a focus on art. The children sculpt, model, construct, and cut block prints. As they do so, they talk together and learn to control both language and form. How these art experiences feed into writing is made clear by the richness of the children's compositions, which are included. This is a book that will give you much to think about and many ideas to try.

Tway, Eileen, "How to Find and Encourage the Nuggets in Children's Writing," *Language Arts* 57:229–304, March, 1980.

Using delightful samples of children's writing, Tway points out nuggets, that is, literary gems, in their compositions. She organizes her discussion into four categories: 1. The *freshness* with which youngsters can view the world that is not available to adults. 2. Children's *naiveté* about what makes a story or their ability to focus on but one part of the story forms the second category. 3. Use of effects to achieve *humor* is described next. 4. The final category is *wisdom*, which children are in the process of developing. Tway ends the article with a list of nuggets to look for in children's writing and a list of strategies to foster growth in writing.

Zutell, Jerry, "Some Psycholinguistic Perspectives on Children's Spelling," *Language Arts* 55:844–850, October, 1978.

In this review of research on spelling, Zutell describes children's development in understanding the orthographic system. Although the research emphasis is on beginning spelling, the recommendations are also appropriate for older children. These recommendations for instruction allow children to discover for themselves the systematic nature of the way words are spelled.

References

Professional Literature

Barnes, Douglas, *From Communication to Curriculum,* Penguin, Harmondsworth, England, 1976.

Britton, James, *Language and Learning,* Penguin, Harmondsworth, England, 1970.

Britton, James, et al., *The Development of Writing Abilities (11-18),* Schools Council Publications, National Council of Teachers of English, Urbana, Illinois, 1975.

Calkins, Lucy McCormick, "Children's Writing," Round Table Discussion, National Council of Teachers of English Conference, Boston, 1981.

Chomsky, Carol, "Reading, Writing and Phonology," *Harvard Educational Review* 40: 287–309, May, 1970.

DeFord, Diane, "Literacy: Reading, Writing and Other Essentials," *Language Arts* 58(6): 652–658, Sept., 1981.

Fitzgerald, James A., *A Basic Life Spelling Vocabulary,* pp. 56–127, Bruce, Milwaukee, 1951.

Graves, Donald H., "An Examination of the Writing Processes of Seven-Year-Old Children," *Research in the Teaching of English* 9: 227–241, Winter, 1975.

Hildreth, Gertrude, "Comparative Speed of Joined and Unjoined Writing Strokes," *Journal of Educational Psychology* 36: 81–102, 1945.

Hillocks, George, Jr., "The Effects of Observational Activities on Student Writing," *Research in the Teaching of English* 13: 23–35, February, 1979.

Horn, Ernest, *A Basic Writing Vocabulary,* University of Iowa Monograph No. 4, 1926.

Huck, Charlotte S., *Children's Literature in the Elementary School,* 3rd ed. updated, Holt, Rinehart and Winston, New York, 1979.

King, Martha L., and Rentel, Victor, "Toward a Theory of Early Writing Development," *Theory Into Practice* 13: 243–253, October, 1979.

McKenzie, Gary R., "Data Charts: A Crutch for Helping Pupils Organize Reports," *Language Arts* 56(7): 784–788, October, 1979.

Richardson, Elwyn S., *In the Early World,* Pantheon, New York, 1964.

Rinsland, Henry D., *A Basic Vocabulary of Elementary School Children,* Macmillan, New York, 1945.

Sager, Carol, "Improving the Quality of Written Composition Through Pupil Use of Rating Scale," *Dissertation Abstracts International* 34:1496A, 1973.

Searle, Dennis, and Dillon, David, "The Message of Marking: Teacher Written Responses to Student Writing at Intermediate Grade Levels," *Research in the Teaching of English* 14: 233–242, October, 1980.

Vygotsky, Lev S., *Thought and Language,* trans. by Eugenia Hoffmann and Gertrude Vakar, MIT Press, Cambridge, Mass., 1962.

Wagner, Betty Jane, *Dorothy Heathcote: Drama as a Learning Medium,* National Education Association, Washington, D. C., 1976.

Washburne, Carlton W., and Morphett, Mabel V., "Manuscript Writing: Some Recent Investigations," *Elementary School Journal* 37: 517–529, 1937.

Winch, W. H., "Print-Script and Cursive-Script in Schools; An Investigation in Neuro-Muscular Readjustments," *Forum Education* 4:123–138, 206–222, 1926.

Children's Literature

Baylor, Byrd, *Hawk, I'm Your Brother,* Charles Scribner's Sons, New York, 1976.

Blos, Jean W., *A Gathering of Days: A New England Girl's Journal, 1830–1832,* Charles Scribner's Sons, New York, 1979.

Butterworth, Oliver, *The Enormous Egg,* illustrated by Louis Darling, Little, Brown, Boston, 1956.

Cooper, Susan, *The Dark Is Rising,* Atheneum, New York, 1973.

Fisher, Leonard Everett, *Alphabet Art: Thirteen ABCs from Around the World,* Four Winds Press, New York, 1978.

Frank, Anne, *Anne Frank: The Diary of a Young Girl,* trans. B. M. Moovart, Doubleday, New York, 1967.

Gasztold, Carmen Bernos de, *Prayers from the Ark,* trans. Rumer Godden, Viking, New York, 1962.

Hickman, Janet, *Valley of the Shadow,* Macmillan, New York, 1974.

Highwater, Jamake, *Moonsong Lullaby,* Lothrop, Lee and Shepard Books, New York, 1981.

Jones, Hettie, ed., *The Trees Stand Shining: Poetry of the American Indians,* Dial Press, New York, 1971.

Jones, Weyman, *Edge of Two Worlds,* Dial Press, New York, 1965.

L'Engle, Madeleine, *A Swiftly Tilting Planet,* Farrar, Straus and Giroux, New York, 1978.

L'Engle, Madeleine, *A Wrinkle in Time,* Farrar, Straus, New York, 1962.

Mendoza, George, *Moonfish and Owl Scratching,* illustrated by Peter Parnall, Grosset and Dunlap, New York, 1971.

Miles, Miska, *Annie and the Old One,* Little, Brown, Boston, 1971.

O'Brien, Robert, *Mrs. Frisby and the Rats of NIMH,* Atheneum, New York, 1973.

O'Dell, Scott, *Island of the Blue Dolphins,* Houghton Mifflin, Boston, 1960.

O'Dell, Scott, *The King's Fifth,* Houghton Mifflin, Boston, 1966.

O'Dell, Scott, *Sing Down the Moon,* Dell, New York, 1970.

O'Dell Scott, *Zia,* Houghton Mifflin, Boston, 1976.

Parrish, Peggy, *Amelia Bedelia,* Harper and Row, New York, 1963.

Schuman, Jo Miles, *Art from Many Hands: Multicultural Art Projects for Home and Schools,* Prentice-Hall, Inc., Englewood Cliffs, N.J., 1981.

Supree, Burton, *Bear's Heart,* Lippincott, New York, 1977.

Uchida, Yoshiko, *Journey to Topaz,* Charles Scribner's Sons, New York, 1971.

Rationale
How to Integrate Language Arts in a Content Area
Selecting a Topic or Theme
Planning for the Theme
Organizing for Work
Recordkeeping
In-class Experiences and Activities that Serve to Integrate
Out-of-class Experiences and Activities that Serve to Integrate
Interpreting the Experience
Sharing Experiences
Opportunities for Assessing

Language as a Content Area
What Teachers Need to Know About Grammar
What Children Could Learn About Language
What Children Can Learn About the Differences Between Oral and Written Language
Choosing Words to Shape Thought
What Children Should Learn About Words

Summary
Suggested Learning Experiences
Recommended Readings
References
Professional Literature
Children's Literature

Chapter 7
Language Arts in the Content Areas

Rationale

The elementary- and middle-school curricula include a group of subjects, sometimes called "content areas," which includes social studies, science, mathematics, and health. Language arts has been often considered to have no unique content; as a result, educators have found it necessary to integrate language arts within the content areas. Language arts does have a specific content, however: linguistic systems, language use, and the history of language.

There are several good reasons for integrating the language arts within the content areas. The content areas provide a place for language use through authentic experiences within a topic or theme. When children produce and rely upon language purposefully, artificial exercises to practice language become unnecessary. A variety of language functions occur with content-area study because the current classwork calls for such diversity. The heuristic function of hypothesizing, tendering a tentative prediction, may appear as observations are made in science or as estimates are made in math. A debate in social studies concerning an individual's rights versus the state's responsibilities may bring in representational (informative) and heuristic functions as dichotomies in the arguments are drawn. Writings can be in the form of a report that explains or describes an event. Personal feelings that arise from an experience can lead to poetic writing. A narrative can evolve from thorough knowledge of an insect or animal through careful observation. Children read not only to satisfy a general interest but also because they want to find out about something specific. Strong, purposeful study in the form of reading takes place.

Another reason for integrating is that language is a medium for learning. Reading about a topic comes quickly to mind, as does listening to reports and resource speakers. But other forms also lead to learning experiences. As we discussed in chapter 4, "Listening and Speaking," speech serves two purposes, communication and reflection. Reflective speech serves the function of learning, for new insights are developed and previously unseen relationships become clarified. Sometimes the language mode is oral; for example, children will discuss among themselves the results of their observations or pertinent information found from reading on a group's topic. As youngsters mature, they can use reflective language, that is, oral and written language for learning. One good way to understand a topic is to write about it, for writing brings about a logical organization of one's knowledge and encourages relationships to be made. Since language will be used when content areas are taught, it is logical to take advantage of their use and extend children's language-arts skills at the same time. Finally, as the curriculum becomes increasingly crowded, teachers become concerned about having enough time for each important area.

How to Integrate Language Arts in a Content Area

One way to use the school day efficiently and effectively is to integrate the subject areas. Although language arts is usually taught separately from math or science, for example, the areas may be studied as they are woven together to form a classroom experience. How the weaving may take place is the subject of this chapter. For each step discussed, an example of an actual fourth/fifth-grade theme will be shown so that continuity in a theme can be seen. We have been telling you *what* to do in an integrated curriculum; now we will focus in on *how* to integrate the curriculum.

Selecting a Topic or Theme

Quite often the topic or the theme of study is determined by the school district's curriculum; however, children's interests are also an important source of classroom experiences. For example, kiteflying in the spring intrigues many children. In studying kites, there might be an investigation of wind, weather patterns, aerodynamics, kitemaking, and even gliders. Math would be included in measurements of size or distance and estimates of the wind's velocity. In social studies a review of the place of kites in Japanese culture and the history of kites around the world could be made. Art may be brought in while designing and decorating kites to fly. The science of winds and weather particular to the spring could be another area integrated into this study.

An event may bring about a theme. One second-grade youngster found a bird with a broken wing. While it was recuperating in the classroom, the teacher began a theme on birds. She placed an empty bird's nest on a corner table in the room near the door; later she added books on birds. Gradually children in the class brought in objects they had found, such as broken eggshells, feathers, and old nests abandoned by their owners. During the study the children took a trip to the zoo and concentrated on the birds there. They observed their favorite birds' behaviors, features, and sounds.

274 Integration of the Language Arts

In another instance a terrific electrical storm occurred during school hours. The sky was dark and the thunder rolled. The teacher decided to move into a study of weather, a unit already in the school's curriculum and science textbook available for the fourth/fifth-grade glass she was teaching.

For a teacher, choosing a theme depends upon several factors. If a topic selected is widely popular, the collection of resources related to it may be gone from the library. The topic may be interesting in and of itself (such as bicycles or pirates) but the resources needed are not available since few books have been written about either topic.

The resources for a theme should include materials written at a variety of levels to meet individual needs. A broad spectrum of genres is needed, including informational books, books of poetry, and fiction. We have placed a bibliography in this chapter to show the variety of literature needed for an effective study. If weather were chosen as the theme, the following bibliography might be selected as the beginning of the library resources.

Selected Bibliography: Weather

Fiction

Barrett, Judith, *Cloudy with a Chance of Meatballs,* illustrated by Ron Barrett, Atheneum, New York, 1978.

Belting, Natalia, "Why There Is Thunder and Lightning," *The Earth Is on a Fish's Back: Tales of Beginnings,* illustrated by Esta Nesbitt, Holt, Rinehart and Winston, New York, 1965.

Bova, Ben, *The Weathermakers,* Holt, Rinehart and Winston, New York, 1967.

Davis, Hubert, compiler and editor, *A January Fog Will Freeze a Hog and Other Weather Folklore,* illustrated by John Wallner, Crown, New York, 1977.

Hutchins, Pat, *The Wind Blew,* Macmillan, New York, 1974.

MacGregor, Ellen and Pantell, Dora, *Miss Pickerell and the Weather Satellite,* illustrated by Charles Geer, McGraw-Hill, New York, 1971.

Shulevitz, Uri, *Rain, Rain Rivers,* Farrar, Straus, New York, 1969.

Tresselt, Alvin, *Hide and Seek Fog,* illustrated by Roger Duvoisin, Lothrop, Lee and Shepard, New York, 1965.

Williams, Jay, *Danny Dunn and the Weather Machine,* illustrated by Ezra Jack Keats, McGraw-Hill, New York, 1959.

Zolotow, Charlotte, *The Storm Book,* illustrated by Margaret Bloy Graham, Harper & Row, New York, 1952.

Nonfiction

Bendick, Jeanne, *Lightning,* Rand McNally, Chicago, 1961.

Bendick, Jeanne, *The Wind,* Rand McNally, Chicago, 1964.

Boesen, Victor, *Doing Something About the Weather,* G. P. Putnam's Sons, New York, 1975.

Bova, Ben, *The Weather Changes Man,* Addison-Wesley, Reading, Massachusetts, 1974.

Branley, Franklyn M., *Flash Crash, Rumble and Roll,* illustrated by Ed Emberley, Thomas Y. Crowell, New York, 1964.

Branley, Franklyn M., *Rain and Hail,* illustrated by Helen Borten, Thomas Y. Crowell, New York, 1963.

Buehr, Walter, *Storm Warning: The Story of Hurricanes and Tornadoes,* William Morrow, New York, 1972.

Cohen, Daniel, *What's Happened to Our Weather,* M. Evans, New York, 1979.

Courtney, William, *What Does a Barometer Do?,* pictures by Len Darwin, Little, Brown, Boston, 1963.

Craig, M. Jean, *Questions and Answers About Weather,* illustrated by Judy Craig, Four Winds, New York, 1969.

dePaola, Tomie, *The Cloud Book,* Holiday House, New York, 1975.

Donnan, John A. and Marcia, *Rain Dance to Research,* illustrated with photographs and drawings, David McKay, New York, 1977.

Keen, Martin L., *Lightning and Thunder,* Julian Messner, New York, 1969.

Lee, Albert, *Weather Wisdom,* Doubleday, New York, 1976.

McGrath, Thomas, *Clouds,* illustrated by Chris Jenkyns, Melmont, Chicago, 1959.

Nelson, Clifford R., *From One Drop of Water,* illustrated by Ren Patterson, Julian Messner, New York, 1970.

Prince, J. H., *Weather and the Animal World,* Thomas Nelson, New York, 1974.

Ryan, Martha, *Weather,* illustrated by Gavin Rowe, Franklin Watts, New York, 1976.

Schneider, Herman, *Everyday Weather and How It Works,* pictures by Jeanne Bendick, Whittlesey House, New York, 1961.

Sears, Rogers, editor, *The World's Weather and Climates,* Bounty Books, New York, 1974.

Shimek, William J., *The Celsius Thermometer,* pictures by George Overlie, Lerner, Minneapolis, 1975.

Simon, Seymour, *Weather and Climate,* illustrated by John Polgreen, Random House Science Library, New York, 1969.

Wolff, Barbara, *Evening Gray, Morning Red: A Ready-to-read Handbook of American Weather Wisdom,* Macmillan, New York, 1976.

Poetry

Brewton, Sara and John E., selectors, *Bridled with Rainbows: Poems About Many Things of Earth and Sky,* decorations by Vera Bock, Macmillan, New York, 1952, pp. 107–124 (23 poems).

Cole, William, editor, *Pick Me Up: A Book of Short Poems,* Macmillan, New York, 1972, pp. 49, 54–57 (6 poems).

Conkling, Hilda, "Weather," *Time for Poetry,* Third General Edition compiled by May Hill Arbuthnot and Shelton L. Root, Jr., Scott, Foresman, Chicago, 1968, p. 162.

Fisher, Aileen, *I Like Weather,* illustrated by Janina Domanska, Crowell, New York, 1963.

Geismer, Barbara Peck and Suter, Antoinette Brown, selectors, *Very Young Verses,* illustrated by Mildred Bronson, Houghton Mifflin, Boston, 1945, pp. 150–167 (17 poems).

Larrick, Nancy, editor, *Piping Down the Valleys Wild: Poetry for the Young of All Ages,* illustrated by Ellen Raskin, Delacorte, New York, 1968, pp. 37–50 (18 poems).

Planning for the Theme

Webbing a theme allows the teacher to think freely about what might be studied and which activities could be incorporated. Through webbing, a teacher can see relationships among subjects possibly not thought of previously. Teacher planning comes first—to consider the possibilities and to determine the theme's richness for study. Teacher-planned webs may be found in the first chapter and in chapter 8, "Literature-Based Language Extensions."

After the initial planning, with some source materials already collected as a beginning, the teacher might choose to plan with the class. The web on page 277 is one that the fourth/fifth-grade combination developed with their teacher on the theme of weather.

This web is noticeably less complex and complete than a teacher-produced web. Resource materials are not noted and few activities are listed, although children often have many good ideas about things to do. But the web does help children see relationships and it does provide a choice of projects for children to pursue in small groups or as individuals. The teacher's role of linking ideas together as they arise from the class is very important, for this

WEATHER

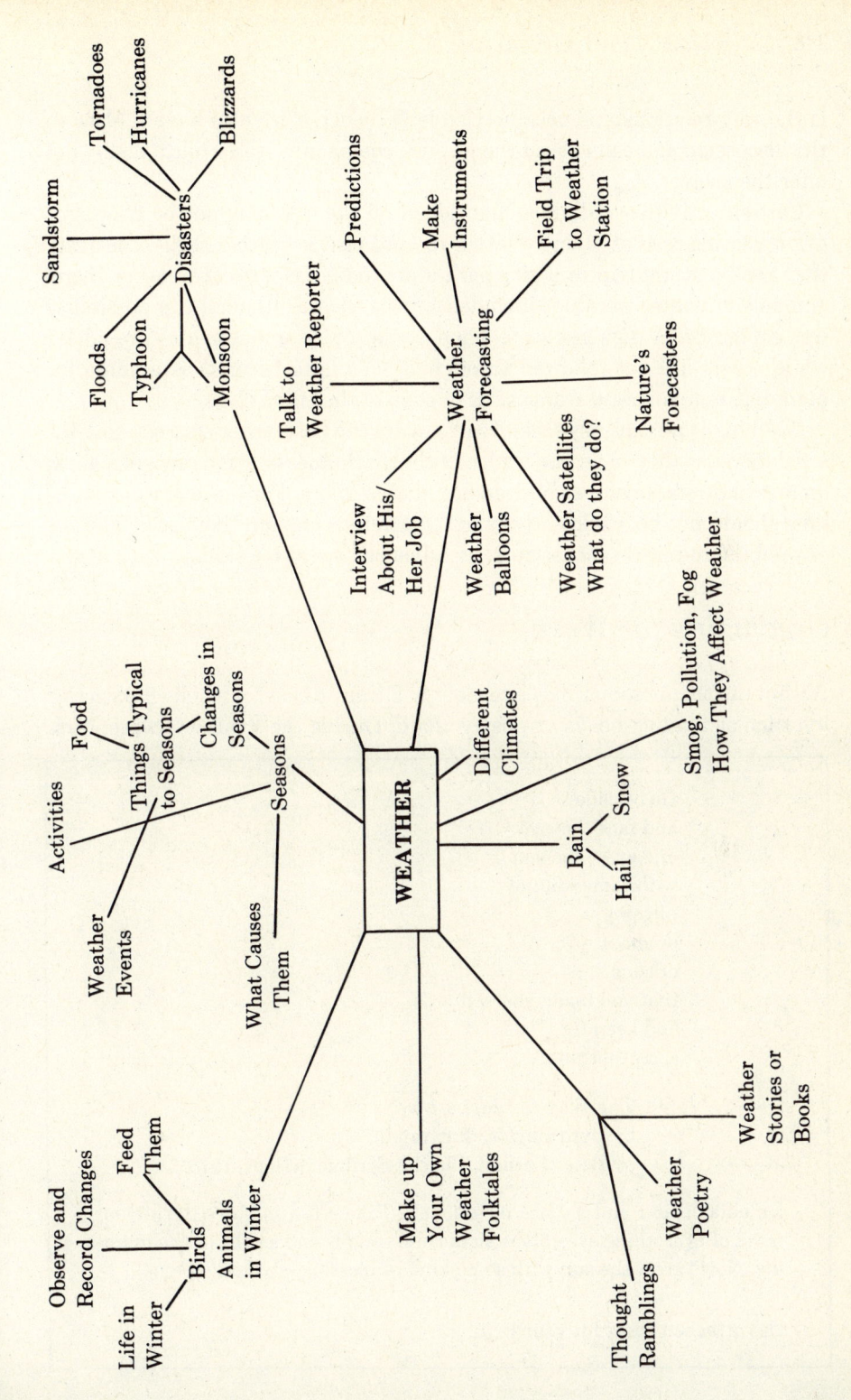

- **Disasters**
  - Sandstorm
  - Tornadoes
  - Hurricanes
  - Blizzards
  - Floods
  - Typhoon
  - Monsoon

- **Weather Forecasting**
  - Predictions
  - Make Instruments
  - Field Trip to Weather Station
  - Nature's Forecasters
  - Weather Satellites — What do they do?
  - Weather Balloons
  - Interview About His/Her Job
  - Talk to Weather Reporter

- **Seasons**
  - Changes in Seasons
  - Things Typical to Seasons
    - Food
    - Activities
    - Weather Events
  - What Causes Them

- **Different Climates**

- **Rain, Hail, Snow**

- **Smog, Pollution, Fog — How They Affect Weather**

- **Life in Winter**
  - Observe and Record Changes
  - Birds
    - Feed Them
  - Animals in Winter

- **Make up Your Own Weather Folktales**

- **Weather Stories or Books**
  - Weather Poetry
  - Thought Ramblings

is the way relationships become visible. Teacher ideas also have a place in the discussion and can extend the webbed theme into areas children may not offer themselves.

Certain activities and areas mentioned on the web may not be done. For example, this class studying weather did not visit a weather station; instead, they took a study trip to a city park and studied aspects of weather there. Animals in winter were not included in this theme although the possibility was contained in the class web. Thus, some topics and activities are added while others are not followed through. A web is to be used as a guide for planning, not as a rigid framework to control the curriculum.

Webbing is not an easy task. Teachers are the best writers or "scribes" for a web because they have knowledge of the disciplines and can recognize hierarchies and relationships children are unable to see. For these reasons, webbing should not be a solo activity for children to plan on their own. The act of webbing requires synthesizing, an advanced cognitive skill.

Organizing for Work

Within the theme sometimes a teacher will want to have a whole-class activity, such as reading books or poetry aloud. During the weather theme, Mrs.

> Go outside
> and face the east
> and greet the sun
> with some kind of
> blessing
> or chant
> or song
> that you made yourself
> and keep for
> early morning.
>
> from: *The Way to Start a Day*
> by Byrd Baylor, illustrated
> by Peter Parnall, Charles Scribner's Sons, 1978.
>
> Go outside and find a place by yourself. Take a few minutes to rid your mind of everything except the sights and sounds and smells of the morning. Now "greet the sun with some kind of blessing or chant or song."
>
> Use attached sheet for your writing.

Blazer, the class teacher, gave all her students a sheet of paper with a quote from Baylor's *The Way to Start a Day* and asked them to go outside. Using their senses the children were directed to greet the sun and write of their experience (see page 278).

Grouping for Work. When working on individual or group projects, the selection can be made in two different ways. Children can make their own choice either openly in whole-group sharing or they can write their topic of study on a card to turn in to the teacher. The card option fosters more individual interest since many times children will choose according to friends' topics rather than make an independent selection.

At other times the teacher may wish to group children with specific purposes in mind. Sometimes children are selected because of the special skills they can bring to a group, such as being a talented artist, a detailed author, or an organizer. Other reasons for teacher selection may be social so that quiet students, for example, might be grouped together so they have a chance to take on leadership responsibilities, or so that children who often work together have the opportunity to know others by working in different groups. A child who continually chooses to work alone may be placed in a group this time. Some youngsters seem to be in a rut, for they always turn to the same activity (such as art) to interpret their findings or always search for a science-directed topic. To move them out of this rut the teacher may place these students in a group whose project will extend them. Another good reason for a teacher to place a student in a group is because of the student's known interest in the topic.

Grouping is a delicate procedure. Many learning opportunities become available in well-functioning groups. A diversity of self-selected and teacher-selected groupings throughout the year makes sure that children get the most out of small-group work. (See chapters 3 and 11 for discussions of different aspects of grouping.)

Managing Space and Time. Besides materials, children need time and space in which to work. A table around which a group could meet, open space in the center of a room, and carrels or individual desks by a wall might meet individual and group needs. Centers for writing, reading, and artwork could be used by members of several groups. If there is free access to the library and materials, the teacher does not need to be interrupted for these mana-

Setting up a room with clearly labeled supplies takes time, planning and errand-running. Classroom results are most positive when children understand how supplies are to be used. Students have a responsibility to keep supply boxes tidy, use them efficiently, and tell the teacher when supplies run low. (Mrs. Harbert's informal classroom, Barrington School, Upper Arlington, Ohio)

gerial duties. This frees teachers to move about the room, consulting with individuals and small groups.

If teachers plan the classroom time flexibly, all children need not do the same thing at the same time; in some schools, however, blocks of time are scheduled rigidly. Flexibility may be incorporated into these schedules by using reading or art time for project work. Even math period could be used for projects; for example, in the weather theme youngsters studied the Celsius scale, learning how to figure centigrade from Fahrenheit, and how to read thermometers and barometers. Blocks of time could be set aside for independent project tasks while the teacher selects small groups with whom to work on other aspects of the curriculum, such as a spelling group, a book discussion, or math group.

Recordkeeping

Keeping tabs on group work can be difficult if a teacher is not well organized. Even young children can help in recordkeeping. There could be a sign-up sheet for long-term plans; children might then check off what they had accomplished each day. Another method is through conferences where the group or individual children meet with the teacher to plan out projects. This is an opportune time for the teacher to serve as a resource for books, ideas, and extensions. The two processes of sign-up sheets and conferences could be combined.

Daily planning might be organized in several different ways. During the morning sharing period, children could state how they are going to spend their project time that day. The teacher could see that materials needed are available. Planning sheets could be turned in by individuals or groups. The teacher might then move from group to group to see how their plans were advancing.

Planning Sheet

Name _____

The topic I'm studying is: _____
_____

Today I plan to: _____
_____

The materials I'll need are: _____
_____

I will work with: _____
_____

The help I need from my teacher is: _____

Anecdotal records of the day's work help the teacher to gain an overview of how each student is progressing. Data need not be added each day but if too many blanks appear, this tells a teacher that that child could be going along unnoticed in class. These notations are informal and really of value for the teacher only. Nevertheless, when parent conferences occur and grading paragraphs are due, the anecdotal records provide specific instances to recount, which may be easily forgotten in busy teaching days. They may also be used to verify "feelings" intuitively drawn about youngsters. The record on page 282 is a week's log of three children. A good sense of each one's involvement in his or her chosen weather project can be discerned.

By encouraging Jamie to write his own report, his teacher, Mrs. Blazer, has evidence of what he had learned and could note his skills in report-writing. The next step for Jamie might be to use several sources within a single report. Look at the three compositions. How might Mrs. Blazer extend Brian? He certainly displays self-motivation and leadership qualities. What can you tell about Cheryl? If Jamie rewrote his composition, what do you think he might change?

Name	March 12	March 13	March 14	March 15	March 16
BRIAN	Working with Jamie on weather satellites. Asked for resource books.	Had mother take him to library for more books. He's really gung-ho!	Asked if he could make model of a satellite. Decided on a drawn model.	Finished model. Is writing report on satellites to accompany picture.	Completed writing. Wants to display work.
CHERYL	Finally chose weather vanes to study. Slow to settle in.	Seems lackadaisical, puttering.		Building a weather vane with Sally. Seems more involved.	Wrote short report but included a lengthy complex sentence! Didn't seem to get into this project. Must help her find some task she is really interested in.
JAMIE	Working with Brian on weather satellites. Seems to be letting Brian take the lead.	Reading book on satellites. Really engrossed!	Letting Brian take the lead. Doing actual sketching with Brian overseeing work.	At my suggestion Jamie is writing own report based on his reading. Both Jamie and Brian are writing side by side, conferring often.	Writing a really lengthy report. Seems pleased with his work. Needs to recopy. Using own words. Really has a good idea of how to write a report.

Weather Satellites

A weather satellite is something that takes a picture of the weather.

The satellite has lots of tools like cameras, radiometer, and various measuring devices. A radiometer instrument is for measuring the energy of the sun. The photographs are sent to the ground by T.V. showing clouds, land form, sea ice hurricane.

On April 1, 1960 Tiros 1 was sent up in orbit. The cameras can photograph up to 4.5 million square miles.

The satellite pictures can spot hurricanes from far out at sea before it hits a ship. Most satellites are owned by the U.S. and don't complete world coverage. Sometime in the future a lot of satellites are going to be sent up by the U.S., U.S.S.R., Europe, and Japan. They will be placed, by the equator and survey the tropics, while others will be around the poles.

Weather satellites are very useful because they can get pictures where other instruments can not.

Jamie

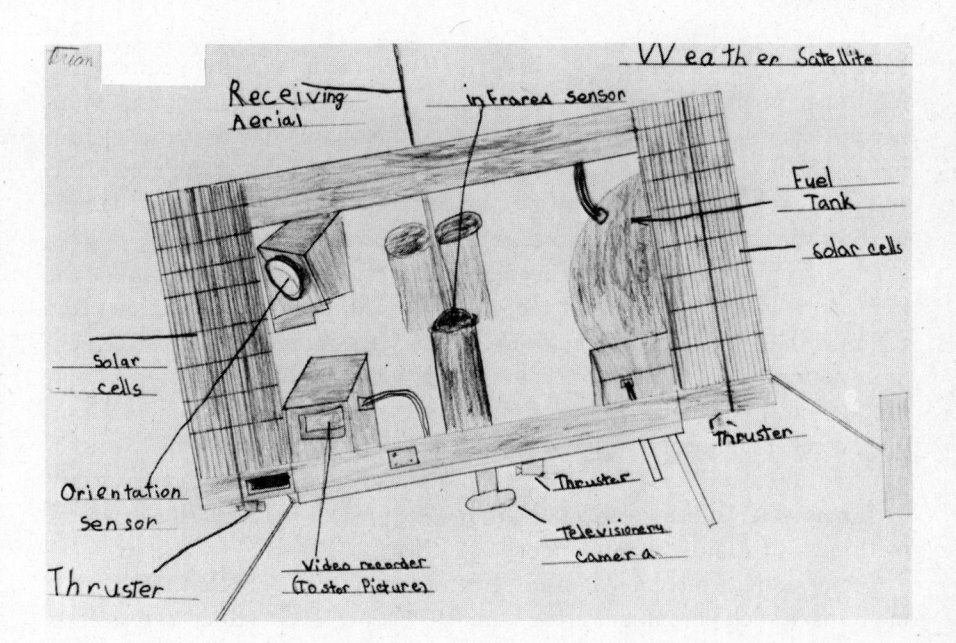

Weather Satellites

Weather satellites look down from space and transmit television pictures of the world below. The pictures show clouds, ice-caps, and snow, as well as land, and water. Weather satellites also detect infra-red rays that come from the earth giving pictures as well as temperature of land, sea, and air. The first Tiros was sent into orbit on April 1, 1960. When one Tiros ceases to operate NASA sends up another one to replace the old one. Tiros 1 was the first satellite designed to photograph weather on the earth.

Brian

Wind Vane

A wind vane shows which way the wind is blowing. The direction of the wind is important because this will tell you which way the wind is blowing and which way a storm or a snow fall will fall, north, south, east, or west. People need to prepare for changes in weather.

Cheryl

In-class Experiences and Activities that Serve to Integrate

All kinds of experiences and activities enhance the integrating process. Living things in the classroom, such as plants and gerbils, give dynamic input because they are always changing. Informal talk may be shared among classmates about these live resources. One young girl took the gerbil's membership in class quite literally. She enjoyed reading to it and even took the time to show the pictures so the gerbil could enjoy them!

Displays on any topic can bring about integration as children examine the items and share their knowledge of the topic with others. One teacher often begins a theme by placing one or two items on a display table. As the children notice the table, they bring in like items to add. A simple example would be one or two leaves and a nut found on a walk around school. Gradually a collection of fall leaves and nuts common to the area could be accumulated to start off a study of leaf types and fruits borne from trees. Children may wish to bring collections that are personal hobbies. Rocks, shells, pictures—all stimulate oral language sharing.

Center activities enhance an integrating process. Rooms that use centers might have such permanent areas as math, writing, art, reading, and science. In addition, a theme center would be available that has specific materials and suggested activities pertaining to current class study. Centers are not places where children perform specific activities; they are resource areas where children have the freedom to explore ideas because the available materials can be used in a variety of ways. Activities may be suggested but they are only a starting point for exploration.

The weather center contained idea sheets to test out. There were books with experiments to try as well as a wide variety of materials. In addition to a thermometer there was a light bulb to be used as a heat source and materials from which children could make a rain gauge. A graph for recording the actual weather was kept here and compared with the *Farmer's Almanac*. Resource books were available. Several books posed leading questions: "Rain falls from clouds; does snow fall from clouds?" In one poetry book, a marker was placed that read "Here is one poem about wind. Can you find another on wind or weather that you like?"

The latter suggestion led several children out of the weather center and into the reading area where they looked through poetry collections to find poems they particularly liked. One youngster wrote her own poetry book to share. Each page was carefully designed and decorated in a variety of art media to reflect the verse written on it. Blue and purple watercolor washes with sparkles were on one sheet; orange, peach, and yellow rubbings lined another, with a bright sun shining; and a collage of tissue-paper snowflakes with cotton clouds adorned yet another. Susie, the author, titled her book after one of her verses: "The Rain Makes Me Shiver." How many specific examples can you find of metaphor use? Which sensory images are the strongest for you as a reader? Susie has relied upon her own sensory experiences for this poetry but obviously has been influenced by poetic language. What kinds of book and poetry selections would you recommend to her based upon this sample of her work?

The rain is falling fast,
it sparkles in the
moonlight and gives me
a chill.

The snow is
cold, it lies on the
ground
like a
twinkling white sheet.

The sun is glowing
bright in my eyes,
it is shining
like a golden crown.

The leaves are
falling fast,
they are many
colors like yellow,
green, brown, and
orange.

The rain is falling
from the sky like
sheets of dazzling
diamonds.

Walking in the
slush is like stepping
on squished tomatoes,
when you stomp on
slushy stuff it squirts
right, left, up, and down.

The rain makes me
shiver, the air is cold
and the wind is blowing
furiously.

The snow is icy cold
against my feet,
there's a chill going up
my back.

The sun is like
a ball of golden
light, it gleams down
on the earth and
keeps us warm.

The wind is blowing
hard, my hair is
swaying in the wind
as the sun goes down.

The snow is
falling hard,
the snowflakes
are the size
of quarters,
I feel like
I'm walking on
a stiff
pillow.

The leaves feel
like paper with
stems in the middle,
when you step on them
they crinkle up.

The rain is shining
bright as it hits the
roof, it sounds like
mice squeaking.

When the leaves fall
all the branches from
the trees are bare, as the
wind whistles
the air is
cool.

The grass is dark
green, when I sit on
the ground the grass
feels like a scratchy
sponge.

The sun is
shining like a gigantic
orange, when it's real
hot it means it's squeezing
warmth on us.

Behind the center was a graffiti board on which weather sayings were placed. "If you don't like the weather now, wait two minutes and it will change." "It's hot enough to fry an egg on the sidewalk!" "Raining cats and dogs." "Pea-soup fog." Children in the class were encouraged to add their own favorite weather adages.

Out-of-class Experiences and Activities that Serve to Integrate

The simplest experience is to step outside the school door and use the playground as the sensory base. The activity where the children went out to "greet the sun" is one good example of this. In the weather theme, *The Cloud Book* was a starting point for observing the movement and shapes of clouds as they passed or hung over the school. Thermometers placed near the building, in the shelter of some bushes and out in the open, told of the influences of shelter versus open space on temperatures. Rain and wind gauges and a weather vane provided further weather information. All of these simple activities encourage talk of comparing, describing, hypothesizing, and the writing of information with tentative conclusions drawn that can be checked in classroom readings.

One class studying architecture walked in a two-block area around the school. They found examples of "dentils," "scales," and other forms of designs. The doors in these old homes were particulary interesting in their details.

Study Trips. Study trips are events that are memorable, not just because they are concrete experiences but because they are experiences shared by the entire group. Shared experiences nurture class interaction. Conversational and working exchanges are based on similar frames of reference, making detailed background information unnecessary. The concreteness of trips provides a basis on which to attach vocabulary labels. Children can bind personal happenings to developing concepts. By participating in a study trip youngsters see the integrated experience as it occurs in a natural setting.

When is the best timing for such a trip? The scheduling may vary. This adventure may begin a theme or culminate it. The middle appears most promising, for once children attain some knowledge of a topic, a trip may stimulate further investigation with renewed interest. If the trip is neither long nor expensive, the group may go more than once.

Study trips can be made to a farm, a grocery store, or a restaurant to see the food development and distribution chain. Some journeys may be simple or confined in their purpose while others are complex, such as visiting a large nearby city. Typical trips of visiting historical sites, museums of art, science, and history, and a zoo can be most worthwhile if defined and refined in their purpose. A visit planned to provide a global view often means that children see little; a focused study, on the other hand, can reveal a great deal. For instance, in an historical site of an older home, one group of youngsters may study food. What kinds were available? How was it prepared and stored? Where did the ingredients come from? Another group may look at social life. What did the family do for entertainment? Who visited and for how long did they stay? How often did visitors arrive? What kinds of games, music, and activities took place in the evenings? Compare these group-study focuses to simply setting children loose to wander around an historical building with no questions in mind and no answers or discoveries with which to return to the classroom.

Some places may be visited more than once for entirely separate purposes.

In the weather unit a park was revisited. The initial trip centered on the combined themes of patterns, movement, and texture to be found in the natural environment. The weather study looked at temperature variation, clouds, and the effects of rainfall.

Although most study trips do include the whole class, not all need to do so. Part of the class may go with a special focus. The remaining students could be left with a team teacher if that is the school organization. Perhaps the principal would take the class on, or they could be dispersed among other classes. When a group has a unique experience they have something special to share with the rest of the class. The language this group needs to use to relate their project requires refinement to achieve clarity. These students must have a clear sense of audience in order to share their trip because the other students have not had their experience.

Study Trip Booklets. A study trip booklet helps to focus observations. A well-prepared booklet offers choice yet provides guidelines so that students are aware of their responsibilities. When parents accompany small groups, the booklets can involve the parents in the learning process. They also help youngsters bring back the observations they have made. The questions elicit at least two kinds of writing: poetic language in thought ramblings and descriptive language in close observations. Imaginative writing is common.

This booklet is usually based upon student and teacher plans about the trip and includes suggested observations with careful questions to guide the observer. There is a page for a thought rambling plus an additional sheet for notes about group plans and work. Space is also given for an individual project, which may be a written description or a sketch or rubbing—perhaps both. Sometimes a schedule for the trip is provided at the beginning. The example is a study trip booklet from the weather unit. Some activities are for the total class. Others are for groups and for individual response.

The sample on pages 289–293 is of a highly structured booklet; not all need to be so directive. By studying the study trip booklets of the children, a teacher can see how an idea arose and was developed into a final product. Working with the children, teachers can assist in the process of developing a written product.

Materials. The kinds of materials available to record the in- and out-of-door activities influence the quality of the experience and language produced as a result. Diversity is the key. In-class recording seems easier, for one would imagine all the media would be present. The organization of these materials is essential. Are they accessible? Clearly labeled? In sufficient quantity?

WEATHER
Study Trip: Darby Creek Metropolitan Park

Name: _____

Take some time to REALLY look around. Sniff the air. Shut your eyes. What do you feel? How are you feeling? What are you thinking? Put those thoughts on paper in the form of a *THOUGHT RAMBLING*.

GROUP PROJECT

What's the Temperature?

Together with 2 or 3 other people, complete the following activity.

Get a thermometer from the teacher.
Remember to write your temperatures in degrees F or degrees C.
You will have to wait about 3 minutes in each place to get an accurate reading.

What is the temperature in an open area?

What is the temperature in a wooded area?

How about the ground? Dig a small hole with your finger or with a stick. Gently put the thermometer in the hole. Be sure to cover the hole back in with the dirt you dug up.

Is there a difference in temperatures between the ground near a lot of vegetation (a lot of plants with roots) and the ground where there are no roots? Check it out.

INDIVIDUAL PROJECT
Choose A or B

A. What type of clouds are in the sky today? Do they look like good-weather clouds or bad-weather clouds? Make a sketch below of the clouds. What color are the clouds? White? Gray? Black? Of what do the shapes remind you?

or

B. Look in an open space. What do you see growing? Dig 6 to 10 inches into the ground. What is the moisture content? Examine the growth beneath a tree. How does it differ from the open space? Dig down 6 to 10 inches. What is the moisture like there as compared to the open space? Now look beneath a shrub. Do the same things. What do you find? What hypothesis can you make?

SCRATCH SHEET

For in- and out-of-door experiences, the types of materials may range from a sheet of paper and pencil for a thought rambling to a camera for recording sequence. Black-and-white film is inexpensive and gives clear results although immediate pictures are fun to work with and provide quick feedback to see if the picture reveals the intended view. Film is especially adaptable to language-experience-type writing. Sketching and drawing materials, which include such items as watercolors, pencils, pastels, oiled chalk, charcoal, and India ink, are helpful. A variety of papers, newsprint, art paper, construction paper, and tissue paper for collage, leads to a variety of interpretations, thus stimulating language for selecting, comparing, and hypothesizing. Media for impressions or molds extend the kinds of records that may be kept. Blueprint paper, plaster of Paris, crayons, and clay help fulfill this goal. Jars and bags for gathering assist specimen collections and aid in making collages.

Interpreting the Experience

Whether it be inside or outside the classroom, close by or at quite a distance, interpreting the experience utilizes many of the language-arts skills. The initial decision is how to share the experience appropriately. Should it be a chart, mural, collage, sketch, writing alone, drama, dance, maps, booklets, or photo display? Each should be accompanied by some writing, except perhaps the drama. The writing may be imaginative: telling a story of what has happened or what might have happened. Perhaps an explanation of how it was done could accompany the work.

Mounting children's products can enhance their value, thus helping to establish the goals of pride and careful work. Some youngsters have difficulty producing art or written compositions. If care is not taken, their work may look weak beside the rest of the class's. Here, a teacher can help by assisting each youngster to do his or her best job and then follow through to aid the product so that all will look as good as possible. Each child needs to make some personal contribution to the theme's display.

Much of the work that goes on during a project is never realized; that is, the work is not placed on display. A teacher who is aware of the processes going on recognizes this. It is the process of making the product that is significant, not the product itself. Thus, keeping records becomes exceedingly important. While interpreting the experience, the reason for going to books becomes apparent. An interest developed is followed. It should be noted once again that much of what is learned is not even shared, let alone interpreted. Choices must be made, and information gained may go unrecognized.

Language Arts in the Content Areas

This mounted picture depicts a tree in winter, a haven for birds, which several girls developed as a part of their weather unit. The writing is an explanation of how they achieved the results of their collage picture. Think of the work that was involved in each step and the discussions that took place to achieve this outcome!

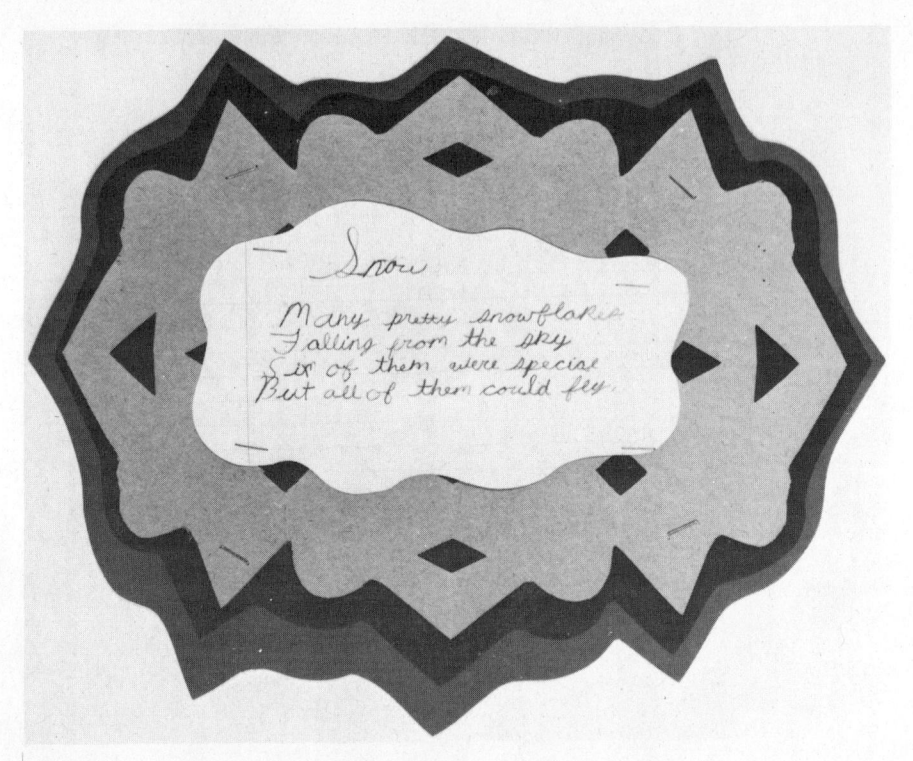

This poem was written by a girl who has some difficulty writing. The teacher-assisted mounting makes this poem look quite special. Confidence is built through pride in one's work.

The time to interpret from a field experience may extend over several days or even a week to several weeks if library resources and other materials are incorporated. One class continued their study of a lake by making a miniature pond in their class that served as further input to their theme. The children's time on projects will vary. Some will be so involved it will be difficult to have them draw conclusions so they can stop their study and move on to another area. Others will finish quickly. Flexible time blocks are of the essence. Is it reading, science, math, or perhaps all? Most youngsters do not need the same lesson.

Sharing Experiences

Display and oral sharing are two ways for children to present information they have learned. Each enhances the child's sense of self-worth. In a display, the quality of work meets the expectations of the teacher. High expectations involve the student in making thoughtful decisions about the content, the audience to be reached, and artistic merit. Working on a display can help to motivate children to put forth their best efforts if the display is attractive. Therefore, time spent on the appearance of the display is worthwhile. Teachers may wish to place some of their own work in a display, particularly at the beginning of the year, to indicate the value they place on this act. This will also model the quality of work expected.

Some writing should appear within each display. A variety of compositions will emerge. Some will explain how the display was made; others will be imaginative narratives. Poetic language of description or feelings may be exhibited. Labels and diagrams may be used.

Oral sharing may be done by an individual or a group. It is an opportunity to read aloud what has been written and a reason to listen to what is being read. Processes used may be explained, data-collection procedures described, and funny incidents told. Oral sharing allows the audience to question and is a time to elaborate on written material. It is a period of peer teaching.

In this simple display on weather, the children have made models of clouds to show the different types and hung them above the bulletin board. Weather maps with keys for reading the symbols, reports, booklets, and thought ramblings with accompanying pictures complete the display. Each youngster, with his or her own work mounted on this board, felt pleased with the effort made. (Mrs. Blazer's classroom, Highland Park School, Southwestern School District, Grove City, Ohio)

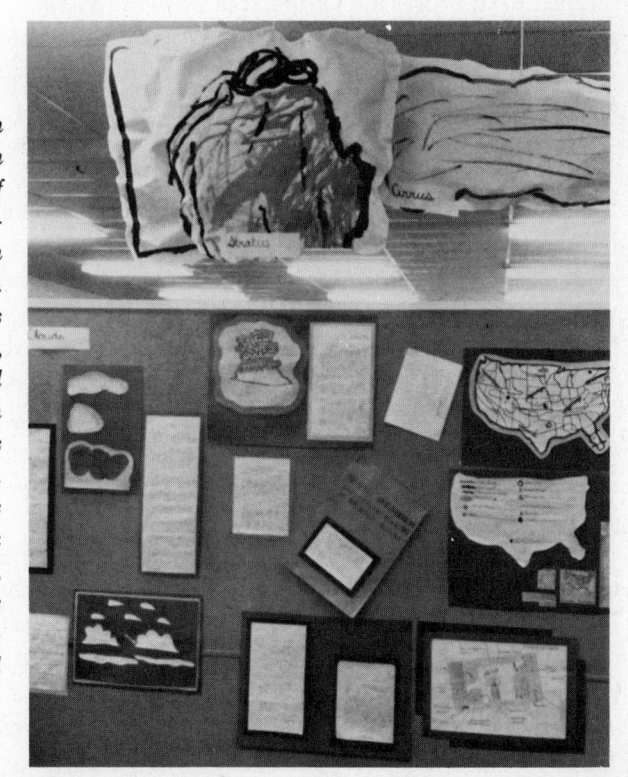

Once again the teacher sets the standard. Courtesy and attention are to be expected but with this expectation the oral sharing needs to be of a quality worth listening to. Constructive group questions and criticisms help to achieve this goal. Stressing what was especially liked or "good" is a positive criticism. Suggestions for trying to present in a different way may be given.

Opportunities for Assessing

Themes generate a functional need for skills. All the skills children need to learn within the school setting may occur naturally in a theme study. Teachers who keep anecdotal records, hold individual and group conferences, and maintain a folder of children's work are able to see and keep track of the development of these skills.

The weather study could serve to illustrate this point. Children learned to read weather maps and understand symbols for weather information. Perhaps these skills will transfer to other kinds of maps and symbols. They learned to interpret a diagram. The weather satellite is one example of this; the "Birth of a Tornado" is another. The real learners in this situation are not those who listened to the report but rather the child who drew the diagrams on the facing page.

This youngster clearly understands the formation of tornadoes. Even if the sequential diagrams were copies, the report obviously was not. To check the level of comprehension the teacher might ask the child to describe the birth of a tornado to another student in the room or to a student from another classroom.

Students read a thermometer and recorded the results. One studied the Beaufort scale. All learned the formula to convert Fahrenheit to centigrade. Specific vocabulary peculiar to weather was acquired, such as Celsius scale, centigrade, cumulus, cirrus, gale, precipitation, kinds of fronts—stationary, warm, cold—and anemometer. All the children will not remember all these terms. But many youngsters will remember many of them, particularly the ones closely tied to their individual or group report.

The students took notes by reading and skimming resource books and newspapers. They listened and reported on TV weather reporters' forecasts. Important study and library skills were practiced. Scott listed the references he used in his report on lightning, showing his ability to bring information together. Probably he cannot synthesize yet, but this is the first important step. Perhaps assistance in using the data chart described in chapter 6 will

Birth of a Tornado

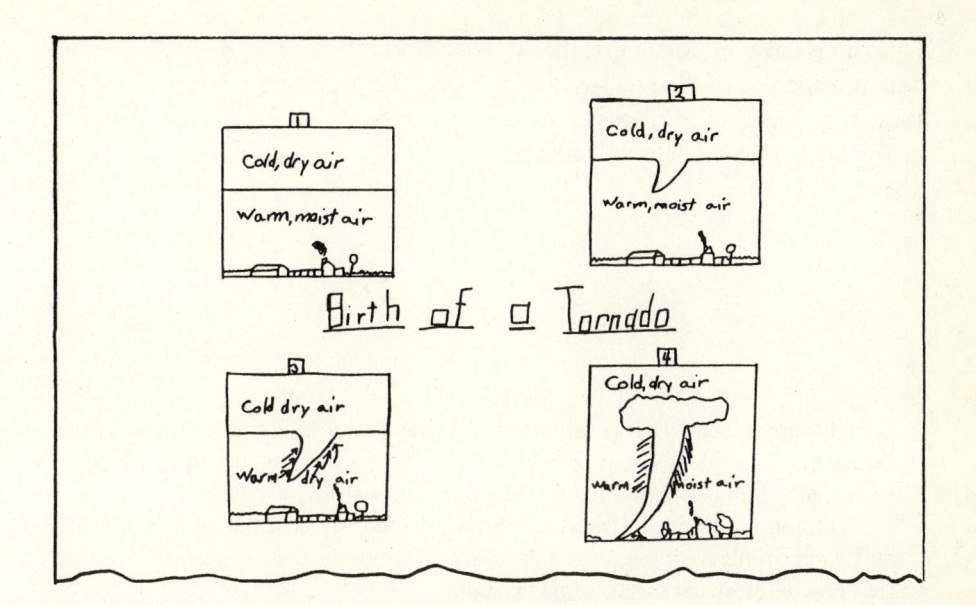

[Panel 1: Cold, dry air above Warm, moist air]
[Panel 2: Cold, dry air dipping into Warm, moist air]
[Panel 3: Cold dry air and Warm dry air with arrows]
[Panel 4: Cold, dry air with funnel extending into Warm, moist air]

Tornadoes are the most fiercest of natural storms. They are masses of spinning air. They last only a few minutes. Cold air is heavier than warm air so when cold air hits warm air it mostly goes under the warm air. A part of the cold air will break into the warm air and makes a funnel shaped section.

The warm air moves into the funnel shaped section and as it moves in it moves around spinning. The air in the tornado goes up to five hundred miles per hour. This makes it like a giant vacuum cleaner. Then it sucks in things and this makes it black so it can easily be seen even far away.

help him develop further skills in reporting. Group-report projects will enhance the use of "language to learn" that the group members will use as they work together to discover more about their topic of study. Such interaction encourages reflective language.

Scott
3/11/80

Lightning is attracted to tall things like trees and buildings and also metal things like cars, planes, and metal buildings. If lightning hits wood it will catch on fire. If it hits metal nothing will catch on fire, nothing will happen.

Lightning is caused by friction. Friction is made of dust particles, snow, ice, and water droplets rubbing together. In strong winds all those things rub together that creates electricity that forms lightning.

There are different kinds of lightning, sheet, heat, and ball. Sheet lightning covers the sky like a blanket. Heat lightning covers the sky like a blanket but it is a weaker color. Ball lightning consists of balls of lightning. They are as small as walnuts or as big as balloons. They last up to 3 to 6 seconds they fall to the ground and explode. Sometimes they roll along the ground untill it hits an obstacle. Ball lightning is the least understood form of lightning. Ball lightning does not appear to be dangerous.

Scott   The Books I Used

1. *World Book Encyclopedia*, V. 12
2. *Storms—from the inside out*
3. *Storms* Irving & Ruth Adler

Children applied critical thinking when they compared the *Farmer's Almanac* predictions to the National Weather Bureau's and compared weather forecasts among the local TV stations. One youngster developed categories for reasons why there is lightning and surveyed the class. Her reasons included: God turning a light switch on and off, Shazam, giant firefly, God striking the devil, and angels looking out of a door in heaven. When she asked other students what they had been told about lightning, they said it was a streak of fire or left-over rain. They said thunder was Mother Nature falling out of bed, Mother Nature clapping her hands, or God tearing down a brick wall. She wrote about her survey:

> I have been working on weather folktales, and I thought it would be intresting to find what our parents tell us or told us what thunder and lightning are. So I took a survey asking people in the building what there parents told them. I went to Miss Frett, Mrs. Keller, Miss Charles and Mrs. Potter's room.

The kinds and functions of language used both orally and written were broad. Language worked naturally to achieve a goal; it was not a purpose in and of itself. Practice was gained in sharing information well, whether it be oral or a written first draft, not as part of an isolated language exercise. Theme studies are truly a way to integrate the language arts.

To assess the total theme, a sheet was developed for children to fill out. The sheet fulfilled two functions: it gave the teacher another view of what each youngster had learned and it gave each child an opportunity for self-evaluation. A follow-up conference based on this completed form by student and teacher would enrich this evaluation experience.

WEATHER EVALUATION

Name _____
Date _____

I'm interested in hearing the kinds of things you've learned about weather. Please answer these questions to help me evaluate your work and the unit.

1. List the names of other people you worked with.
2. What was the topic you were studying?
3. Did you write about this topic *and* do an illustration or other type of extension? Yes   No
4. List three things you learned from your topic:
   1.
   2.
   3.
5. List three things you learned from listening to other people share their weather projects.
   1.
   2.
   3.
6. Why is studying the weather important?
7. How would you grade your project?

   Excellent   Good   All right   Not my   Poorly
                                  best work   done

In this first section of the chapter we have shown why language arts is an integral part of content-area studies and how you as teachers can use these opportunities to extend children's growth in language. Language growth is not necessarily the outcome of all curricular activities. The teacher needs to plan and work with children to establish a learning community that supports the development of language skill.

The following section is removed from the first discussion because it deals solely with the study of language itself. The teacher's role is not to interject language learning but rather to help students learn more about the nature of language itself. Language is part of the world about them and therefore worthy of study.

Language as a Content Area

The focus of this text has been to show that children develop proficiency in a language not by talking about it but by using it. However, there is also a reason for children to examine language itself, to explore the way language works, which, we wish to point out, does not suggest that children need to learn grammatical rules. For years grammar was emphasized because it was said to improve children's ability to write or to learn a foreign language even though research strongly suggested that these reasons for grammatical study were unfounded. Boreas (1917) found a higher correlation between achievement in grammar and mathematics than between achievement in grammar and composition or oral language abilities. A number of other researchers have found that a knowledge of English grammar does not aid one's ability to learn a second language. Finally, both Miller (1951) and Macaulay (1947) found that even when grammar is carefully taught, little grammatical knowledge is retained over time. What these researchers were studying was the effect of teaching grammar rules such as:

The verb form *was* is used with singular subjects.
The verb form *were* is used with plural subjects and with the pronoun *you*, even if it refers only to one person.

Such prescriptive rules, which tell students how they should form their utterances, have very little, if any, effect on a student's language.

What Teachers Need to Know About Grammar

While children do not need to learn grammar rules, teachers do need to know something about them. Because of the influence of the "back-to-the-basics" movement, children's language-arts textbooks are including large segments on the teaching of grammar rules. A problem exists because grammar is a word with different meanings for different people. We are using the term "grammar" to mean a set of rules that illustrate how language works. Even so, disparity occurs because there are different sets of rules with different purposes. Classroom teachers, who in all probability will receive a set of language-arts textbooks for their children to use, need to know the most common models of grammar to better understand and thus better use the classroom texts. The decision may be to refer to the texts only as resources rather than initiating language study or to use only particular sections of the texts.

Three types of grammar have had the most influence on classroom practice: traditional, structural, and transformational-generative. Traditionally grammar has been viewed as analyzing language by labeling parts of speech, diagraming sentences, and choosing between correct and incorrect speech patterns. The objective of a grammar class was to teach students how they ought to talk and write: a prescriptive approach. Since those who wrote the first books on English grammar had a strong background in Latin, they described English in terms of Latin structure. Cases were discussed, even though English, unlike Latin, is not inflected for case. Verb tenses were described as they were in Latin, making for a less than perfect match.

Structural linguists took a different view by approaching language as a science. To them grammar was not prescriptive but rather descriptive, describing how people actually do speak. Classes of words are discussed functionally; for example, a noun is not defined as the name of a person, place, or thing, but rather in terms of how it behaves. Therefore, a noun is a word which can be made plural or possessive and may be preceded by determiners, such as "the," "an," or "a." Sentences are grouped by basic sentence patterns that can be changed by expansion or substitution. In other words, to analyze sentences, structural linguists look at surface structure. Sentences are grouped by pattern types; for example, all the following sentences have the same pattern:

Birds sing loudly.
Children play happily.
Martha sews beautifully.

Other linguists, who use a transformational-generative grammar model, point out that this kind of analysis does not explain ambiguities that occur. For example, the sentence "We are starving children" can have two very different meanings. Transformationalists suggest that the language we hear and read is the surface structure of language, but there is also a deep structure. Understanding the deep structure can explain the relationships of these sentences, all of which have very different surface structures, but which are obviously related by meaning:

The boy hit the ball.
Did the boy hit the ball?
The ball was hit by the boy.
Was the ball hit by the boy?

Transformationalists use insights to develop a model of language that can account for such relationships. They see grammar as a set of rules that will generate all of the grammatical sequences of a language and none of the ungrammatical ones. To analyze sentences, showing and discovering the relationship between surface and deep structure, "tree" diagrams are used. The focus of this particular grammar is to explain how language might be generated. This theory provided the basis for much of the early work in the sixties on child language acquisition.

Other significant grammar models exist that have influenced language research such as case grammar, but these models do not appear within children's language-arts textbooks even though findings based upon these theories may influence the kinds of activities being recommended for children.

What Children Could Learn About Language

Just as children explore the phenomena of their world so too they can explore language. Children who hypothesize, question, and explain as they work with batteries and bulbs to learn about electricity will use language in many of the same ways as they try to find out just how far you can extend one single sentence.

Within the linguistic system there exists much flexibility. Sentence patterns can change from active to passive and elements within a sentence can be moved about. One need not instruct children in techniques for using language flexibly; however, it can be worthwhile to help them become conscious of the grammatical knowledge they have already acquired. Chomsky (1980) proposes "linguistic awareness sessions." Such sessions should not be based on worksheets or workbooks; rather, they should spring from the children's own oral and written language. As children learn to manipulate sentences they have spoken and written, they can become increasingly aware of the structure of English.

Language Explorations for Primary-grade Children. In English, word order is extremely important. Children who are native speakers use word order effectively. The following explorations springing from children's own language simply bring certain aspects of language systems to the level of awareness. An experience story written by a group of second-graders contained the following sentences:

Bobby fed the baby goat.
The big goat chased Mrs. Snow.

The teacher cut the sentences apart so the children could move words about to make new sentences. They giggled at the images the new sentences created:

> The baby goat fed Bobby.
> Mrs. Snow chased the big goat.
> The goat fed baby Bobby.
> Big Mrs. Snow chased the goat.

They discovered that certain word arrangements were not possible. One does not say such things as:

> Goat the Bobby fed baby.
> Mrs. the big goat chased Snow.

Such manipulations of sentences make the relationship of word order to meaning explicitly clear.

The teacher can help children see that certain kinds of words will fit into certain slots in a sentence by taking a sentence from their own writing, removing one word, and asking them to think of other words that might possibly fill that slot.

> Bobby fed the goat.
>   pets
>   watched
>   sits on

They will find some words such as "little" and "barn" are not possible entries for that particular slot and that other words cannot be selected unless other words are also added, such as "plays with" or "looks at." Using the very same sentence, the children can work to find words to fill another slot.

> Bobby fed the goat.
>   my
>   Tom's
>   that

If children are permitted to expand this sentence, they will find that they can say, "the great big goat" or "the brown and white goat" but not "great big the goat," which suggests that modifying words have a systematic word order.

While categorization of words is helpful, learning the traditional definitions of the parts of speech is not. To know the old textbook definition of a noun as "the name of a person, place, or thing" is not as helpful as knowing that one word can serve a variety of functions depending on its placement in a sentence. The word "spring," for example, has a different function in each of the following sentences: "The deer will spring away if startled." "Spring is the gentle season." "It was a spring day." Children will enjoy searching for words that can switch categories such as "pet," "box," "ship," and "book." A realization that words may have different meanings in different positions is knowledge that is much more valuable than being able to recite that "a noun is the name of a person, place or thing."

Language Explorations for Middle-grade Children. Language explorations for older children can help them develop a greater sensitivity to the nuances of meaning that language can express. This aspect of language has been beautifully described in Hunter's book *A Sound of Chariots*. In this book, Bridie, a young girl, has written an essay, "A Description of the Sea," to be turned in to her teacher. Hunter writes of Bridie's efforts:

> ... she had taken time over it, lovingly choosing and picking among her pirates' treasure of words for the ones that had the right sound and color about them, carefully fitting them together like a mosaic in one penciled draft after another till the final pattern had been achieved (p. 45).

When the essay is returned, her teacher has covered it with red marks, changing words and word order, which infuriates Bridie because the "corrections" would change the "feel" of the essay. Her fury is so great that she defies her teacher and refuses to rewrite the passage. The teacher whips Bridie for insolence, but the punishment is interrupted by the headmistress who stops the whipping and asks to see the essay. Bridie had written "And waves like green broken glass fell jaggedly down." The sentence had been changed to read, "broken green glass." When the headmistress asked if there were any real difference in the two wordings, Bridie tried to explain:

> "Broken green glass—it's just ordinary, just what it says. 'Broken green glass.' A bottle, a dish, anything ordinary."
> "Well, the other way," she tried again, "it's *not* ordinary anymore because the sound has a sort of pattern to it. You know—like the notes of a song, rising and falling. And changing the order of the words to 'green broken glass'—well it makes them look different, mysterious all of a sudden ... as if they had a sort of magic about them ..." (p. 47).

This kind of sensitivity to words grows from both an input of literary language and the opportunities to play with language, to move words about in order to create a certain texture in one's writing. The teacher's selection of books to read aloud whose language has such beauty of phrasing will provide the literary input.

Secondly, children need to be given time and assistance as they work with their own writing. For example, children can be helped to see how meaning is shaded by the arrangement of phrases within a sentence. Taking a sentence like "The boy saw the cat at the window," children can move the prepositional phrase to create the new sentences "The boy at the window saw the cat" and "At the window the boy saw the cat." To discover how moving this one phrase changes the emphasis of the sentence, children can create the questions that each sentence could answer.

Which boy saw the cat?
The boy at the window saw the cat.

What did the boy see?
The boy saw the cat at the window.

Where did the boy see the cat?
At the window the boy saw the cat.

The development of a sense of the "purposefulness" of word placement can bring about an awareness of how meaning can be clarified and sharpened by the way a sentence is shaped.

Languages not only vary from country to country but also from region to region within a country. Just as it is important for children to accept those who speak another language, so too is it important for them to accept people who speak a different dialect. Miel (1967) conducted a study designed to see how schools in suburban communities prepare children to live in a world peopled by men and women of different nationalities, races, religions, and economic backgrounds. She found that

> ... the child of suburbia ... tends to be a striver in school, a conformist, and above all a believer in being "nice," polite, clean and tidy. Besides dividing humanity into the black and the white, the Jew and the Christian, the rich and the poor, he is also apt to classify people as "smart" or "dumb," "clean" or "dirty" and "nice" and "not nice" (p. 43).

She found that the latter categories were often based on the way a person spoke. People who did not speak English or who spoke with an accent were frequently viewed as "not nice." Helping children learn that dialects are a part of language, that, indeed, everyone speaks a dialect, can help them to accept speech that varies from their own. Further, any exploration of dialect should help children discover how dialect adds a richness to language.

Dialectical differences are more than quaint and amusing because each dialect has its own power and own beauty. Still's book *Jack and the Wonder*

Beans is a delightful retelling of "Jack and the Beanstalk" in Appalachian dialect. The dialect gives the tale a fresh and wonderful flavor:

> The giant waked and took after him. And did Jack skedaddle! You could of shot marbles on his shirt tail (1977, unpaged).

A comparison of this tale with an original version can help children see how dialect can create a special texture in writing.

What Children Can Learn About the Difference Between Oral and Written Language

Written language is not "talk written down." If oral language were written down, it would often appear to be ungrammatical since speakers do not necessarily use complete sentences. A speaker may start out to say something one way and then shift mid-sentence, creating a verbal erasure. Because of this there may be subjects that do not agree with predicates and pronouns with no referrents. At other times one word or a sentence fragment makes up a completely intelligible response when the dialogue that surrounds it is taken into account. For example, "What are you giving your mother for her birthday?" Response, "A book." There is no need to answer in a complete sentence; in fact, such a sentence may sound awkward or unnatural in the conversation. The fabric of the dialogue contains much meaning that need not be stated or restated.

A technique to help upper elementary children look at the differences between oral and written language is to have them tell a story into a tape-recorder, then write that story down. The oral and the written versions can be compared. In which version were the sentences longer or shorter? Was the vocabulary the same? How did each version begin and end? Another way to examine the difference between oral and written language is to see how authors write conversation. In the book by the Cleavers, *Where the Lilies Bloom,* Mary Call talks to Mr. Connell about her plans to collect and sell medicinal plants:

> "You going to turn wildcrafter, Mary Call? Sure enough?"
> "Yes, sir," I said. "Sure enough. And so I need to know the prices you and the botanist will pay and should we look for everything or just some things?"
> "Oh, look for everything," crowed Mr. Connell and hopped over to the wall and yanked down a price list from a hook. "But right now it's the time for leaves. Boneset and deer's-tongue and catnip and wintergreen and o' course the witch

hazel. Then comes fall you go out and dig for your roots. Bark you can go after any time. Looka here. You see this? Ginseng is bringing thirty dollars a pound right now. Thirty dollars a pound, Mary Call!"

(1969, p. 53)

In looking at this passage to see how the authors caught the flavor of oral language on the printed page, you can see the use of dialect:

"looka here"
"sure enough"
"come fall"

Some phrases are punctuated as sentences:

"Boneset and deer's-tongue and catnip and wintergreen and o' course the witch hazel."

"Thirty dollars a pound, Mary Call."

Some words have been spelled in a way to reflect the way speech sounds:

"o' course"
"looka here"

If you were to rewrite what Mr. Connell said without the use of conversation, the passage would sound quite different. It could read:

Mr. Connell told Mary Call to look for every kind of plant she could find. He said that it was just the right time to look for leaves such as boneset, deer's-tongue, catnip, wintergreen, and witch hazel.

Just as the Cleavers conveyed the way a conversation sounded, so are all who write able to show how the written text should sound if read aloud. Punctuation is the convention used to mark the pauses that segment language. Wherever a speaker would pause in discourse, a mark of punctuation is needed in a written text. A period signals a stop and a probable drop in intonation. A question mark signals a stop and generally a rise in intonation. Commas, semicolons, and colons signal briefer pauses. This relationship between oral language and punctuation is an important one for children to discover. Children's writing, often free of the needed punctuation marks, can be read aloud with the proper intonation and pauses. The children may then mark punctuation to reflect what they are hearing.

Choosing Words to Shape Thought

Persuasive Language. Language can also be varied purposely in order to slant a message and to persuade to a point of view. Advertisers and editorial writers select words with care in order to change people's thinking. It is frequently suggested that children study the various propaganda techniques used by the writers of advertisements. These techniques are:

Snob appeal	Transfer
Name-calling	Testimonial
Glittering generalities	Bandwagon
Plain folks	

Children can collect ads and then decide how the writer is trying to persuade them to purchase the product, according to the categories of propaganda techniques.

Another approach that would help children focus upon particular words is to have small groups of children collect ads for one particular type of product. They can list the words used most frequently to describe their products. Several groups of children collected these words found in ads for four different types of products:

Cigarettes	*Toys*	*Appliances*	*Cosmetics*
new	imagination	safe	enriched
taste idea	thrills	most efficient	precious oils
⅓ less tar	educational	new	makes a difference
99% tar free	fun-packed	automatic	soft
pleasure	lovable	carefree	silkier
better taste	huggable	space-saving	plus
cooler	safer	more powerful	nourishes
ultra light	most popular	easy to clean	creamier
slim	learn	adjustable	protects
	love	easier	noticeably
	newer	most convenient	gentler
	soft	guaranteed	more natural
		larger capacity	new

In the discussion that followed, children were able not only to identify the qualities deemed most important for each type of product, but also to note how language was used to display the benefits of each group of products. Comparison was used frequently:

creamier   easier
best buy   better than
safer than   lowest
most powerful

The most powerful word they decided was the word "new." It appeared in all categories, not once but many times. The children also compared the way the ads were written. The most information-packed ads were the ones for appliances; the ads with the least text were those for cigarettes. Children were quickly aware of why this was so.

With this knowledge in mind the children wrote their own ads for a selected product. While it is not necessary for children to become apprentice ad writers, it is important for them to become aware of how language is used to persuade and influence. In exploring the way others have used language and most of all in writing their own passages of persuasion, children can become more critical in their listening and in their reading.

Metaphor. While comparison is used in ads to make a potential buyer prefer one product over another, the writer can use comparison to create an image in the reader's mind. The poet frequently compares one thing in terms of another. Worth (1976), for example, compares a safety pin to both a fish and a shrimp. Holman (1973) sees a person in an elevator as a bubble being sipped up through a drinking straw.

The poet's use of metaphoric language can lead children to see how they can use comparison in their own writing. Some comparisons are old and tired ones, so shopworn that they have become clichés:

quiet as a mouse
good as gold
slow as molasses
poor as a church mouse

A graffiti board is a good place to collect clichés. Later children can select a cliché and rewrite it in a variety of ways. Molasses does pour out of a jar slowly, but are there other things that also move slowly?

What Children Should Learn About Words

Language is not static. It changes and grows. The slang of today will be dated in three or four years. Words like "groovy" and "hip" are as outmoded for today's youngsters as such expressions as "twenty-three skidoo" and "the cat's meow." Some words drop out of language. A look at nursery rhymes will let children find words that are rarely if ever used in current speech. One seldom talks of

tuffets	gruel
curds and whey	pease porridge
victuals	counting houses

Some words have changed meaning over time. The word "nice" today is simply a word of approval, but at one time it meant simple, foolish, or ignorant. The word "silly" today is applied to someone who is foolish. Years and years ago it meant innocent, happy, blessed, or prosperous.

One can see history in the changes in the English language. The long Roman occupation of the British Isles is marked by place names such as Lancaster, Chester, Worcester. All have as part of their name a derivation of the Latin word *castra,* which means "camp."

The Anglo-Saxon occupation of Britain was the beginning of English as it is known today. Many of the most common English words are Anglo-Saxon, words such as "drink," "sleep," "come," "be." When the Normans invaded England in 1066, they brought with them their religion, government, and a more elegant life-style. While the language of the peasant remained Anglo-Saxon, the language of that of the court became French. The French added more than 10,000 words to the English language at that time—words that reflect the Normans' status as rulers of government, church, and court life, such as:

government	saint	robe
nation	religion	satin
jury	vestry	dance
justice	prayer	dinner

But it is not only invasion that brings words from one language into another. Languages borrow words from other languages. This can easily be seen if one looks at the way food words have entered English.

coffee	Arabic
sauerkraut	German

pizza	Italian
chile	Spanish
tea	Chinese
candy	Persian
squash	Native American
soufflé	French
bagel	Yiddish
goulash	Hungarian
sukiaki	Japanese
borscht	Russian

In addition to discovering words that English has borrowed from other languages, it is interesting for children to learn what words other nations have borrowed from English. Despite strenuous efforts by the Académie Française to keep the French language from becoming Anglicized, English words are liberally sprinkled in French speech, with "Franglais" words such as:

le blue jean	*le rock*
le weekend	*le jazz*
le snackbar	*le knockout*
le self-service	*le cowboy*
le sandwich	*le businessman*
le hot dog	*le parking*
le hamburger	*le camping*

Languages also grow because new discoveries, new products, and new ideas need a label and, therefore, a new word must be coined. Terms such as "astronaut," "food processor," "microwave," "stereo," and "women's lib" were all coined after World War II.

There are many books that can help children find out about the history of language and of words. A few of these books are:

Asimov, Isaac, *Words from History,* Houghton Mifflin, Boston, 1968.
    Two hundred fifty words that have their roots in history, such as "marathon," "sabotage," "cravat" are identified and their stories given.

Grenfeld, Howard, *Summer Is Icumen in: Our Ever Changing Language,* Crown, New York, 1978.
    Shows how the English language has changed over ten centuries.

Horowitz, Edward, *Words Come in Families,* Hart, New York, 1977.
    A look at root words as the building blocks of language.

Hunt, Bernice Kohn, *The Watchamacallit Book,* illustrated by Tomie dePaola, G. P. Putnam's Sons, New York, 1976.
A delightful compendium of labels for those objects usually called "thingamajigs," such as the little piece that holds on a lamp shade or the metal rim that holds a gem in place on a piece of jewelry.

Laird, Charlton and Laird, Helene, *The Tree of Language,* World, New York, 1957.
Contains a brief history of English along with a collection of "word stories."

Lindquist, Lilly and Wachner, Clarence, *General Language: English and Its Foreign Relations,* Holt, Rinehart and Winston, New York, 1962.
Shows how many languages have contributed to English. Written with the purpose of providing introductory experiences with foreign languages.

O'Neill, Mary, *Words Words Words,* Doubleday, New York, 1966.
Verses about words—their nuances and their power.

Schwartz, Alvin, *Chin Music: Tall Talk and Other Talk,* J. B. Lippincott, New York, 1979.
A wonderfully amusing collection of the funny words people have made up such as "snitch," "busticate," and "dudfoozled."

In addition to considering how words enter a language, children can become aware of how words enter their own vocabularies. Just as words come into a language because there is a need for that particular word, so too do words enter a person's vocabulary. New experiences create a need for new vocabulary. When children have an opportunity to try out the art of pottery, they will have a need to talk about a potter's wheel, glaze, slip, and kilns.

New experiences can also extend and deepen meanings for words that are already in someone's vocabulary. While "jump" is a word in the vocabulary of even very young children, experience and wide reading will broaden their understanding of that word through the years. They will find that not only can they jump, but they can jump rope, jump bid, and jump someone's checker. It is possible to jump town, jump bail, jump the gun, and jump a claim. Film can jump and trains can jump the track. If you are quick, you can get the jump on someone else, but eventually you will reach the jumping-off place.

Words are related in a number of different ways. Synonyms are words that mean the same thing (shout and yell, cry and weep, complete and finish). Antonyms are words that are opposite in meaning (hot and cold, short and tall, lazy and energetic). Homographs are words that look the same but sound different and have different meanings (The dove sat on the nest./He dove into the pool.). Homophones are words that sound the same but have different spellings (son and sun, air and heir, reign and rain). Children enjoy collecting such words. Homonyms are the basis for puns. From third and fourth grade on up, children delight in this kind of word fun.

Another way of helping children see relationships of words is to examine affixes. For example, once children figure out that "bi-" means "two" they can see that they know the meanings of a large family of words:

bicycle	binocular
bifocal	bipartisan
bilateral	bisect
biplane	bicentennial
biped	bivalve
bilingual	bicolor

Word webbing is another way to search out relationships. All the words listed that begin with the prefix "bi-" are examples of one kind of a relationship. Words can also be related thematically. The web on page 317 is a thematic one developed around the word "apple." The group that developed this web did so by searching their experiences to find "apple connections."

Another kind of web will send students to dictionaries and books on language to search for historical connections, to books on language and to literature to look for metaphorical connections. This kind of web has a cognitive base.

Summary

Language study is a discipline just as the sciences, mathematics, and social sciences are disciplines. Children use and live in a language environment from which they can make inquiries about the nature of language, its systems, and its uses. The purpose of such study is not to produce linguists any more than the study of a science must produce scientists. Rather, the goal is to respond to student interests about the language they use and help them discover attributes about this discipline. We are proposing that children can *use* language to learn about language. Language as a topic of study is worthy of close examination because it is the most powerful tool humans possess. For further ideas of language phenomena to study, see chapter 2.

Suggested Learning Experiences

1. As a group, visit a site you feel would be a good place for children to explore. Try to stay away from the usual zoo or museum trips and instead

APPLE

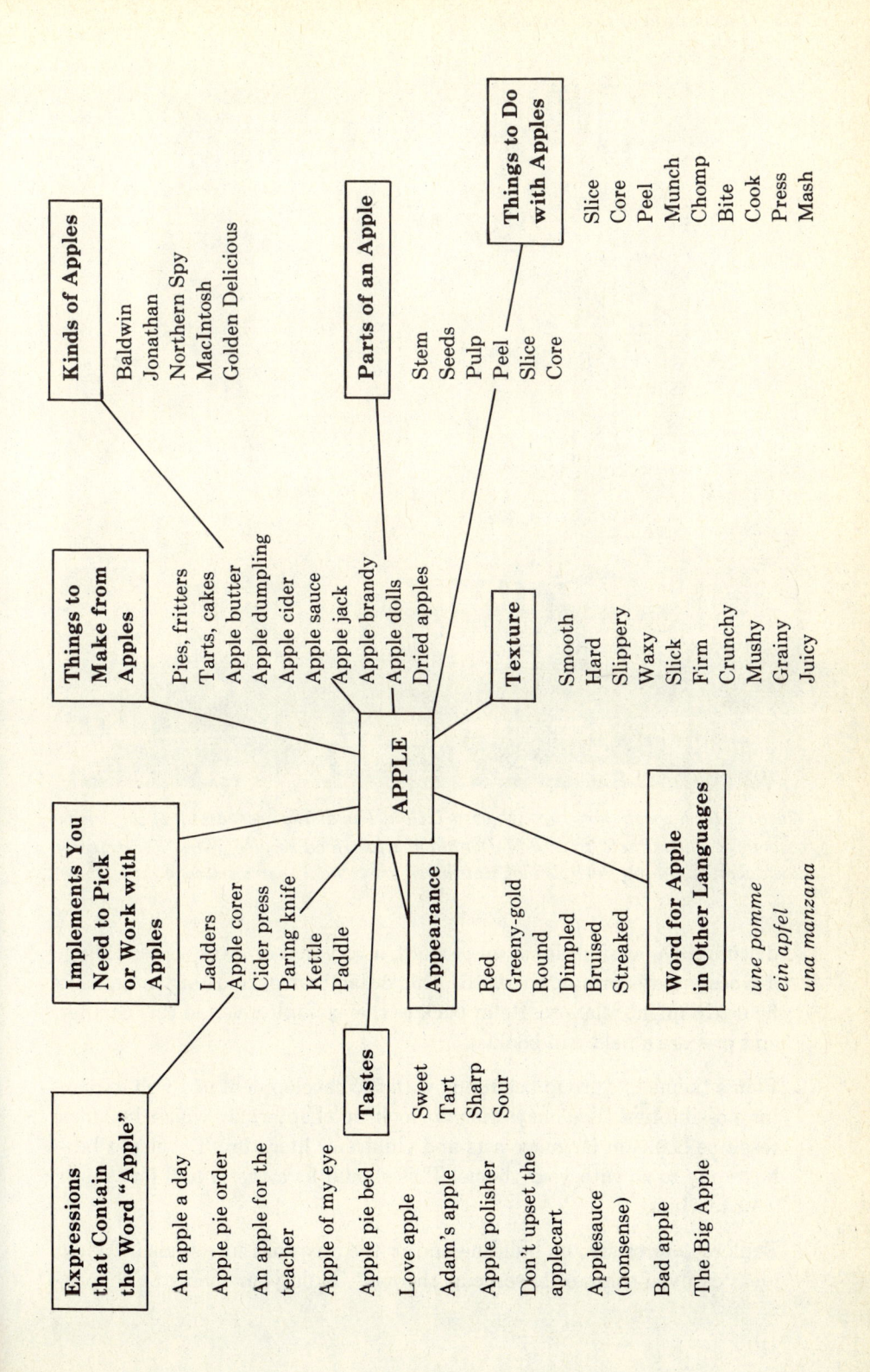

Expressions that Contain the Word "Apple"
- An apple a day
- Apple pie order
- An apple for the teacher
- Apple of my eye
- Apple pie bed
- Love apple
- Adam's apple
- Apple polisher
- Don't upset the applecart
- Applesauce (nonsense)
- Bad apple
- The Big Apple

Kinds of Apples
- Baldwin
- Jonathan
- Northern Spy
- MacIntosh
- Golden Delicious

Things to Make from Apples
- Pies, fritters
- Tarts, cakes
- Apple butter
- Apple dumpling
- Apple cider
- Apple sauce
- Apple jack
- Apple brandy
- Apple dolls
- Dried apples

Parts of an Apple
- Stem
- Seeds
- Pulp
- Peel
- Slice
- Core

Things to Do with Apples
- Slice
- Core
- Peel
- Munch
- Chomp
- Bite
- Cook
- Press
- Mash

Texture
- Smooth
- Hard
- Slippery
- Waxy
- Slick
- Firm
- Crunchy
- Mushy
- Grainy
- Juicy

Word for Apple in Other Languages
- *une pomme*
- *ein apfel*
- *una manzana*

Appearance
- Red
- Greeny-gold
- Round
- Dimpled
- Bruised
- Streaked

Tastes
- Sweet
- Tart
- Sharp
- Sour

Implements You Need to Pick or Work with Apples
- Ladders
- Apple corer
- Cider press
- Paring knife
- Kettle
- Paddle

Words enter a vocabulary through association. The display reveals all of the words associated with a field trip to McDonald's, a fast-food service. (Mrs. Kerstetter's classroom, Highland Park School, Southwestern School District, Grove City, Ohio)

discuss such possibilities as an orchard, a very new or a very old building, a grocery store, or a lumberyard. Think about what kinds of themes this field trip might relate to. Refer back to the example given in this chapter and prepare a field trip booklet.

2. Plan a theme in a group beginning with the development of a web to plan for possibilities. You may wish to look at chapter 11, which includes resource books in language arts and children's literature. Develop a bibliography to go with your theme. This should be a useful tool for you in your teaching.

3. Explore your classroom building and/or the area that surrounds it. What ideas can you think of to serve as themes? Could your theme be shapes,

patterns, and textures; architecture; the old and the new? Divide into groups and explore one aspect of the theme you have selected. Interpret the information you gathered and the experiences you had for the rest of your class. What will you share orally? Which forms of art will you use? How will you display your work? What kinds of writing will be shared with others?

4. In a group or as an individual, develop a word web that may show the historical development of a word, cognitive relationships of words, or a web of synonyms. You may wish to read the writings of Dale and of Platt, which are included in the suggested readings for this chapter.

5. Examine several different children's language-arts textbook series. Decide which kind of grammar is the basis for their instructional program. How did you ascertain this? What would you as a teacher do with the section on grammar in each series?

Recommended Readings

Chomsky, Carol, "Developing a Facility with Language Structure" in *Discovering Language with Children*, ed. Gay Su Pinnell. National Council of Teachers of English, Urbana, Ill., 1980.

Chomsky proposes the use of "linguistic awareness sessions" that will permit children to think about language in an objective way. These sessions should not be based upon worksheets or workbooks, but should instead spring from children's own oral and written language. Chomsky suggests several types of language explorations that will help children see their own language from a fresh perspective.

Dale, Edgar, "The Word Game: Improving Communications," Phi Delta Kappa Education Foundation, Fastback 60, Bloomington, Indiana, 1975.

The term "vocabulary" is considered broader than a set of words. Dale considers vocabulary development to be language development, concept development, and an ongoing process that never ends. With this larger view of vocabulary, Dale recommends ways to extend vocabulary and reveals how words are related, a key to learning their meaning. This interesting booklet contains facts about how language works and where usage may result in unintended humor.

Hennings, Dorothy Grant, "A Writing Approach to Reading Comprehension," *Language Arts* 59:8–17, January, 1982.

This article is particularly appropriate to the chapter you have just read. Hennings points out that most youngsters are prepared to read and write narratives but are totally unprepared to deal with expository texts. She suggests that writing informational (expository) materials prepares a youngster to read such material, for it informs the child how the author structures his or her knowledge. To her credit Hennings explains how to help youngsters organize data into expository structures. Using schema theory as the overarching rationale, this article gives an illustration of how an integrated approach strengthens learning in the different modes.

Levstik, Linda S., "Using Adolescent Fiction as a Guide to Inquiry," *Theory into Practice* 20:174–178, Summer, 1981.

Youngsters ten years old and older are beginning to pose important questions about social concerns, moral issues, and value systems. Levstik suggests how children's literature and social studies can be related in ways that will provide a basis for young adolescents to develop greater sophistication in inquiry at a point in their lives when they are very motivated to do so. The author proposes a number of ideas that are truly related to the language-arts curriculum, including interviews, discussion, role-playing, book comparisons, and journal-writing.

Platt, Nancy, "Webbing Words—Weaving Connections," *Ohio Reading Teacher* 14:7–11, January, 1980.

In this article Platt describes how webbing words can help children learn more about the language they use, such as how language changes over time, the influence of foreign cognates, the development of metaphors, and meaning relationships. She includes several word webs to illustrate her points.

References

Professional Literature

Boreas, Julius, *Formal English Grammar and the Practical Mastery of English,* doctoral thesis, University of Minnesota, 1917.

Chomsky, Carol, "Developing a Facility with Language Structure" in *Discovering Language with Children,* ed. Gay Su Pinnell, National Council of Teachers of English, Urbana, Ill., 1980.

Macaulay, William J., "The Difficulty of Grammar," *British Journal of Educational Psychology* 27:153–162, 1947.

Miel, Alice, *The Shortchanged Children of Suburbia,* Institute of Human Relations Press, New York, 1967.

Miller, Helen Rand, "What If They Don't Know Grammar?," *English Journal* 40:525–526, 1951.

Children's Literature

Baylor, Byrd, *The Way to Start a Day,* illustrated by Peter Parnall, Charles Scribner's, New York, 1978.

Cleaver, Vera and Cleaver, Bill, *Where the Lilies Bloom,* Signet Books, New American Library, New York, 1969.

dePaolo, Tomie, *The Cloud Book,* Holiday House, New York, 1975.

Holman, Felice, "Elevator" in *I Hear You Smiling and Other Poems,* Charles Scribner's, New York, 1973.

Hunter, Mollie, *A Sound of Chariots,* Avon Books, New York, 1972.

Still, James, *Jack and the Wonder Beans,* G. P. Putnam's, New York, 1977.

Worth, Valerie, "Safety Pin" in *More Small Poems,* Farrar, Straus and Giroux, New York, 1976.

One Child's Version of a Well-known Tale

Reasons for Literature in the Language Program
Literature as Input to Language
Literature as Experience
Literature as a Stimulus to Language Output

Literature in the Classroom
Listening to Literature
Reading in Literature
Talking about Literature
Writing from Literature

Integrating Literature into the Language-Arts Program
An Example of a Literature Web
Assessment

Summary

Recommended Readings

Suggested Learning Experiences

References
Professional Literature
Children's Literature

Chapter 8

Literature-Based Language Extensions

One Child's Version of a Well-known Tale

The Three Little Chickens

David

Once upon a time there were three chickens. And there mother hen told them that they must go and build there own egghouse. Now the first chicken didn't like to work too hard so he built himself a wood egg.

The second didn't like to work very hard either so he built himself a twig egg. And put in a CB and TV

But the third chicken liked to work and he built himself a steel beam concrete egg that looked like a castle.

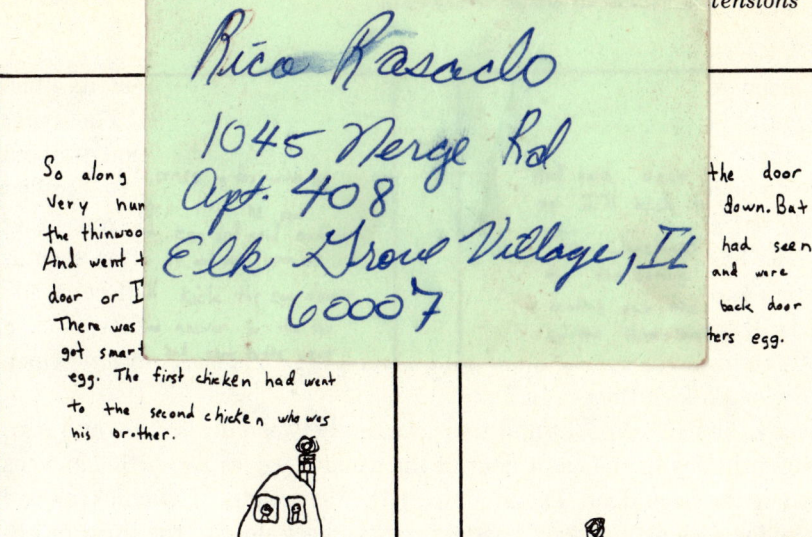

So along [...] the door
very num[...] down. Bat
the thinwoo[...] had seen
And went t[...] and were
door or I[...] back door
There was [...] ters egg.
got smart[...]
egg. The first chicken had went
to the second chicken who was
his brother.

And that egg was built like a castle. The fox went to it and couldn't reach the door because it had a mote and it was very deep. He tried to jump but missed. And started swimming but one thing he didn't know was the mote had pirahna in it.

And the fox got ate and the chickens lived happily ever after.

The End

Rico Rasaclo
1045 Nerge Rd
Apt. 408
Elk Grove Village, IL
60007

A person reading the preceding story learns a great deal about its nine-year-old author, David, who has obviously heard the story "The Three Little Pigs" not once but many times. He is knowledgeable enough about stories to be able not only to play about within the framework of a familiar folktale but also to weave into his writing information gleaned from other stories he has heard. He is aware that foxes, like wolves, are often seen as tricksters and that chickens belong to the category of "good, well-behaved" animals. David also has a sense of story language: "Now the first chicken didn't like to work so hard so he built a wood egg." He uses refrain: "Open the door or I'll kick the egg in."

David knows about books and the close ties between illustration and text. He shows the fox at the front door of the wooden egg as two little chickens scurry out the back door. The accompanying text reads, "The chickens had seen the fox coming and were heading out the back door to the third brother's egg." Like any good author David makes the form his own by weaving in his own perception and experiences; for example, the second chicken not only built a twig egg, he also installed a CB and a TV. The piranha's fierce voracity, information David probably acquired from television, had such an impact that he uses it to bring his story to a dramatic finish. David's reasoning about how things are constructed is demonstrated through careful drawings that show how the eggs were put together and how props are used to hold each oval construction in a steady position. He also is able to show through language his understanding of the properties of certain materials. The fragile eggs are made of "thin wood twigs," while the castlelike egg is made of "steel-beamed concrete." Finally, David has a sense of the demands of authorship. He already has the ability to sustain a story line, work within a story framework, and yet make the story uniquely his own. He is able to put together a book with care and attention to detail; detail in language, in illustration, in print, and in format. David knows how to use literature as a springboard for his own creative expression.

What is next for David? How could a teacher help extend this youngster's language skills? David is capable of progressing in many language areas at this time. His own interests can provide some guidance but his teacher needs to help direct his growth. He has a strong sense of story but does not use much rich descriptive language. Perhaps David needs to hear literature with strong imagery and practice that language by describing a concrete experience such as an event or an observation. Another direction would be for the teacher to share a range of folktales with David so that he can make comparisons among the tales and learn more about variation among stories from different cultures. Since he has already gained enough knowledge about folktales to update one, perhaps this child is ready to move on to another genre, such as realistic fiction.

From David's story it is easy to see the powerful force literature can exert on the language of children. In other chapters of this book the role of concrete experiences has been central. In this chapter the main focus is upon only one kind of language input—that which comes from literature.

Reasons for Literature in the Language Program

Literature as Input to Language

Literature as language input deserves special attention. One only has to read a book such as Lionni's *Swimmy* to realize why any language-arts program must have a strong literature component. Swimmy, a very small fish, travels through the depths of the ocean, where he encounters marvel after marvel:

> He saw a medusa made of rainbow jelly ... a lobster, who walked about like a water-moving machine ... strange fish, pulled by an invisible thread ... a forest of seaweeds growing from sugar candy rocks ... an eel whose tail was almost too far away to remember ... and sea anemones, who looked like pink palm trees swaying in the wind ... (unpaged, 1963).

Literature offers language as unlike the ordinary language of everyday life as is an elegantly cut crystal goblet from an old jelly jar that serves as a water glass. The jelly jar serves the utilitarian purpose of holding a liquid so that one can drink comfortably. The crystal goblet serves the same purpose, but because of its beauty and the artistry of its design, it is worthy of being preserved and passed on to future generations. The author of a literary work uses the same words that are available to any other user of language, but uses them with the care and precision of an artist to create a unique statement.

It is as children listen to, read, and talk about books that they become aware of the artistry of writers. Writers tell their tales in language that is written rather than oral. They, therefore, can plan what they want to say, set down their words on paper, and return to them again and again to revise and polish.

The shape of the language often becomes part of the message itself. When

Alexander says that he has had "a terrible, horrible, no good, very bad day [Viorst]," the piling of adjective upon adjective conveys the day's misery as no single adjective could. Sometimes the writer juxtaposes elements of language in order to create an effect. When Dazzle, a peacock, decides he will be lord of the jungle, the lion questions Dazzle's qualifications for this lofty position. He is given the following response:

> "Because I am more beautiful," said Dazzle, and he stood up, stretching his magnificent tail for all to see. "I am exquisite from quill to tip, which is more than I can say for you...." (Massie, 1969, unpaged).

Dazzle's elegant language, "exquisite from quill to tip," juxtaposed with the childish petulance of "which is more than I can say for you," does a great deal to let the reader see the outward magnificence and the inward shallowness of Dazzle at the same moment.

The writer can use language to create a mood or to foreshadow what is to come. In the prologue to her book *Tuck Everlasting*, Babbitt does just that.

> The first week of August hangs at the very top of summer, the top of the livelong year, like the highest seat of a Ferris wheel when it pauses in its turning. The weeks that come before are only a climb from balmy spring, and those that follow a drop to the chill of autumn, but the first week of August is motionless, and hot (1975, p. 1).

The motifs of a circle and of life that appear throughout the book are introduced. It is in reading and listening to such passages that children can become sharply aware of the power of the written word.

Literature as Experience

One kind of experience the teacher can offer is concrete—the gerbils in the classroom, the trip to the farm, the mapping of the schoolyard. Such experiences give children material to talk, read, and write about. A second type of experience is offered by books. Books can permit the reader to move into inaccessible worlds. One can travel back in time with Jean Fritz to find the answers to such questions as *And Then What Happened, Paul Revere?*, *Why Don't You Get a Horse, Sam Adams?*, and *Can't You Make Them Behave, King George?* Madeleine L'Engle in *A Wind at the Door* helps the reader become so tiny that he or she can enter the body of the seriously ill Charles Wallace, thus able to attack the evil forces that are destroying the small boy.

Literature can give one the opportunity to see the world through a different set of glasses, changing the reader's perspective. Norton, in her book *The Borrowers,* lets the child discover what the world looks like when you are only inches high and live in a world peopled by "human beans." The poet often helps one to see the commonplace in fresh and delightful ways. The experience of walking along a dark path guided by the yellow beam of a flashlight becomes new after reading:

FLASHLIGHT

My flashlight tugs me
through the dark
like a hound
with a yellow eye,

sniffs
at the edges
of steep places,

paws at moles'
and rabbits'
holes,

points its nose
where sharp things
lie asleep—

and then it bounds
ahead of me
on home ground.   (Thurman, 1979, pp. 8, 9)

Literature, then, lets readers live lives other than their own and explore worlds to which they could never travel. Huck writes:

Vicariously, he will experience other places, other times and other life styles; he may identify with others, or find his own self-identity; he may observe nature more closely or from a different perspective; he will encounter the thrill of taking risks and meeting mystery; he will endure suffering; he will enjoy a sense of achievement, and feel he belongs to one segment or all humanity. He will be challenged to dream dreams, to ponder and to ask questions of himself (1979, p. 5).

Not only does literature let children take journeys; it lets them repeat those journeys. When children return to literature for a second look, they can examine it in greater depth and make comparisons. Children who have read *Dazzle,* the story of a peacock who lost its glorious tail to the jaws of a lion, might be led to read fables of Aesop and La Fontaine to look for other animals whose pride was their downfall.

One can return again and again to a book to let the lovely sounds of its language slip over the tongue. Young children will respond to the lullaby quality of Brown's *Goodnight, Moon.* Very quickly they will be able to join the reader in the gentle recital of soft farewells:

> "Goodnight comb
> And goodnight brush
> Goodnight nobody
> Goodnight mush
> And goodnight to the old lady whispering hush" (unpaged, 1947).

Literature is a way of learning. Just as the children observing the hamster cage learn a great deal about the habits of hamsters and are then able to discuss and write about what they have learned, so too do books open the doors to learning. Children can read about the internment of the Japanese during the Second World War in a history text. However, reading *Journey to Topaz* (Uchida) will let them share Yuki's experience in one of those internment camps in such a way that they will need to talk about it, write about it, and find out more about it.

Literature as a Stimulus to Language Output

Literature, because of the way it is produced, has inherent qualities that make it a rich source of language input. In addition, there is the power that is released when reader and text interact. Iser (1978) views reading as a dynamic process in which the reader sets the work in motion, an act that awakens reader response. One aspect of this interaction between text and reader that can strongly influence the language of children is that of response to literature to which much attention has been given. Rosenblatt views the author's text much as a piece of music. A Bach fugue remains black notes on a white page until the musician interprets those notes. A text, then, is not truly complete until it has a reader. Rosenblatt writes:

> The literary work exists in the live circuit set up between reader and text: the reader infuses intellectual and emotional meanings into the pattern of verbal symbols, and these symbols channel his thoughts and feelings. Out of this complex process emerges a more or less organized imaginative experience (1976, p. 25).

The author's message is a dynamic one, getting its life from both the reader and the writer.

When a child reads a story alone and later discusses that story with others, the author's message takes on a new shape, a new perspective. The child does not have or need to have the ability to examine a work of literature analytically, as a critic would, but instead interprets the author's message in light of his or her own background of experience. Discussions with other children who have read the same book but who bring to that book a different set of experiences may help reshape the child's understandings. Comparisons of books with similar themes, dramatizing a section of a book, and reinterpreting a book through art are all experiences that require children to dip back into an author's work for another look in order to explain their views or support their point.

Response to literature provides a strong foundation for language extension. It is as children respond to books through drama and writing that they acquire literary language and extend their vocabulary. When they use literature as a springboard for their own writing, they can begin to focus on the form and texture of language. Sharing poetry helps them actualize their own sensory images. Finally, literary experiences intensify their own experiences and thus help them to value more deeply their own reactions to the things they see and touch and feel. When children perceive that their feelings and ideas are valuable, they will wish to share them through talk and through writing. This chapter is included in our language-arts text because we see literature as the richest kind of language input and as experience different from any other. Literature gives children something to listen to, to read in, to talk about, and to write from.

Literature in the Classroom

Listening to Literature

For many years parents have been admonished to read to their children, especially during the preschool ages. Everyone knew that it was a good idea but little concrete evidence was available to prove that reading aloud to children made a difference in their reading achievement. This claim has now been verified not only for preschool children but also for school-age youngsters. In her studies of children who began reading before entering school, Durkin (1966) found that early readers were consistently read to by their parents; Clark (1976) made a similar discovery about young, fluent readers. Hall, Moretz, and Staton (1976) reported that children who begin to write early have been read to not only by their parents but also quite often by older siblings. Sostarich (1974) found that active sixth-grade readers had been read to as children.

The way that parents read to their children relates to the child's scores on prereading predictive tasks. Flood (1977) visited families and asked parents to read to their youngsters as they usually would while he tape-recorded the sessions. There was a significant relationship between number of words spoken by the child, number of questions answered and asked by the child, warm-up preparatory questions posed by parents, post-story evaluative questions, positive reinforcement by the parents, and the child's scores on prereading predictive tasks of letter and word recognition, vocabulary, and visual discrimination. Time taken before, during, and after reading a story enhances the child's learning about books, words, and print.

Cohen (1968) investigated whether a program of reading aloud to school-age children influenced their verbal achievements. She selected a group of high-quality literature books and developed a manual of accompanying activities and story-reading techniques for teachers to use. The findings revealed a significant growth in vocabulary, word knowledge, and reading and listening comprehension. Extending Cohen's research, Cullinan, Jaggar, and Strickland (1974) studied the effects of reading aloud to primary-grade children when follow-up activities were included or omitted. Although language gains were found for both groups, higher scores came from the group with language activities following the reading.

Strickland (1974) looked at the effect that verbal versus nonverbal activities following an oral reading session had upon speakers of black dialect. Both groups retained their ability to produce the black dialect; however, the oral language follow-up group made significant gains over the nonverbal group in their control of standard English. Using book language provides an opportunity to practice standard English forms.

Knowledge of literature, both an indirect measure of having been read aloud to for younger children and expanding reading experiences for older children, relates to linguistic sophistication. Chomsky (1972) found the Huck "Inventory of Children's Literary Background" to have the highest correlation with language development of the six- to ten-year-old youngsters she studied.

Reading aloud to children helps them to develop a sense of story. Applebee (1978) posits that children learn to expect specific actions from certain character types: foxes are sly; wolves, hungry; a witch, wicked. As children become more familiar with stories, their storytelling becomes more complex. This knowledge of story structure, story language, and character types assists youngsters as they read. Many folktales are conventionally structured in "threes"; for example, three tasks are given to the hero. "There was once in a land far away" tells a listener and reader that a story is beginning; thus, print becomes predictable. In Frank Smith's (1978) terms, there exists a "reduction of uncertainty" for readers as they meet the printed page.

This knowledge of story can begin quite early. One four-and-a-half-year-old, Beth, drew this picture of a witch. She told her mother, "This witch is a mean witch." Beth wrote out the frightening sounds emanating from the

witch's mouth, which adults might spell as "eh, eh, eh ..." and included approprite story language: "Beware, my pretty!" Obviously, she has had a good deal of contact with children's literature. The influence of her having been read aloud to is clear. What should a parent do with a youngster like Beth? More of the same! She is progressing well, using the rich literature environment about her.

Other evidence of literary effect may appear in play situations of drama, dolls, and storytelling. These kinds of practice provide youngsters not only with the needed experience of retelling but also with the opportunity to conjure up new stories and meld familiar characters and plots together in different ways.

Selecting Literature. Selecting literature to read aloud may be based on several premises. Usually it is a good idea to choose a book slightly beyond the child or children's reading level, for youngsters' listening comprehension extends beyond their own reading abilities. In this way the listeners have the opportunity to grow in vocabulary and story knowledge more than their own reading would offer them.

Reading aloud gives a teacher the opportunity to share literature children may not read on their own. Some older youngsters avoid picture books, believing they have gone beyond that level of reading. Yet many authors and illustrators create such books with the older reader in mind. *Dawn* by Shulevitz, with its economy of words and lovely watercolor illustrations that expand as the light of day reaches the scene, calls for sophisticated interpretation to gain appreciation of the book's beauty. Lobel's *Fables,* the 1981 Caldecott Award winner, is appropriate for middle- and upper-grade youngsters who can understand morals and the humor contained in the book, for these children have reached that cognitive level of development. *The Magician of Cracow,* a Polish legend retold by Turska, is quite similar to the story of Faust: a magician agrees to go with the devil, provided certain conditions are met. The intricately detailed illustrations and cleverness of the magician's actions require a broad background only older children can have acquired. Cavemen, Aztecs, the Congo, China, pharaohs in Egypt, Pueblo cornfields in New Mexico, and mountains in Peru are brought together in Byrd Baylor's singing words and Peter Parnall's exquisite drawings for *The Way to Start a Day.* Older children may grow from the experience of having literature such as this shared with them.

Poetry must be read aloud for two basic reasons. First, most poetry is written to be heard. The spoken words combine to make a special aesthetic experience.

Winter Alphabet

Bare branches of trees
brush strokes of Chinese pictograms
marking the parchment sky.

On the ground
Queen Anne's lace brown shriveled
Egyptian hieroglypha
waiting to be deciphered.

My breath in the air
smoke
signalling from a tepee.

    Eve Merriam (1973, pp. 20, 21)

Secondly, if not consciously made a part of the literature program, the enjoyment of poetry can be lost. Appreciation of poetry is learned.

Children enjoy the sounds words make. *The Poetry Troupe,* compiled by Wilner, contains a fine collection of poems meant to be read aloud by both teachers and children. Poems with concrete subjects that children can relate to are a good beginning. For example, most children have had experiences with cats and can relate to Fisher's anthology of cat poems, *My Cat Has Eyes of Sapphire Blue,* realistically illustrated by Marie Angel. Humor may draw in older youngsters not yet poetry enthusiasts. Narratives such as "Colonel Fazackerley" and "I Saw a Jolly Hunter" (Causley, 1973) delight students. As more poetry is shared with children and used to convey special sensory experiences in words, children will acquire a taste for, a positive attitude toward poetic language and literature.

Some books do not need to be read aloud, for children will read them for themselves. The Atwaters's classic *Mr. Popper's Penguins* is one example of such a book and Blume's *Tales of a Fourth Grade Nothing* is another.

At times books to be read aloud may be chosen to introduce a new author to the class, such as Betsy Byars. In this instance, *Summer of the Swans* or *After the Goat Man* might be read. A new genre may be introduced. *Mrs. Frisby and the Rats of NIMH* by O'Brien could initiate fantasy. A new topic may be brought into the class by sharing a book. *Everyone Knows What a Dragon Looks Like* by Williams might lead a class from a typical interest in dinosaurs to dragons, a rich field in literature.

Not all books need to be read in their entirety. New books and authors may be introduced by the teacher's reading a part of the selection. Another way for the class to discover Byars is for the teacher to read the beginning of *The 18th Emergency,* in which Benjie dashes home, sure that Marv Hammerman, Toni Lionni, and a boy in a black sweatshirt are going to kill him. Benjie's "terrors" continue! Cleary's delightful characters, Beezes, Ramona, and Henry Huggins, could be introduced by reading a portion of *Henry Huggins,* and other books in which these characters take center stage can be made available to the class.

The need to hear literature read aloud has already been discussed in regard to poetry; however, some prose also has poetic quality. *The Seeing Stick* by Yolen is a good example:

> Once in the ancient walled citadel of Peking there lived an emperor who had only one daughter, and her name was Hwei Ming. Now this daughter had carved ivory combs to smoothe back her long black hair. Her tiny feet were encased in embroidered slippers, and her robes were woven of the finest silks. But rather than making her happy, such possessions made her sad (1977, unpaged).

The richness of metaphoric and rhythmic language appears in the fantasy *When the Sky Is Like Lace* by Horwitz, beautifully illustrated by Barbara Cooney.

> Because on bimulous nights when the sky is like lace, the trees eucalyptus back and forth, forth and back, swishing and swaying, swaying and swishing—in the fern-deep grove at the midnight end of the garden (1975, unpaged).

Mollie Hunter is a master of the oral tale tradition. Her keen ear for language of the story is revealed in the beginning sentences of *A Stranger Came Ashore:*

> It was a while ago in the days when they used to tell stories about creatures called the Selkie Folk.
>
> A stranger came ashore to an island at that time—a man who gave his name as Finn Learson—and there was a mystery about him which had to do with these selkie creatures. Or so some people say, anyway . . . (1975, p. 1).

Rich language is not limited to storybooks. Author-illustrator Adkins uses poetic prose in *Inside: Seeing Beneath the Surface* to convey to his readers the notion of how to see in uncommon ways. "Your two eyes just *look,* at shapes, colors, movements, but your inner eye sees, putting sense and sight together. A good word for sensible sight is *vision*" (1975, pp. 6, 7).

Reading a book aloud allows a class to discuss a book that some children might not be able to read on their own but all can understand. Some books seem to require discussion, for it is through such interplay that children may become more aware of major themes and subtleties of the text. Fantasy seems to call for such discussions. Babbitt's *Tuck Everlasting,* so beautifully structured, uses symbols eloquently and leaves each reader with the questions "Would you have chosen everlasting life? Would you have made the same decision as Winnie?"

In *The Dark Is Rising,* Cooper makes great use of symbols in a tale of high fantasy that requires previous experience with the literature of fantasy. Will Stanton, the hero of this story, represents the forces of good in his struggle against evil as time stands still during a raging battle. This complex story can be discussed at a variety of levels, the discussion itself revealing the depth of the book. Themes may be drawn out from individual children's appreciation of the text and also through interaction with the teacher and the rest of the class.

Literature also should be read aloud for the sheer enjoyment of sharing a book experience, for the laughter, delight, and appreciation of a quiet moment. Books and poems that are shared must be made available to the class so they can reread stories and poems. Other books by the same author might be made available; for example, if *Tuck Everlasting* were read aloud, other Babbitt books such as *The Search for Delicious*, *Knee Knock Rise*, and *The Eyes of the Amaryllis* could be displayed. If a time fantasy book were shared, other fantasy books on time could be made available—L'Engle's *Wrinkle in Time*, Boston's *The Children of Greene Knowe*, and Bond's *String in the Harp*. This availability of books both read and related to books read promotes reading among children.

Sharing Literature. Reading aloud to children has been established as beneficial to youngsters' oral language development and reading achievement. But *how* should literature be read aloud? Oral reading is an art, an art that can be acquired. To ensure that youngsters have the best experience, the teacher should read the material over first. Oral practice helps far more than silent reading.

1. How might intonation and phrasing aid the story line?
2. When should a page be turned so that there is no break in a sentence?
3. If a picture book is being shared:
   a. Which illustrations will be shown?
   b. Are some too small for the group to see?
   c. Do your hands hide part of the picture?
   d. Can the entire group see the page or do you need to move the book around so that all can see?
4. How can the children be involved? At the least, eye contact could be maintained through frequent recognition of the audience.
   a. Are questions helpful or would they distract the audience from the mood of the story?
   b. Are student comments appropriate; do they personalize the tale?
   c. Are there refrains or chants in the story that invite children to join in?
   d. Does the story call for movements? The teacher's slight beginnings may encourage the class to enter in.
5. How do children respond? Stories that children love bear rereading. A teacher must listen to the children.
   a. Do they ask to hear a poem once again?
   b. Is there a favorite part that the class wishes to have repeated?

Not all stories need to be *read* aloud. Some tales should be learned so well that the teacher can tell them without a book. Teacher storytelling has a special place in the classroom, for it encourages child involvement and also child storytelling. Storytelling is generally done without props because it increases the intensity of this experience in a way that is rarely duplicated. Eye contact is at its fullest and audience feedback can help guide the teller easily. Using a flannelboard to tell a story decreases the closeness of audience contact but has the added value of providing children with the pieces with which they can retell the story. The props are only an aid to child retelling if the teacher leaves the materials out for children to use and schedules time for free activities. A single prop and puppets may also be used in storytelling. Once again, their availability to youngsters encourages the retelling.

Poetry sharing is an art. Some poems might be memorized by the teacher for the same values in audience contact as storytelling. Children will naturally memorize their favorite poems if they hear them over and over. A poetry tree could be made from a branch stuck in a can filled with sand. The twigs could hold new poetry discoveries as well as old favorites. Children could collect poems on a class theme, creating a class poetry book. Youngsters could share their favorite poems, practicing reading them into a tape recorder.

Reading aloud literature in the classroom as an integral part of the daily schedule holds great value for the language arts. Selections must be made with care and a knowledge of the literature available. Accessibility of such selections is essential to child language growth.

Reading in Literature

Selecting Books for the Classroom Library. Selecting books for a classroom library is one of the most important decisions that a teacher makes to encourage reading in literature. Taking research on children's reading interests into account can serve as one initial basis for classroom book selection before the teacher becomes acquainted with a new group of children. The collection will change during the year because each class has its own personality and unique interests, which teachers can find when they become acquainted with the class. Another point is that children's interests change over time; they grow and mature, becoming aware of new areas that intrigue them. Finally, each child has his or her particular set of interests that come from a variety of factors. In the last analysis it is the child's singular interests that are the most important to the teacher in working with each student.

Investigators of children's interests have centered on such factors as age, sex, intelligence, and socioeconomic level. Very young children seem to like stories about children their own age, home, and family (Burton, 1956; Purves and Beach, 1972). Friendly animals are also appealing. Little or no sex difference in interests occur at this early age (Harris, 1962). In addition, children from six to eight enjoy fairy tales. Favat (1977) believed this interest relates to their stage of child development. He analyzed fairy tales with Piaget's theory of cognitive growth and found that fairy tales represent the child's conception of the world. Children are comfortable with the predictability of the tales and the patterns that reappear. The simplicity of the stories matches youngsters' simplistic view of the world about them.

Middle-grade youngsters, third- and fourth-graders, become interested in adventure, animal stories that are realistic, humorous tales, and fables (Burton, 1956; Purves and Beach, 1972). Informational books gain popularity. Sex differences may become noticeable (Harris, 1962). The reading of series books such as Nancy Drew and "The Little House" books may begin.

Upper-grade students continue their interest in adventure. Biography and mysteries become increasingly popular (Burton, 1956; Purves and Beach, 1972). Girls will read boys' books; but boys may not read a girl's book (Hanna and McAllister, 1960). These marked differences have subsided in recent years; perhaps one of the reasons might be that many current books are not marked as a "boy's" or a "girl's" book; for example, those by Byars and Paterson. Another change has come from altering attitudes toward sex roles. Male figures are showing more tenderness, once thought a feminine trait. *William's Doll* by Zolotow is an example of this. Girls' books are more appealing to boys because no longer does the heroine have to alter tomboyish ways. Becoming a "lady" in the stereotypical fashion does not have to be the resolution to the story's problem. For example, Claudia in Konigsburg's *From the Mixed-up Files of Mrs. Basil E. Frankweiler* remains strong and inventive.

Intelligence, defined as achievement in reading, does seem to influence reading interests. Better readers go through the reading stages faster but still follow the same sequence (Harris, 1962). Significantly, there is no gravitation toward quality literature (Cleworth, 1958; Norvell, 1950), for taste in literature is learned (Brown, 1965). Good readers read at all levels of difficulty—easy, current-reading level, and frustratingly difficult. These youngsters have no fear and will tackle any book that interests them.

Lower achieving students often have less mature interests than others their age. However, their interests are commonly above their reading level. This can create problems if the teacher does not have books at a variety of reading levels on the same topic. Less able readers are more apt to choose easy-to-read books, not daring to fail at more difficult ones. Sometimes, however, these youngsters will select very difficult books for show. A strong interest in a topic can spur a reader of any ability to work through difficult books, so freedom of choice is important.

Socioeconomic level has been examined by Johns (1973) as he looked at the interests of inner-city children. Some educators recommended realistic fiction that depicted inner-city settings and characters, for they felt it would help children from this background identify with the stories. Johns found that inner-city children preferred stories with middle-class settings, characters, and positive group interactions. The point of a variety of books available from which children may choose is reinforced by this study. Socioeconomic level does not determine interests.

Book selections should not be determined solely by award-winning literature. Schlager (1978) analyzed books given the Newbery Award according to their library circulation records and characteristics of child development as presented by Piaget and Erickson. She found a strong, positive relationship between the story protagonist's problems and actions and the developmental characteristics of middle-grade students. When youngsters could identify with the book, they read it. Rarely circulated Newbery winners did not display a middle childhood perspective.

Adult choices of poetry for children do not always match children's choices. Terry (1974) found that many traditional classics assembled for children are not liked. Youngsters enjoy contemporary poetry dealing with familiar experiences. Humor, rhythm, and rhyme in poetry are appreciated, but complex imagery is not. Perhaps the most significant finding was the most regrettable: teachers rarely read poetry to children nor do they encourage the writing of poetry.

Probably the best source for choosing books to place in a classroom library is the teacher's knowledge of students' specific interests, reading levels, and available children's books. The collection should contain three to five books per student if there is a school library within the building. Larger numbers are required if no library exists within the school. Some principles of selection are:

The inclusion of books representing a variety of genre to encourage a widening breadth of children's experiences with literature;

The bringing in of newly published books to generate excitement from crisp pages and shiny covers and to introduce living authors' works. These authors may be written to and even heard on occasions when they visit the community;

The establishing of a range of books according to child interests, reading levels, and experiences. The range needs to extend beyond current child levels to encourage and allow growth;

The choice of quality books to assist children's development of taste in literature. Books rich in language feed into language growth. Realistic characters showing depth rather than cardboard stereotypical characters facilitate an understanding of human problems and interpretative thinking.

Chapter 11 contains resources for teachers to use in selecting and keeping current with children's literature.

Setting Up a Context for Reading. The scheduling of time is one of the most important considerations in establishing a context conducive to reading. Children need time to select books and to browse. This allows them to scan titles which may intrigue them and enter into a book to determine whether they wish to read it. Browsing can encourage children to try a new type of book, for it demands no commitment to check the book out and read it in its entirety.

When teachers schedule Sustained Silent Reading (SSR), a consistent block of time is set aside for all in the class to read, *including* the teacher (McCracken and McCracken, 1972). The silence of intense absorption with reading prevails. The program begins with a small amount of time—perhaps only ten minutes—and expands as children's attention span grows. Older classes may read for 30 to 40 minutes, some even longer. Even very young children can participate in SSR by looking through books, finding pictures to interpret, choosing stories they wish to have read to them, or "reading" books they have heard.

An essential part of SSR is children's freedom to select books for themselves. A sharing period commonly follows. This brief, informal period allows children and their teacher to tell others of interesting characters or events in their stories. A particularly fascinating paragraph or page may be read aloud to let others know the author's style, a funny event, or a rich, descriptive scene. Teachers can judge the success of the program in their classrooms by how their students react to SSR time. Do they eagerly reach for their books? Are they involved in their reading? Are there some youngsters who keep reading when the time is over?

Flexible classroom scheduling permits children to read often if they choose. Some enjoy reading for long periods of time, while others like shorter times but perhaps choose to read more often. Short books may be finished in fifteen minutes but longer books may so involve the child that an extended period of time is needed to find out what happens. When the selection is finished, many children prefer to do something different before returning to reading and they should be permitted to do so. This type of arrangement also encourages children to read purposefully. For example, if a youngster is working on a project of constructing a farm and if there is sufficient time, the child may turn to books for ideas on the specific architecture of barns or the size of corrals. By making time periods flexible, teachers help children to integrate their activities one with the other, the goal of the language-arts program.

Another part of the context for reading is the physical room arrangement. Books on display invite reading. When teachers arrange for quiet places in the room, children can take flights into literature, leaving the classroom behind. Comfortable chairs are conducive to reading. Sofas often become the place where two or three youngsters can read a book together or they can read separate books but with the physical companionship of others. Rugs in the book area are a good place to sprawl out, lean on elbows, and become immersed in a story.

The grouping of books can make selection easy for children. Broad categories probably can be used with no need for alphabetizing. Classroom collections are small enough for this freedom. The general collection might be divided into picture books, story anthologies, poetry, informational books, reference books, chapter books, and books written by class members. Additional groupings could be books on a topic of current study, books that have been read aloud plus other books related to those read, special-interest books for a small group of children (such as books on mice in chapter 1), and new books.

Part of the reading context is established by the teacher's attitudes and expectations.

Questions for Teachers to Consider in Establishing a Reading Context

1. Is reading considered to be a valuable experience or something to do when all other work is completed?
2. Does the teacher share his or her interest in books and arrange for the children to share theirs?
3. How well can the teacher match books with children? In this instance not only knowledge of the child is needed but also knowledge of children's literature.
4. Has the teacher kept abreast of current literature to share with the class and with children who have special interests?
5. Are children encouraged to exchange ideas about books with each other and with their teacher?

Sometimes students are encouraged to read vast numbers of books with contests to see who reads the most titles, but the quantity of books is not as

These two pictures depict two different reading centers. The first provides a clear view of how a reading area may be set up to invite student participation. Notice how many books are on display, thus inviting their being handled. The picture above shows a reading center in use. Both interactional and individual response to books are invited by the setting. (Mrs. Harbert's and Mrs. Monaghan's informal classrooms, Barrington School, Upper Arlington, Ohio)

important as the reading experience itself. When reading becomes an accumulative race through titles, children quickly learn to select short books and skim rather than savor the words. Races cut off the opportunity to reread books, and thus may prevent children from gaining fluency in reading and finding aspects not found before. Britton (1978) states there is a place and a need for both close and wide reading. By wide reading Britton means that the child should find pleasure in reading many and varied books. Close reading refers to the pleasure the child can find in savoring the language and themes of a particular book in some depth. Classrooms should foster both kinds of reading.

Hepler (1982) studied fifth- and sixth-grade student responses to literature in a classroom where literature comprised the total reading context; no basal readers were used. She found reading to be a social experience rather than an isolated act. Just as interaction in oral language supports growth in oral and written language skills, interaction in reading appeared to support growth in reading skills. Hepler's findings have many implications for teachers.

Children have a strong influence on each others' response to literature. They provide information to each other about the book if they have read it and about the author's other books. They encourage peers to read a book by saying, "That's really good!" or "Ooh, I loved that book!"

Children have a need to be recognized for their actions in order to become readers. They take pride in logs kept about the books they have read, in the number of books completed, and in being the first person in the class to read a book. Children also like to be recognized when they begin reading in a new genre or see parts of a story in a different way, such as reinterpreting a character or viewing an event as being more or less significant in the total scheme of the story.

To engage deeply in reading, children need time. A class of students includes some who start the year reading; others may not become committed to books for several months. Students have cycles of reading, going on "binges," then centering on other activities. They do return if time is allowed and the atmosphere encourages reading.

Book discussions provide children with an opportunity to expand their knowledge about a book. A book discussion may be thought of as revisiting the book where children may talk with others about their interpretation and experience with the story. They can question others about parts they did not understand or discover whether classmates viewed a character or event as they did.

"A legacy of past satisfactions" associated with reading supports children's growth in reading. Hepler found that the teacher needs to accept the books children select even if those books are not ones the teacher might recommend. Children seem to generalize teacher behaviors and if one selection is not accepted, then maybe none will be. Children prefer the positive, so book criticism for this age group is nonproductive. If the youngsters do not like a book, they do not want to talk about it. If they do like a book, they wish to speak only about the parts they like, ignoring aspects that are not appealing.

Children can find their own way through books without literary vocabulary to use as "handles." They may stumble, appearing inarticulate to an uninitiated adult, but children are able to discuss and study literary aspects of a book if given enough time and if the setting is an accepting one. Sophisticated concepts of theme, characterization, or plot may likely occur as children discuss, but the terms commonly used in English literature classes will not appear unless imposed by the teacher. Specific vocabulary is unnecessary at this time, for the concepts must be developed first.

Classroom activities comprise part of the reading context. Besides the selection and actual reading of books, an important segment of the reading experience is the sharing activity. The following two sections on "talking about" and "writing from" literature will explain how to help children make their reading memorable and how such projects will extend children's skills in the language arts. It is through the follow-up activities that the reading of a book becomes part of an integrated language-arts experience. In addition, these activities are a good way to introduce many books in the classroom, for peer influence can motivate reading.

Art projects may be worked upon individually or jointly. If done in the art center, both situations will contain opportunities for a variety of language uses such as planning, hypothesizing outcomes, comparing colors, materials, and shapes, evaluating, and simply interacting as a way to develop social skills. Each project would include some writing, telling about the book, and providing information on the title and author.

Here are a few ideas children might enjoy.

Make a diorama of the setting of a story.

Construct a peepbox of a scene out of a shoe box.

Design a mobile of important characters and props in the story.

Draw a TV show that runs on a scroll across the front of a box.

Create a poster, possibly a collage, to advertise the book to others.

Collect items mentioned in a book and develop a museum display with appropriate labels. (A leaf from the vine in "Jack and the Beanstalk," Baby Bear's porridge bowl, a lock from Rapunzel's hair, etc.)

Make a game from the story—board style, cards, etc.

Stitch a character or scene in brightly colored yarns on burlap.

Put up a mural showing the setting and events of the book (this would be a good group project).

Oral language activities provide children with large-group experiences. Some may be spontaneous; others may require planning and practice, as can be seen in this sampling.

Do role-playing of a character in a new situation or tell selected parts of the story from a minor character's point of view.

Use puppets to explain or be characters in the book.

Hold a television show where favorite authors or characters are interviewed.

Have a telephone conversation between characters within a book or characters from two different but related books.

Give a sales pitch for the book as a carnival barker or TV announcer.

Participate in a panel discussion on books with similar themes, characters, or settings.

Dramatize an event in the story either in a group or alone.

Writing about a book can come easily, for many of the ideas in the book stimulate new thoughts and such writing will invite book language. Several ideas for writing follow.

Write a newspaper account of an event in the story.

Develop a diary that one of the characters might have kept.

Make up a letter from one character to another.

Extend the story by telling what further adventures might occur.

Write to the author of a favorite book to tell of your choice and ask questions that may have arisen.

Develop a class newspaper with story events reported and books advertised.

Use the style of a book as a model to write your own: for example, Burningham's *Would You Rather . . .* or Viorst's *Alexander and the Terrible, Horrible, No Good, Very Bad Day.*

Talking About Literature

Story Retelling: An Oral Response. One of the earlier types of oral response that children make to books is to retell a story they have heard. Five-year-old Kristy told her teacher the tale of "The Shoemaker and the Elves."

Kristy: The man was making shoes and when they and when they and when the man when the man was finished he went to bed and then when they woke up they saw a pair of shoes lying on the table. The elves made them.

Teacher: Who?

Kristy: The elves. And then when they come back in, those guys stayed up and watched them. 'Cept the next night they stayed up and then made a pair of shoes and pants and a lit . . . some hats and then they danced out the door and then and then he just had one more pair of of . . . left to make two more shoes and then four more.

Teacher: And then what else?

Kristy: And then they danced out of the door.

Teacher: Who danced?

Kristy: The elves 'cause they had a pair of . . . so, so they won't be so they didn't have no clothes on.

Kristy showed a good degree of sophistication for a five-year-old. Whereas many children her age might have started off by telling the end of the story since that would be the last thing they heard, Kristy moved back to the beginning. She remembered the names of the characters (shoemaker and elves) and used them. She repeated words frequently, a strategy that gave her time to think ahead. She had not yet developed a sense of audience, blithely using words like "he," "them," and "those guys," and leaving it to the listener to figure out to whom those words referred. While Kristy was able to convey a sense of what the story was about, she left out whole chunks of the story. She centered her retelling on the elves, probably because that aspect of the tale was most enchanting. She stopped several times and only the teacher's promptings caused her to extend her retelling. Kristy needs many experiences to retell stories; perhaps a flannelboard experience would give her the assistance she needs to add detail in the retelling. Drama may provide help to her as she elaborates and extends characterization through her concentration of one role rather than on all.

Compare Kristy's retelling with the retold tale of Meg, a sixth-grader. Meg had read a folktale by the Grimms, "Cherry, or the Frog Bride." She told the story to a group of friends and she began the retelling as follows:

> In this kingdom lived the King and his three sons and an old woman and her daughter named Cherry. And the three sons were sent out by the King to discover wisdom in the lands around the kingdom. And as they were going on their adventure they met this girl named they saw this girl named Cherry. Well, before this happened, this mother ran out of cherries to give this girl. She was named Cherry because she liked cherries so much and that was the only thing she ate. And the mother finally had to go to this nunnery and that was nearby to get these cherries for the little girl because for the girl, because she would eat nothing but cherries. And the mother was too poor to buy them. So she was taking cherries from the nunnery. And the Abbess saw but she wasn't angry. So later on these three princes were going through this village where the mother and her daughter lived. And they saw Cherry combing her hair in the village and they all thought that she was lovely and all wanted to marry her. So they started fighting over her. And the Abbess came out and caught them fighting over her and sought revenge by turning Cherry into an ugly toad.

Meg continues her story, which goes on at some length. She recounts the trials of the princes in much detail, concluding the retelling in this fashion:

> ... So the prince got up and started back home. And on the way back this little coach passed him that reminded me of the coach in Cinderella with the little mice and things on it. He didn't even think anything about it because he was too worried about not being able to accomplish this task. As he went around this bend where the coach had gone he found the coach like it had turned into in Cinderella with the prince and the coachmen.

> So he took Cherry back. And even though the maidens were very pretty that his older brothers brought back as soon as the king saw Cherry, he awarded the kingdom to his youngest son. And his son married Cherry and they lived happily ever after.

The first thing one notes is the length and the complexity of Meg's retelling in which no part of the story is left untold. Meg has a strong sense of audience. As she begins her story she has the king's sons setting off on a journey where they will find Cherry. Meg quickly realizes that there is a bit of information about Cherry that the listeners need to know if they are to follow the story, so she backtracks in order to include it. Meg sustains her retelling with no prompting and retells the story in exact sequence. Her sentences are more complex syntactically although she strings them together with conjunctions. Furthermore, her syntax patterns frequently reflect those found in written language, such as:

In this kingdom lived the king....

They all set out again and took the same roads as before, the two eldest sons taking the nice ones and the youngest taking the swamp.

As he went around the bend where the coach had gone....

Meg uses the vocabulary she has acquired from her reading in appropriate and precise ways: "nunnery," "abbess," "sought revenge," "awarded," and "maidens." She sees relationships between stories. In a technique approximating stream of consciousness, she shares the image that comes to her mind when a coach becomes a part of the story: " ... that reminded me of the coach in Cinderella with the little mice and things." Finally, Meg was able to keep a group of friends enthralled with her retelling from start to finish. Perhaps Meg's retelling skills could be assisted through the use of a tape-recorder so that she could listen to herself for self-evaluation. As with the younger child, drama may be a helpful avenue to concentrate on characterization. This is a good time to compare oral retelling with written versions to see if she is able to translate her oral skills into written form.

These two retellings were juxtaposed in order to convey how literary input strengthens children's language. As the children are given a rich input of literature, they begin to control more and more completely the conventions of story—the organization of the tale, the patterns of various genre. Fed by author's language, vocabulary becomes much more extensive. This linguistic development will be seen in both children's oral and written language.

Stages in "Book Talk." Talk seems to flow naturally from books. At the very earliest stages children's talk about books may be mostly pointing out and naming objects they recognize in a book's illustrations. Books such as Oxenbury's *ABC of Things* or *Anno's Counting Book* will encourage the child to do just that. Young children will enjoy retelling a story they have heard. Folktales such as "The Three Billy Goats Gruff" and "The Little Red Hen" with their predictable patterns and refrains invite children to retell. Newer books such as Rayner's *Mr. and Mrs. Pig's Evening Out* or Preston's *Where Did My Mother Go?*, which follow the folktale pattern, are good choices for "read-aloud" books at this stage.

Children in first and second grade still have a view of the world that is limited by their egocentrism. At this stage they are ready to relate stories they hear to events in their own lives. For example, they will be able to talk about *Leo, the Late Bloomer* (Kraus) and to relate to Leo's difficulties in learning to eat neatly, to draw well, and to read at all. Many children will sympathize with Peter, whose furniture was repainted pink and handed down to a new baby sister in the book *Peter's Chair* (Keats). Familiar experiences, such as the loss of a tooth by Sal in *One Morning in Maine* (McClosky), will bring forth a torrent of talk about the children's similar experiences.

Third- and fourth-graders are becoming less egocentric. At this point they can begin to look at the world through someone else's eyes. They are empathetic and ready to discuss how others might feel. Stolz has written two books that would help children to move into this kind of discussion. *A Dog on Barkham Street* is the story of Edward, a boy whose life is made miserable by Martin, the bully who lives next door to him. A second book, *The Bully of Barkham Street,* is the same story but told from Martin's point of view. Other kinds of book comparisons will also be a source of interest to children at this stage. Many of the books by Lionni, such as *Swimmy, The Biggest House in the World, Fish Is Fish,* and *Alexander and the Wind-Up Mouse* have a similar theme—the importance of being oneself.

Other children in fifth, sixth, and seventh grades will be reading some books that have layers of meaning. *Tuck Everlasting* (Babbitt), for example, can be read simply as a good fantasy, or it may be looked at in the light of characterization as the reader examines how Winnie Foster grows and changes. Another layer is the theme of the cycle of life—from birth to death, represented symbolically by the wheel that appears over and over in the text. High fantasy books such as *The Dark Is Rising* (Cooper) and *A Wizard of Earthsea* (LeGuin), which have at their center the struggle between good and evil, will challenge the reader to think, to reexamine, and to talk.

Book Discussions. Discussion, talking together in small groups about a topic of mutual concern, is a vital part of a language-arts program. Moffett and Wagner (1976) have stated, "It is through discussing that learners face the challenge of defining, clarifying, qualifying, elaborating, analyzing and ordering experiences, concepts, opinions or ideas, thereby developing their thinking and verbalizing skills for reading and writing" (p. 74).

Books provide an ideal basis for such discussion. When children have read the same book they have shared a special kind of experience, which is both sustained and complete. They followed a narrative from start to finish and have shared not only the story but also the language and the thinking of the author. A book permits a discussion to take place from the point of view of the spectator. You can discuss the actions, emotions, and values of a book character with far more objectivity than you are able to discuss your own actions or feelings. With book in hand, children can justify and elaborate, because they can always return to the text to support their views when they need to. A book discussion, then, offers special opportunities for children to sharpen and hone their ability to exchange ideas with others in a small-group setting.

Some book discussions can be held by the children themselves without the aid of a teacher once they become aware of what happens in a book discussion. Such groups may arise from a shared interest, as when a group of children who enjoy reading horse stories gathers to talk about books by Marguerite Henry. In chapter 4 of this text a discussion of the book *The Cay* (Taylor) is presented. That discussion was held without a teacher present. However, there are also occasions for a book discussion to include the teacher. The teacher can help children to explore a book in greater depth than they might be able to do on their own.

One teacher was working with a small group of fifth- and sixth-graders, all of whom had read L'Engle's book *A Wrinkle in Time* and wanted to talk about it. This is a powerful and complex book. On one level it is the suspenseful story of three children, fourteen-year-old Meg Murry, her five-year-old brother Charles Wallace, and her friend Calvin, who set off on a search to find the Murry children's father, a scientist who has been missing for some time. The children find Mr. Murry, but to do so they have to journey to another planet in another galaxy. They do this by "tessering"—that is, by moving through time and space in the fifth dimension. On this level the book is a rousing good tale of science fiction.

On another level, *A Wrinkle in Time* is a story of how light can conquer darkness. Camazotz, the planet where Mr. Murry is being held prisoner, is a planet that has surrendered to the dark. Everyone is controlled by the powerful brain of It. Children even skip rope and bounce balls to the throbbing rhythm set by It. On yet another level this is a book about the power of love. It is Meg's love that helps her vanquish It in a struggle for the mind and body of Charles Wallace. Implicit in the text is the love of God for His world and for those whom He has created.

Before the book discussion, the teacher webbed out the possibilities for discussion in order to be able to move flexibly with the children's ideas (page 352). Webbing was used as a way for the teacher to organize his own thoughts so he could more easily relate to the children's ideas about the same book.

The process of webbing assisted the teacher to plan a few questions that might help the children move back into the story by refreshing their memories. He also planned a few questions that would lead the children more deeply into certain aspects of the book or help them to look at the book from a different perspective. The questions he jotted down all focused on the strengths of the book.

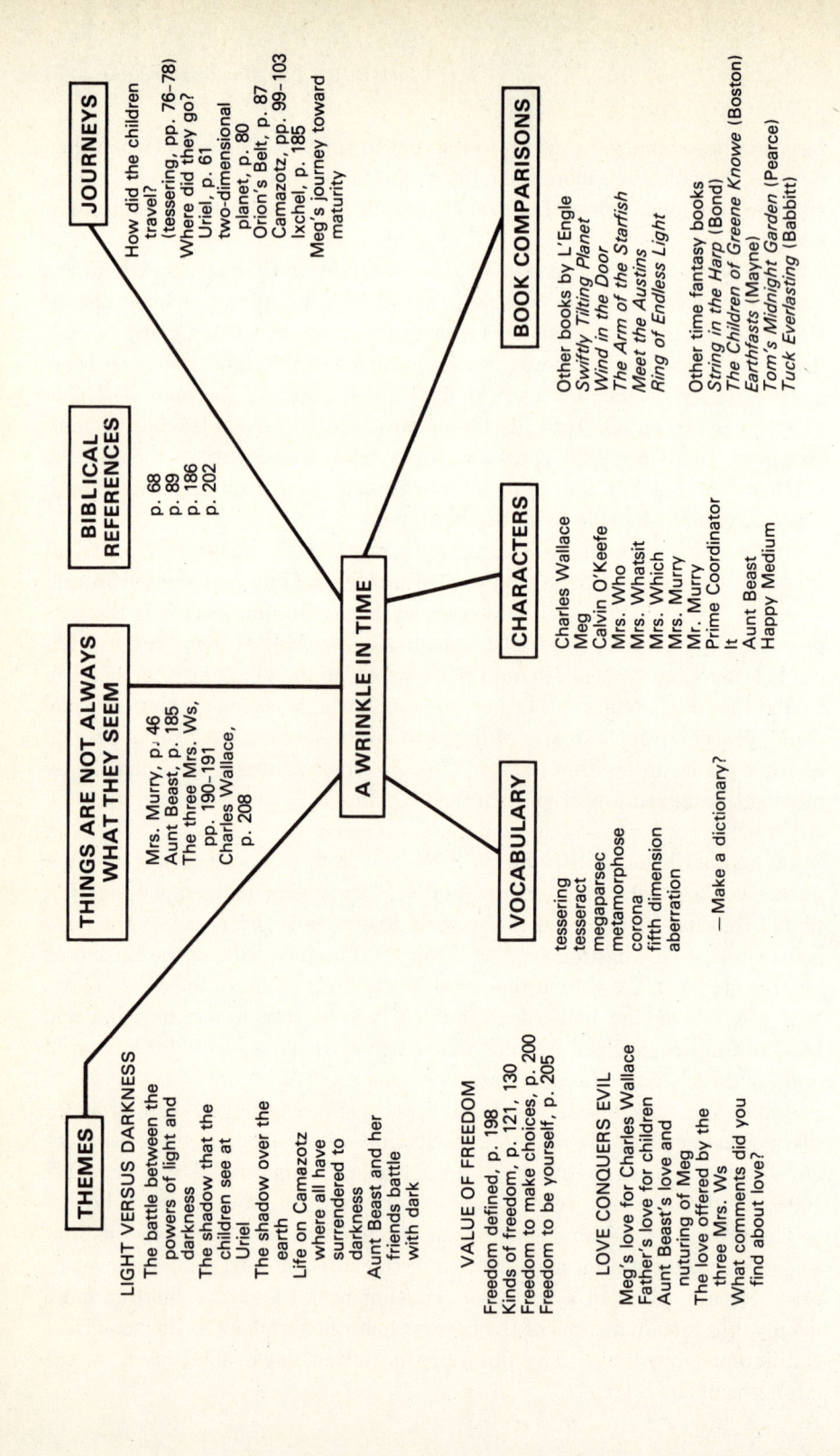

A WRINKLE IN TIME

JOURNEYS
- How did the children travel? (tessering, pp. 76-78)
- Where did they go?
  - Uriel, p. 61
  - two-dimensional planet, p. 80
  - Orion's Belt, p. 87
  - Camazotz, pp. 99-103
  - Ixchel, p. 185
- Meg's journey toward maturity

BIBLICAL REFERENCES
- p. 68
- p. 89
- p. 186
- p. 202

THINGS ARE NOT ALWAYS WHAT THEY SEEM
- Mrs. Murry, p. 46
- Aunt Beast, p. 185
- The three Mrs. Ws, pp. 190-191
- Charles Wallace, p. 208

CHARACTERS
- Charles Wallace
- Meg
- Calvin O'Keefe
- Mrs. Who
- Mrs. Whatsit
- Mrs. Which
- Mrs. Murry
- Mr. Murry
- Prime Coordinator
- It
- Aunt Beast
- Happy Medium

BOOK COMPARISONS
- Other books by L'Engle
  - Swiftly Tilting Planet
  - Wind in the Door
  - The Arm of the Starfish
  - Meet the Austins
  - Ring of Endless Light
- Other time fantasy books
  - String in the Harp (Bond)
  - The Children of Greene Knowe (Boston)
  - Earthfasts (Mayne)
  - Tom's Midnight Garden (Pearce)
  - Tuck Everlasting (Babbitt)

VOCABULARY
- tessering
- tesseract
- megaparsec
- metamorphose
- corona
- fifth dimension
- aberration

—Make a dictionary?

THEMES

LIGHT VERSUS DARKNESS
- The battle between the powers of light and darkness
- The shadow that the children see at Uriel
- The shadow over the earth
- Life on Camazotz where all have surrendered to darkness
- Aunt Beast and her friends battle with dark

VALUE OF FREEDOM
- Freedom defined, p. 198
- Kinds of freedom, p. 121, 130
- Freedom to make choices, p. 200
- Freedom to be yourself, p. 205

LOVE CONQUERS EVIL
- Meg's love for Charles Wallace
- Father's love for children
- Aunt Beast's love and nuturing of Meg
- The love offered by the three Mrs. Ws
- What comments did you find about love?

1. Who were the characters in the story? What is special about each character?
2. This is the story of a journey. Can you tell me about this journey? Was there more than one journey?
3. Several characters were not what they seemed to be at first. Can you think of any characters who were like that?
4. How would you react:

   to Mrs. Whatsit when she said, "We want nothing from you that you do without grace ... or that you do without understanding" (p. 195)?

   to Mrs. Murry when she said, "I've learned you don't have to understand things for them to be" (p. 23).

   to It, when he said, "I in my own strength am willing to assume all pain, all responsibility, all the burden of thought and decision" (p. 121).

   to this statement about Meg: "It was she who was limited by her senses, not the blind beasts, for they must have senses of which she could not even dream" (p. 182).
5. This is the story of many battles. Which battles do you remember? How were they won or lost?
6. What made the story seem real to you?
7. How does Meg at the end of the book differ from Meg at the beginning of the story?
8. If you asked Madeleine L'Engle to define evil, what do you think she would say? What do you think she would say about love?

The amount of preparation done by this teacher does not mean that he took the major role in the discussion nor that he used all the questions he wrote. The questions are to be used sparingly—only when needed. They are asked not to prod children into saying what the teacher wants to hear, but to get an honest response about how the children feel and what they think. The chief task of the teacher is to listen. A listening attitude and the value he places upon the thoughts shared by children will help them to expand their talk and their thinking.

Activities with Books that Can Lead to Talk. Talk about books can take place throughout the day. Children may want to tell a friend about a book they have read or the teacher may share a new book he or she has discovered. Events that occur during the day may call forth talk about books. When one third-grader's brother brought in his pet snake to show the class, the book *Crictor* by Ungerer was happily recalled. The children looked at the long snake coiled in his cage and wondered at length if he could do all

354 *Integration of the Language Arts*

the things that Crictor could—serve as a jump rope, a kite's tail, form letters and numbers.

As children extend books many different kinds of talk will be used. One group of children made a diorama of the town square in *Strega Nona* (dePaola) just as the pasta begins to coil about the statues, fall into the fountain, and slither up the church steps. They had lengthy discussions on making things to scale. Much time was spent on trying out materials to use for pasta—real spaghetti, dry and cooked, yarn, paper strips, and string all were tried. Questions were raised, positions set forth, decisions were made; later, the children shared their project with another class. They retold and shared the book and described how they went about making their project. A wide variety of language functions were made possible because of the cooperative nature of this project.

Another group of children in Mrs. Stewart's fifth-grade class developed a game from the book *Why Mosquitoes Buzz in People's Ears* (Aardema). This is the tale of a mosquito whose innocent remark to an iguana creates chaos in the jungle. The design of the game was influenced by the colorful illustrations. The children decided a board game would be best because they could make the curvy snake be the path that players must follow. The markers were the different animals that appeared in the story and the mosquito became the spinner. The cards the players were to draw took much time to devise. In writing the instructions on the cards the children made use of the African words that occurred in the story. The rules for playing the game were difficult to write. The game was tried out a number of times with the result that the rules were resequenced and amended until the children were able to be sure that players could play the game with no outside assistance. At the very end of the book is an illustration showing a large hand squashing a mosquito. The only text is the word KPAO! Note how the children incorporate this aspect of the book into their game.

Think of the language used to decide how the game would be played. The act of making the game drew the children back again and again to the book, thus deepening the youngsters' understanding of the text.

Mosquito!

Rules:

Each player shuts his eyes and draws a marker from the bag.

Green gets to be Iguana and hold Iguana during the game. He starts *first*.

Tan gets to be Rabbit and hold Rabbit while he plays. He starts *second*.

Brown gets to be Monkey, and hold him while he plays. He starts *third*.

Orange gets to be Mother Owl and hold her while he plays. He starts *last*.

Each player spins in turn. He must go down as many cards as Mosquito sends him when he stops on a number. He must then read the card aloud, and follow directions.

Those landing on Lucky Seven get to move seven spaces forward.

After a card is used it is placed on the bottom of the deck.

The first player to pop off the Python's tail becomes Mother Owl. He gets to hoot three times for the sun to come up.

The second player to pop off the Python's tail becomes King Lion. He roars three times to declare himself King of the Jungle.

The third player to pop off the Python's tail becomes Crow and gets to call out

Punish the Mosquito!
Punish the Mosquito!
Punish the Mosquito!

The player still on the board gets to *KPAO* a very very small mosquito that only he can see on the unlucky loser's left hand.

POOR MOSQUITO!!!
_____
_____

Dramatic Expression. Drama provides another avenue for extending children's language through literature. It is immediately necessary to make a distinction between "theater" and "drama." The term "theater" suggests a written script to be memorized, sets, costumes, and a performance before an audience. The term "drama," on the other hand, is more likely to be an improvised, cooperative, creative adventure that requires no sets, no costumes, and no audience. Brian Way (1967) writes, "Theatre is largely concerned with *communication* between actors and an audience; drama is largely concerned with *experience* by the participants, irrespective of any function of communication to an audience" (p. 3).

Drama should be an integral part of any language-arts program, for it lets the child focus upon oral language in some very special ways. Dramatic representation requires that the voice be used to convey emotion and to delineate character. It calls for an exploration of the power of stress, pitch, and volume of voice. Since drama is a cooperative venture; the actors must listen attentively to each other in order to build upon what has been said. Drama, then, provides a real need to speak clearly and distinctly. In addition, attention must be given to register. A king does not talk the same way a scullery maid does nor a soldier like a little boy. Taking on a role in a drama requires an ability to take on other registers.

While drama can grow from many sources, children's literature is particularly rich. Stories can provide a base for developing narrative, for creating a character, and for language upon which children can build. Drama leads children back into a book. As children work together to interpret a story, they gain a new perspective and their understanding of the author's message deepens.

The teacher beginning drama with a class will probably want to begin in small ways. One of the first steps into drama is pantomime—conveying ideas without words through posture, movement, gesture, and expression. An example of how the teacher might do this can be seen in the work one teacher did with the book *Strega Nona*. In one part of the book Big Anthony, the apprentice to Strega Nona, invites all the townspeople to Strega Nona's home where he will serve them pasta from the magic pasta pot. The children and the teacher talked about serving spaghetti. They discussed the qualities of spaghetti that made it hard to serve: its slipperiness, its length, the thinness of the strands, and its heat. They then talked about the size of the pasta pot, which they agreed would be much bigger than the saucepans their mothers use. Children then demonstrated how Big Anthony moved as he reached into the pot to swirl up hot masses of pasta to serve each person. Other ideas of pantomine that might grow from that same scene in the story are:

Someone watching Big Anthony serve, following the apprentice's gestures with his eyes.

Someone waiting in line to be served who is getting hungrier and hungrier.

A little girl waiting in line trying to see over the heads of the crowd.

A small boy carrying away a very large bowl of steaming hot pasta.

Another source of pantomine is to think about how people in the story might move. Anthony is not portrayed as being very energetic. How might he hoe the garden? Strega Nona is a round grandmother witch. How would she be walking as she set off to see her friend, Strega Amelia? When the magic pasta pot overflowed, it eventually covered the town square with a thick layer of warm, slippery spaghetti. How would you have to walk across the square if you were a schoolboy? If you were a dainty young woman with long skirts? Pantomime can also be a cooperative effort; for example, how might a group work together to build a barricade to keep the pasta out of the town?

A next step into drama is improvising dialogue. Again, it is better to begin in a small way. Rather than act out whole stories, begin with small bits of dialogue. This narrow focus lets the children think about how people would talk and move and how they would react to what others say, without having to move a story forward. Suggestions for such bits of dialogue that might grow from *Strega Nona* are:

What do you think happened when Big Anthony applied for the job at Strega Nona's house? What might she have asked him? What would he have told her about himself?

Who might have been waiting in line to be served pasta?—a nun? the mayor? a mischievous little girl? a mother with a hungry child? relatives of Big Anthony? What might they talk about while they wait?

After such beginnings, children will be able to act out sections of the story and eventually, if they wish, the entire story. Sometimes improvisation can go beyond the text. For example, while the text ends with Big Anthony eating up all the pasta, the aftermath of the "pasta inundation" would have continued. The mayor might have been faced with an angry man who had lost his prize grape arbor to the spaghetti flood, or a priest concerned about the damage to his church's pipe organ. Children could look at the story from another point of view. Strega Nona would probably want to tell Strega Amelia about what had happened or Big Anthony in his later years might want to tell his grandchildren about this part of his life story.

By beginning with small pieces of drama, everyone can have a go at it, for nothing is fixed. Such activities accomplish what Heathcote calls "building belief." As children think about the way a witch would move, or what a person might say or do in a given situation, they strengthen their creative abilities. They must call upon their own experiences and observations. "Drama happens because they, like all other beings, have a fantastic capacity—the ability to identify" (Wagner, 1976, p. 33).

Role-playing is another way children can share their ability to identify with a character. Sometimes characters from one book might wish to talk with characters from another book. Karana in *Island of the Blue Dolphins* (O'Dell), survived all alone on a Pacific island for eighteen years. Julie in *Julie of the Wolves* (George) survived alone through the long Alaskan winter by becoming part of a pack of wild wolves. If Julie and Karana met, surely they would have tales to share and questions to ask.

Puppetry is another form of dramatization that creates a real need for language. The creation of puppets, if done cooperatively, is the basis for much talk and decision-making. Puppets may be created from a variety of materials and in a variety of ways. They may be as simple as a sock slipped over a hand with a face drawn on with marking pens, to more elaborate creations of papier mâché with beautifully sewn costumes. One group of third-graders had a wonderful time making puppets of nursery-rhyme characters. Nursery rhymes told by the puppets were shared with the kindergarten class. Later in their own classroom, these third-graders put their puppets together to discuss similar problems.

> Jack Sprat's wife who lived in a pumpkin shell and the Old Woman who lived in a shoe got together to discuss the difficulty of finding good housing.
>
> Humpty Dumpty and Jack and Jill discussed their falls and the medical care they received.
>
> Mary's little lamb and the black sheep who said "Baa baa" talked over their daily activities to see how they varied.

Another technique for dramatization of books is "Story Theater." This is described by Moffett and Wagner (1976, pp. 111–117). As the text of a story is read or narrated the actions of that story are shown in pantomime. For example, if the story of the Three Bears were read, one child could be Goldilocks and in appropriate places show how she peeked into the house, how she gingerly tried two bowls of porridge, and how she gobbled up Baby Bear's porridge. Other actors would show Father Bear's annoyance, Mother Bear's dismay, and Baby Bear's disconsolate weeping.

Thus drama helps children deepen their understanding of story. Drama slows the story down and gives children a chance to think about the "hows" and the "whys" of an action. It permits them to elaborate, to add detail, to compose dialogue, and to demonstrate emotional and sensory experiences through gesture and voice. Moffett and Wagner suggest this experience with drama is a bridge to writing. They write:

> Generally an important relationship in the process of writing is that of drama to narrative; drama elaborates narrative and narrative summarizes drama.... By improvising dramas for narrative sketches and, conversely, by writing narrative summaries of improvisation, pupils can grasp the abstractive relationship between these two orders of discourse (1976, p. 102).

Writing from Literature

Hearing and reading good children's literature will influence children's writing. Literature provides the input of language and imagery. Through hearing stories children begin to take on the literary conventions of beginnings and endings and of the patterns of various genres. As they discuss books, they begin to see how the author delineates a character, details a setting, or evokes an emotion. Literature gives children a sturdy platform from which they can launch their own writing efforts.

Books that Provide a Story Frame

Mrs. Blocher had shared Viorst's book *Alexander and the Terrible, Horrible, No Good, Very Bad Day* with her class. One girl in the class later wrote about her own dreadful day using Viorst's framework. There is the same reporting of dreadful happening after dreadful happening. The language closely approximates the style found in the book; however, the experiences are her very own, now seen in a new light and presented humorously to an audience.

Today was a Terrible Horrible No good vary bad day. first I spill jelly allover my pants and had to change. Then during jym a lutten pot on my pants. And I had to miss jym.

Thats how my terriBLe, Horrible no good vary Bad day started out then when I went to put the pin in my pants If my zipper Broke then I knew it was going to Be a terriBle Horrible, no good very Bad day. When I was going to miss Blockes my shoe came untied and I triped down the stetps. a terriBle, no good, vary baddoy, is when you cant even walk down the steeps.

When I got home from school I had to do the dishes, I hate to do the dishes,
I had to do the livengroom and seuip the floar,
Thats a terriBle, no good verry Bad day.
When I was ridding my skateBord I fell and cut my knee and had to get stiches.

have you every had such a terriBle, horriBle, No good, very Bad day? When I got home from the hospelet I fill and buied my lip.

What a terriBLe horriBLe No good varry Bad day

Mrs. Blocher responded to Sharon's story. This is the note she attached to the writing when she returned it to the little girl.

> Sharon, I hope you don't have too many such terrible, horrible, no-good days. It really was a bad one! It reminded me of the bad day I had when I got locked out of my house on a cold, rainy day. My books were getting wet. I was hungry and cold. Worst of all I had to wait *one hour* for my husband to come home and let me in. It *really* happened to me! Did your bad day really happen to you?
>
> It might be fun to think about a terrific, wonderful, fantastic, super-good day. Do you think that would be easier or harder to write about than Alexander's day?

In her response Mrs. Blocher did not evaluate or rate Sharon's writing; instead, she responded to what the child had said. The teacher's comments let Sharon know that she appreciated the way the child had used the Viorst framework for her story by sharing an experience of her own. Mrs. Blocher's comments not only established a dialogue between teacher and child, but encouraged further writing.

There are many books that can help children develop a framework for telling a story. After sharing books like *The Turtle and the Two Ducks: Animal Tales retold from La Fontaine* (Plante and Bergman) and the book *Fables* in which Lobel invents his own pithy and humorous fables, children will begin to develop a feeling for the fable genre. They will perceive that fables are characterized by brevity, animal characters who act out a universal truth, and are concluded by a moral maxim. Such input will permit children to experiment with fable form.

Jim and the Beanstalk by Briggs is a delightful retelling of the folktale "Jack and the Beanstalk." Briggs's version of the tale takes place years later when the giant is much older. He has lost his hair and his teeth, and his eyesight is failing. *You Can Go Jump* (McLenighan) is a retelling of the tale of the frog who returns the golden ball the princess has lost. The version is told in the vernacular of today using a cartoon style. When the frog is finally turned into a handsome prince, he tells the demanding princess that she can "Go jump!" *Red Riding* (Merrill and Solbert) is the story of Red Ridinghood as told by a little girl to her younger brother who constantly interrupts her with questions and with his own interpretations. Such books as the aforementioned will encourage children to feel free to try their own rewriting of familiar tales. Knowing a story framework gives children the security they need to experiment, elaborate, and personalize.

One middle-grader had read Monjo's book *Grandpapa and Ellen Aroon*, a tale told through the eyes of Thomas Jefferson's granddaughter. When Irene finished reading the story, she developed an ABC book based on what she had learned. Her writing reflects not only knowledge of the ABC format, but also the language of Monjo's book.

Anastacia. The fancy name my older sister wants to be called.

Blue Ridge Mountains. What you can see from Grandpapa's portico.

Chair. Grandpapa's leather "whirlagig" chair that swirls around.

Books that Extend Children's Use of Words

The extensive vocabulary used by authors can spill over into children's writing. After hearing *A Wrinkle in Time* read aloud, a group of fourth-graders returned to the book and developed a chart they labeled "*Wrinkle in Time* Words." This focus upon the vocabulary of Madeleine L'Engle helped them explore new words that might expand their own writing vocabulary.

Wrinkle in Time Words

inexorable	tangible	intangible
naive	muted	aloft
exultation	serenely	infinity
corona	tentatively	illumination
insolent	dimension	reverberated
resilience	arrogance	fascination
simultaneously	billions	vulnerable
peril	sonorous	substantial
monotonous	authoritative	preconditioned

The imagery found in some books makes them excellent choices for reading aloud. *Swimmy* and *When the Sky Is Like Lace,* which were mentioned previously, are examples of books in which the author has used words to create images in the reader's mind. In her book *Walk with Your Eyes,* Brown captions her lovely color photographs of nature in ways that help children see images. A close-up view of a dried leaf is seen as a "leaf map." A breathtaking photograph of the gigantic curl of a wave is captioned, "You can slide down the green glass curve of a wave" (1979, unpaged). Hoberman's *A House Is a House for Me* creates images that add new dimensions to the word "house":

The cookie jar's home to the cookies.
The breadbox is home to the bread.

My coat is a house for my body.
My hat is a house for my head
	(1978, unpaged).

Such books can help ignite the child's imagination. One kindergartner, after hearing *A House Is a House for Me,* announced with a smile that "arms are a house for a hug, a hug!" Well-selected books read aloud and discussed with children can help them to focus on the flow and the sound of written language and to see that their vision of the world can be put into words.

Books that Motivate Writing

In addition to providing input, books can motivate children's writing. The book *Kickle Snifters and Other Fearsome Critters* (Schwartz) is a catalogue of strange and wondrous animals. There is the "Rubberado," who bounces from place to place, and the "Side-Hill Gouger," whose uphill legs are much shorter than his downhill legs. Such a book simply invites readers to join in the fun and invent some of their own animals.

Other books involve the reader so deeply that shared emotions need to be expressed. After hearing *Julie of the Wolves* read aloud, one sixth-grader wrote a diary that Julie might have kept. He returned to the book again and again telling Miss George he wanted to get it "just right." The intensity of his involvement with the loneliness that faced Julie is apparent in his journal. Read the journal closely. What extrapolations did this young writer make from the story? Think about how you might extend this youngster. What kind of conference would you hold with him? Which books should he be reading next? Could this experience be a lead-in to diary-style books such as *My Side of the Mountain* (George) or other survival stories such as *Call It Courage* (Sperry)?

July 1st

Dear Diary,

Today I ran away from Daniel. He is meaner than I thought. I stopped at Pearl's and got a sleeping skin, food and needles.

I was scared when I thought about the long walk to Point Hope, then getting to San Francisco. What would I do if I ran out of food? Where would I sleep? Would I make it?

I just went along wondering and hoping. I am now Miyax, not Julie. I built a mud hut on top of a little hill, close to a pond. I also had some matches, a cooking pot and a backpack which I hadn't mentioned before.

July 2nd

Dear Diary,
 Today I met the wolves. I named the leader Amaroq, then Silver, Nails, Jello, and the pups Kapu, Sister, Zit, Zat, Zing. I was scared of them at first, then I discovered that they were very shy creatures. My food is almost gone. I have to try to talk to Amaroq to get food. My father Kapugen, the hunter, talked to wild animals once, but he never told me how. I guess I'll have to watch what they do and copy them. But how?

July 3rd

Dear Diary,
 I am surprised at how hard it is to communicate. It is hard to keep watching the wolves. I keep thinking which is worse, Daniel, or hunger, or loneliness? I can't seem to find an answer. I just might as well give up. It's no use hoping that I'll get something to eat or even get to Point Hope. What scares me most is dying out here in the wildness. Can't I learn to speak wolf or is it impossible? Every day I get hungrier and hungrier. Will I live?

July 4th

Dear Diary,
 I am progressing. I think I know the wolf word for anger. It is a growl and lips curled up with teeth showing, and eyes slitted. I have practiced it a lot. I might be able to learn more from Kapu, the oldest, funniest, and ringleader of all the pups. I hope he teaches me good enough, so I can tell Amaroq about how hungry and starving I am. If not, I will be left heart-broken.

July 5th

Dear Diary,
 Today it rained. The wolves didn't go out, neither did I. I have to patch a part of my roof since it rained in. After the rain stopped, I went to a pond which was nearby and got some water. I gathered caribou droppings and lit a giant fire. I found some seeds on the ground and on the flowers. I ate them. It only filled a little corner of my appetite. I felt tired, so I took a short nap. When I woke up it was raining again. I fell back asleep and when I woke up, I heard the wolves coming back from a hunt. They had no meat.

July 6th

Dear Diary,
 The wolves stayed in the cave all of today. Then I remembered about the long hunt yesterday and decided they were sleeping. I gathered seeds and caribou droppings. It took time to get used to this but I liked it. I spotted a prairie fox

today, which is unusual as they should be sleeping. This may be the last entry. I can't find another piece of paper. I hope not.

July 7th

Dear Diary,
I am learning the wolf language quickly. Kapu and his mother were out and I watched them. I was filled with joy when I discovered how easy the wolf language is. I know this is the last entry, unless I can find something else to write on. Goodby.

The pleasure of sharing books with children provides one of the very best ways to extend their repertoire of language and to help them become sensitive to the way words can be used to produce an image or to sketch a feeling. It assists the child to take on the structures that separate written language from spoken language.

Integrating Literature into the Language-Arts Program

As can be seen by the prior discussion, literature is rich with ideas for extensions in the language arts. Huck (1979) suggests webbing as a way for finding the various directions a student might take from a book.

> The more planning that is done to discover all the possibilities in a book, the freer the teacher will be to follow children's interests and extend their understandings. Rather than being restricted to a single lesson plan, which might not meet the needs of the particular group being taught, the leader who has thought through the potential of a particular book may explore as many aspects as seem worthwhile for the developmental level of the children (p. 721).

An Example of a Literature Web

The web was on page 366 developed from the book *The Great Gilly Hopkins,* written by Katherine Paterson. This is the powerful story of a girl, Gilly, who was deserted by a young mother, made a ward of the court, and shifted from foster family to foster family. Gilly, a survivor, becomes wise in ways to manage and manipulate people. But through all her trials, her dream never changes. She yearns for her mother, Courtney, to return from the commune where she is living and to build a new life for the two of them. When

THE GREAT GILLY HOPKINS

RELATED LITERATURE

CHILD ABUSE
Rainbow Jordan by Childress
The Pinballs by Byars

STRUGGLE TO GROW UP
Julie of the Wolves by George
My Own Private Sky by Beckman
18th Emergency by Byars
From the Mixed-up Files of Mrs. Basil E. Frankweiler by Konigsburg

RELATING TO ADULTS
After the Goat Man by Byars
The Cay by Taylor

OTHER BOOKS BY PATERSON
Angels and Other Strangers
Bridge to Terebithia
Jacob Have I Loved
The Master Puppeteer
The Sign of the Chrysanthemum

GETTING TO KNOW THE AUTHOR

Find Paterson's acceptance speech and biography in *Horn Book*
Read write-ups in *N.Y. Times Book Review* and *Language Arts*
Paterson's craft—trace development of Gilly through her story
"Maggie's Gift"
Paterson's work as a translator in *The Crane Wife* (Yagawa)

RELATED POETRY

"Zada to Baby" by Livingston
"Thumbprint" by Merriam
"Intellectualism" by Giovanni
"Me" by Danny
"Boys Don't Cry" by Martinez

DISCUSSION

What might have happened if Gilly had run away?
Compare to TV drama of *The Pinballs* (Byars)
Debate ending:
It had to end that way because . . .
It shouldn't have ended that way because . . .

WRITING

Gilly's diary
A letter from Ernest T. to Gilly
Newspaper article about Gilly's being picked up at bus station as a runaway
Social worker's report on Gilly
Maime Trotter's diary
Letter from the Grandmother to Courtney after her visit to see Gilly
Graffiti board of words to describe characters
Rewrite the ending

DISPLAY

Collection of comments about Gilly by people who knew her
Items that were special to Gilly
Information about Paterson
Book display other books by Paterson; books related to *The Great Gilly Hopkins*

TO CONSTRUCT

A diorama of two living rooms—Maime's and the Grandmother's

Gilly is sent to live with Maime Trotter, her life is changed. Gilly is not able to manipulate Maime. Walls that Gilly had built around herself to shield her emotions suddenly begin to crumble. This is a book about love, about families, and about growing up; a book that children will want to read and to talk about.

Obviously, a great many activities could come from the reading of this book if teachers make the books and materials available. A full variety of extensions occur only after children have had many experiences with books and the opportunity to share their reading in a number of ways. Not all activities from a web will or even should be done. This would tire children to boredom! But teacher knowledge of what may develop from a book helps plan for student interests and may be a source for suggesting extensions to children who need a new direction.

Webbing need not be limited to a single book at the core. Literature webs can be developed around themes such as "survival" or "becoming" or concepts and topics may be similarly planned out; for instance, the topic "mice" was webbed in the first chapter. Other webs appeared in chapters 1, An Integrated Language-Arts Program: A Rationale" and 7, "Language Arts in the Content Areas" and will be discussed in chapter 10, "Program Planning and Evaluation."

Assessment

In assessing how effectively literature is being used to extend language, a teacher must have a way of assessing how children are interacting with and responding to books. One researcher who examined children's responses to books is Hickman (1979). She used an ethnographic approach to explore children's responses to literature in natural classroom environments. She spent four months in classrooms from kindergarten through grade five as a participant-observer to identify the variety of ways children respond to books and to see if she could find any pattern of behavior that seemed to be related to classroom context.

Hickman categorized her observations into several groups. These categories have implications for language-arts teachers who wish to focus attention on children's interaction with books in order to assess their own classroom practices. Following is an observation guide based upon Hickman's six categories of response. This guide is one tool that pre-service and in-service teachers could find useful as they look at children's behavior in a classroom setting.

An Observation Guide to Literature in the Language-Arts Program

Listening Behavior

1. Child listens attentively to stories read aloud to a small group.
2. Child listens with attention to stories read to the whole class.
3. Child shows enjoyment of stories by laughing, commenting, body attitude.

Contact With Books

1. Child takes opportunities to browse through books in the reading corner or library.
2. Child keeps books at hand.
3. Child becomes intently involved with a book.

Sharing Books

1. Child chooses to read with other children.
2. Child seeks opportunities to share books with others.
3. Child is willing to discuss a book he or she has read with an adult.

Oral Responses

1. Retelling

    a) Child is able to retell a story he or she has read in sequence.
    b) Child's retelling includes story conventions such as traditional beginnings and endings.
    c) Child's retellings show an influence of the syntax and vocabulary of the written language.

2. Book Discussion

    a) Child is an attentive and active participant in a small-group book discussion.
    b) Child's contributions to the discussion show an ability to relate other books read and experiences he or she has had to the book under discussion.
    c) Child listens to what others have said and builds upon their comments.
    d) Child's comments help move the discussion forward.

3. Drama

    a) Child can dramatize his or her understanding of story actions through pantomime.

- b) Child is able to speak clearly and distinctly in doing improvisational dialogue.
- c) Child is able to use voice expressively to convey character and mood in improvisational drama.
- d) Child is able to listen to others in order to build together a dramatic improvisation of a story heard or read.

4. Extending Books
   - a) Child is able to use language in such cooperative book extensions as murals, dioramas, constructions, and gaming in order to:
     —ask questions
     —share information
     —make wishes known
     —come to a group decision
   - b) Child is able to share and explain a book project he or she has made:
     —with a small group
     —with the whole class
     —with an adult
     —with a group outside the class

Written Response

1. Child is able to write a summary of a book he or she has read or heard.
2. Child is able to use a literary model as a basis for his or her own writing:
   —by extending a story he or she has heard or read
   —by combining different stories to make his or her own new tale
   —by using an author's or a genre's story framework
3. Child's writing reflects the literary conventions used by authors.
4. Child's writing reflects the syntax and the vocabulary that can be found in children's literature.

As you use the guide you will become more aware of just how, when, and where children are interacting with books, you can begin to build upon each child's strengths. Children who like retelling stories can be provided with opportunities to tell stories to younger children, or perhaps to move into drama as another way to retell. Children who spent time browsing might profit from being able to interact with the teacher about some of the books which they are seeing. Input such as "If you like *Tales of a Fourth Grade Nothing* (Blume), I think you'd like this one about Henry Huggins, too" may help the child connect with a new book and author. Children who enjoy books, but whose extensions of books are a bit sparse, might be assisted to extend books with the support of a small group, or provided with more opportunities to share extensions others have done.

If you find that many children are looking at books but not becoming engrossed with books, you may wish to allow more time for children to make selections. You may also decide to take a more active role in helping children choose their literature since they may be missing connections between themselves, their prior readings and interests, and the books before them. If you discover that few children are sharing books with each other, you may decide to review the class's room arrangement. There may be few places where children can gather comfortably around books to talk.

Response to literature may include sharing a book with each other as these two middle grade students are doing in the classroom loft. Each has his own book but can interact with the other during their reading time. (Mrs. Monaghan's informal classroom, Barrington School, Upper Arlington, Ohio).

Summary

A language-arts program that does not have a strong literature component would be an impoverished program, for literature brings into the classroom rich vocabulary, imagery, and language shaped by an artist's mind. Literature enriches the experience of children and has the ability to let them view the world with a different, wider, or finer focus. Therefore, it allows children to discuss or write about old notions with a fresh perspective. Language is stimulated by hearing and reading stories and poetry, for books offer children models for writing, a platform for drama, and a basis for discussion.

Your ability to select and introduce children to quality literature and to provide a context that encourages children to read, listen to, and talk about books will be central to developing a strong language-arts program. As you assess children's interaction with books through close observation, you will be able to use books flexibly so that children's individual strengths and interests can be extended to lead to new learnings.

Recommended Readings

Huck, Charlotte, "Literature as the Content of Reading," *Theory into Practice* 16: 363–371, December, 1977.

> Too often children's literature is viewed as the "icing on the cake," a treat to be offered when the "real" work of the classroom has been completed. Huck sees literature as central both to the child's development as a caring, wondering person and as a fluent, enthusiastic reader. She provides a strong rationale for integrating literature within the total curriculum and suggests a variety of ways to achieve that goal.

Lamme, Linda, "Reading Aloud to Young Children," *Language Arts* 53: 886–888, November/December, 1976.

> Lamme describes a study in which a number of primary teachers were videotaped as they read to their students. Her findings form a good set of criteria to use as you read to children. Although the title limits the audience to young children, we believe the recommendations could be extended to older youngsters. For example, books for middle-grade students have few refrains or chants for easy child involvement, but especially at this age, children can discuss a character's intent, relate what they might have done in the same situation, and predict events to come. These acts too will involve the students in the story.

Ross, Ramon, R., *Storyteller,* Charles E. Merrill, Columbus, Ohio, 1972.

The author uses marginal notes to "talk through" the preparation of one story with the reader, raising questions about voice, pointing out interesting story details, and suggesting times to involve listeners. Suggestions are also given on how to practice and to share stories. There are separate chapters on the use of flannelboards, puppets, and choral reading. This is a readable and helpful book that invites you to join the age-old rank of storytellers.

Somers, Albert B. and Worthington, Janet Evans, *Response Guides for Teaching Children's Books,* National Council of Teachers of English, Urbana, Illinois, 1979.

A "response guide" is a series of suggestions for extending and exploring one particular book. It includes a summary of the narrative, suggestions for ways to move into that book, discussion questions, and ideas for drama, artwork, or writing that might be used to extend the reading. The authors have selected 27 books ranging from picture books, such as *Where The Wild Things Are* (Sendak), to stories for older readers, such as *Call It Courage* (Sperry).

Suggested Learning Experiences

1. Select a folktale you would like to learn and to share with children. The book *Storyteller* (see "Recommended Readings" above) will be of help as you prepare and practice the story. Tape-record your story and analyze your retelling. Listen for phrasing, voice quality, expression, and smoothness. How would you change your retelling? Share your story with a group of children. How does this experience compare with reading a book aloud to children?

2. Develop a card file of children's books you would like to use in your own classroom. On each card include the bibliographic entry, a brief annotation, and any ideas for extending the book that have occured to you. Categorize the books in ways that you find useful. Some categories might be: Books that Invite Drama, Story Frames for Writing, and Books with Poetic Language. Or you might wish to develop a poetry file. For sources you may wish to consult the books on literature cited in chapter 11.

3. Using the "Observation Guide for Literature in a Language-Arts Program" (page 368) spend a morning or afternoon in a classroom where books are shared frequently and are widely accessible. Try to find out as much as you can about children's interaction with books. You may wish

to focus on one or two children or to compare children. Organize what you have learned in a way that can be shared with the class. Discuss with the class or a small group within the class how you as a teacher would use these findings. Do your classmates agree or disagree with your recommendations for instruction?

4. Go into a classroom and find out which books are being read and passed around the class. If you think any of these books merit an in-depth book discussion, plan a series of questions that could serve as a resource pool in talking about the book with these children. Evaluate the discussion, keeping in mind whether it is the first book discussion these children have ever had or whether they are accustomed to discussing books frequently. An alternative plan is to bring into the classroom multiple copies of a book you find compelling, that children would enjoy, and that has literary merit. Invite several youngsters whom you feel would enjoy the experience to read the book and discuss it with you. You may wish to extend this experience by developing a literature web using the book as a theme focus.

5. Examine the book *Response Guides for Teaching Children's Books* (see "Recommended Readings," page 372). Develop a similar guide for a book you would like to share with children. Would you use the same format? If not, what would you delete or add? Try out your guide with an appropriate group of youngsters. Reassess your guide. What changes would you make now?

6. Select a book you think would be a particularly rich source for a variety of language experiences. Develop a web that builds on the strengths of that book. You may wish to work in teams and use resources cited in Chapter 11.

References

Professional Literature

Applebee, Arthur N., *The Child's Concept of Story,* University of Chicago Press, Chicago, 1978.

Britton, James, "The Nature of the Reader's Satisfaction," pp. 106–111 in *The Cool Web* eds. Margaret Meek, Aidan Warlow, and Griselda Barton, Atheneum, New York, 1978.

Brown, E. J., "Interest, Motivation, and Incentives," *Catholic School Journal* 65:44–45, October, 1965.

Burton, William H., *Reading in Child Development,* pp. 360–410, Bobbs-Merrill, Indianapolis, 1956.

Chomsky, Carol, "Stages in Language Development and Reading Exposure," *Harvard Educational Review* 42:1–33, February, 1972.

Clark, Margaret M., *Young Fluent Readers,* Heinemann, London, 1976.

Cleworth, Maud C., "Appraising Reading Interests and Attitudes in Grades Four Through Six" (reprinted from *Evaluation of Reading,* University of Chicago, December, 1958).

Cohen, Dorothy H., "The Effect of Literature on Vocabulary and Reading Achievement," *Elementary Education* 45:209–217, February, 1968.

Cullinan, Bernice E.; Jaggar, Angela; and Strickland, Dorothy, "Language Expansion for Black Children in the Primary Grades: A Research Report," *Young Children* 29:98–112, January, 1974.

Durkin, Dolores, *Children Who Read Early,* Teachers College Press, New York, 1966.

Favat, F. André, Child and Tale: The Origins of Interest, *NCTE Research Report No. 19,* National Council of Teachers of English, Urbana, Illinois, 1977.

Flood, James E., "Parental Styles in Reading Episodes with Young Children," *The Reading Teacher* 30:864–867, May, 1977.

Hall, Mary Anne; Moretz, Sarah; and Staton, Jodellano, "Writing Before Grade One: A Study of Early Writers." *Language Arts* 53:582–585, May, 1976.

Hanna, Geneva, and McAllister, Mariana K., *Books, Young People and Reading Guidance,* Harper & Row, New York, 1960.

Harris, Albert J.. *Effective Teaching of Reading,* pp. 284–309, McKay, Chicago, 1962.

Hepler, Susan I., Patterns of Response to Literature: A One-Year Study of a Fifth and Sixth Grade Classroom, doctoral dissertation, The Ohio State University, Columbus, 1982.

Hickman, Janet, Response to Literature in a School Environment, doctoral dissertation, The Ohio State University, Columbus, 1979.

Huck, Charlotte S., *Children's Literature in the Elementary School,* 3rd ed. updated, Holt, Rinehart and Winston, New York, 1979.

Iser, Wolfgang, *The Act of Reading: A Theory of Aesthetic Response,* The Johns Hopkins University Press, Baltimore, 1978.

Johns, Jerry L., "What Do Innercity Children Prefer to Read?" *The Reading Teacher* 26:462–467, February, 1973.

McCracken, Robert A. and McCracken, Marlene J., *Reading Is Only the Tiger's Tail,* Lewswing, San Rafael, California, 1972.

Moffett, James and Wagner, Betty Jane, *Student-Centered Language Arts and Reading, K-13: A Handbook for Teachers,* 2nd ed., Houghton Mifflin, Boston, 1976.

Norvell, George W., *Reading Interests of Young People,* Heath, Chicago, 1950.

Purves, Alan C. and Beach, Richard, *Literature and the Reader: Research in Response to Literature, Reading Interests and the Teaching of Literature,* National Council of Teachers of English, Urbana, Illinois, 1972.

Rosenblatt, Louise M., *Literature as Exploration,* 3rd ed., Noble and Noble, New York, 1976.

Schlager, Norma, "Predicting Children's Choices in Literature: A Developmental Approach," *Children's Literature in Education* 9:136–142, Autumn, 1978.

Smith, Frank, *Understanding Reading,* 2nd ed., Holt, Rinehart and Winston, New York, 1978.

Sostarich, Judith, A Study of the Reading Behavior of Sixth-Graders: Comparison of Active and Other Readers, unpublished Ph.D. dissertation, The Ohio State University, 1974.

Strickland, Dorothy S., "A Program for Linguistically Different Black Children," *Research in the Teaching of English* 79–86, Spring 1974.

Terry, Ann, Children's Poetry Preferences: A National Survey of Upper Elementary Grades, *NCTE Research Report No. 16, National Council of Teachers of English,* Urbana, Illinois, 1974.

Wagner, Betty Jane, *Dorothy Heathcote: Drama as a Learning Medium,* National Education Association of the United States, Washington, D.C., 1976.

Way, Brian, *Development Through Drama,* Longman, London, 1967.

Children's Literature

Aardema, Verna, *Why Mosquitoes Buzz in People's Ears,* illustrated by Leo and Diane Dillon. Dial Press, New York, 1975.

Adkins, Jan, *Inside: Seeing Beneath the Surface,* Walker, New York, 1975.

Anno, Mitsumasa, *Anno's Counting Book,* Crowell, New York, 1977.

Atwater, Richard and Atwater, Florence, *Mr. Popper's Penguins,* illustrated by Robert Lawson, Little, Brown, Boston, 1938.

Babbitt, Natalie, *The Eyes of the Amaryllis,* Bantam, Des Plaines, Illinois, 1979.

———, *Knee Knock Rise,* Farrar, Straus, New York, 1970.

———, *The Search for Delicious,* Farrar, Straus, New York, 1969.

———, *Tuck Everlasting,* Farrar, Straus and Giroux, New York, 1975.

Baylor, Byrd, *The Way to Start a Day,* illustrated by Peter Parnall, Scribners, New York, 1977, 1978.

Beckman, Delores, *My Own Private Sky,* Dutton, New York, 1980.

Blume, Judy, *Tales of a Fourth Grade Nothing,* illustrated by Dale Roy, Dutton, New York, 1972.

Bond, Nancy, *String in the Harp,* Atheneum, New York, 1976.

Boston, L. M., *The Children of Greene Knowe,* illustrated by Peter Boston, Harcourt Brace Jovanovich, New York, 1964.

Briggs, Raymond, *Jim and the Beanstalk,* Coward-McCann, New York, 1970.

Brown, Margaret Wise, *Goodnight, Moon,* illustrated by Clement Hurd, Harper & Row, New York, 1947.

Brown, Marcia, *Walk with Your Eyes,* Franklin Watts, New York, 1979.

Burningham, John, *Would You Rather . . . ,* Crowell, New York, 1978.

Byars, Betsy, *After the Goat Man,* Viking, New York, 1974.

——, *The 18th Emergency,* Viking, New York, 1973.

——, *The Pinballs,* Harper & Row, New York, 1977.

——, *Summer of the Swans,* Viking, New York, 1970.

Causley, Charles, "Colonel Fazackerley," in *Figgy Hobbin,* illustrated by Trina Schart Hyman, Walker, New York, 1973.

Causley, Charles, "I Saw a Jolly Hunter," in *Figgy Hobbin,* illustrated by Trina Schart Hyman, Walker, New York, 1973.

Childress, Alice, *Rainbow Jordan,* Coward, McCann, New York, 1981.

Cleary, Beverly, *Henry Huggins,* Morrow, New York, 1955.

Cooper, Susan, *The Dark Is Rising,* Atheneum, New York, 1973.

Danny, "Me," in *I Heard a Scream in the Street: Poems by Young People in the City,* selected by Nancy Larrick, Dell, New York, 1970.

dePaola, Tomie, *Strega Nona,* Prentice-Hall, Inc., Englewood Cliffs, New Jersey, 1975.

Fisher, Aileen, *My Cat Has Eyes of Sapphire Blue,* illustrated by Marie Angel, Crowell, New York, 1973.

Fritz, Jean, *And Then What Happened, Paul Revere?,* illustrated by Margot Tomes, Coward-McCann, New York, 1973.

——, *Can't You Make Them Behave, King George?,* illustrated by Tomie dePaola, Coward-McCann, New York, 1976.

——, *Why Don't You Get a Horse, Sam Adams?,* illustrated by Trina Schart Hyman, Coward-McCann, New York, 1974.

George, Jean C., *Julie of the Wolves,* illustrated by John Schoenherr, Harper & Row, New York, 1972.

——, *My Side of the Mountain,* Dutton, New York, 1959.

Giovanni, Nikki, "Intellectualism," in *Ego-tripping and Other Poems for Young People,* illustrated by George Ford, Hill, New York, 1973.

Hoberman, Mary Ann, *A House Is a House for Me,* illustrated by Betty Fraser, Viking, New York, 1978.

Horwitz, Elinor Lander, *When the Sky Is Like Lace,* illustrated by Barbara Cooney, Lippincott, New York, 1975.

Hunter, Mollie, *A Stranger Came Ashore,* Harper & Row, New York, 1975.

Keats, Ezra Jack, *Peter's Chair,* Harper & Row, New York, 1967.

Konigsburg, E. L., *From the Mixed-up Files of Mrs. Basil E. Frankweiler,* Atheneum, 1967.

Kraus, Robert, *Leo, the Late Bloomer,* illustrated by José Aruego, Windmill Press, New York, 1971.

L'Engle, Madeleine, *Meet the Austins,* Vanguard, New York, 1960.

———, *A Ring of Endless Light,* Farrar, Straus and Giroux, New York, 1980.

———, *A Swiftly Tilting Planet,* Farrar, Straus and Giroux, New York, 1978.

———, *A Wrinkle in Time,* Farrar, Straus, New York, 1962.

———, *A Wind in the Door,* Farrar, Straus, New York, 1973.

———, *The Arm of the Starfish,* Farrar, Straus, New York, 1965.

LeGuin, Ursula K., *A Wizard of Earthsea,* illustrated by Ruth Robbins, Parnassus, Berkeley, California, 1968.

Lionni, Leo, *Swimmy,* Pantheon, New York, 1963.

———, *Alexander and the Wind-up Mouse,* Pantheon, New York, 1969.

———, *The Biggest House in the World,* Pantheon, New York, 1968.

———, *Fish Is Fish,* Pantheon, New York, 1970.

Livingston, Myra Cohn, "Zada to Baby," in *No Way of Knowing: Dallas Poems,* Atheneum, New York, 1980.

Lobel, Arnold, *Fables,* Harper & Row, New York, 1981.

Martinez, Lydia, "Boys Don't Cry," in *I Heard a Scream in the Street: Poems by Young People in the City,* selected by Nancy Larrick, Dell, New York, 1970.

Massie, Diane Redfield, *Dazzle,* Parents, New York, 1969.

Mayne, William, *Earthfasts,* Dutton, New York, 1967.

McClosky, Robert, *One Morning in Maine,* Viking, New York, 1952.

McLenighan, Valjean, *You Can Go Jump,* illustrated by Jared D. Lee, Follett, Chicago, 1977.

Merriam, Eve, "Thumbprint," in *A Poison Tree and Other Poems,* illustrated by Mercer Mayer, Scribners, New York, 1977.

Merriam, Eve, "Winter Alphabet," in *Out Loud,* Atheneum, New York, 1973.

Merrill, Jean and Solbert, Ronni, *Red Riding,* Pinwheel, New York, 1973.

Monjo, Ferdinand N., *Grand Papa and Ellen Aroon, Being an account of some of the happy times spent together by Thomas Jefferson and his favorite granddaughter,* illustrated by Richard Cuffiari, Holt, Rinehart and Winston, New York, 1974.

Norton, Mary, *The Borrowers,* Harcourt, Brace Jovanovich, New York, 1952, 1953.

O'Brien, Robert C., *Mrs. Frisby and the Rats of NIMH,* illustrated by Zena Bernstein, Atheneum, New York, 1971.

O'Dell, Scott, *Island of the Blue Dolphins,* Houghton Mifflin, Boston, 1960.

Oxenbury, Helen, *Helen Oxenbury's ABC of Things,* Franklin Watts, New York, 1972.

Paterson, Katherine, "Maggie's Gift" in *Angels and Other Strangers,* Crowell, New York, 1979.

———, *Bridge to Terebithia,* Crowell, New York, 1977.

———, *Jacob Have I Loved,* Crowell, New York, 1980.

———, *The Great Gilly Hopkins,* Crowell, New York, 1978.

———, *The Master Puppeteer,* Crowell, New York, 1975.

———, *The Sign of the Chrysanthemum,* Crowell, New York, 1973.

Paterson, Katherine, articles about:
  Buckley, Virginia, "Katherine Paterson," *Horn Book* 54: 368–371, August, 1978.
  Jones, Linda T., "Profile: Katherine Paterson," *Language Arts* 58: 189–196, February, 1978.
  "Talk with a Winner," *New York Times Book Review,* pp. 52+, April 26, 1981.

Pearce, Philippa, *Tom's Midnight Garden,* illustrated by Susan Einzig, Lippincott, New York, 1959.

Plante, Patricia and David Bergman, *The Turtle and the Two Ducks: Animal Tales Retold from La Fontaine,* illustrated by Anne Rockwell Thomas, Crowell, New York, 1981.

Preston, Edna Mitchell, *Where Did My Mother Go?,* illustrated by Chris Conover, Four Winds Press, New York, 1978.

Rayner, Mary, *Mr. and Mrs. Pig's Evening Out,* Atheneum, New York, 1976.

Schwartz, Alvin, *Kickle Snifters and Other Fearsome Critters,* illustrated by Glen Rounds, J. B. Lippincott, Philadelphia, 1976.

Sendak, Maurice, *Where the Wild Things Are,* Harper & Row, New York, 1963.

Shulevitz, Uri, *Dawn,* Farrar, Straus and Giroux, New York, 1974.

Sperry, Armstrong, *Call It Courage,* Macmillan, New York, 1940.

Stolz, Mary, *The Bully of Barkham Street,* Harper & Row, New York, 1963.

———, *A Dog on Barkham Street,* Harper & Row, New York, 1960.

Taylor, Theodore, *The Cay,* Doubleday, New York, 1969.

Thurman, Judith, "Flashlight," in *Flashlight and Other Poems,* Atheneum, New York, 1979.

Turska, Krystyna, *The Magician of Cracow,* Greenwillow, New York, 1975.

Uchida, Yoshika, *Journey to Topaz,* illustrated by Donald Carrick, Scribner, New York, 1971.

Ungerer, Tomi, *Crictor,* Harper & Row, New York, 1958.

Viorst, Judith, *Alexander and the Terrible, Horrible, No Good, Very Bad Day,* illustrated by Ray Cruz, Atheneum, New York, 1972.

Williams, Jay, *Everyone Knows What a Dragon Looks Like,* illustrated by Mercer Mayer, Four Winds, New York, 1977.

Wilner, Isabel, compiler, *The Poetry Troupe: An Anthology of Poems to Read Aloud,* Scribners, New York, 1977.

Yagawa, Sumiko, *The Crane Wife,* translated by Katherine Paterson, Morrow, New York, 1981.

Yolen, Jane, *The Seeing Stick,* illustrated by Remy Charlip and Demetra Maraslis, Crowell, New York, 1977.

Zolotow, Charlotte, *William's Doll,* illustrated by William Pene du Bois, Harper & Row, New York, 1972.

One Second-Language Learner in a Classroom

The Need for All Teachers to Know About Second-Language Learning

Bilingual Approaches to Helping Second-Language Learners

A Framework for Helping LEP Children
Cultural Considerations
Linguistic Considerations
Social Considerations

Role of the Classroom Teacher
Input
Environment
Concrete Experiences

Assessment of Oral Language

The Role of the ESL Teacher

Moving into Print
Learning to Read a Second Language
A Writing Experience in One Bilingual Classroom
Selecting Books for LEP Children
Suggestions of Books for LEP Children

Summary

Suggested Learning Experiences

Recommended Readings

References
Professional Literature
Children's Literature

Chapter 9
Second-Language Learning and the Language Arts

One Second-Language Learner in a Classroom

It was shortly after the first wave of Vietnamese refugees arrived in the United States in the mid-70s when Thuy, a 10-year-old Vietnamese girl, was brought into Mrs. Sullivan's class. Thuy was small and delicate with large, solemn eyes and an immediate smile. Because she was so tiny and spoke no English, the principal decided that the child would be placed in Mrs. Sullivan's second grade rather than in the fourth grade with children her own age.

Thuy received a warm reception from the children in Mrs. Sullivan's class; everyone wanted to help take care of her. While Thuy's lack of English worried the teacher, she was delighted at how happy the child seemed in her new school. The little girl was attentive, obedient, and always smiling. Mrs. Sullivan requested help to learn what would be the best way to help Thuy learn English. She had questions about how to approach reading. It was difficult to find enough time to give Thuy assistance in English and yet not neglect other students. Even though she was a bit frustrated, Mrs. Sullivan felt she could muddle through until help of some sort arrived. She often commented to other teachers about what a delight it was to have Thuy in her class: "Her smile lights up our room. If we could only get the language problem licked!"

But Mrs. Sullivan's perceptions of Thuy were to be changed sharply. One day as she helped Thuy sort through her papers, the teacher saw a picture that the child had drawn showing a man standing in a rice paddy with a helicopter hovering overhead. A straw hat shaded the man's face but did not hide the very large tears that were falling from his eyes. As she gazed at the picture, the teacher realized that Thuy's smile covered some deep emotional scars and that the child's major needs were not linguistic ones.

Help from various sources did arrive. A church agency put her in touch with people who were assisting the Vietnamese community. She got help from students at a nearby university who were learning to teach English as a second language. She also wrote for and received materials from the Center for Applied Linguistics (3520 Prospect Street, N.W., Washington, D.C. 20007) and the National Clearinghouse for Bilingual Education (1300 Wilson Boulevard, Rosslyn, Va. 22209).

After reading these materials, Mrs. Sullivan decided that Thuy should be placed with children her own age to develop social skills. By being placed in a grade level two years below her own, Thuy's knowledge of such nonverbal information as mathematics was not developing as it should have been. In fact, Thuy was being limited in using the knowledge she had already acquired.

The Need for All Teachers to Know About Second-Language Learning

Mrs. Sullivan is not alone, for increasingly there is a strong need for teachers who are able to work with the culturally different child. Certain areas of the United States have long had a need for such teachers. In the East and Southwest there are large populations of Hispanics; there are also many speakers of Native American languages, such as Navaho, in the Southwest. In California many Asian children are enrolled in public schools. New England and Louisiana have numerous communities where French is the first language. New England also has many Portuguese. The arrival of several large waves of refugees—Indo-Chinese, Haitians, Cubans, and Dominicans—has made it much more likely for teachers across the country to have in their classroom an LEP (Limited English Proficiency) child, for these populations tend to be more mobile. While migrant workers from the South follow the growing season northward, some other groups arrive for resettlement in one city and then disperse gradually.

In school systems with large, fairly constant populations of children whose first language is not English, bilingual education programs are usually established. While such programs may vary greatly, the purpose is to provide teachers and curricula in order to permit children to learn new concepts in their first language at the same time they are acquiring English as a second language. This type of education was supported by the Bilingual Education Act of 1968. By the year 1980, federal bilingual education programs alone were handling some 500,000 children. Not included in this number were the many programs supported by local funding.

In some areas, however, the non-English-speaking population is less constant. Universities and colleges, for example, often attract many foreign students representing different language groups, whose children will attend local schools. One kindergarten teacher in such a college community had twelve children in her class who did not speak English. They represented a wide variety of language groups: Hausa, Chinese, Arabic, Japanese, Spanish, Italian, and Icelandic. Such children may attend a school for several years while their parents complete a degree; then they will return to their homelands. In these cases a school would not be able to afford to provide bilingual programs for each language group. The school can arrange for instruction in English as a second language (ESL) and, when possible, supply teacher aides who are native speakers.

This chapter will address the needs of teachers who, within the regular classroom setting, are working with children of limited English proficiency. Such teachers often have little help available either in materials or assistance. They do have questions, such as the following examples that were raised in a workshop:

> How can I possibly help Kim Su learn English when I have 32 other children in the class?
>
> What do you do about grades? I am required to give grades. If I do give fair grades, Nhat will fail everything.
>
> What should I do about parents? Yoko's mother insists on staying in the classroom. I think Yoko would learn English more quickly if her mother were not there.
>
> There are three Puerto Rican children in my room. They insist on sticking together. What can I do to make them a part of our class?
>
> How do you send important information home when the parents of the child you have in your room speak only Arabic?

Bilingual Approaches to Helping Second-Language Learners

There are a variety of ways to help children who enter school speaking a language other than English. In one approach used in many bilingual programs in the United States, children are taught subject matter in their native language and also given instruction in English as a second language. This kind of instruction continues for several years until the children are able to receive the majority of their instruction in English. In this way, LEP children do not fall behind their English-speaking peers while they are acquiring English as a second language. Further, they are taught to read and write in their dominant language. This approach is viable when a number of students share the same first language. In schools where students come from a variety of different language backgrounds or in schools that have only one or two children who speak a language other than English, such an approach would be costly and difficult. In these situations, efforts are usually concentrated upon helping children to acquire English. Frequently a teacher is hired to work with non-English-speaking children on a pull-out basis; that is, the children leave their regular classroom and go to work with the ESL teacher for a specified period of time.

Another approach is the "immersion program," in which children are immediately put into the situation of receiving all their instruction in their new language. This type of program has been found to be successful in Montreal, for example, where English-speaking parents made a decision to have their children taught in French so that the children could acquire a second language. These immersion programs, largely voluntary, are designed for middle-class children who speak the majority language and who wish to add on a second language. Immersion programs for minority children of the non-dominant culture, where the focus is upon replacing one language with another, have not been as successful. These programs are a "sink-or-swim" proposition. Therefore, simply plunging LEP children into an English-speaking classroom with no assistance does not give those children the kind of support they need in order to succeed.

A Framework for Helping LEP Children

The focus of this chapter is not to discuss the role of the specialist, i.e., the trained bilingual teacher or ESL teacher, but to discuss the kind of language-arts program that can be developed for LEP children in a regular classroom with the teacher who has had no specialized training. Even in schools where there are ESL specialists, the child only spends a small portion of the day with that specialist; the largest amount of time is spent in a classroom with the regular classroom teacher. If these regular teachers are to assist LEP children, they will want to consider the special cultural needs, language needs, and social needs of these children.

Cultural Considerations

Understanding children's cultural background is as important as understanding their language. Here are some accounts of cultural effects on children's behaviors found in the school. Hall (1959) tells the story of the Navaho child who arrived in school with greasy black dirt on his face. The teacher took the child to the restroom and made him wash his face. The boy ran away from the school in tears. What the teacher did not know was that the marks on the little boy's face had been placed there by the medicine man and were part of a cure for the child's sister, who was very ill.

The Japanese do not express affection by the frequent touching and kissing that so often accompany warm feelings in this culture. One Japanese woman said she could not remember being kissed by her father. Therefore, when at the age of six she entered an American school and was greeted by the teacher with a warm embrace, she was terrified. "It was behavior I simply did not expect, especially from a teacher," she recalled.

Navaho children come from a culture that values cooperation rather than competition. These children will wonder why they can not help each other with tests and will not respond well to educational practices that rely wholly upon competition to motivate children to learn.

Vietnamese children are often perceived by their teachers to be happy and well adjusted because they are obedient, quiet, and smiling. While in the American culture a smile usually signals delight, interest, and affection, the Vietamese smile can also be used to mask shyness, anger, fear, or confusion. A booklet published by the Center for Applied Linguistics points out:

> Many foreign teachers in Vietnam have been irritated and frustrated when Vietnamese students smile in what appears to be the wrong time and place. They cannot understand how the students can smile when reprimanded, when not understanding the lessons being explained, and especialy when they should have given an answer to the question instead of sitting still and smiling quietly. These teachers often thought the students were not only stupid and disobedient, but insolent as well. One thing they did not understand was that the students often smiled to show their teachers that they did not mind being reprimanded, or that they were indeed stupid for not being able to understand the lesson (Binh, Diller, and Sutherland, 1975, p. 18).

While these surface aspects of a culture are important, the deeper and less easily perceived influences of a culture are of equal importance. Children from different cultures may have learning styles that do not match standard school procedure. They may have ways of interacting with adults that differ from those the Anglo teacher would expect; their school goals may not match the goals set by the mainstream community. These areas of culture clash create problems for both child and instructor.

Research in this area is relatively new, but already there are findings that can give some guidelines to those working with culturally different children.

Vera John (1972) worked with children on a Navaho reservation in New Mexico. She noted that these children have a visual approach to their world:

> Though by urban standards life is poor on the reservation, many children raised in that vast area of desert and mountain develop slim and strong bodies, and they learn to care for animals at an early age. Through these efforts they develop a keen and observant eye for motion. . . . [They] learn by looking. They scrutinize the faces of adults; they recognize at great distances their families' livestock. They are alert to danger signs of changing weather or the approach of predatory animals (p. 333).

However, when these children arrive in the classroom, instruction is often focused upon their ability to speak and write. Frequently ignored are their finely honed skills of observation. Dumont (1972), who studied the way Sioux children interacted with teachers and with peers, found that these boys and girls, often labeled "silent," proved to be talkative in situations that did not single them out as performers, but instead let them interact with peers in small groups as they worked cooperatively on an interesting task.

Cazden, in examining bilingual Spanish/English classrooms in Chicago, found a need not only to examine what children and teachers were saying but also to focus upon the total context of the discourse. She discovered that before getting down to the day's work the Hispanic children and their bilingual Hispanic teacher took time to socialize with much touching, patting, and hugging. The teacher used terms of endearment and made inquiries about the health of the child and members of their families. These children's needs for a fairly lengthy socialization time before settling down to work contrast with the American view of the well-organized teacher who smoothly and efficiently settles into the day's routine.

A teacher who is meeting the needs of the culturally different child in the classroom will want to do more than celebrate *Cinco de Mayo* with Mexican-American pupils or study famous Native American leaders with Navaho children. The more important questions to answer are: How do groups function in that culture? What distance is required between adult and child? How do children learn at home? What goals do the family and the community have for their children?

Professional books can provide some answers and the Center for Applied Linguistics offers a variety of resources for many different language groups. The community itself will provide opportunities for teachers to learn. The teacher can tune into the ethnic community's concerns through reading its newspapers and by becoming involved in community projects such as neighborhood fairs and festivals. Getting to know those who work in agencies that provide support services to the ethnic group often can lead to new insights.

Visits to the homes of children can do much to make the parent feel welcome in the school and help the teacher better understand the child.

Nancy Martine, a young teacher beginning a new job in an inner-city school where almost all her children were Puerto Rican, made such visits. She wrote in her journal:

> Made 3 home visits in the afternoon. Mayra and Maria's (the twins') mother has two younger ones, a *small* house, and no husband. She is on welfare and is dreaming of being able to return to Puerto Rico where all her family still live. She is very sweet-natured, just like the twins. She insisted upon serving us orange juice. Alma and Armando's mother wasn't expecting us, but was friendly and warm. Looks a lot like Alma. She has seven children—again, no father in the house. She had to leave in five minutes so we couldn't talk much. Visited the Torres' home last—*both* parents in the home. The house is nicely furnished, well-kept, *preciosa*. All three of the Torres children are well cared for. The parents have a lot of interest in what is going on at school. They are really anxious to be involved. They were both *very* friendly. This home was much like a home in a middle-class suburb—not what I would have expected in the inner city. The visits have really helped me understand the children so much better.

This teacher's interest in parents continued. Parents were invited to see children's work, to attend small class programs. The relationship grew so strong that children, parents, and the teacher got together in midsummer for a picnic at the lakeshore. By the end of her year Nancy had developed a good sense not only of the shared values and customs of the Puerto Rican families in her area but also of the differences from family to family. She had seen how parents and children interacted and how children were disciplined. She knew the kinds of foods her pupils liked to eat and they knew her likes. They delighted in introducing her to fruits and vegetables she had never before eaten. She had firsthand knowledge of the extended family, for grandparents, toddlers, cousins, and even cousins' fiancés would attend some of the gatherings. She was not surprised when Carlos arrived at school one morning sleepy and yawning to tell her that his grandmother had arrived the night before from Puerto Rico bringing gifts of coffee. He had sat up late visiting and sampling the coffee and then couldn't fall asleep. The teacher knew what a special and important occasion it had been and simply sent Carlos to the nurse's room for a nap.

Linguistic Considerations

One important consideration in helping a child learn another language is a realization of the amount of time it takes to acquire a language. A traveler who has studied French or Spanish for three or four years is shocked upon arrival in Paris or Madrid to find out how little he or she is able to comprehend and how difficult it is to make even very simple requests at a hotel or railway station. FLES (Foreign Language in the Elementary Schools) was very popular in the 1950s and 1960s and can still be found in a number of school systems. Parents, administrators, and teachers alike are delighted if, after a year of instruction in French, fourth-graders are able to sing several French songs, count to 100, act out some brief dialogues, and know a few expressions of *politesse*. On the other hand, teachers of children who speak a language other than English are often pressured to offer the children all their instruction in English as quickly as possible. The children are expected to keep up with a peer group made up of children who have spent their entire young lives acquiring English.

The person who moves into a culture where another language is spoken quickly acquires fluency in certain aspects of that language. The wife of one foreign-language professor who has had to spend time in a number of countries reports that she can quickly become fluent in what she calls "housekeeping language." She said, "I can shop and get what I need, tell a repairman what problems I am having with a washing machine, and let the drycleaner know that I need my dress back by Wednesday and no later. What is frustrating is that I can't really discuss the ideas that concern me, or share some delightful adventure I've had. It's just so hard to get those things across in the way you want to. I sometimes feel as if there's a part of me—the most important part—that our new, non-English-speaking friends will never know."

What this professor's wife was feeling so keenly was the difference between talk that is supported by context and talk that is relatively context-free; the difference between the discussion of commonplace, everyday matters as opposed to the discussion of complex ideas. A lack of context and an increase in abstraction put an additional burden on both speaker and listener. This shift from language that is supported by the context to language that is not often marks a dramatic difference between home language and school language. Wells (1981) points out

> Whereas most talk—and most learning—in the home arises out of contexts of practical activity, often ones which the child himself has initiated, a great deal of learning in school, and the talk associated with the tasks through which that learning is planned to take place, is largely teacher initiated and involves contexts which are unfamiliar to the child and ones which in many cases are also relatively abstract. The result is that, for many children, strategies that have proven effective for interpreting and learning from the very varied situations that occur in

the home are less effective at school and in some cases are even counter productive (p. 19).

Cummins (1981) has suggested one way of viewing the content of the communication act, which focuses both upon context and message. This mapping of language can be of value to classroom teachers as they consider the kinds of language proficiency that some common classroom activities require.

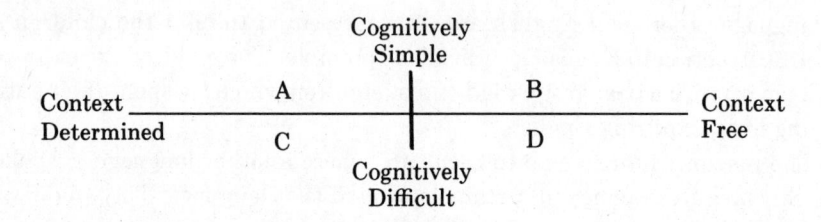

```
                    Cognitively
                      Simple
                         |
  Context _____A_____|_____B_____  Context
  Determined       C     |     D           Free
                         |
                    Cognitively
                     Difficult
```

In area A, the topic would be embedded in the context and would be cognitively simple. For example, an explanation of how to set a table, which takes place in the dining room with all the materials needed for table setting in full view, would be bound by the context and would require little background knowledge. The topic of discussion in area B is also cognitively simple, but is not bound by the context. An example of this kind of focus could be the recounting of an adventure one had on a shopping expedition. The context does not determine the topic under discussion, but the ideas are not difficult ones and are within the realm of experience of both speaker and listener. Area C could be exemplified by the talk that takes place during a science experiment. The materials are at hand and determine what happens, but the ideas explored may be quite complex and introduce new learnings. In area D can be found topics that exist in many textbooks, such as a discussion of the political and economic conditions that led to the Second World War, written by a distant author and containing abstract and complex ideas.

This grid does not mean that communication falls neatly into four discrete compartments; Cummins himself would propose a blending or shading of areas. However, it does suggest that because children are able to use language with a fair degree of ease and fluency in contexts that support the topic under discussion and that permit them to draw upon knowledge and concepts they have already acquired, it does not follow that their language will be as facile in other situations. Yet children who exhibit fluency in some situations are frequently expected to display it in all situations; for example, to read textbooks dense with content or to listen to and absorb formal lectures. When working with LEP children there are especially strong reasons to provide many diverse, concrete experiences to support concept development as well as vocabulary development. Too frequently the teaching of labels is equated with the teaching of language, and all too often these children are given assistance only until they are able to communicate about their everyday needs and concerns.

Social Considerations

One important consideration needed in working with the language-different child is a realization of the wide variation found in these language learners. Lily Wong Fillmore (1976) studied several five- to seven-year-old children who were acquiring English in a bilingual school setting. The most successful learners were those who were anxious to play with others; the least successful were shy and quiet children who liked to play and work alone. Fillmore discussed the differences between five-year-old Nora, the child who learned the most language, and seven-year-old Juan, who learned the least language during the year. Juan was a child who wanted to be in control of any play situation; therefore, he always sought out and played with Spanish-speaking children. He tended to avoid the children who spoke English. Nora, on the other hand, loved to play with others and quickly learned a few formula phrases to get into the games. She sought out English-speaking children and was not afraid to try out whatever English she knew with them.

Fillmore pointed out three social strategies that children who are successful language learners seemed to employ. First, they were willing to join a group of English speakers and act as if they understood what was going on, even if they did not. Second, they learned and used a few well-chosen words, which gave the impression that they understood the language even if they did not. They used phrases like "Oh goody!" "Look here!" and "My turn next." Finally, they counted upon friends to help them out if they did not understand. They had trust in the good will of others.

Muriel Saville is currently doing research on the acquisition of a second language by foreign children who are enrolled in an American multicultural school. She is finding that some children who are making good progress in English are not necessarily the ones who seek out social interaction with English-speaking children. One of the students who made the greatest gains in English, for example, ignored opportunities to speak with children, but actively sought out occasions to interact with adults. Another child in this study said very little for six months and then began speaking with much effectiveness. These studies by Fillmore and Saville-Troike suggest that teachers need to be aware that different children may use very different strategies as they move into a new language.

Children will also have different motivations to acquire a second language. Migrant children who live in an isolated community and know that they will be leaving the school at the end of the growing season have quite a different feeling about acquiring English than do middle-class children whose parents are political refugees from Cuba. The Navaho, whose family feels a strong tribal pride and plans to remain in the Navaho community, is going to feel less keenly the importance of English than the Vietnamese child whose family has left Vietnam and knows that they will not be returning.

All of the aforementioned social considerations will affect the time it takes for the child to become fluent in a second language. They will also affect the amount of fluency acquired. Learning style, personality, and culture may all affect how children set about acquiring a second language. While teachers will want to provide many and varied opportunities for children to work together, these same teachers can expect that some LEP children will be willing to take immediate risks in order to communicate, while others may wish to listen and reflect for a much longer period of time before plunging into the sea of language.

Role of the Classroom Teacher

What, then, is the role of the classroom teacher who is neither an ESL specialist nor has the time to be? A teacher who was quoted earlier in this chapter asked, "How can I possibly help Kim Su learn English when I have 32 other children in the class?" The answer she was given is, at the same time, both simple and complex. "You don't have to teach Kim Su so that she will *learn* English. You need to provide the kind of linguistic input and create the kind of environment that will permit her to *acquire* English."

Input

Babies acquire language; they are not *taught* language. This acquisition process occurs not only because people talk to the baby as if the infant understands what they are saying but also because those who talk to babies alter their language in some interesting ways. They speak more slowly, restrict their vocabulary, and use short sentences. They often repeat what the baby has said and expand the utterances. Freed (1980) found that people talking to adult foreigners do many of the same things that mothers do when talking to babies, but for different reasons. When mothers repeat and expand the baby's utterance, they do so in order to keep the interaction going. When native speakers talk to adult foreigners, repetitions and expansions are generally used as clarifiers. Fillmore (1976), in her work with Spanish-speaking children, found that children as young as five years old will simplify their speech when talking to a child who does not share their language.

Krashen (1981) has developed what he terms the "input hypothesis." He theorizes that individuals acquire a second language by getting linguistic input that is just a bit beyond them. In other words, the input is easy enough for them to follow, but it also provides some new vocabulary and structures. If the students understand the input and if there is enough input, eventually they acquire the structures and vocabulary they need. Krashen suggests that presenting lessons in which grammar is carefully segmented is not necessary and may even get in the way of a person "acquiring" a second language.

Finally, input must be attended to. If a subject under discussion is not of interest, listeners will tune out. If, on the other hand, listeners have a high degree of interest in what is being said, they will listen attentively even when the conditions make listening very difficult. Language learners tend to act the same way. Friedlander, Jacobs, Davis, and Wetstone (1972) studied the linguistic input of a 22-month-old girl who was as fluent in Spanish as she was in English. While the little girl's father spoke only Spanish to her, the rest of her language input was from English speakers. The researchers found that the father's interactions made up only 4 percent of the language the child heard each day. This finding seemed strange since the child spoke Spanish just as well as she spoke English. Upon closer examination, it was discovered that the father's language was directed to the child, while much of the English the little girl was hearing was directed not at her, but at others.

Teachers who use most of their teaching time talking to the whole class or to large groups of children will not alter their language to meet the needs of the LEP child. If they were to do so, the rest of the class would tune them out. It is vital that teachers arrange for situations that permit the LEP child to talk with them or other adult English speakers in a one-on-one situation. These sessions do not have to be lengthy, but they should be frequent. Parents and older children can be of great help here. Situations such as the following could arise naturally during the school day:

> Walk around the playground with the child. Talk about who is swinging, who is pushing the swings, and who is jumping rope. Help the child by naming some of

the things he or she is seeing, but don't merely talk in labels. Such conversations provide a great deal of language in which the child has a high interest, for it is about enjoyable activities and familiar people. One can also help the child to learn how to enter into the play of other children.

At milk time, let the child help. Tell her to whom she should give milk, where to get the straws, how to pass the wastebasket to collect the empty cartons, and where the wooden milk carrier goes.

Gym class provides opportunities for wonderfuly active ways to develop understanding of prepositions as children crawl *through* the tunnel, climb *up* the rope, slide *down* the pole, balance *on* the beam, and skip *around* the circle.

Share a book with the child and take time to talk about the illustrations.

Another way the teacher can provide valuable input is to assure that what LEP children are hearing is not only within their grasp, but will stretch them beyond their current level. In other words, provide language that is comprehensible yet not too simple in structure and vocabulary.

The teacher's ability to build upon the LEP child's interest can provide similar opportunities. A child who enjoys model building will be able to follow with interest and good comprehension a demonstration of model building given by another child. An avid soccer player will listen intently to instructions by the coach. The youngster's understanding of the game will help in predicting what the coach will be saying and in comprehending language that contains new vocabulary and structures.

One value of home visits is that it permits the teacher to discover some of the child's interests outside the classroom. Observation during the school day can also help the teacher discover the kinds of activities the child chooses and the types of tasks that the child finds most absorbing. When a youngster returns to the bookshelf again and again to search out books on dinosaurs or remains absorbed all morning at a carpentry task, the teacher can build upon those interests.

A sense of the child's cognitive level assists the teacher in making curricular decisions. A bright LEP ten-year-old given math workbook pages designed for a second grader will be able to handle the simple addition and subtraction, but will be wasting time that could be used to much better advantage.

Just as important as the teacher-child interaction is the child-child interaction. In discussing how children grow in their use of the mother tongue, Shuy suggests that

> ... children will learn the important [language] functions without teacher models at all. They will learn them, if they learn them, with models whom they admire

from their peer environment. This is how the major language learning has taken place throughout time. There is little reason to expect it to change now (1981, p. 174).

The LEP child can participate in many activities that call for both cooperation and communication with English-speaking peers.

When young children work together with large blocks, there is a need to ask for "the big, long block" or to make a request, such as "Put this block on top."

Magnets and a bag of objects will have children guessing which objects will stick to the magnet and which ones won't.

Baking cookies will provide opportunities to talk about how to measure the butter, who should break the eggs, and how long to stir the batter.

Making a mural together, as opposed to painting separate pictures, calls for decision making. "Where should we draw the building?" "What color should we paint the fence?" "Shall we paint birds flying in the sky?"

Opportunities to interact with both children and adults are important to the language development of the LEP child. Peck (1978) studied the discourse of Angel, a Spanish-speaking child who was acquiring English, as he interacted with Joe, an English-speaking child, and also as he interacted with an adult. By contrasting these two types of discourse, Peck found some interesting differences. When Angel talked with Joe, he received a wide variety of input, such as songs, sound effects, language play, parodies of songs, and imitations of TV figures. Joe teased Angel at times and sometimes used language to pretend. Angel was called upon to respond in a variety of ways and he needed to question Joe in order to join in. With the adult, the language input was less varied. However, Angel was able to initiate topics of his own choosing, which was difficult for him to do in child-child discourse. The adult listened and responded to Angel's meaning, questioning him to make sure she understood his intent. Peck states, "One overly blunt way to characterize the difference between the child-child and the child-adult discourse would be to say that Angel struggles to learn, or understand the other child's language, but that the adult works at trying to learn and understand Angel's language" (p. 399). This strongly suggests that classroom environments that limit child-child interaction are cutting off a rich source of language input for the LEP child. In addition, classrooms in which teacher talk is usually directed to the whole class or to groups of children are rooms in which the LEP child is being deprived of needed one-to-one exchanges with adults.

Children naturally gather to discuss work, play, or events in their lives. When an LEP child becomes a member of the class, that child is pulled into the communication framework. Freedom to interact is essential. (Mrs. Daley's classroom, Cranbrook Elementary School, Columbus, Ohio)

Environment

Krashen (1976) has discussed the different kinds of contributions made by formal and informal environments to language learning. The formal environment is one that provides for conscious learning of the second language; the focus is upon the language itself. In other words, one learns the rules about forming the future tense in French and then practices using these rules. Such conscious understanding of how the language works acts as a "monitor" in Krashen's terms. In other words, as the language learner starts to form an utterance, the monitor intrudes and the learner applies the rules previously learned in order to shape that utterance. A person who uses the monitor too little has ill-formed speech. A person who overuses the monitor says little.

In contrast, informal environments for language learning are those where the focus is not upon the language, but upon using the language to meet some purpose of the learner—to play a game, to purchase something, to socialize. Informal environments imply more than exposure to language; they require intensive involvement on the part of the learner. Both formal and informal environments contribute to second-language learning, but their contributions are made in different ways. The regular classroom teacher may not have the background, expertise, or time to do formal teaching of English. However, the classroom is filled with opportunities for the informal acquisition of language if the environment is arranged properly. To encourage second-language learning, the classroom should invite interaction.

Fillmore found that the five- to seven-year old Spanish-speaking children whom she studied all made good strides in English during the year she observed them. Although these children received no formal English instruction, they did have a wide variety of opportunities to interact with English-speaking children in contextualized situations. She found these children used several cognitive strategies as they worked their way into English. These strategies were:

1. The children assumed that what people were saying was directly relevant to the ongoing situation.

So, if a child is holding a bag of marbles and saying something, the second child might assume that she is being invited to play marbles.

2. The children learned a few stock expressions and started to talk.

In other words, the focus of these Spanish-speaking children was not upon learning individual words and then putting those words together in patterns, but rather upon seizing a whole expression that would get them into the action, expressions such as: "Give me one," "My turn next," and "Ready, set, go!"

3. They looked for patterns that recurred in the language structures they knew.

Fillmore reports how Nora began with a formal phrase: "How do you do dese?" At the beginning she used the question only in this fixed way. At this point it stood for many meanings. Later she was able to use the same phrase but added on words and phrases to make meaning more precise.

How do you do dese	little tortillas?
	in English?
	September *por mañana*?

Still later the "do dese" was seen as an element that could be removed. Nora was then able to come up with sentences such as:

How do you	like to be a cookie cutter?
	make the flowers?
	gonna make these?

This progression shows how sophisticated Nora has become in her ability to use language.

4. Children made the most use they could of the language they had.

If the only food word the child knows is "cookie," for a while he may let "cookie" stand for all foods. If the only question the child can ask is "What's that?," it may be used for all questions.

5. The children spent their major effort on getting across meaning and saved refinements of language for later.

If the child can say "He play marbles," she does not concern herself immediately with the verb inflection that marks third-person plural and the inflection used to mark past tense. Rather, she is pleased to communicate her message. Meaning comes first; refinements come much more slowly.

The environment the school can provide is a rich and varied one. It includes not only the classroom but the playground, the lunchroom and the immediate neighborhood, as well as experiences of the broader community through study trips. Each provides a place for a variety of interactions with English-speaking children and adults. The arrangement of the classroom itself can either encourage or discourage the interaction of children. Small tables where children can work together encourage talking and sharing, in contrast to rows of desks that discourage children's talk.

It is especially appropriate when working with LEP children to arrange the room so that many different kinds of materials are available that will invite the children to work, to manipulate, and to create. LEP children will be unable at the very beginning to ask for materials they need for they will not realize all the options available to them unless materials are in view.

A teacher might consider arranging:

—An art table that has, in addition to the usual paints, crayons, and clay, a box with textured material for collage—such as scraps of fabric, yarn, lace, and ribbons—materials for stitchery projects, small boxes and cartons for constructions, pastels, chalks, and food colors for creating colorful work.

—A listening center where there is a record player with recordings of music of all kinds and stories. A tape-recorder with tapes of books with the book available. Blank tapes can be placed in the center so that LEP children can try out their new language and share their mother tongue with others.

—A corner could be made into a play store complete with cans and boxes of food and a cash register with a dollar's worth of real change. This will become the basis for dramatic play as children buy and sell the items in the store. For the LEP child it will also be an introduction into such cultural items as breakfast cereal and U.S. currency.

In addition, the teacher can have on hand such other materials as a doll house with furniture and a doll family, a dress-up box, a well-stocked picture file, table settings and cooking utensils, a set of toy telephones, and carpentry tools. All of these materials support play and, as we have pointed out throughout this text, play supports language development. Lindfors (1980) also holds this view and states that play has a special value for the LEP child, for it "... maximizes the opportunity for the crucial ingredients to children's language growth: contextualized language that is easily understood, active participation in language-filled situations, the accumulation of useful formulas, establishing and maintaining of social relations, the opportunity to experiment" (pp. 420–421).

Concrete Experiences

It is clear that the kinds of experiences that are valuable for LEP children are equally valuable for English-speaking children. Shared experiences can provide the basis for much language input as children talk to each other and to adults in order to discuss what they are doing and what they have made. The language input provided each child will be varied to suit that child's needs. From the common experience will come an output of oral and written language that will reflect the differences in linguistic development of the children. The following is an example of one such experience.

A second-grade class took a trip to the farm to study farm animals. Before the trip, story books were shared, such as *Rosie's Walk* (Hutchins), *Petunia* (Duvoisin), and *No More Baths* (Cole), as well as a variety of informational books about farm animals. During their visit to the farm, the children petted the sheep, goats, a baby chick, and a mother hen. They held a piglet, milked a cow, and rode the old farm horse. Upon their return to school, the day at the farm inspired much talk and also became the basis of much writing. Pictures were painted and labeled; stories were written and shared; and a big class book was made and bound.

The LEP children in this class acquired much from this trip. They learned not only the labels that English speakers attach to such animals as sheep, goat, goose, and cow, but discovered much more. They developed an understanding of the relative size of these animals, heard the sounds the animals made, and saw the way each moved. They touched the animals, feeling the soft, downy back of the baby chick and the smooth, slick hide of the horse. Upon their return, they were not able to share everything they had learned with words, but they could deepen and share their new-found understandings in other ways. Working with English-speaking children they could use their bodies to show how the different animals moved—the way the rooster strutted, the pig rooted, and the duck waddled. They could match animal sounds with the animals found in the toy farm set. They could categorize animals in a variety of ways by moving around pictured or toy animals:

Big animals/small animals
Big animals/bigger animals /the biggest animal
Animals with fur/animals with feathers

Artwork provided another way for the LEP children to display the knowledge they had acquired from their trip. For example, to answer the question "What kinds of feet did the different animals have?" the children could draw or model with clay the horse's hoof, the pig's cloven hoof, the duck's webbed foot, and the chicken's claw. A collage could convey what they had found out about the textures in the barnyard. A mural might best permit them to show their knowledge of the sweep of the farm—the barn, the busy barnyard, the chicken coops, the duck pond, and the meadow.

A set of wooden farm animals and a toy barn would promote socio-dramatic play. Stories read before the trip could be reread or retold and new books introduced. After meeting a goat face to face, children might enjoy the opportunity to act out "The Three Billy Goats Gruff." LEP children would be able to participate in all these activities, by joining in at times when they feel comfortable to do so and being able to work in ways that do not require verbal sophistication. The oral language and writing of the other children would provide rich input. Even though the stories and discussions might contain new vocabulary and unknown structures, the shared experience of the trip to the farm would help the LEP child to comprehend.

Most people recognize the need for concrete materials at the primary level. Such materials are just as appropriate at upper levels for all children but most particularly for the LEP child. The older child who is acquiring English as a second language will be developing more complex cognitive structures, often without the facilitating use of language.

While the fluency of LEP children in English may be limited, their cognitive abilities are not. A fifth-grade class studying electricity might work with batteries, bulbs, wires, and switches. Often the children will set their own problems to research. One question they might wish to try to answer is: What kinds of materials conduct electricity? Opportunities to work with concrete materials will let LEP children explore problems that interest them and that will develop their abilities to ask and seek answers to questions.

Compare this kind of problem solving with reading a history text that discusses the causes of the Civil War. In addition to such difficult vocabulary as "emancipation," "abolition," and "secession" are words which, at the surface level, would seem to have one meaning, but in this specific instance have another, words like "underground railroad," "Yankees," and "carpet baggers." There are geographic place names, such as "Appomattox," "Bull Run," and "Gettysburg." Finally, there are many abstract terms that are difficult to grasp or explain fully, such as "freedom," "justice," and "state's rights." The vocabulary just discussed reveals the need for the teacher to adjust classroom experiences so that LEP children can work in situations where they have a comprehensible context and are able to deal with the concrete when necessary.

Assessment of Oral Language

Assessing children's levels of language development is an important part of any language-arts program, particularly a program designed to include LEP youngsters. It is too easy to assume that LEP children cannot say anything at all, or that they are able to understand far more language than they actually do. After the child feels at home in the new school and is comfortable with the teacher, some informal assessments can be made. One way to begin would be to sit side by side with the child and look through a picture book, such as an ABC book. Perhaps the child will volunteer words she knows; if not, the teacher can often get a sense of her listening vocabulary with questions such as:

"Show me the cat."
"Where is the boy?"
"Show me the yellow flower."
"Where is the black cat?"

Note that none of these questions call for a verbal response. All the child needs to do is point.

Other questions can be answered by responding with an action. Commands can be given in a gamelike manner. It sometimes makes the task easier if an English-speaking child works with the teacher, for he can then serve as a model to the LEP child on how to play the game. Such commands as the following might be used:

Stand up.   Sit down.
Pick up the book.   Open the box.
Put the book on the desk.   Give me three pencils.
Go to the door.   Show me the red pencil.
Open the door.   Show me the biggest pencil.

Often quiet children have acquired surprisingly large amounts of receptive language. It is important to remember that comprehension precedes production. Listening comprehension, therefore, will be far greater than speech production.

If the child shows that she understands some language, the teacher will need to get an idea of her ability to speak. A few short questions can help give the teacher a general idea of the child's degree of fluency. It is best to begin with simple questions that require brief answers:

What is your name?
How old are you?
Where do you live?
What color is your shirt?
How many books are on the table?

If the child is able to respond to these questions with a word or two that demonstrate her understanding, the teacher can later try some questions that call for a longer response:

Tell me about your family.
What do you like to do after school?
Tell me about this picture.

The procedures described above are best performed in a relaxed, pressure-free manner. However, any kind of situation where language is called forth on command, even commands given in a warm and reassuring way, may not give a fair sampling of what the child is able to do. The teacher will wish to observe the child in a variety of settings to see how, where, and with whom the youngster talks. The teacher will also want to watch for interests and personality traits that could affect the ease with which the child will acquire a second language. The following check list, influenced by suggestions given by Tough (1976) for observation of young children, may help you determine the level and growth in communication of LEP children in your classroom.

Oral Language Observation Guide for the Language-Different Child

Listening Behavior
1. Child appears to listen to the talk of other children who try to initiate a conversation.
2. Child listens to children and to teacher in small-group activities.
3. Child is attentive in such whole-class activities as story time.

4. Child attempts to respond with an appropriate action when given directions or an invitation to play.

Speaking Behavior
1. Child seems willing to speak
   — to a friend
   — with small groups of children
   — in a whole-class situation
   — with an interested adult
2. Child initiates a conversation
   — with a friend
   — in a small-group setting
   — with an interested adult
   — in a whole-class situation
3. Child is able to use language
   — to ask for help
   — to ask questions
   — to make wishes known
   — to share information
   — to socialize
   — to regulate the behavior of others

Personality Characteristics
1. The child seeks out other children
   — for assistance
   — to work on class projects
   — on the playground
   — in the lunchroom
   — on the way to and from school
   — after school
2. When given a choice the child seems to prefer
   — working alone
   — working with a good friend
   — working with a small group
   — working with the assistance of an adult

Interests
1. When given choices the child prefers
   — looking at books
   — creating something with paper or clay
   — constructing something
   — vigorous activity
   — playing with others
   — listening to stories or records
   — _____
   — _____
   — _____

404 Integration of the Language Arts

> 2. Topics or themes which seem to have caught the child's interests are
> — _____
> — _____
> — _____
>
> *Home Language*
> 1. In the home the language most spoken by the mother is _____
>   most spoken by the father is _____
>   most frequently used is _____
> 2. The wishes of the parents concerning the language of the child are __

As you use this observation guide, you will find it helpful to code your responses according to the language used. For example, a red check mark could indicate the child's first language and a blue check mark could represent English. This coding will make it easier to identify patterns. Some children may use their home language in the lunchroom and on the playground and use English only in the classroom, while others may be attempting to use English both to socialize and to learn.

One value of this kind of observation guide is that it can give a truer and more complete measure of the child's language competence than more formal measures are likely to, for it helps teachers to look at language in a variety of settings. Frequently, children who are silent in the classroom may be assumed to have little ability to communicate, even though they are able to use language very effectively in other settings.

An assessment of the child's oral language can help teachers provide the kinds of experiences that a child needs and is ready for. A child who enjoys listening to stories on records can be given the opportunity to listen to favorite tales again and again, manipulating flannelboard figures as she does so. This will help reinforce meaning and also build up her store of language. A child who uses language to ask for help but does not yet share information or socialize can be drawn into small-group activities that will allow him to do both. Surveying children to find out the kinds of pets they have might grow out of a class study of animals. The survey will call for interaction with many children and will also demand repetitive language: "Do you have any pets?" and "What kind of pets do you have?" After gathering the information, the children can work together to develop a graph, a task that will not only call for the LEP child to share the information he has gathered but to do so in a way that elicits much repetitive language: "John has a dog," "Becky has a cat," and "Ramon has four fish."

After the child has been in the classroom for a longer period of time and has heard numbers of stories read aloud, story retelling can be a valuable assessment tool. Carlos, a ten-year-old, had arrived from Santiago, Chile only four months before this retelling was made. His teacher, Mrs. Nunn, selected the book *Strega Nona* (dePaola) to read to Carlos. This is the story of an Italian witch who hires Big Anthony to work for her. She warns him not to touch her magic pasta pot. Later he hears her chanting to the pasta pot and watches as it magically fills with mounds of pasta. Unfortunately, Big Anthony does not see Strega Nona blow three kisses to the pot, which stops the flow of pasta. Naturally, Big Anthony tries out his own brand of magic as soon as Strega Nona leaves the house to visit a friend. But, since he is ignorant of the power of the three kisses, he almost buries the village in pasta. This is a book whose delightful illustrations illuminate the humor of the tale.

After the story was read aloud to Carlos, he retold it. As you read this retelling think about how the language differs from that of a native speaker. Are there aspects of the language that strike you as non-native? How much is it like the retelling of young native English speakers?

> When the witch go to see her sister, he, Big Anthony, take—touch—the pasta pot and he make a spaghetti and he give to everybody and say coming with bowls, forks, spoons, knife, and plates and for eat pasta, spaghetti, and when we say to stop the pasta, he don't did the three kisses and the pasta out of and never finished and everybody put beds and tables and all for the pasta and no pasta don't pass for the city and when the witch back, she did stop the pasta and what for Big Anthony did that. She say he eat all pasta and for she likes sleeping in the bed in she home, and when he eat, he would fat, fat, and more fat, and when he finish in the night, he finish very fat and he eat all the spaghetti.

In analyzing Carlos's retelling, it is clear that he comprehended most of the tale, relating it in sequence and including the relevant detail of the three kisses, which are so vital to the plot. His retelling showed that Carlos indeed had a sense of story. He used the language he had to convey meaning. His storytelling became most detailed when he was able to list all the items the townspeople used to eat the pasta—"bowls, forks, spoons, knife, and plates." Carlos also used every clue he could to gain meaning. He had asked to have the word "pasta" clarified for him when the story was being read; it was identified as "spaghetti." During his retelling Carlos then used these two words interchangeably. In the story Strega Nona visits her friend, Strega Amelia. Carlos called them sisters, possibly making an assumption based on their similar names or on their similar appearances in the illustration. The pictures also helped Carlos extend his understanding of the story. The text ends with Strega Nona handing Big Anthony a fork and telling him to eat up all the pasta that now fills her house. The picture that follows has no text, but shows an exhausted Big Anthony with a very round stomach. So Carlos is going beyond the text when he says, "When he eat, he would fat, fat, and more fat, and when he finish in the night, he finish and he finish very fat and he eat all the spaghetti."

In several places in this retelling it is easy to see that Carlos is using his knowledge of Spanish as he acquires English. Foreigners working at learning a new language develop an interlanguage, a stage between two languages, during which the learners are attempting to use what they already know about their own language to create order and system in the new one (Selinker, 1972). This interlanguage can be seen in the way Carlos is applying his understandings of Spanish to English. For example, Carlos says "for eat," a direct translation of the Spanish *para comer*. In English we would say that something "passes through the city" but Spanish speakers would say *pasar por la ciudad*, making it easier to understand why Carlos tells us that "no pasta don't pass for the city." When Carlos says "What for Big Anthony did that?" he is directly translating *para qué* as "what for." *Para qué* is one of a number of ways Spanish speakers can ask the question "why"; however, this particular expression has the precise meaning of "for what reason," which is the thought that Carlos wishes to express here. When Carlos brings his retelling to a dramatic finish by saying of Big Anthony, "He would fat, fat, and more fat," the child is once again demonstrating his knowledge of Spanish, for the verb *engordar* encompasses the whole idea of becoming fat, an idea that must be expressed in English by both a verb and an adjective. It is clear to see that Carlos's language is not simply a faulty imitation of the English he is hearing, but instead a sophisticated meshing of his knowledge of one language he already knows with the input he is receiving in a second language.

Carlos is able to get meaning across despite the fact that his control over the language is limited. He uses verbs, but does not inflect them. He uses a nominative pronoun where a possessive pronoun is called for, which is what young children do as they acquire their mother tongue. Like young children, he does not need to have his errors corrected at this point. He needs to be applauded for his ability to communicate and given the time and the opportunities to hear and speak much more English.

If a teacher wanted to extend Carlos's learning from what was found in this retelling, the story could be reread to him as often as he wanted to hear it. It could be taped so that he could listen to the tape by himself and at the same time follow along in the text. Carlos might enjoy another Strega Nona story, *Big Anthony and the Magic Ring*. While he will enjoy hearing these

By allowing an LEP student to look at illustrations of stories read in class, that student can formulate the words which go along with the story. This child is being given the freedom to explore a book and generate his own version of a story to go along with that book. (Mrs. Weisent's classroom, Cranbrook Elementary School, Columbus, Ohio)

stories with groups of children, it would also be good for him to be able to have stories read aloud just to him. In a one-to-one situation he will feel free to stop the reader and ask questions or talk about what he is hearing. Since Carlos is ten years old and is able to read and write very well in Spanish, he might find it fun to make a cartoon of Strega Nona and Big Anthony. He could dictate what is to be written in the speaking balloons above their heads.

The Role of the ESL Teacher

Even when the classroom teacher develops an environment to provide optimal support for the child who is acquiring English as a second language, it is still important to have the aid of an ESL specialist. The ESL specialist is trained to teach English to speakers of other languages and can provide for an intensive exploration of the new language in a small-group setting. As discussed earlier in this chapter, language directed to the child is extremely important. If an ESL specialist is not available, the teacher can make use of parent volunteers or older children. These assistants can work with the LEP children in a variety of ways: sharing books, taking walks, baking cookies, building a birdhouse, or doing an art project. Any interesting activity that provides a basis for language would be useful.

One way of providing help to the untrained volunteer would be to use language boxes. A language box contains materials selected around a theme. In addition, there are several cards that suggest questions to be used for discussion. These cards and materials are all placed in a shoe box, which has been covered attractively with adhesive paper. The aide can then talk with the child about the various items that are in the box.

One such set of materials are those focused on traffic. In the box are a map of the neighborhood drawn on a piece of muslin; small buildings made of blocks and representing homes, school, stores, church, movie theater, and post office; and a series of cardboard traffic signs.

In addition to the materials there are three cards. The first suggests ways the tutor could work with a child who is just beginning to acquire English. The second card contains suggestions for the intermediate child. The third card lists some activities that can extend the language and the cultural understandings of both the LEP child and English-speaking classmates. If the tutor has the aid of an English-speaking child, that child can serve as a model for response.

As you examine the materials in this box can you think of materials you could gather for similar boxes? You might wish to focus on clothing, grooming, transportation, foods, or sports.

TRAFFIC BOX

Beginning Card

Vocabulary   street   store   post office
              corner   church
              block   bus
              house   car
              school   theater

Structures

    A. Show me High Street.
        (Child points to High Street on the map.)

    B. Show me the church.
        (Child points.)

    C. Put the car on High Street.
        (Child does the action.)

    D. What is this?
        (It's a car.)

    E. Is this the store?
        (No, it's the school.)

    F. Where's the theater?
        (On Main Street.)

Intermediate Card

Vocabulary   change   go down the street
              turn   go across the street
              lost   stop
              address   go
              closer   left
              farther   right

Structures

    A. What is your address?
        (195 Spruce Street.)

    B. How do you go home from school?
        (Child points to map. Eventually child can "talk his or her route," e.g., "I go down Spring Street and turn left on Spruce.")

    C. What do cars do when the light changes to yellow?
        (They slow down.)

D. Which is closer to the school, the church or the post office? (The church.)

Activities Card

A. Children can give each other directions and manipulate cars to respond.

B. Map can be made of local area. Pictures of each child's house can be placed at appropriate places on the map. Children can give directions for getting to someone's house, while a child traces the route with his or her finger.

C. Take a walk to find the signs and traffic lights near the school.

D. A game can be played with road signs. Children can act out what a car would do.

E. Role-play a policeman and a lost child or a motorist asking for directions.

F. How do traffic rules vary? Compare countries by exploring such items as: police officer's dress, which side of the road you drive on, kinds of taxis, and at what age you can learn to drive.

A very good exercise is to have English-speaking children think of the kind of language they would need in a variety of situations. These children can then develop boxes to be used in the classroom; for example, a box with a variety of tools, or one that contains toy vehicles such as cars, trucks, and planes. These homemade kits can be one way of providing help to the untrained language tutor. For examples of such materials see "Language in a Shoebox: English as a Second Language" (Allen, 1976).

Moving into Print

Learning to Read a Second Language

When Cristi, the kindergartner described in chapter 5, arrived in school, she had spent five years living in an English-speaking world with English-speaking parents. She had seen a great deal of print around her and probably had watched her parents read. Quite possibly she had visited libraries and been read to every day. The experiences of the LEP child will not match those of Cristi. While all LEP children will have limited proficiency in the oral use of English to some degree, they will vary widely in their experiences with print. The Navaho child who speaks only Navaho at home may have seen much English print in stores, on TV, and on labels. Carlos, the ten-year-old from Chile, had seen little or no English print before his arrival in the U.S.A. However, he was a fluent reader of Spanish and had had many rewarding and happy experiences with books. Some children of Hispanic migrant workers may have developed a fair degree of fluency in the speaking of English since they return to an English-speaking community year after year. However, it may well be that they have not had the experience of seeing their parents read much or of having had books read aloud.

As teachers work with the LEP child, they will want to be aware of the child's background with print. The child needs to have an oral base in the language before being asked to write or read. The young refugee who comes from a small Southeastern Asian village where the illiteracy rate is very high will need much language and many experiences with books before that youngster can be expected to move into print. Carlos, who is a fluent reader of Spanish, will probably be ready and able to work with some forms of written English very quickly.

A phonics approach to reading is particularly difficult for the LEP child because there are phonemic differences between languages. In Spanish, for example, there is no phonemic contrast between the sounds represented by "sh" and "ch." Spanish speakers will have trouble first hearing and then producing the contrasts that English speakers produce in such minimal pairs as:

ship/chip
share/chair
shin/chin

In English there are at *least* 11 vowel distinctions, as in:

beet	bet	cut	pole
bit	bat	cool	cute
bait	bite	cot	

Contrast this with the Spanish language, in which only five vowel distinctions are made. Therefore, the Spanish-speaking child will have difficulty in hearing the differences between such words as:

sheep/ship
raid/red

mad/made
full/fill

Other aspects of language will also provide differences that are confusing to the person learning to speak and read a second language. Word order differences can make prediction difficult. Intonation differences can make reading aloud a problem, for some languages, such as French, do not use stress for emphasis as the English language does. Finally, the lexicon can present problems. In English there are two different words for the appendages attached to hands and feet. On the hands one has fingers and on the feet one has toes. In Spanish the same word is used for both. One has *dedos* on one's hands and *dedos* on one's feet.

Saville and Troike (1973) point out the fact that words may also be distributed in different ways. For example, in English the word "water" can be used in several ways. You can drink a glass of water or water the lawn. The water company can send out a man to read the water meter. So the word "water," depending upon position, can be used as a noun, a verb, or an adjective. In French, on the other hand, a lake would be filled with *eau*. One would go out to *arroser* the lawn. Waterskiing is *ski nautique,* and a water wheel is a *roue hydrolique*.

One of the best approaches to reading for LEP children is the language experience approach, which was described in chapter 5. This approach lets the children use the language they already control and helps them to discover how the oral symbol relates to the written symbol. While the language experience approach builds upon the child's own experiences, the basal text that is designed for middle-class American readers can create problems. Arab children may not be able to understand stories that center on concern over Spot, the pet dog, since dogs are not treated in this manner in their culture. A story about a birthday party may be confusing to the child who comes from a culture where birthdays are not celebrated, but Saint's days are.

Language experience can help LEP children avoid many of the difficulties that could be caused by a basal reading text. Because the children are using language they have already acquired to write about experiences they have had, there will be no mismatch between the children's conceptual and linguistic understandings and the materials that they are reading.

A Writing Experience in One Bilingual Classroom

A teacher in a third-grade bilingual classroom opened a coconut with her children one day. The youngsters made three holes with a hammer and nails so that the juice could trickle out, giving everyone a taste. The shell was cracked and the coconut meat (copra) was dug out and shared. The children were then asked for words to describe the coconut. In this particular classroom all of the children spoke Spanish and were at a variety of stages in their acquisition of English. These are the words they listed and later categorized:

Sound/escuchar

como agua
like wine
waves on the beach (Lizette)
espumoso (Marcos)

Touch/tocar

áspero (Mayra)
razgosa (Marcos)
like a bird's nest (Armando)
como los palos viejos (Marcos)
dura

Sight/ver

brown
black (Maria)
blanco
like a bowling ball with three holes (Armando)
redondo (Maria)
peludo (Marcos)
se parece de leche (Marcos)

Smell/oler

a ron
a whiskey
like mild

Taste/saborear

a coco
water
a ron
a gin
It makes my mouth hot. (Richard)

Copra

like nuts
good (Maria)
como piña colada (Marcos)

delicioso
crunchy (Lizette)
bad—*sabe de jabón*
dulce
like candy (Richard)

As can be seen in the above contributions, the children were at very different levels of language development. Lizette enjoys using English. Her contributions of "crunchy" and sounds like "waves on the beach" show an interest in finding just the right word to share her thoughts. Richard was comfortable with English, but his vocabulary was not yet very rich: "It makes my mouth hot" and "like candy." Marcos was a lively participant whose contributions, all in Spanish, show an ability to describe observations precisely. Maria's brief contributions were expressed in both English and Spanish.

Regular classroom teachers might not be able to work in quite this way, but they could provide opportunities for children to express their thoughts in their own language from time to time. A bilingual aide or a bilingual parent could assist in taking dictation from younger children and translating for older children. Often universities can provide bilingual students who can help in the classroom for periods of time each week. In this way, there would be opportunities for children to express themselves fully. One chafes at the bonds that language limitations can create. Being able to communicate in one's mother tongue is a relaxing moment of freedom.

At a later time this same bilingual teacher played an orchestral selection and had the children close their eyes and imagine they were doing something as the music played. Lizette chose to write in English and wrote:

> I want to the sky and I veth the sky and I felat lik I was in the air and I feta higher and thet felat rel good in me then i sol lot of thens thet I owas wanted to see.

She read her story aloud as follows:

> I went to the sky and I was the sky and I felt like I was in the air and I flew higher and that felt real good in me. Then I saw lot of things that I always wanted to see.

From this writing, the first thing to be noted is Lizette's willingness to and pleasure in expressing her feelings in English. Some spelling differences are predictable ones for a Spanish speaker, "want" for "went," "thet" for "that," and "thens" for "things." Such errors can be traced back to differences between the Spanish and English vowel system. The majority of spelling errors, however, are quite similar to the ones English-speaking children would make when first beginning to write:

"felat" for "felt" (an overenunciation)
"ove" for "of" (as it sounds)
"owas" for "always" (as it sounds)
"rel" for "real" (developmental)
"sol" for "saw" (as it sounds)

While the language used is limited, Lizette is able to get her feelings across—"and thet felat rel good in me." Lizette does not need spelling errors corrected at this point but needs to be praised for the expressive content of her writing and offered opportunities that provide a context for many more writing experiences. Lizette is moving into the use of print in English with enthusiasm and self-confidence. She needs to be supported in her explorations.

Marcos shared the same musical experience with Lizette, but chose to respond in Spanish. He wrote:

Estaba en las nubes estaba volando por el cielo con un aire limpio y suave. Estaba volando en una alfrombra y la música se oía por todo el mundo. Todo estaba tranquilo los pájaros pitando en el tono de la música. Estaba por las nubes y las nubes me abrazaban y todo el mundo entero me quiera. Y los árboles contentos porque a todo el mundo entero le agradaba la música y la tranquilidad.

*Por las nubes
me encontraba*

I was In the Sky

Translation

I was in the sky. I was flying through the clear, smooth air. I was flying on a rug, and the music was heard by everyone. All was tranquil. The birds whistling to the tune of the music. I was in the sky and the clouds embraced me and the whole world loved me. The trees were contented because the whole world loved the music and the tranquility.

Marcos had a lot to say and he could better get his meaning across in Spanish. But his interest in exploring English appears in the title, written in both Spanish and English.

The stories of Marcos and Lizette illustrate the need for children to write in the language in which they feel most comfortable. Writing can be translated and shared, but if children are always required to express their thoughts, ideas, and feelings in a language in which they lack the vocabulary and structure to do so, the writing task becomes an intolerable burden.

Selecting Books for LEP Children

In working with LEP children it is important to plan a program that involves them with books in a variety of ways, for text and illustrations provide an input of language as well as a basis for talk and for writing. Illustrations are of utmost importance, since clear and uncluttered pictures can help these children to develop vocabulary and concepts. Many storybooks have illustrations that convey much of the tale. There are also a wide variety of wordless picture books available. Some information books have richly detailed illustrations, which impart vast amounts of information, while others give step-by-step instructions on how to do something, with pictures so exact that they can be followed with little need for text.

The language of certain books is especially helpful to LEP children. Cumulative tales provide repetition of phrases. Poetry, as do stories with chants and rhythmic language, invites the child to join in. The predictable patterns of folktales encourage children to retell these stories and thus offer an opportunity for sustained oral language.

Some books are windows to other cultures. Realistic fiction, folktales, poetry, historical fiction, biography, and information books can all illuminate another culture's view of life. Children whose language and heritage are different from those of their classmates often feel set apart. Sharing books that illustrate aspects of the non-English-speaking children's culture can benefit both these children and their English-speaking peers.

The book list that follows is a sampling of some of the kinds of books that can provide the support LEP children need as they interact with text.

Suggestions of Books for LEP Children

Books that Develop Concepts and Vocabulary

>Anno, Mitsumaso, *Anno's Counting Book,* Thomas Y. Crowell Co., New York, 1975.
>>A very special counting book. The page for zero shows barren, snowy hillsides. Page by page the seasons change and the landscape is transformed as roads, trees, and houses are added with each succeeding number. A counting book that even older children will find absorbing.

>Burningham, John, *Seasons,* Jonathan Cape, Ltd., London, 1969.

Rich, luminous color make these seasonal scenes delightful. Tree branches dusted with frost are lacy against a dark winter sky; leaves flame in autumn. The text is simple and limited to a few unobtrusive words on each page.

Hoban, Tana, *Over, Under and Through,* Macmillan Publishing Co., New York, 1973.
 Black-and-white photographs are used to help children develop spatial concepts. Clear, large pictures show a cat *on* a window sill, berries *in* a basket, and a child crawling *through* a pipe. A valuable tool, since prepositions are most difficult for the person acquiring English.

——, *Push Pull, Empty Full,* Macmillan Publishing Co., New York, 1972.
 Clear black-and-white photographs illustrate opposites. *Empty* and *full* are shown by two gumball machines, while *in* and *out* are demonstrated by an obliging turtle.

Rockwell, Anne and Rockwell, Harlow, *The Toolbox,* Macmillan Publishing Co., New York, 1971.
 The contents of a toolbox are explored and shared in colorful and simple pictures. Such words as "hammer," "clamp," and "plane" are illustrated. The text is minimal.

Spier, Peter, *The Food Market,* Doubleday, New York, 1981.
 Numerous detailed pictures of things that happen in a supermarket, as well as the many items that are sold there, make this a particularly useful resource for vocabulary development. This book is one of a series, printed on heavy cardboard and cut in the shapes of various village buildings. Other books in this series are: *The Fire House, Bill's Service Station, My School, The Pet Store,* and *The Toy Store.* The sophistication of the drawings would attract older as well as younger students.

Wildsmith, Brian, *ABC,* Franklin Watts, Inc., New York, 1963.
 The illustrations in this prize-winning book have the glowing, extravagant color of stained glass. Each page has only one object to illustrate the letter.

Books Whose Illustrations Tell the Story

Barrett, Judi, *Animals Should Definitely Not Wear Clothing,* illustrated by Ron Barrett, Atheneum, New York, 1970.
 The author proves her point by showing how silly a giraffe would look with six neckties draped along his neck and the problems a hen wearing slacks would have when it came to egg-laying time. The humor lies in the preposterous pictures. Children of all ages will laugh at this book.

Hutchins, Pat, *Titch,* Macmillan Publishing Co., New York, 1971.
 This story for younger children depicts the problems of being the smallest

person in the family. The simple story, well conveyed by the illustrations, allows an opportunity for developing the concepts of big, bigger, biggest and high, higher, and highest.

Hutchins, Pat, *Rosie's Walk,* Macmillan Publishing Co., New York, 1968.
　　Rosie the hen goes for a walk blissfully unaware that she is being followed by a wily fox. Rosie's walk is pleasantly uneventful but the fox's walk is disastrous. Since his eye is on the hen he bumps into a post, falls into a pond, and knocks over a beehive. The pictures tell two stories, while the very brief and simple text recounts only one—that of Rosie.

Kraus, Robert, *Herman the Helper,* illustrated by Jose Aruego and Ariane Dewey, E. P. Dutton, Inc., New York, 1974.
　　Herman, a tiny octopus, is most helpful. We see him designing a seaweed bonnet for his aunt, helping his uncle build a ship in a bottle, and finally washing his hands—all eight of them! The vivid and humorous illustrations should charm young children.

Sendak, Maurice, *Where the Wild Things Are,* Harper & Row, New York, 1963.
　　This well-known book is one that non-English speaking children can enjoy. Though they may miss the beauty of the language, the author's use of space and color makes his monsters seem to dance across the page. The smile on Max's face speaks most clearly of his character!

Shulevitz, Uri, *Dawn,* Farrar, Straus and Giroux, New York, 1974.
　　This book is a visual poem. An old man and his grandson sleep under a tree by a lake in a world that is a deep, cool blue. Picture by picture we see dawn unfurl. This is truly a picture book the older children can appreciate.

Books with Repetitive Language

Hogrogian, Nonny, *One Fine Day,* Macmillan Co., New York, 1971.
　　This Caldecott Award winner is based on an Armenian folktale. Fox has to ask others for help in getting his tail sewn on. Over and over he must repeat his request. The lovely illustrations tell much of the story.

Kent, Jack, *The Fat Cat,* Scholastic Book Service, New York, 1971.
　　A hungry cat gobbles up not only the gruel, but the pot it was cooked in and the old woman who cooked it. He goes on his way gobbling up all he meets until he finally bursts, freeing all the people upon whom he had dined. The last picture shows him smaller and wiser with a neat bandage on his stomach. The pictures delight children as they watch the cat grow to blimplike proportions. A cumulative tale that invites children to chant along with the reader.

McGovern, Ann, *Too Much Noise,* illustrated by Simms Taback, Houghton Mifflin, New York, 1967.
　　An old man, annoyed by the creaks and squeaks of his house, goes to a wise man for help. The man tells him to get a cow. When this fails to improve the

situation he is advised to get a donkey. So it continues till he has a house full of animals. Young children love to help out by making the sounds for each animal.

Wordless Picture Books

dePaola, Tomie, *Pancakes for Breakfast,* Harcourt Brace Jovanovich, New York, 1978.
   A little old lady decides to make herself a sumptuous breakfast of pancakes. When, after immense trouble, she finally gathers all her ingredients, her cat and dog manage to spill them. The day is saved by kindly neighbors. A recipe for pancakes, the only text in the book, could serve as the basis for a cooking lesson.

Goodall, John S., *Creepy Castle,* Atheneum, New York, 1975.
   A gallant mouse and his lady friend explore a deserted castle. There they are trapped by a villainous rat. Richly detailed pictures convey the story of their escape. The author's use of half pages adds to the fun and the suspense.

Hoban, Tana, *Look Again!,* Macmillan Publishing Co., New York, 1971.
   This book, a visual puzzle, will involve and excite children of all ages. A "peep hole" page lets the child see a small portion of a photo. When the page is flipped the whole object can be seen. An excellent book for the child who does not yet read.

Mayer, Mercer, *Frog Goes to Dinner,* Dial Press, New York, 1974.
   A little boy's pet frog hops into his pocket as he is getting ready to go out for dinner with his family. Chaos results as the frog leaps from a lady's salad into a gentleman's champagne. Rollicking fun for all ages.

Spier, Peter, *Noah's Ark,* Doubleday, New York, 1977.
   Spier gives us a new view of Noah's voyage depicting the immensity of Noah's task of caring for so many animals in such a small space. While the story of the flood may not be a part of some children's cultural heritage, the humorous detail of the illustrations should amuse all children.

Turkle, Brinton, *Deep in the Forest,* E. P. Dutton and Co., New York, 1976.
   A curious bear wanders into a small cottage in the forest. He finds a table set with three bowls marked Papa, Mama, and Baby. What follows is a reverse tale of Goldilock's adventures. Even children who don't know the story of *The Three Bears* will laugh at the antics of the cub as he cavorts about the house.

Ward, Lynd, *The Silver Pony,* Houghton Mifflin, Boston, 1973.
   This lengthy wordless picture book tells the story of a lonely young farm boy who conjures up in his imagination a beautiful winged horse. On the back of this silver horse he has many adventures but finally returns to the real world, where he receives a real pony. Ward's black-and-white drawings are both forceful and delicate. An absorbing book for older children.

Informational Books

Adkins, Jan, *Inside: Seeing Beneath the Surface,* Walker and Co., New York, 1975.
    The artist uses cross sections to give us a look inside of an apple pie, a fountain pen, and an airplane. These beautifully detailed drawings give children a new way of viewing the world. The language of this book is rich, but the illustrations alone carry a powerful message.

Adkins, Jan, *Toolchest,* Walker and Co., New York, 1973.
    All sorts of tools are examined and explained—tools for measuring, shaping, boring, and cutting. The illustrations are profuse and executed with exquisite attention to detail. While the well-written text is for the mature reader, the illustrations are a marvelous resource for the child interested in building.

Emberley, Ed, *Ed Emberley's Great Thumbprint Drawing Book,* Little, Brown and Co., Boston, 1977.
    Emberley shows children how to use their thumbprints to create such delightful creatures as fish, birds, spiders, and even a worried pig. Step-by-step pictures are given. The text is confined to labels.

Grillone, Lisa and Gennaro, Joseph, *Small Worlds Close Up,* Crown Publishers, New York, 1978.
    Spectacular photographs made by using an electron scanning microscope give close-up views of such items as salt, cork, and the edge of a razor blade. Much information is conveyed dramatically.

Macaulay, David, *Castle,* Houghton Mifflin Co., Boston, 1977.
    The building of a thirteenth-century castle is shown. Each step in the construction is drawn with fine attention to architectural detail. Four other books by Macaulay will also interest children. They are *Underground, Cathedral, City,* and *Pyramid.*

Books in the Child's Native Language *(Spanish)*

Griego, Margot C.; Bucks, Betsy L.; Gilbert, Sharon S.; and Kimball, Laurel H., *Tortillitas Para Mama,* illustrated by Barbara Cooney, Holt, Rinehart and Winston, New York, 1981.
    These Latin American nursery rhymes and lullabies are presented in both English and in the original Spanish. Cooney's illustrations link the rhymes to different sections of Mexico and offer a tapestry of rural Mexican life. A book rich in sound, color, and texture.

Kouzel, Daisy, *The Cuckoo's Reward: El premio del cuco: A Folktale from Mexico in Spanish and English,* illustrated by Earl Thollander, Doubleday and Co., New York, 1977.
    This legend of the Mayan Indians tells how the cuckoo lost her bright colors

and her beautiful song. Bright watercolors illustrate the text, which is printed in Spanish and English side by side. It would be helpful to have tapes made both in Spanish and English for children to use in the listening corner.

Pomerantz, Charlotte, *The Tamarindo Puppy and Other Poems,* illustrated by Byron Barton, Greenwillow Books, New York, 1980.

These delightfully different poems are not translated but are written in two languages, English and Spanish. Each poem has an interplay of both languages, allowing children to enjoy the sounds and patterns of each language in a unique way.

Books in English about the Child's Native Culture

Kha, Dang Manh, *In the Land of Small Dragon: A Vietnamese Folktale,* told by Dang Manh Kha to Ann Nolan Clark, illustrated by Tony Chen, Viking Press, New York, 1979.

This Vietnamese version of Cinderella is retold in the traditional metric form used in that country and the rhymes are interspersed with Vietnamese proverbs. The beautifully detailed illustrations underline the cultural aspects of this tale.

Miles, Miska, *Annie and the Old One,* illustrated by Peter Parnall, Little, Brown and Co., Boston, 1971.

This is the moving story of the love of a little Navaho girl for her grandmother. The grandmother tells Annie that her time for death is near and that she will die when the rug she is weaving is completed. Annie tries to stop death by stealthily undoing each day's weaving. Culturally one sees the unity of the Navaho and the land, the pride in craftsmanship, and the deference to elders. Perhaps, more significantly, one sees the universality of love and death.

Supree, Burton with Ann Ross, *Bear's Heart,* J. B. Lippincott, Philadelphia, 1977.

In 1874 Bear's Heart, a Cheyenne, was captured and sent to a military prison in Florida. He recorded all that happened in a series of colored drawings, beautiful in their childlike simplicity. The text tells of the white men's attempts to teach Bear's Heart their ways. The moving Afterword by Jamake Highwater tells of Bear's Heart's return to his tribe. With his white man's clothing and new ways he was seen as a misfit by his own people.

Yashima, Taro, *Crow Boy,* Viking Press, New York, 1955.

A frightened Japanese boy, Chibi, starts his school life. The other children make fun of him because he is different. An understanding teacher helps Chibi to share his special talents. The theme of the book is a strong one, which could help children to better understand the feelings of those who are set apart in some way. The illustrations, rich in cultural details such as Japanese handwriting, the abacus, and a luncheon of a rice ball, could lead to explorations into Japanese life.

Summary

As children work at acquiring a second language, they go about it using many of the strategies they used in tackling their first language. They look for meaning and for system. They expect language to be used purposefully. They hypothesize and test, thus developing a tacit grammar. Therefore, the same kind of contexts that support first-language development will support second-language acquisition. This does not mean that LEP children should simply be immersed into the English-speaking classroom to sink or swim. Attention must be given to cultural and social differences, particularly as they might affect learning. Opportunities should be provided for language input that is within the child's grasp. Such children need to be able to practice language structures in meaningful situations. Above all they need to be given time to develop fluency and confidence.

LEP children, because of their knowledge of a language other than English, add a special dimension to the total language-arts program. In a very concrete way they can help the monolingual English-speaking child become aware that English is only one language among many. Teachers who provide for cross-language sharing can help all children begin to develop a sense of the capabilities and the beauty of a language system other than their own. Above all, as children communicate with those whose background and language differ from their own, there is a real need to explain, to question, to clarify, and to modify. All of these will help children to develop an increasing control over language.

Recommended Readings

Allen, Virginia, "Foreign Languages in the Elementary Schools: A New Look; A New Focus," *Language Arts* 55: 146–149, February, 1978.

   This article presents the other side of the coin, for it looks at teaching a second language to English speakers in an English-speaking society. Allen reviews past practices in FLES (foreign languages in the elementary schools) and proposes changes. She believes that if FLES is to succeed it needs to become an integral part of the language-arts program, and suggests ways that this might be accomplished.

Edelsky, Carole and Hudelson, Sarah, "Language Acquisition and a Marked Language," *NABE Journal* 5: 1–15, Fall, 1980.

   FLES offered in classes where there are children who are native speakers of the language being taught would seem to provide the optimum environment for learning that language. Edelsky and Hudelson studied such a first-grade classroom in a school system that had as its goal that all children would develop skills in two languages. This study, a replication of an earlier one by these researchers, suggests strongly that the political position of the second language is a powerful factor in its acquisition.

Rodrigues, Raymond J. and White, Robert H., *Mainstreaming the Non-English Speaking Student: Theory and Research into Practice* (TRIP) booklet, NCTE and ERIC/RCS, Urbana, Illinois, 1981.

This booklet offers a variety of suggestions of ways teachers can individualize instruction for the LEP child: a learning packet with precise instructions for a number of language activities appropriate for students from elementary through high school; a sample plan for an open language experience; as well as a number of examples of assessment techniques. Written in response to the needs of regular classroom teachers who are working with LEP children, this publication provides some sound advice.

Saville-Troike, Muriel, *A Guide to Culture in the Classroom,* Rosslyn, Virginia: National Clearinghouse for Bilingual Education, 1978.

This exploration of the relationships among language, culture, and education, while written with the bilingual teacher in mind, is a valuable resource for all teachers. Saville-Troike helps the reader probe beneath the superficial to discover the kinds of cultural information that is crucial. The section "Questions to Ask About a Culture" is an excellent basis for developing a broader understanding of the many aspects of culture that relate to language development and to classroom practice.

Urzuá, Carole, "A Language Learning Environment for All Children," *Language Arts* 57: 38–47, January, 1980.

Urzuá proposes that since all children have similar expectations about what language is, how it works, and why people communicate, language-arts environments should be the same for all children, those who speak English natively and those who are acquiring English as a second language. The author demonstrates that the interactive, supportive, responsive environment needed for all children will support LEP children in ways that will help them acquire a second language as they did their first. A strong rationale is given, with many implications for the teacher of language arts.

Suggested Learning Experiences

1. Using the observation guide in this chapter, spend one morning or afternoon in a classroom observing one LEP child the entire time. In which situations does the child feel most free to enter? Where is he inclined to be more tentative in language use? As a teacher, what kinds of experiences would you propose for this child?

2. Select a folktale that has not been read to the child before. Read the story to an LEP child, letting her sit beside you so that she can see the illustrations. Ask her to retell that tale to someone else in the class. Tape the

retelling and transcribe it. How does her retelling compare to the one done by Carlos, discussed on pages 405–407? What has the child learned about English? How is she relying on her prior language knowledge? How did the illustrations in the book assist her interpretation?

3. Using the sample suggested in this chapter, develop a language box for LEP children. You may work either alone or in small groups to do this. You may find that you need to think about which structures in English you would focus upon. If so, a book such as Robinett's *Teaching English to Speakers of Other Languages* might be a helpful resource. After you have developed the box of materials and the cards, take them to a school where LEP children are enrolled. Try out the materials. Do you see any need for change? What did you learn about the materials? What did you learn about the children with whom you worked?

4. If no LEP children are enrolled in nearby schools, talk with college students who have had to learn English as a second language. Ask them to discuss their experiences with you. What was the most difficult cultural adjustment they had to make as they moved into an American school setting? What were their most trying linguistic experiences? Are there still situations in which they feel a need to adjust?

References

Professional Literature

Allen, Virginia Garibaldi, "Language in a Shoebox: English as a Second Language," *Instructor* 86:81–85, August/September, 1976.

Binh, Duong Thanh; Diller, Anne-Marie; and Sutherland, Kenton, *A Handbook for Teachers of Vietnamese Students: Hints for Dealing with Cultural Differences in Schools,* Arlington, Va.: Center for Applied Linguistics, 1975.

Cummins, James, "Four Misconceptions about Language Proficiency in Bilingual Education," *NABE Journal* 5:31–46, Spring, 1981.

Dumont, Robert V., Jr., "Learning English and How to be Silent: Studies in Sioux and Cherokee Classrooms," pp. 344–369 in *Functions of Language in the Classroom* eds. Courtney B. Cazden, Vera P. John, and Dell Hymes, Teachers College Press, New York, 1972.

Fillmore, Lilly Wong, *The Second Time Around: Cognitive and Social Strategies in Second Language Acquisition,* Ph.D. Dissertation, Stanford University, Stanford, Calif., 1976.

Freed, Barbara, "Talking to Foreigners Versus Talking to Children: Similarities and Differences," pp. 19–27 in *Research in Second Language Acquisition* eds. Robin Scarcella and Stephen D. Krashen, Rowley, Mass.: Newbury House, 1980.

Friedlander, B.; Jacobs, A.; Davis, B.; and Wetstone, H., "Time Sampling Analysis of Infants, Natural Language Environments in Their Home," *Child Development* 43:730–740, September, 1972.

Hall, Edward L., *The Silent Language,* Greenwich, Conn.: Fawcett Publications, Inc., 1959.

John, Vera P., "Styles of Learning—Styles of Teaching: Reflections on the Education of Navaho Children," pp. 331–343 in *Functions of Language in the Classroom,* eds. Courtney B. Cazden, Vera P. John, and Dell Hymes, Teachers College Press, New York, 1972.

Krashen, Stephen D., "Formal and Informal Linguistic Environments in Language Acquisition and Language Learning," *TESOL Quarterly* 10:157–168, June, 1976.

Krashen, Stephen, "Some Consequences of the Input Hypothesis," paper presented at the Fifteenth Annual International Conference of Teachers of English to Speakers of Other Languages, Detroit, March, 1981.

Lindfors, Judith Wells, *Children's Language and Learning,* Englewood Cliffs, N.J.: Prentice-Hall, Inc., 1980.

Peck, Sabrina, "Child-Child Discourse in Second Language Acquisition," pp. 383–400 in *Second Language Acquisition,* eds. Evelyn Marcussen Hatch, Newbury House, Rowley, Massachusetts, 1978.

Robinett, Betty Wallace, *Teaching English to Speakers of Other Languages,* University of Minnesota Press, Minneapolis, 1978.

Saville, Muriel and Troike, Rudolph C., *A Handbook of Bilingual Education,* revised edition, Washington, D.C., Teachers of English to Speakers of Other Languages, 1973.

Selinker, Larry, "Interlanguage," *IRAL,* 10:201–231, August, 1972.

Shuy, Roger, "Learning to Talk Like Teachers," *Language Arts* 58(2):168–174, February, 1981.

Tough, Joan, *Listening to Children Talking: A Guide to the Appraisal of Children's Use of Language,* Schools Council Communication Skills in Early Childhood Project, Schools Councils Publication, London, England, 1976.

Wells, Gordon, *Learning Through Interaction: The Study of Language Development,* Cambridge University Press, Cambridge, England, 1981.

Children's Literature

Cole, Brock, *No More Baths,* Doubleday, Garden City, New York, 1980.

Hutchins, Pat, *Rosie's Walk,* Macmillan Publishing Co., New York, 1968.

Duvoisin, Roger, *Petunia,* Knopf, New York, 1950.

dePaola, Tomie, *Big Anthony and the Magic Ring,* Harcourt Brace Jovanovich, New York, 1979.

———, *Strega Nona,* Prentice-Hall, Englewood Cliffs, New Jersey, 1975.

Soft, light white
Rocky, slushy
Cold snow.

The Snowman
By
David John

The Snow Book
by
Gillian and Krista

The Deepest
Snow
by Wesley

PART 3
Organization and Evaluation of the Language-Arts Program

Rationale for Planning

Developing Long-term Plans
An Example from One School District
An Example of One Teacher's Focus

Developing Short-term Plans
An Example of One Class's Planning
Role of Weekly Plans

Developing an Integrated Program
The Beginning
Differences Between a Unit and a Theme

Communicating the Language-Arts Program
Other Teachers and the Principal
Parents

Evaluating the Program
Plans
The Ongoing Program

NCTE Guidelines

Summary

Suggested Learning Experiences

References
Professional Literature
Children's Literature

Chapter 10

Program Planning and Evaluation

This text has focused on the development of an integrated language-arts program. In each chapter the emphasis has been on:

1. interrelating the language arts with each other and with the total curriculum
2. meeting the differing abilities and interests of children within the context of a rich and diverse program
3. building upon and expanding the linguistic abilities of all children
4. evaluating the progress of both children and teachers as learners in the classroom
5. establishing a learning context conducive to language growth

Such a language-arts program does not just happen; it is much more than a haphazard series of interesting and worthwhile experiences. An integrated language-arts program is cohesive and provides for continuing growth. The development of such a program takes effective planning.

Rationale for Planning

Planning has been seen by some as a needless expense of time, a job done only to satisfy a principal or a university instructor, with little relationship to the real tasks of the teacher. But planning is neither filling in squares on a time sheet nor writing behavioral objectives. Planning is not done simply to enable a substitute teacher to take over if necessary; rather, planning is a way of thinking, a way of approaching problems.

In order to develop a strongly cohesive language-arts program, teachers need to have firmly in mind some broad, overarching goals that let them envision the kinds of long-term experiences children need. Broad goals will let teachers balance experiences. There should be many opportunities to explore literature, but there should also be an emphasis on concrete and authentic experience. Reading should not be emphasized to the neglect of writing or writing to the neglect of oral language opportunities. While some whole-class work is extremely valuable, this should be balanced by many occasions when children work in small groups on individual projects.

As teachers look at their programs as a whole, they can work on integrating the language arts across the curriculum. The goals of a language-arts program regarding critical listening, debate, and discussion match the goals of a social studies curriculum. Mathematics provides opportunities for a wide variety of language functions. Integration has both a horizontal dimension and a vertical dimension. As teachers think through their program, they will want to consider what learnings and skills the children are bringing with them as they enter the classroom. They will also want to lay a foundation for future learning that will come when the children move out of their classroom. Children who are required to do work that they perceive as needlessly repetitive quickly become bored and frustrated, as do children who are asked to do tasks for which they have been poorly prepared. If children are to see themselves as able learners, they need to be aware that they are indeed progressing in knowledge and in ability. A teacher, then, needs an awareness of sequence.

But teacher goals should not be seen as hurdles over which all children must jump. If children are to learn well, their interests and their needs must be an integral part of the language-arts program. This means that the program must be flexible enough to allow for different learning styles, different abilities, and even goals that differ from the teacher's own. A language-arts curriculum, then, cannot demand that all children do the same tasks with a comparable amount of success. Instead, the program should foster growth in diversity.

Such a program cannot be drawn with fine, precise lines of India ink. Rather, it should be sketched with broad charcoal lines that can be rubbed out, changed, and even smudged a bit. Teachers and children need to feel free to adjust, to change, to move in new directions. Barnes sees the curriculum as communication:

> When people talk about "the school curriculum" they often mean "what teachers plan in advance for their pupils to learn." But a curriculum made only of teachers' intentions would be an insubstantial thing from which nobody would learn much. To become meaningful a curriculum has to be enacted by pupils as well as teachers. . . . By "enact" I mean come together in a meaningful communication—talk, write, read books, collaborate, become angry with one another, learn what to say and do. . . . In this sense curriculum is a form of communication (1976, p. 14).

Developing Long-term Plans

Long-term plans are nothing more than a map of the directions a class may go during the year. In making long-term plans there are several important considerations. First, the teacher must think of the developmental stages of the children in the classroom. Some learning activities would be inappropriate for younger children because their attention span is still fairly brief. Certain kinds of activities may be inappropriate for the preadolescent who has become self-conscious about physical size and appearance.

Expectations of parents should be taken into account. If children are to develop to their fullest, parents and the schools will have to work together. Teachers should not assume that their goals and the parents' goals will always mesh. Some parents, who may adamantly demand a focus on the so-called "basics" will be concerned and upset if aspects of the language arts that they consider vital seem to receive little attention. In all probability the "basics" are still as significant a component of the curriculum as they have been historically. However, by integrating subject areas, the emphasis on such areas as writing or reading may become obscured. In this instance, teachers have a clear responsibility to explain their program to parents with concrete examples of how important competencies are being included during class activities.

The teacher's own goals are extremely important. One school year should not simply be a repetition of the previous one. Each year is an opportunity for the teacher to develop new strengths and to enlarge areas of expertise. Teachers who are involved in professional organizations, who read journals and books in their field, will have fresh ideas they wish to try. Teachers should also build upon their own interests and abilities. A teacher with an artistic bent will want to integrate art activities with the language-arts program. A teacher who has a strong interest in the out-of-doors could use this knowledge to enrich the curriculum.

Finally, there are the requirements mandated by the state and by the local school system. Many states provide guides that suggest how much time must be devoted to specific curriculum areas at different grade levels. School curriculum guides often incorporate state goals into more specific objectives for their particular system. Textbooks also have a sequence of concepts and skills to be presented to children. These learnings are often displayed on scope and sequence charts, which outline the skills and show where in the text series that skill is introduced, practiced, and reviewed.

An Example from One School District

At first, all of these considerations can make long-term planning seem an impossibly bulky task. However, it becomes much simpler if one example is examined. One curriculum guide (Columbus Public Schools, 1977) lists the following goals for children in language-arts programs in the primary grades:

    I. Students will expand their repertoire of language functions in a variety of situations.

    II. Students will become critical, receptive, and appreciative listeners.

III. Students will become effective speakers and will respect and appreciate the speech of others.

IV. Students will enjoy and value good literature as a result of rich learning experiences.

V. Students will be able to express ideas clearly and creatively, share and evaluate their own writing, and develop skills and attitudes that foster appreciation and enjoyment of written expression.

VI. Students will expand their understanding of the mass media (newspapers, magazines, television, and films) and will learn to use media for primary and supporting presentations.

VII. Students will understand that language reaches out through nonverbal channels to communicate meaning that words alone cannot convey and recognize that nonverbal language is a part of a comprehensive language program.

VIII. Students will recognize the value of correct spelling and will develop the appropriate skills needed to improve written language.

IX. Students will recognize the value of legible handwriting and will develop the appropriate skills and attitudes needed to develop a writing style that is easily read.

Under each broad goal is listed a number of objectives for both the teacher and the student. The goals and objectives are general rather than specific. General goals permit integrated programs to grow, while narrower goals tend to segment learning. One broad literary objective is to explore the sounds of poetry. This goal allows for: listening to poems read aloud, searching together for poems where the sound is a vital part of the poet's message, using the rhythms of poetry as a basis for movement and dance, using the voice expressively to share a poem, and trying out the poet's role. A narrower objective, such as "Children will be able to identify poems in which the poet has used onomatopoeia," requires little of the teacher or of the child. Here the attention is given not to the wholeness of the poetry experience but to examining a very small fragment of the poet's craft.

An Example of One Teacher's Focus

Goals and objectives are not tied to textbooks; rather, they are designed to illumine the school's philosophy. Far from restricting teachers, they liberate them from having to slavishly follow a text. Teachers can meet the objectives in ways they find most suitable for them and for their classes. For example, a teacher whose own particular interest was to provide a wide variety of drama experiences for a third-grade class would find that some aspects of goals I, II, III, IV, VI, and VII could be met. In addition, the teacher could also be meeting many specific objectives under those goals. To look more closely, the following are the objectives for Goal III. Those objectives that are starred could easily be met within the framework of drama.

Goal III: Students will become effective speakers and will respect and appreciate the speech of others.

Teacher's Objectives

*1.0 Create a climate of respect for individual speech patterns

*2.0 Provide situations for purposeful speaking

*3.0 Promote appreciation of oral language

*4.0 Facilitate acquisition of what has been called "written edited American English" through exposure to literature and free oral response to it

Student's Objectives

*1.1 Express confidently their thoughts and feelings

1.2 Apply rules of courtesy for group discussions

*1.3 Accept the unique language styles and dialects of others

*2.1 Increase effectiveness in group communication by actively participating

*2.2 Participate in individual speaking; e.g., monologue, storytelling, sharing

*2.3 Participate in creative dramatic situations through role-playing, improvising, and fantasizing

*2.4 Apply register switching to meet a variety of speaking situations

*3.1 Use oral language for a variety of purposes

3.2 Recognize the beauty that exists in language

*3.3 Develop oral language through music, art, drama, and movement

*4.1 Identify situations where standard American English is appropriate

*4.2 Acquire ability to employ the use of standard American English

	4.3 Acquaint themselves with traditional and modern classics in literature
*5.0 Help students learn the mechanics of speaking	5.1 Recognize the ingredients necessary for effective discussion; e.g., understand, contribute, listen, stay to the point, summarize
	*5.2 Articulate sounds and words clearly, adjust rate of speech to achieve effectiveness, and adjust volume according to the situation
	*5.3 Use pitch, juncture, and stress for emphasis
*6.0 Assist students in identifying kinds of problems in oral communications	*6.1 Assist each other through constructive criticism
	6.2 Identify particular speech needs and integrate learned skills into daily usage
	6.3 Generalize the importance of the services rendered by the speech therapist and nurse

K-3 Curriculum Guide and Source of Study, Columbus Public Schools, pp. F-3a–F-3c, Columbus, Ohio, 1977.

The same teacher could also look at the scope and sequence chart of the language-arts textbook series to search for sections where drama is treated. Sections such as those on pantomime and puppetry could be used, as they fit in with class plans.

Developing Short-term Plans

At this point, webbing can help the teacher map out connections. As he webs he can connect short-term goals to long-term ones, children's interests to their needs, and past learnings to new learnings. The mouse web, discussed in chapter 1, as well as the many other webs included in this book, show how the teacher can make these connections.

An Example of One Class's Plans

The teacher does not plan alone, for pupils are planners also. Pupil planning is much more than the opportunity to choose among activities previously selected by the teacher. It is a way of having language arts spring from children's own interests and concerns. One group of fourth-graders was dismayed by a newspaper article describing how the bitterly cold weather had made it impossible for birds in the area to find food. As a result many birds had died. The children's decision to feed the birds sparked a number of activities.

> They researched ways to build bird feeders.
> They had group discussions on the kinds of bird feeders they wished to build.
> They met with the principal to explain their plans and to find where they might place bird feeders.
> They called a ranger at a nearby park to find what kinds of food to give the birds.
> They decided to involve the community in their efforts by preparing a handbill describing what people could do to help birds survive the long, cold winter.
> They organized groups for the production and the distribution of this handbill.

In order to meet their own purposes, these children used language in a number of ways: explaining, questioning, researching, writing to persuade,

Planning with the teacher is a focused event where each concentrates on the project or task to be accomplished. It is highly personal and bonds teacher and child together as can be seen in this photograph. (Miss Enciso's informal classroom, Barrington School, Upper Arlington, Ohio)

and writing to share information. But more than this, the planning itself was an intensely valuable experience. It is as children plan that they become independent decision-makers by examining ideas, defending views, weighing various alternatives, and taking upon themselves the responsibility for a project. Thus, children's planning is in itself an important part of a language-arts program.

The teacher's role is to support and assist children in their efforts. Children and teacher can meet together daily to plan for the day's activities. The teacher whose class worked on feeding the birds mapped out the afternoon project time as follows:

Children's Groups	*Activity*	*Materials*
Handbill Group		
Sal, Rick, and Leslie	Proofread copy and put on ditto master	Dittos, dictionaries, children's language-arts textbooks, copy of the sample handbill
Mark and Karen	Work on designs for border of handbill	Materials in art center and colored dittos
Tammy, Kelly, Meg, Joel, and Paul	Work with map of school district to divide up distribution routes	District map School directory
Feeder Group		
Beth, Fred, and David	Work at carpentry bench Finish sawing and sanding	Materials at carpentry bench
Molly and Tim	Stain feeder	Stain and brushes at the sink area
Spelling		
Connie, Sam, Diane, and Julie	Work with cards on *cvc* and *cvce* spelling patterns	Word banks Newspaper to look for words Blank cards
Finishing		
Ted	Work on story	
Gail	Bind book	Bookbinding materials in writing center

A cursory glance at these plans might lead some people to the conclusion that little language arts was going on that particular afternoon. However, the teacher had language-arts goals in mind and was quite aware of how those goals were being met. Sal, Rick, and Leslie had met with their teacher the day before to talk about proofreading. They were going to have one child read the text of the handbill aloud while the other two children examined the copy for punctuation. Then each child was to examine his or her copy, circling all the words about whose spelling they had a question. Such words were to be compared, discussed, and checked in a dictionary.

Mark and Karen were working on a design for the border of the handbill, trying to match design to message. They had looked at illustrated ads and decided they needed a design that would be eye-catching and that would also add to the message. Mark and Karen's language included comparisons, descriptions, and hypothesis testing. The group that was working on handbill distribution was using map-reading skills as well as the skills needed to find addresses in the student directory.

Those children working on sawing, sanding, and staining the feeders would undoubtedly have time for lots of social talk as well as heuristic language, which hypothesizes about outcomes. The next day they would be using another kind of oral language when sharing what they had done. The teacher selected groups carefully. Fred is a shy child who is not a strong student, but he is extremely adept with tools. Working with Beth and David, he will have a chance to take the leadership role. Molly is a very bright little girl, but she almost always chooses to work alone. This task is one where she could learn to enjoy working with others.

It would appear as if the children who are working with the spelling materials are cut off from the bird-feeder project. This is not so. Their turn at the carpentry table will come the next day. As for this particular afternoon, they were working to develop their knowledge of spelling based upon particular needs the teacher had noticed in their writing.

Ted began a story in the morning and became so engrossed that he asked to be allowed to continue this work during project time. Gail's bookbinding is the completion of a writing task, a story she had worked on over several days. The story had been illustrated, recopied in her finest handwriting, and was now ready for "publication."

When teachers have developed long-range plans and have well in mind the overarching goals, they can write their plans briefly and still be confident that they are planning well. This kind of planning helps the day go smoothly. Children know what they are to do, where they will work, and with whom. Teachers are able to organize time, space, and materials so that children can work well. At day's end this planning can help focus the evaluation of the children's work. Children can judge their own progress and take pride in goals when they themselves have helped set those goals.

Role of Weekly Plans

Weekly plans are also important, for they let the teacher see the week as a whole. It is one way to keep track of class schedules and appointments that must be kept at specific times. Times of meetings with the art teacher and gym classes can be recorded, as well as such teacher duties as playground supervision or lunchroom duty. Weekly planning also helps the teacher organize and balance the days, and permits one activity to flow smoothly into the next. Such planning will prevent a series of activities that all require intensive writing. It can also prevent the confusion that occurs when an activity that requires a high level of movement follows a similar activity; for instance, improvisational drama should probably not immediately follow an exciting volleyball game. Weekly schedules allow teachers to plan around the changes that each week brings.

Weekly plans also help teachers to arrange time so that those aspects of the curriculum that are central receive the proper amount of attention. In the weekly plan shown on page 440 the teacher has begun by blocking out periods for things to be done at specific times. It is easy to note the concern with language interaction and with the wide use of literature. The large blocks of time free the teacher to use them for projects, for introducing and practicing subject specific content, and for integrated activities.

Developing an Integrated Program

The Beginning

Moving from a schedule of separate subjects to an integrated curriculum need not be difficult. The process can be gradual. One way to begin is to use groups already established in the class, such as reading groups. One group could be selected to work on a literature theme. Even though the theme is carried out by only a few children, others in the class will note what is happening. Something new is usually of interest so the rest of the class will eagerly anticipate their work in themes. This group-by-group entry into an

Weekly Planning Chart

Monday	Tuesday	Wednesday	Thursday	Friday

9:00–10:00
Block Time

9:00–9:45
9:45
Art
Reading Aloud

10:00–10:15   Recess

10:15–11:15
Block Time

11:15–11:30   Reading aloud time of continuing book, picture book, poetry   11:00–11:45 Music

11:30–11:45   Clean-up

11:45–12:45   Lunch

12:45–1:15   SSR — Last five minutes sharing of books read

1:15–2:15
Block Time

1:15–2:00
Physical
Education

2:15–3:00   Clean up and evaluation of day, sharing time of ongoing and completed projects, reminders for next day's work sessions

integrated language-arts curriculum may take six weeks to two months to establish.

The beginning time may come from the reading/language-arts block. As themes become broader, encompassing more curricular areas, time may be drawn from all subjects so that a specific block is scheduled as an integrated theme time. Adjustments in the evolving schedule can be made from an assessment of the students' activities. The amount of attention given to an area in a theme would indicate a decrease in the scheduled time for a separate subject. Perhaps a later theme will provide for more learning experiences in a slighted area to achieve a balance.

Broad themes can come from children's interests or from problems they wish to explore. Themes might also come from a topic to be studied in a subject area. The arithmetic text itself could serve as one classroom source in addition to other class texts that could be reviewed to see how they might be used. A study such as measurement in arithmetic could be extended to include the history of measurement. Would each youngster's yard, measured from the outstretched hand to the nose, be the same? Why are there twelve inches in a foot? Shoe sizes discourage thoughts of uniformity in measuring without such agreement. Besides many interesting informational books available on measuring, there exist related books of fiction. *Inch by Inch* (Lionni) is a delightful picturebook of an inchworm's adventures. In Steig's *Abel's Island,* Abel measures using his mouse's tail as a measuring unit. There are many activities involving children's measuring, such as computing the size of the classroom or taking dimensions of its door and windows. Perhaps mapping skills could be exercised and extended by mapping the room to scale or building a model of the school, depending upon the age of the students involved. Some children may wish to build an item and will need to measure carefully to make all the sides fit. In social studies the issues of changing to metric could be explored, discussed, and debated. Why does the public resist the change when other countries are using the metric system? Is the government's program to change to metrics a worthwhile goal? Who benefits from the change? Who might be harmed by it?

Differences Between a Unit and a Theme

A unit begins with the teachers knowing what is going to be taught. Pupils are allowed to plan but only within the teacher's predetermined framework. A unit lasts for a set period of time, which is divided into three types of activities: initiating activities, which pose the problems to be studied; projects that serve to answer questions that have arisen; and a culminating activ-

442 *Organization and Evaluation of the Language-Arts Program*

ity to bring the unit to a conclusion. Most often a unit is the curriculum for the entire class in contrast to a theme, which may be for a small group.

A theme may be considered as an organism that can change direction, move, and grow while it is occurring. There exists no set framework as there is in a unit; rather, a theme provides flexible guidelines in which the teacher and students share responsibility for future directions. Thus, students take on a greater share of the planning and make more choices about their work. Some children may drop out of a theme quickly, their interests sated with little involvement. Others will pursue one or more projects within a theme for long periods of time. The result is that more than one theme will be occurring at the same time. A new one may begin while another goes on. Some portion of each theme usually remains through the year so that children can refer to a prior experience as part of their classroom context. For example, a child's model may remain standing; a piece of display may stay in a prominent location; and collections of student writing may be placed in the class library.

Children brought in simple machines from their own homes as a basis for study such as egg beaters, can openers, and cork screws which can be seen in the first picture. The theme of simple machines evolved from the children's contributions. Notice in the picture on the right how the screw demonstrates the display full of student writing about this topic. (Mrs. Harbert's informal classroom, Barrington School, Upper Arlington, Ohio)

Communicating the Language-Arts Program

Programs work best in a congenial, supportive atmosphere. Good communication builds such a context.

Other Teachers and the Principal

For those in the school building, displays, so valuable for children's learning, also provide a means to communicate what is going on in a classroom. Teachers and students in other classes will be interested in hall displays. They can find out which topics are being explored, how artwork was done, and gain new information. Sharing projects in another class and with the principal is an additional way to communicate.

Classrooms may develop their own newsletters and distribute them around the school. This is a good experience for the class reporters, giving them a real audience for their writing and allowing the members of the school to learn what others are doing. The school itself may establish a magazine or weekly newspaper not only to send home but also to provide a system of communication within the school.

Classes can serve as audiences for each other and may decide to work together on a project. Study trips could be planned where classes of the same age learn to work together, or where younger and older students are paired for mutual gain. Teachers who exchange ideas with their colleagues reap the benefit of new ideas and may find resource people on their own staff.

Parents

No one is more concerned about the children than their parents, who have nurtured and loved their children from their first breath. Their commitment to the child is lifelong. It is important that schools include parents in the educational program. One aspect of this involvement is to keep parents informed about the ongoing activities of the classroom. Many teachers extend open invitations to parents and grandparents to visit classrooms. This kind of warm, welcoming attitude on the part of teacher and administrator can be the basis for strong ties between home and school. However, many mothers now work outside the home and many children now attend schools outside their own neighborhood. Casual and impromptu school visits are no longer as possible as they once were.

Newsletters. Newsletters are another way to keep parents informed and to provide children with a wider audience for their accomplishments. One first/second-grade teacher, Mrs. Hodges, begins the year by writing the newsletter herself. On Friday morning the class discusses with her what they have done during the week, and then the children decide which events would be most important to tell their parents. This review helps children see relationships among their daily actions. The following newsletter was sent home early in the year. Notice how Mrs. Hodges has used children's names to personalize the week's activities. Both the children and their parents will attend closely, reading the newsletter carefully. The child's concrete poem included at the end helps to heighten the interest and is a beginning step toward developing pupils' ability to meet a broad audience. The schedule included at the end is important, for it informs parents which days their children meet with special teachers. Parents can ask their children about these classes and they will also know when they can come for a visit in the classroom.

October 5

Insects Insects Insects

Discoveries

Todd discovered that the buckeye butterfly has purple spots on its wings that make it easy to identify. When Andy looked for insects around his house, he discovered an open cocoon and he said it was soft. Scott found out that Doug's praying mantis has three legs on each side. The front legs are in a praying position. Laura said, "That's where they get their name." Doug noticed his praying mantis turns green and brown. David D. watched the praying mantis eat a grasshopper. He says that they like to eat insects. Kelli found out that fireflies will light at night and during the day they go to sleep.

Papier-mâché

A group of us are making the creatures from *James and the Giant Peach* (Dahl). The giant peach ended up on the Empire State Building. James got to live in the peach stone. The insects all got jobs in New York City.

Poetry

Doug made a concrete poem about a ladybug. Jennifer D. made a stitchery on burlap of a ladybug. A concrete poem is written around the thing you are writing about.

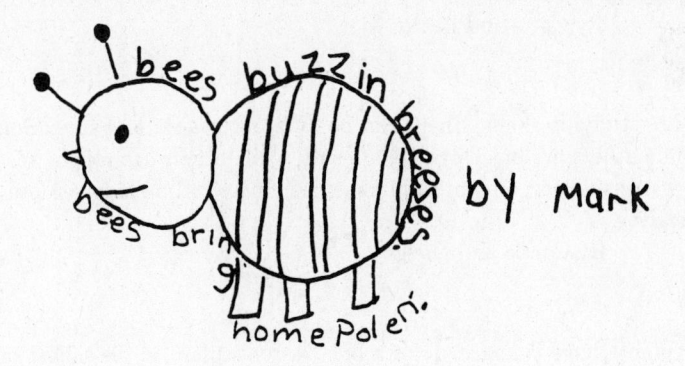

bees buzzin breezes
bees bring
home polen.
by Mark

Schedule	Monday	Tuesday	Wednesday	Thursday	Friday
	Music 1:00–1:30	Library 9:00–9:30	Music 2:00–2:30	Gym 12:30–1:00	Art 12:30–1:30
		Gym 1:50–2:20			

Later in the year children can begin writing their own articles for the newsletter. As before, Mrs. Hodges discusses with the class on Friday morning significant events of the week but, at this time, pairs of children choose to write a report of their choice. As the couples complete their writing, they revise and proofread their material. Finally it is brought to Mrs. Hodges for a conference. Sometimes revisions are necessary; at other times editing occurs; and maybe no changes are made at all. Over the noon hour Mrs. Hodges types the newsletter on a ditto and runs it off so that the children can take it home to their parents that afternoon "hot off the presses." This report-writing is a fine experience for the youngsters and truly results in an integrated language-arts experience. The newsletter that follows illustrates the children's work. Think of all the questions parents will want to ask their youngsters after reading this newsletter!

May 4

Room 19 Newsletter

Chicks

The chicks that we have will start to hatch on Monday. We will probably have some chicks running around the incubator. Someone dropped one of the eggs. It was egg No. 6. One of the eggs died, so we got to crack it open. We got to see the leg, the eye, and the wing.

By Catie and Becky

Shells

We are studying shells. Shells can be different shapes and sizes. Some can be big, while others are bigger. Some are soft, while others are rough. We are going to get water snails in our caterpillars' cages. Some can be bivalves and some can be univalves.

By Carrie and Doug

Plants

Our plants have changed quite a bit. Darren's plant is the tallest one. It is 1 foot, 4 inches tall. Amy L. did an experiment with a bag over her plant and it worked. Nine people went over to Chad's garden and planted some radishes, peas, and lettuce.

By Darren, Mimi, and Kent

Little People's Farm

On Tuesday, May 8 we are going to Little People's Farm. We are going at 10:00 and coming back at 2:30. We are going by bus. We need to bring a sack lunch and we need to wear grubby clothes. We need to bring 10 cents for milk or a canned drink.

   By Jennifer and Jeff

Our New Author

 We have a new author. Her name is Louise Fatio. She was born in Switzerland. She got married to Roger Duvoisin. He illustrates books for writers. Louise moved to the United States with Roger. She loves pets and to travel and to tour other places. Her first book was *The Happy Lion*.

   By Jennifer and Laura

Chrysalises

 Our caterpillars are making chrysalises. Sarah's died when it was in the middle of making its chrysalis. Most people's have made a chrysalis. They hang like a j. It will take 10 days to get out.

   By David and Gannon

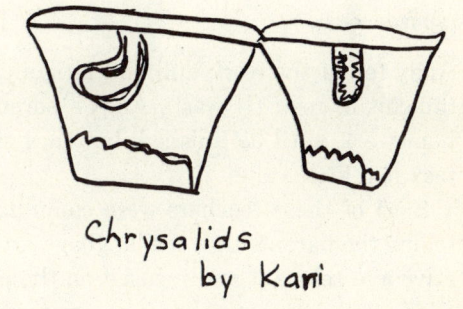

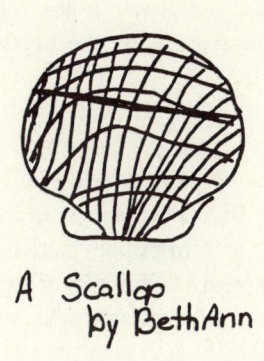

A Chick by Jon

Chrysalids by Kari

A Scallop by BethAnn

Homework. Homework, whether the teacher is aware of it or not, is one very important way for a teacher to communicate with parents. This can best be shown by comparing two homework assignments given to two different sixth-grade children in two different schools. Leslie's assignment was to find out how Christmas was celebrated in the "old days." Father and Mother were both interviewed about their childhood Christmas customs. Grandparents were called and their memories invited. The evening, one of talk, sharing, and laughter, produced a notebook full of data, which later became part of a classbook. The project was a lengthy one. Parents were interested participants of each step of the process and were delighted when they finally were able to read the finished product.

Another homework experience was that of Andy, whose assignment was a list of 20 words. He was to look up a definition for each, copy each word 10 times, and then write a sentence for at least 10 of the words. The word list began:

infectious
inferior
infuriate
ingenious
ingenuous

Andy found the work dull and fatiguing. He complained that the ditto was difficult to read (It was!). Andy's parents were firm that he stick with his homework until he finished, but they too were frustrated, for they felt the task had little value.

Both of these teachers were communicating with parents. The first was telling the parents that the language-arts program in Leslie's school was creative and relevant and focused on the needs and interests of the individual child. The second teacher was communicating a sad poverty of ideas, a lack of understanding of the learning process, and a disregard for the needs of individual children.

It is rare that one can use the terms "always" and "never" when talking about working with children, but homework should *always* be purposeful and *never* be used as punishment. There are some valuable kinds of homework for elementary-grade children. They can use their homes as sources of information, as Leslie did with her interviews on Christmas traditions. Meaningful practice is another good use of homework. Children who are working on learning to spell certain sight words can take these words home for additional practice. Along with the word list should go a sheet that suggests effective ways for parents to help the child with spelling. Finally, the home provides a very special audience. A book read in class can be taken home to be shared and talked about, not only with parents but with brothers and sisters.

Conferences and Notes. Communication with parents is more than "telling" them in a variety of ways what is happening at school. Home/school communication is interaction in which parents contribute to a dialogue. One of the best ways to do this is through the parent–teacher conference. However, the mother of one first-grader reported rather ruefully after her first such conference, "I guess I have a lot to learn. I went to the conference with so many things I wanted to tell the teacher about Mike, and all I did was listen to her talk about a child called Michael, who didn't sound anything like the boy we know at home!"

The child at home and the child at school are often different in many ways. It is vital for teachers to learn as much as they can about the "at home" child. One teacher found that the boy who was seen as uninterested in reading had a strong interest in science and did enormous amounts of reading in that field at home.

Teachers can prepare for conferences by talking with children about what they would like to share, pulling together folders of each child's work, and even displaying some of the books that the children are reading or have read. The teacher can plan to focus part of the conference on finding out from the parents their concerns, their impressions, the child's home activities, and family interests.

Sending notes home to parents is another way of inviting dialogue. Too often notes are sent home only to report failure. Such notes are sometimes more irritating than helpful. One mother said, a bit angrily, "How can I make him finish his work at school? I'm not there!" Notes that report accomplishments of all kinds are much more useful to both child and parent.

Evaluating the Program

Plans

One way to begin a program evaluation is to review the long- and short-term plans that have been made. The same criteria that were used to develop the program are appropriate to evaluate it:

Is a balance planned among all of the areas of the language arts?

Do the students have a variety of experiences and activities within their school days so that interest is maintained and a broad program of student choice is available?

Is there a balance between literary and concrete experiences?

Were past experiences taken into account as new activities were planned?

Are differences among all children recognized in the planning? How is this element provided for in the curriculum?

Is there evidence of children's needs and interests taken into account in the plans?

Do individual, small-group, and large-group activities appear in the plans?

Will the program meet school district and state requirements?

Were the plans adhered to so closely that flexibility could not occur? Or were they strayed from to the extent that the plans were unrecognizable and major objectives were missed in a formless program?

The Ongoing Program

Sometimes the plans can look quite good but the actual program is very ineffective. Imaginative ideas do not always result in creative experiences. For this reason the ongoing program needs to be evaluated in addition to the plans:

Are children using all of the language arts in purposeful ways?

Was there an integration of all the areas as occurs in natural language use?

Do some children continually select the same type of activity (for example, writing poetry) so they have limited learning experiences?

Was language used in a variety of ways to meet real needs found in authentic, natural events?

Did the class gain confidence in using language, seeing it as a tool for themselves?

Are the children willing to try new language styles?

Can the youngsters be seen moving forward in language development or are they staying at the same level?

Is there evidence that the pupils are involved in the decision making of class events and their own work?

Do students become involved with extended interests over a period of time?

Did the children enjoy the language arts, learning to appreciate skill in language use?

Program evaluation needs to be a continual process, not all of which need be formal. Teachers often consider the teaching day or week and revise according to the assessments made. However, formal evaluation of the language-arts program should take place periodically. If this is not accomplished, the curriculum may meander, achieving little.

NCTE Guidelines

Sometimes you may wish to evaluate your total program, framing questions such as the ones we have suggested. At other times you may wish to focus in on one aspect of your program, such as writing, to see how your language-arts program is functioning in that area. A committee of the National Council of Teachers of English has developed a set of guidelines to use in evaluating a language-arts program. The guidelines are comprised of lists of questions that help teachers to think about their own programs. Since we consider these guidelines to be most useful, we have included them within this chapter. The list is a lengthy one to read through, but quite interesting if one has a specific interest or need. We recommend that you look over the entire set of questions and select one area to read through. You will find that the questions may direct your thinking to aspects of the classroom curriculum you may not have considered before.

Guidelines to Evaluate the English Component in the Elementary School Program

NCTE Committee: Alba Allard   Ruth Steinmetz
                 Inez Bishop   Allaire Stuart
                 Naomi Chase   DeWayne Triplett
                 Evelyn Luckey   Lois Williams
                 Dorothy Menosky   Yetta Goodman
                 Clara Pederson

Much has been learned about child language in the last ten years. The fields of linguistics, psychology, psycholinguistics, and sociolinguistics are involved in ongoing research in child language learning, resulting in knowledge and principles about language and thinking. These principles must be taken into consideration in the organization and evaluation of any language-arts curriculum. Additionally, the great diversity in America, reflected in any school system through differing values, attitudes, and concerns of parents, teachers and the community must also be recognized during the process of curriculum evaluation, expansion, or change.

The questions and statements in these guidelines should stimulate thinking and discussion on the part of school personnel, which considers both the latest principles suggested by scientists interested in all facets of child language and the diversity found within their own school system. The guidelines should lead local school committees to thorough evaluation of their language-arts curriculum so that it builds on the language strengths children have when they come to school. Building on these strengths will help children expand their learning in all areas of language arts.

The horizontal divisions of the guidelines are concerned with the various areas of the language-arts curriculum. The first is concerned with the *general* aspects of the language arts, which must be considered in an integrated fashion. Following the general concerns are sections that deal with specifics for each of the major areas of the language arts: listening, speaking, reading, and writing. Each area has been considered separately because we believe each deserves consideration for appropriate time in the curriculum. Sometimes, because of various pressures or because of the emphasis in commercial materials, too much time is spent in one area of the language-arts curriculum to the neglect of another.

The guidelines are also categorized vertically, with columns of concerns for: 1) individual and group differences, 2) principles of language learning, and 3) objectives and evaluation.

In each section the guidelines are presented as a statement of concern, followed by questions. This format allows for flexibility in the use of the guidelines. We have circulated these questions among language-arts supervisors, teacher educators in language arts, and elementary school teachers. They represent the thinking of many people. In answering the questions relating to the overall statement, a committee may generate objectives that are best for their local needs.

As these guidelines were disseminated it became obvious that the whole area of viewing experiences—the child's active involvement with perceiving a variety of stimuli in the environment—enhances language development and learning. We have attempted to integrate viewing experiences as part of many of the considerations in developing a language-arts curriculum. However, greater consideration needs to be given to viewing and its implications for curriculum. Language arts is an umbrella to all aspects of the elementary school curriculum. Languaging is integrally involved in art, music, physical education, science, math, social studies, and human relations. This must be kept in mind in developing an exciting, integrated curriculum that will make learning a whole, real-life experience for children.

GENERAL ASPECTS OF THE LANGUAGE ARTS

Concern for Individual and Group Difference

The language-arts program must be interesting to attract and involve students.
1. What experiences which involve children's senses and physical activity are the major focus of the program?
2. How are students involved in understanding the purposes for activities?
3. How are students involved in setting their own purposes?
4. What choices or options are provided for learning experiences?

The language-arts program must involve the affective domain of students.
1. How are empathy and understanding of others encouraged?
2. How does the program help students become aware of beauty?
3. How does the program encourage students to expand their knowledge of the world?
4. How does the program increase the students' ability to understand themselves and the world in which they live?

Provisions must be made for individual and group differences.
1. How does the program take into consideration the ethnic, racial, and cultural differences of students?
2. How does the program take into consideration the social and economic differences among students?
3. How does the program take into consideration students' attitudes toward sex roles?
4. How does the program take into consideration the dialect and language background of students?
5. How does the program take into consideration differences in ability and interest of students?

Learning is accommodated best when there is an interrelationship among the various language arts of listening, speaking, reading, and writing.
1. How are speakers helped to become aware of their audience?
2. In what ways do student audiences recognize their roles in the speaking-listening exchange?
3. What opportunities are there for student writers to read their own products of writing as well as the composition of others?
4. What is done to help student writers produce with readers in mind?

Learning is accommodated when there is an interrelationship between the language arts and other areas of the curriculum such as science, social studies, mathematics, music, art, drama, physical education, and home arts.
1. In what ways are other subject matter areas involved in developing the programs for language arts?

2. How are the materials and texts of other subject matter areas used with understanding about language and thought development?
3. How are viewing experiences used to help develop language and thought?

Children's literature must be an integral part of all the language arts.
1. In what ways through listening, reading, and viewing are children involved in knowing and enjoying children's books and their authors?
2. What provisions are made through speaking, writing, or other expressive forms for children's responses to literature?

A variety of media must be used in the language-arts curriculum.
1. How are media such as photographs, drawings, paintings, three-dimensional objects, film strips, and tape recorders used to enhance the curriculum?
2. What is done to assure that the media used is most appropriate for the activity?
3. How are libraries and learning centers used as focal points for small groups and individual learning activities?

Concern for Principles of Language Learning

The language-arts program must be based on how children learn language.
1. How does the program reflect the latest scientific knowledge about language?
2. In what ways do the activities planned for children reflect how language is acquired and developed?
3. What is done to assure that information about language which is presented to students is consistent with the latest scientific knowledge?

The language-arts program must be based on how students develop thought processes.
1. How does the program reflect the latest scientific knowledge about how thought processes develop in children?
2. In what ways do the activities planned for children reflect how students learn and acquire concepts?
3. In what ways does the program provide time for children's thought processes to develop?

The language-arts program must provide opportunity for application of learning.
1. In what ways is consideration given to the diversity of language experience?
2. In what ways is consideration given to the diversity of language development?
3. What provisions are made so all learning experiences are related to settings or concerns that children know and understand?

Listening

Listening activities must attract and involve students.
1. What is done to assure that an appropriate amount of time is given to listening activities?

2. What provisions are made for a variety of listening activities with one or two other children, in small groups, or in large groups?
   a. What provisions are made for listening to recorded materials that include both visual and nonvisual experiences?
   b. What provisions are made for listening to selections read by the teacher, other adults, and other students?
   c. What provisions are made for listening to stories told by the teacher, other adults, and other students?
   d. What provisions are made for listening during field trips, programs, or other audience settings?
3. How is listening outside of school encouraged and integrated into the instructional program?
   a. What opportunities are there for students to interview parents, siblings, community leaders, and others and share what they have learned with classmates?
   b. What opportunities are there for students to report about games, trips, television shows, radio programs, plays, or concerts?
4. How are students involved in the selection of the musical records, narrative records, and tapes they wish to use?

A variety of experiences must be made available for listening related to the social, cultural, and economic differences.
1. In what ways are field trips and other investigative experiences planned to enhance awareness and understanding of others?
2. In what ways are books, stories, records, tapes, and films related to the backgrounds and experiences of the students?

Once students are comfortable in their learning environment, listening experiences should be planned to help them expand their background and experiences.
1. How are language differences introduced?
2. How are cultural differences introduced?
3. How are new concepts and ideas introduced?

Listening experiences must be based on how students learn language.
1. How does the curriculum present the target language or dialect as an alternative form without stressing its superiority?
2. In what ways are students provided with listening experiences that introduce a wide variety of language styles and dialects?
   a. Are experiences with formal and informal language differences provided?
   b. Are various dialects provided?
   c. Are the language styles of different age groups provided?
3. If the language or dialect of the student is different from the language or dialect used by most teachers, what activities are provided to help the student gain receptive control over the target dialect or language before other kinds of performance are expected? For example:
   a. Are musical and narrative rec-

ords and tapes representing a variety of dialects available?
  b. Are there varied listening experiences with peers who speak the target dialect or language?
  c. Are there varied listening experiences with adults who speak the target dialect or language?

Listening experiences must be based on how students develop thought processes.
1. What opportunities are students given to learn through listening activities prior to the expectancy of achievement in other language-arts areas?
2. What opportunities are there for the student to learn to listen with an open mind?
   a. Are group discussions encouraged in which positions may be questioned, compared, and evaluated whether they are stated by an authority in a particular field, a teacher, or a peer?
   b. Are group discussions encouraged in which propaganda presented through various media (television, records, tapes, photographs, tape recorder, films, filmstrips, etc.) is evaluated and questioned, including reactions to loaded words, analogies, slogans, sarcasm, patriotic appeal, and status appeal?

A variety of means should be employed to assess listening.
1. In what ways are nonverbal responses used to assess listening?
   a. Through facial expressions and body language.
   b. Through reactions to music, narrative records, and story telling.
   c. Through peer conversations.
   d. Through reactions to sounds of different intensity, pitch, and rhythm.
   e. Through constructions based on oral instructions.
   f. Through ability to play games or perform job responsibilities based on oral directions.
   g. Through visual images that may accompany language.
2. In what ways are students' acquisition of concepts and meanings assessed?
   a. Through interaction with peers.
   b. Through observation of large and small group discussions.
   c. Through students' graphic illustrations, artwork, written work, science experiments, or other constructions.
3. In what ways are nonclassroom experiences used to assess listening?
   a. From the playground or street play.
   b. From reactions to television, radio, or movies.
   c. From related information by parents, siblings, peers.
   d. From stories about family experiences.
4. In what ways are verbal responses used to assess listening?
   a. Through oral retellings.
   b. Through written reactions.
   c. Through dramatic activities

such as role-play and puppetry.
5. How are individual conferences with students used to assess growth in listening?

Students must be involved in developing learning objectives.
1. How are students involved in setting new goals?
2. How are students involved in planning group experiences for listening?
3. How is the student involved in planning individual listening experiences?

Speaking

Speaking activities must attract and involve students.
1. In what ways are students who are not yet proficient in writing permitted to use speaking as the major medium for communication and learning?
2. What is done so that speaking experiences involve more time in the classroom than writing experiences?
3. What is done so that students have opportunities to select and plan various kinds of oral language experiences and settings?
   a. Are students involved in their choice of audience?
   b. Do students choose their subject matter for speaking?
   c. Do students choose the time for their own speaking?
   d. Are a variety of settings provided for speaking?
4. What opportunities are there for students to talk to other students as much as they talk with adults?
5. How does the program encourage sharing of ideas, experiences, and activities among students?
6. Are role playing and creative drama integral parts of all of the curriculum including language arts?

Students should be encouraged to use with dignity a variety of dialects.
1. Are diverse dialects permitted in role-playing, folk singing, and storytelling?
2. How are students helped to view all dialect differences with respect?
3. How are students whose speech represents one dialect given opportunities to talk with children and adults who speak other dialects?

Speaking activities should occur in curricular areas other than that of language arts.
1. How are speaking experiences provided in the areas of social studies, science, humanities, and literature?
2. What opportunities are provided for students to talk about viewing experiences they have had both in and out of the school setting?

Speaking experiences must be based on how students learn languages.
1. In what way does the program focus on the student developing language fluency rather than on concern for an arbitrary correctness?
2. How are students given opportunity to interact frequently with their peers in speaking situations?

3. How is the legitimacy of language diversity recognized?
    a. When students are talking, are they encouraged to use their own dialect without correction or rejection?
    b. What does the teacher do to understand children who speak a different dialect or language?
4. What opportunities are there for students to speak informally more often than formally in the classroom?
5. In what way does the teacher differentiate between speech problems and language difference?
    a. Are speech immaturities recognized and permitted to develop into adult forms without pressure?
    b. Are dialect differences and language differences due to foreign language influences recognized and respected as the student's home language and not treated as a speech problem?

Speaking experiences must be based on how students develop thought processes.
1. How and when are students given time to consider the principles of effective discussion?
2. In what ways are they given opportunities to implement these principles?
3. How are students encouraged to plan questions that are appropriate for various situations?
    a. Are they given opportunities to ask questions about what they read and what they hear?
    b. Are they given opportunities to develop questions for interviews with peers and adults?
    c. Are they provided with opportunities to discover what kinds of questions are most appropriate for different settings?
4. What opportunities are there for vocabulary growth to be a part of understanding concepts as opposed to learning meaningless labels?

A variety of means should be employed to assess speaking.
1. What procedures are there to keep samples of students' oral language over a period of time to establish growth?
2. How are conferences with the individual student used to assess growth in speaking?
3. How are observations of the students' interaction with peers observed?
4. How is the use of oral language by students observed?
    a. In front of the whole class.
    b. With one other student.
    c. Within a small group of students.
    d. With an adult.
    e. Behind a stage or puppet.
    f. In play, game, or sport situations.
    g. In formal learning situations.

Students must be involved in developing learning objectives.
1. How are students involved in setting new goals?
2. How are students involved in planning group experiences for listening?

3. How is the student involved in planning individual speaking experiences?

Reading

There must be reading materials available for a range of reading abilities, interests, tastes, and racial and cultural backgrounds.
1. What materials or help is provided in selecting and purchasing a wide variety of materials?
2. How are students involved in selecting a variety of materials?
3. Are there textbooks available for resource material in content areas such as history, science, mathematics, music, and art?
4. In what way are trade books given as significant a role in the reading program as basal texts where the latter are built into the curriculum?
5. In what ways is children's literature given a significant role in the reading program?

Reading must be interesting and enjoyable to the individual student.
1. How are students involved in sharing their responses to reading with others to stimulate others to expand their reading?
2. In what ways does the teacher motivate students to broaden reading experiences?
3. How is sufficient time provided so each student can become involved in silent reading?
4. How are opportunities for sustained silent reading planned and carried out?
5. In what ways are magazines, newspapers, and other nonbook reading materials used in the school curriculum to make reading a current and vital process?
6. How does the program provide for self-selection of both reading experiences and reading materials?
7. How are materials written by students used as part of the classroom reading materials?
8. What opportunities are there for sharing what has been read?

A variety of reading opportunities must be provided.
1. What provisions are made so that plays, radio scripts, and other drama forms are part of the reading program?
2. How are choric reading and other kinds of unison or assisted reading part of the reading program?
3. What is done to assure a variety of audiences for oral reading?
4. How are televised productions planned to be a part of a reading-viewing program?

Reading experiences must be based on how students learn language.
1. What provisions are made for more silent reading than oral reading as students progress through the grades?
2. Is oral reading used *only* for a specific purpose? For example:
   a. When a reader wishes to describe a situation or event?
   b. To interpret a character or a characterization?
   c. To support or elaborate ideas during discussion?
   d. To read words that are vivid in imagery?
   e. For diagnosis by the teacher?

3. When students read orally are they permitted to use their own dialect?
4. How are the reading materials selected so that they represent a variety of language styles and dialects?

Reading experiences must be based on how students develop thought processes.

1. When informational materials are used, what nonreading experiences are provided as a basis for extending concepts and vocabulary prior to reading?
2. Is there opportunity to extend and expand on new concepts through many viewing experiences in addition to reading, such as films, filmstrips, television, taking pictures with a camera, and microscopes?
3. What experiences are provided to permit students to apply the knowledge acquired through reading to nonreading situations?
4. What experiences are provided to encourage students to integrate previous knowledge with what they are reading?
5. What experiences are provided so that students can question, challenge, and criticize the authenticity and accuracy of written materials?
6. How are students helped to use reference materials, libraries, guides, signs, and other practical written material whenever they fit naturally into the learning experience or curriculum?

Students must be involved in developing learning objectives.

1. How are students involved in setting new goals?
2. How are students involved in planning group experiences for speaking?
3. How is the student involved in planning individual speaking experiences?

A variety of means should be used to assess reading.

1. What opportunities are there for students to read without the teacher's help to discover what a reader can do independently?
2. What procedures are there to keep samples of students' reading over a period of time to establish growth?
3. How are individual conferences with students used to assess reading?
4. How is comprehension used as the main criterion for assessing reading?
5. In what ways are non-paper-pencil responses used to assess reading?
   a. Through ability to dramatize from reading.
   b. Through following written directions.
   c. Through carrying out experiments.
   d. Through construction following written directions.
   e. Through cooking following recipes.
   f. Through sharing reading experiences with others.
6. What variety of options do students have to share books with others?
7. How are reading experiences at

home or in the library used in reading assessment?
8. How are judgments about a child's reading made primarily from silent reading assessments?
9. What is done to consider errors in oral reading only if they disrupt the meaning of the text?
10. If oral reading is used to assess dramatic or expressive oral reading, what kinds of opportunities do the students have to read the material silently and to practice prior to the assessment?

Writing

Writing activities must attract and involve children.
1. In what way are writing experiences built upon oral language activities?
2. What plans are there for many and varied writing experiences?
3. How is the program organized so that students are permitted to write when they want to?
4. What provisions are made so that students have the right to keep their writing private if they wish to do so?
5. In what ways do students share their writing with others when they wish to do so?
6. How are students' responses to literature used for creative writing?
7. How are art and music used to stimulate or to accompany creative writing?

8. How are various media used in conjunction with creative writing?
9. What opportunities are there for children's writing to include both practical and creative expressions?
10. How are children involved in the editing process?
11. What opportunities are there for children to see their own writing published at least in classroom style?

A variety of writing experiences must be provided.
1. How are student logs encouraged?
2. What time is provided so that teachers can respond to logs and other writing experiences?
3. What options or ideas are available for children to write about?
4. How are children encouraged to use their own ideas for writing even though a standard kind of assignment has been made?
5. Are products of children's writing not copied unless the students want to for the purpose of sharing?

When teachers have students with dialects different from their own, they must take this into account when thinking about the growth of the child in the areas of syntax, usage, mechanics, spelling, etc.
1. How does the teacher encourage children whose writing reflects a knowledge of the rules of their own dialect?
2. How are students encouraged to write in many styles and to use a variety of language structures?
3. How is discussion about language

planned so students understand it as an area of discovery, exploration, and inventiveness, not as something which has a prescribed set of rules?
4. Are students who demonstrate they can spell the specified words or write in the appropriate style excluded from lessons related to such skills?

Students must always write with a purpose in mind.
1. What efforts are made so that students always write with a purpose they understand?
2. How are students involved in setting their own purposes for writing?
3. How are children introduced to a variety of appropriate writing styles to use at times when they are needed to help achieve specific purposes?
4. What different kinds of writing experiences are encouraged? For example:
   a. Dictation
   b. Writing directions
   c. Reporting
   d. Story writing
   e. Letter writing

Writing experiences must be based on how students learn language.
1. How is the time spent on writing activities related to the children's ability to write?
2. Is more time spent on writing as a process than on the mechanics of writing (handwriting, punctuation, spelling, grammar)?
   a. Are handwriting and spelling programs integrated and related to writing experiences?
   b. Are handwriting, spelling, punctuation, and grammatical activities for practice of specific skills used only for students who provide evidence that they are having such specific problems?
   c. In what way does the handwriting program focus on legibility for the sake of communication rather than on exact reproduction of models?
   d. Is editing and rewriting encouraged only when there is a stated purpose for final copy?
3. Are the students always encouraged to express their ideas in writing and not stifled by concern for mechanics?
4. Are students encouraged to use a variety of styles and structures and to experiment with forms as they write?

Writing experiences must be based on how students develop thought.
1. What opportunities are there for students to get feedback from peers and other adults, as well as teachers, in relation to the ideas written?
2. How is the student encouraged to use writing to express reactions to ideas—to criticize, to compare, and to question the ideas of others?
3. What opportunities are there for students to express themselves in writing in all areas of the curriculum?
4. How are students helped to write formal reports that are based on actual experiences?
5. What opportunities are there for students to talk about what they will write about?

Students should be encouraged to participate in creative writing frequently.
1. Are there opportunities for writing to take place daily?
2. Are students given opportunities to share their writing with others *only* if they wish to do so, and get reactions to their ideas?
3. What suggestions are provided to encourage students to write personal feelings and opinions?

A variety of means should be employed to assess writing.
1. What procedures are there to keep samples of student's writing over a period of time to establish growth?
2. What is done to focus the evaluation of writing so that teachers react mostly to students' ideas?
3. How are informal pupil-teacher conferences used to encourage freedom of expression and to stimulate ideas?
4. What is done to assure that mechanics of writing are evaluated only in terms of a final copy?
5. How are initial baselines established for each child for continuous development in spelling, handwriting, punctuation, and other mechanics?

Students must be involved in developing learning objectives.
1. How are students involved in setting new goals?
2. How are students involved in planning group experiences for writing?
3. How is the student involved in planning individual writing experiences?

Concern for Objectives & Evaluation

There must be continuous evaluation of the language-arts program.
1. In what ways is the language-arts program evaluated?
2. What provisions are there to evaluate on a periodic and regular basis?
3. In what ways is the evaluation related to objectives based on concern for individual and group differences?
4. In what ways is the evaluation related to objectives based on principles of language learning and the thinking process?
5. What is done to see that the objectives are clearly stated and understood by teachers?
6. How are the methods evaluated to see if they are suitable to the children?
7. How are teachers involved in the evaluation of the program and in setting significant and relevant objectives?
8. After evaluation, how are new objectives developed and current ones modified or dropped if they are no longer applicable?
9. How are modifications and changes in the program brought about to comply with new or changed objectives?
10. In what ways do objectives show concern for long-range goals as well as specific immediate needs and concerns?
11. How are students involved in the evaluation of their own work and in setting their own objectives?

12. How does evaluation consider both cognitive and affective domains?
13. How does the evaluation program relate to stated objectives?

There must be continuous evaluation of materials and packaged units.

1. What measurement devices are used to evaluate materials and packaged units?
2. How is the worth of commercial material determined?
3. In what ways is there consideration of whether equally effective teaching can be done by less costly means?
4. In what ways have the materials proved to be worthwhile for the students?
5. In what ways do the materials contribute positively to the student's learning?
6. How do the materials encourage language development in children?
7. How do the materials encourage the development of thinking in students?
8. How do the materials encourage creativity in students?
9. How do the materials make provisions for individual needs, interests, and personal choices for the students?
10. How do the materials create curiosity in the students and encourage independent activity?
11. How do the materials encourage further exploration so the students will want to study various aspects in greater depth?
12. In what ways are the materials consistent with current knowledge in the field of language and language learning?
13. What evidence is there that the materials have been written with concerns for growth and development?
14. How do the students show that they are interacting with materials?
15. In what way are materials assessed on the basis of content, authenticity, and accuracy?
16. In what way are materials assessed to avoid stereotypes or misconceptions about ethnic, cultural, racial, or sex groups?
17. What is done to make sure that a wide range and variety of materials are available?
18. What is done to make sure that trade books or multi-texts are used whenever possible in preference to a single text or program for all students?
19. How are the materials assessed to see that they are appropriate for the linguistic and cognitive development of the children who use them?

"Guidelines to Evaluate the English Component in the Elementary School Program," *Language Arts,* October, 1976. Copyright © 1976 by the National Council of Teachers of English. Reprinted by permission of the publisher and the author.

Summary

An integrated program cannot be neatly prescribed. It may be comforting at times to be told to practice step one until all children reach a certain level of proficiency and then to proceed to step two; however, language learning is too complex and too important to fit such a segmental model of learning. An integrated program demands that teachers bring to it their own professional judgments: a sense of the wholeness of language, a knowledge of how oral and written language are acquired, and an understanding of the ways children develop and learn. Using such a background, teachers can mesh their knowledge with requirements mandated by the schools in order to develop a sound program. An integrated program balances children's interests with their needs, school requirements with teacher objectives, oral language with written language, and individual work with group work.

Beginning teachers may feel the need to rely more heavily on the school's guidelines and on the scope and sequence charts developed for the text series. At first the beginning teacher may choose to move in small ways to integrate aspects of the curriculum. Social studies provides opportunities to read and discuss biographies and historical fiction. Mathematics offers a base for children to use oral language to hypothesize and to explain. As teachers acquire more experience and confidence, they will become more flexible and more adept in their ability to make connections between children's interests, their own objectives, and the goals of the language-arts program.

Planning the language-arts curriculum not only provides direction but also encourages freedom. When plans are made, the teacher and students may decide whether to follow those plans, how closely to adhere to them, or if new plans should be proposed. Plans not only tell where a class is going but they may also tell where the class has been and, on this basis, new directions may be found.

The curriculum is not limited solely to in-class activities. The learning context includes the entire school, children's parents, and even the community in which all this takes place. One way to establish a positive context is to have good means of communicating with others. Displays, visits to and from other classes, and newsletters are all good communicating modes. Subtle means of communication include the kinds of homework assigned, requests made of parents, and the class's attitude toward its school activities.

Evaluating the curriculum causes the teacher to look at both the plans and what actually occurred. Evaluation is a time for reflection. The language-arts curriculum need not be judged as "bad" or "good" but rather could be seen as a series of actions that may need to take on new emphases or may require different experiences. Evaluation is an important part of teacher growth.

Suggested Learning Experiences

1. Examine a curriculum guide from a nearby school system. Look across the broad goals. Are all the areas that you consider to be significant covered by these goals? Study the more focused objectives. Take one area, as we did using drama, and see how many of these objectives could be covered across goals within one integrated view of a language-arts component.

2. Collect report cards from the school systems surrounding you. What can you learn about the kind of language-arts program in each system? Then study the curriculum guides for each. Are the two items in agreement?

3. As an individual or in pairs, talk with an experienced teacher about the way he or she communicates with parents. Which modes do they find most effective in establishing a positive rapport? What specific problems have they met? Share your findings with a small group in the class to find common teacher concerns and effective teacher strategies of communication. As a group, can you develop a list of suggested actions for teachers who wish to establish positive relationships with the home?

4. If you have the opportunity (for example, if you are participating in a field-based program), work on gaining an overview of a week's activities, possibly by looking at the teacher's plans, talking with children, and observing daily work accomplished. At the end of the week, gather a group of the students together to discuss the week's accomplishments and events. Depending upon the age of the students and their writing proficiency, either accept their information for dictated articles or divide them into small groups to write up the class news events. Show the results to the classroom teacher for final editing and approval. Type or print the articles on ditto and run off copies.

References

Professional Literature

Barnes, Douglas, *From Communication to Curriculum*, Harmondsworth, Middlesex, England: Penguin Books, Ltd., 1976.

"Guidelines to Evaluate the English Component in the Elementary School Program," NCTE Committee, *Language Arts* 53: 828–838, October, 1976.

Children's Literature

Dahl, Roald, *James and the Giant Peach,* illustrated by Nancy Burkert, Knopf, New York, 1961.

Lionni, Leo, *Inch by Inch,* Astor-Honor, New York, 1960.

Steig, William, *Abel's Island,* Farrar, Straus and Giroux, New York, 1976.

Role of the Teacher
The Teacher as a Resource
The Teacher as a Professional

Professional Resources
Journals
Books
Children's Literature Textbooks

Children's Classroom Resources
Language-Arts Textbooks
Magazines
Newspapers
Book Clubs
Book Fairs and Book Stores

Resources from Outside the Classroom
Television
Parents and Grandparents
Library Media Centers

Summary

Suggested Learning Experiences

Chapter 11
Instructional Resources

There are myriad resources available to teachers and students; this chapter focuses on two—human and commercial resources. A classroom is most effective when a wide variety of sources are included as a part of the curriculum. Teachers have the major responsibility to search out and make available these information sources. The human resource file begins with teachers and their students; then it extends beyond the classroom to the entire school population and to the community at large. The commercial resources include textbooks, library materials, and other media. The interaction of human and commercial resources helps form the most productive language-arts curriculum. How can the program be expanded? One way is through new materials and a variety of human resources. In addition, teachers may join professional organizations, attend their conferences, and read their journals to keep current in the field of language arts and to discover material that can serve as a source for new ideas to incorporate in the classroom.

This chapter describes the teacher as a resource, the teacher as a professional, and other resources for classroom use. The annotated lists of professional journals, books, and student periodicals are meant to serve as a handbook to acquaint the language-arts teacher with the available commercial resources and sources of new thinking in the area.

Role of the Teacher

The Teacher as a Resource

One instructional resource in the classroom is the teacher; this is not to diminish the role and input of each student. Teachers as well as children bring interests and talents into the classroom. In addition, teachers have an expertise in child development and knowledge of the curricular structure and goals. They respond to teaching situations with a combination of feelings and facts.

Teachers respond to children both verbally and nonverbally to create an environment that gives confidence so that the student will feel comfortable experimenting with oral and written language. Teachers are not stamped from a single mold. They can show enthusiasm in unique ways. For instance,

This chapter was developed by Diane Driessen.

one successful teacher may be outgoing and quick to laugh while another one may be reserved and react quietly. Both can be effective.

Children tend to have a high regard for their teachers. They often quote them at the dinner table or give support to a position by beginning with "My teacher says...." Trust is also demonstrated when children share intimate family details, much to the amazement of the teacher. As a compliment, they may take on a teacher's physical mannerisms, speech patterns, word choices, even hairstyle and dress! Sometimes seeing a teacher in an unexpected public place, such as the library or grocery store, creates excitement. Children are surprised to see that their teacher is a person who does many of the same everyday living activities as they and their families.

Teachers' interests, hobbies, travel, and education can serve as sources for an enriched curriculum since enthusiasm toward a subject is contagious. A talent in dancing can lead to teaching folk dances during a unit of study about Mexico. A jogger can use recess time to involve some students who express a desire to try the exercise. A teacher can bring a guitar to accompany class sing-alongs. Field trips to art museums, concerts, and factories can be ways to share interests. Hobbies can be sources for holiday gift-making. The teacher's trips to exotic and common places could provide a basis for study if the teacher and students share a common interest. A teacher brings a great deal to a unit on Japan if he or she has visited that country and can relate events experienced during the travel and bring items acquired during the stay. Teacher film accounts could help to personalize the study and lead children away from stereotypical concepts. Even a teacher's weekend camping trip can stimulate student interest when rocks, plants, or a map of the hiking trail are brought into the classroom. By involving students in their lives, teachers show that they are persons who explore, create, share, and interact with their environment; perhaps student knowledge of teachers as people could help them to see learning as an exciting, lifelong process.

Some teachers we know have even extended the classroom walls into their own homes. Jeff, a first-grader attending a Sunday tea in his teacher's apartment to culminate a unit on families, announced to his parents that it was time to leave. "Teas are not like birthday parties, you don't play games. You have polite conversation, some punch, a few cookies, and then go." Clearly, Jeff was sensitive to the new social context and eager for his parents to meet the different requirements. In the past, his parents were the ones who had such concerns; now Jeff was assuming this responsibility.

One teacher invited small groups of students to dinner, thus providing them opportunities for a variety of language experiences. She gave the dinner guests the task of planning the menu, shopping for the food, and preparing the dishes, which placed them in a position that requires a wide use of language. Interacting with students in social situations gives teachers a chance not only to share themselves but also opportunities to learn more about their students. It permits teachers to observe and listen to children in different environments. Knowing students well assists the instructional effectiveness of the teacher.

Many teachers visit their students' homes. The students' homes and their parents provide sources that give the teacher a better understanding of children's backgrounds and experiences. By extending themselves to the parents, teachers build a cooperative relationship that establishes cohesion between home and school. To go back to the first chapter, this home/school relationship brings together more closely the familiar and the new, an essential for learning. Periodic notes or telephone calls to announce an accomplishment help build positive feelings.

The Teacher as a Professional

The teacher is also cast in the role of a professional. As a professional, the teacher is expected to fulfill certain responsibilities. These responsibilities lie at the local, district, state, and national level. A variety of choices are available to teachers; for instance, choosing to serve on committees at any of the levels. Locally, the teacher may plan programs and curriculum or select textbooks.

Professional Resources

Two national organizations specifically dedicated to the language arts are the National Council of Teachers of English (NCTE) and the International Reading Association (IRA). NCTE "focuses on the major concerns of teachers of English and language arts, and offers teaching aids, advice, direction, and guidance to the members." Each year NCTE sponsors a fall national convention and spring combined sections meeting that rotate their geographical locations. A membership allows the holder a choice of section in which to vote—elementary, secondary, or college—and any section journal—*Language Arts, English Journal,* or *College English.* In addition, teachers can subscribe to the Council's *Research in the Teaching of English,* which is of interest to teachers at all levels. A discount on NCTE publications and registration fees for conventions and conferences are also membership benefits. More information and a catalog of publications are available from NCTE, 1111 Kenyon Road, Urbana, Illinois 61801.

The IRA "encourages study of the reading process, research, and better teacher education and promotes the development of reading proficiency...." The IRA sponsors a spring national convention as well as regional meetings at various geographical locations throughout the country. Membership includes a choice of journals—*The Reading Teacher, Journal of Reading,* and *Reading Research Quarterly*—and discounts on publications and registration fees for conventions and meetings. More information and a catalog of publications are available from IRA, 800 Barksdale Road, P.O. Box 8139, Newark, Delaware 19711.

Journals

A variety of professional journals in addition to the ones published by NCTE and IRA are available as resources in the language arts. The articles in the journals keep the teacher informed about trends, research findings, ideas to try in the classroom, and new professional and children's books. They also provide a source for teachers to publish their own or their students' writing. A selected list of journals of interest to the language-arts teacher includes the following:

Journals Published by NCTE

Language Arts. National Council of Teachers of English, 1111 Kenyon Road, Urbana, Illinois 61801.

Language Arts publishes theme issues (Writing, Children's Literature, Reading, Language-Arts Essentials, etc.) monthly September through November and January through May. The articles focus on concerns of those interested in promoting language arts in preschool through middle-school years. Regular departments include reviews of recent children's literature, a profile of a children's book author/illustrator, viewpoints from outside the profession, "Research Update," "ERIC/RCS Reports," reviews of professional resources and instructional materials, and responses to questions that teachers ask. *Language Arts* also invites classroom teachers to submit manuscripts. They accept a variety of formats, including children's writing and drawing.

English Journal. National Council of Teachers of English, 1111 Kenyon Road, Urbana, Illinois 61801.

The focus of *English Journal* is on any phase of English teaching or any subject of interest to the English teacher in the middle, junior, or senior high school. Thematic issues deal with current topics and concerns, such as humor in the classroom and teacher burnout. The journal accepts manuscripts relating to upcoming topics. (Topics are announced five to eight months before publication.) Poetry by teachers and students is accepted. Regular features include "News and the English Profession," letters from readers, reviews of professional and student publications and young adult literature, "Junior High/Middle School," "Research," "The Language Game," and "Electronic Media."

Research in the Teaching of English. 1111 Kenyon Road, Urbana, Illinois 61801.

Four times a year (February, May, October, and December), *RTE* publishes current research in the areas of English and language arts. An abstract highlights the essentials of each article. The references that follow provide sources for further study. Once a year a selected annotated bibliography of research is included. The studies are organized by subject categories: "Language," "Literature and Media Study," "Writing and Teacher Education" and level groupings: "Preschool and Elementary"; "Secondary"; "College and Adult"; and Research Reviews."

Journals Published by IRA

The Reading Teacher. International Reading Association, 800 Barksdale Road, P.O. Box 8139, Newark, Delaware 19711.

Articles focus on reading, language arts, and children's literature at the elementary-school level. The journal is published monthly October through May with a winter supplement. Regular features include "Interchange," an ideas exchange; "Clip Sheet," a review of current instructional practices and materials; "ERIC/RCS"; "Critically Speaking," which reviews books for children, classroom materials, and professional books; and "Research Views." *The Reading Teacher* welcomes manuscripts from classroom teachers.

Journal of Reading. International Reading Association, 800 Barksdale Road, P.O. Box 8139, Newark, Delaware 19711.

This journal is published monthly October through May for those interested in the teaching of reading at the secondary school, college, and adult levels. Articles are written to "exchange information, give opinions on theory, and relate research to practice." The areas of language arts and literature are also covered. Regular features include a readers' exchange of ideas, reviews of adolescent fiction, nonfiction, and professional books, an essay about research, and "ERIC/RCS."

Reading Research Quarterly. International Reading Association, 800 Barksdale Road, P.O. Box 8139, Newark, Delaware 19711.

Published four times a year, this journal presents recent research in the area of reading improvement, "especially through instruction and supervision in the schools." An abstract in English, French, and Spanish precedes each article. Regular features include letters to the editors, reactions to recently published articles, and "Commentary," authors' reactions to recently published articles.

Instructional Resources   475

Journals about Children's Literature

Bulletin of the Center for Children's Books. The University of Chicago Press, 5801 Ellis Avenue, Chicago, Illinois 60637.

This journal contains critical reviews of children's books for preschool through high school levels. The books are discussed by an advisory committee before being reviewed. Both recommended and nonrecommended titles are included. The *Bulletin* is published monthly except August.

The Calendar. Children's Book Council, Inc., 67 Irving Place, New York, New York 10003.

The CBC is headquarters for National Children's Book Week and a center for children's book promotion. For a one-time fee of five dollars, members will receive a lifetime subscription to *The Calendar*. This small brochure is packed with useful information. Regular features include "Up to Date with Books," which highlights recently published books pertaining to a monthly theme, and "Materials Available," which presents many free materials, including booklists, bookmarks, posters, and author/illustrator biographical sheets.

Children's Literature in Education: An International Quarterly. Agathon Press, Inc., 15 East 26 Street, New York, New York 10010.

This journal is published four times a year "for librarians, teachers, writers, and concerned parents." An editorial committee is maintained both in the United Kingdom and the United States. Topics of the articles range from indepth studies of books and authors to interviews and articles by authors and illustrators. The purpose of the journal is to "promote lively discussion of books for children and young adults, to heighten professional awareness and understanding of this literature and its use."

The Horn Book Magazine. Park Square Building, 31 St. James Avenue, Boston, Massachusetts 02116.

This magazine was founded in 1924 and remains an excellent source for keeping current in the area of children's literature. Contributors for the six-times-a-year publication include authors, illustrators, librarians, and educators. The book reviews of recommended titles are categorized by stories for young, intermediate, and older readers. Also reviewed are books "Of Interest to Adults," audio-visual materials, science books, and "adult books of interest to high school readers." "The Hunt Breakfast," a regular feature, provides notes of interest to the children's book world, which include information about the contributors and staff and announcements of awards and conferences. The Newbery and Caldecott Award acceptance speeches are printed in the August issue each year.

School Library Journal. R. R. Bowker Company, Subscription Dept., P.O. Box 13706, Philadelphia, Pennsylvania 19101.

Issued monthly except June and July, this periodical is published for children, young adults, and school librarians. Teachers may be interested in the specialized bibliographies and review sections. Reviews written predominantly by librarians include audio-visual materials and books for preschool through high school.

The WEB: Wonderfully Exciting Books. The Ohio State University, Room 200, Ramseyer Hall, 29 West Woodruff, Columbus, Ohio 43210.

Published four times a year, this periodical provides reviews of currently published books. The reviews written by classroom teachers, professors, and graduate students in children's literature include responses from children and suggestions for extending books. Also, in each issue a "web of possibilities" on various themes gives teachers ideas for developing units across the curriculum.

In addition to the selected list of national publications, many states and regional areas publish informative journals that are of interest to the teacher.

Books

A variety of books are available to aid the teacher in the language arts. For instance, bibliographies and indexes are good sources for planning a theme that integrates the curriculum. These resources acquaint the teacher with a wide range of materials that extend the use of the textbook, enhance the theme's scope, and better serve to meet the needs of the learners. They provide annotated lists of fiction, nonfiction, print, and nonprint materials. An annotated and categorized list of resources pertinent to the language arts follows:

Language Arts

Barnes, Douglas, *From Communication to Curriculum,* Harmondsworth, Middlesex, England, 1976.

Barnes states that the kind of personal and conversational interaction that exists between teacher and student is an important aspect of the learning process. He includes transcriptions of conversations in the classroom to use as instructional devices for the reader. The power of using language to learn is expounded.

DeStefano, Johanna, *Language, the Learner and the School,* John Wiley and Sons, New York, 1978.

This book is divided into two major sections. The first deals with language structure, development, and variation. The second discusses classroom applications of this knowledge. The text is helpful as background information for the teacher making decisions in the language arts.

Lindfors, Judith Wells, *Children's Language and Learning,* Prentice-Hall, Inc., Englewood Cliffs, N.J., 1980.

The author has drawn together knowledge and research in areas of language acquisition, language variation, communicative competence, and second-language learning. Information is presented so that teachers may make informed instructional decisions about both classroom environment and program. She has included many samples of children's speech.

Marland, Michael, *Language Across the Curriculum,* Heinemann, London, 1977.

Called an "Implementation of the Bullock Report in the Secondary School," this book gives teachers specific ideas in extending middle-grade students' language. The sections on oral language are particularly helpful to language-arts teachers.

Rosen, Connie and Harold, *The Language of Primary School Children,* Penguin, Baltimore, Md., 1973.

Language arts for the primary-school child is described within the British school setting. The significance of context to the learning process leads the discussion. Within this framework the language arts are drawn as children work in the school situation. Examples of children's language are given.

Wagner, Betty Jane, *Dorothy Heathcote: Drama as a Learning Medium,* National Education Association, Washington, D.C., 1976.

Wagner describes and details the philosophy and instructional techniques of Dorothy Heathcote, professor of drama at the Institute of Education at the University of Newcastle-upon-Tyne, Great Britain. Heathcote sees drama as problem-solving. Wagner has made Heathcote's exciting approach available to teachers.

Weeks, Thelma E., *Born to Talk,* Newbury House, Rowley, Mass., 1979.

Weeks describes how children learn "to produce language that works—how to communicate what they intend to communicate." This sociolinguistic perspective is strongly woven throughout the book. Although the audience is general, the author has references to a wide range of research investigations, including studies focused on the nonverbal aspects of language.

Selecting Books for Children

Adventuring with Books: A Booklist for Pre-K–Grade 6, new ed., Mary Lou White, ed., National Council of Teachers of English, Urbana, Illinois, 1981.

This is an annotated list of 2,500 recommended children's trade books published from 1977 through 1980. Older titles without annotations are included at the end of each major category to balance the subject. The bases for selection include interest for the child, literary merit, equitable treatment of minorities, and the recognition of quality books of the past. The genre and specific topic categories aid teachers in discovering books about a theme and planning for instruction. In addition to books for children, a section is devoted to professional books about children's literature.

Best Books for Children: Preschool through the Middle Grades, John T. and Christine B. Gillespie, R. R. Bowker Company, New York, 1978.

Approximately 10,000 recommended titles in print through the end of 1977 are organized into categories in this volume. Brief annotations serve as an aid for giving reading guidance and in preparing bibliographies. Biographical, title, and author-illustrator indexes complete this bibliography.

Children's Catalog, 13th ed., Barbara E. Dill, ed., The H. W. Wilson Company, Bronx, N.Y., 1976.

This is an annotated bibliography of recommended books covering all subjects for preschool through sixth-grade children. Published every five years with annual supplements, this reference tool is divided into three parts: Dewey Decimal "Classified" Catalog; "Author, Title, Subject, and Analytic Index"; and "Directory of Publishers and Distributors." This is used as a guide for book selection, purchasing, and developing subject-area themes.

The Elementary School Library Collection: A Guide to Books and Other Media, 12th ed., Lois Winkel, ed., Bro-Dart, Newark, N.J., 1979.

This annotated bibliography is divided into three sections: "Classified"; "Indices" (author, title, and subject); and "Appendices." The recommended materials include books, periodicals, filmstrips, recordings, transparencies, study and art prints, and kits. The grade level coverage is from kindergarten through sixth grade. Professional resources are also included.

Junior High School Library Catalog, 4th ed., Gary L. Bogart, ed., The H. W. Wilson Company, New York, 1980.

Similar in format and purpose to the *Children's Catalog,* this book is intended primarily for seventh, eighth, and ninth grades, with some overlapping to the elementary and senior high grades.

A Multimedia Approach to Children's Literature, 2nd ed., Ellin Greene, compiler and ed., American Library Association, Chicago, 1977.

This is a selective list of films, filmstrips, and recordings based on children's books for use with ages preschool through eleven. Brief annotations and ordering information accompany the alphabetical arrangement.

Reading Ladders for Human Relations, 6th ed., Eileen Tway, ed., American Council on Education, Washington, D.C., 1981.

This annotated bibliography is compiled "to advance the cause of better human relations." The five ladders—"Growing into Self," "Relating to Wide Individual Differences," "Interacting in Groups," "Appreciating Different Cultures," and "Coping in a Changing World"—are subdivided into subcategories and age ranges from preschool through high school. Most of the titles have been published since the fifth edition; however, a few earlier outstanding titles are included in the sixth edition. Inclusion criteria include good literature that is positive and fair in the presentation of all people. This specialized booklist aids parents, teachers, and librarians in book selection.

Subject Guide to Children's Books in Print, R. R. Bowker Company, New York.
Published annually, this is a listing of all books for children currently in print that are available in the United States and can be classified by subject. The subject heading format makes this a source for teachers developing topical bibliographies. Citations give pertinent ordering information. A companion volume is *Children's Books in Print* (date): *An Author, Title and Illustrator Index to Children's Books.*

Specialized:
The Bookfinder: A Guide to Children's Literature About the Needs and Problems of Youth Aged 2–15, Sharon Spredemann Dreyer, Volume I, 1977; Volume 2, 1981, Circle Pines, Minnesota.
These reference books describe and categorize current children's books according to psychological, behavioral, and developmental topics of concern to children and adolescents. The split-page format allows the user to view the subject index while browsing through the annotated section. Volume I annotates 1,031 books and Volume 2 annotates 723 books published between 1975 and 1978.

Children and Poetry: A Selective, Annotated Bibliography, 2nd ed., revised, compiled by Virginia Haviland and William Jay Smith, Library of Congress, Washington, 1979.
Hoping to make poetry as natural and harmonious to the fifth grader as it is to the preschooler who responds freely to the rhythm and rhyme of nursery rhymes, the compilers have annotated a selective bibliography. Included are "rhymes as well as more serious poetry, the old as well as the new works originating in English as well as translations from all over the world."

A wide variety of bibliographies on specific topics are available. A sample listing includes:

Fantasy for Children: An Annotated Checklist, Ruth Nadelman Lynn, R. R. Bowker, New York, 1979.

Index to Collective Biographies for Young Readers: Elementary and Junior School Level, 3rd ed., Judith Silverman, R. R. Bowker, New York, 1979.

Notes from a Different Drummer: A Guide to Juvenile Fiction Portraying the Handicapped, Barbara H. Baskin and Karen H. Harris, R. R. Bowker, New York, 1977.

World History in Juvenile Books: A Geographical and Chronological Guide, Seymour Metzner, The H. W. Wilson Company, New York, 1973.

Indexes
Children's Book Review Index, Gary C. Tarbert, ed., Gale Research Company, Detroit, 1975.
This is a source for finding reviews of children's books that have appeared

in over 380 periodicals. The format is the same as that of *Book Review Index.* Each citation includes author's name, book title, reviewing publication, volume, date, and page number. Also includes a title index.

Index to Fairy Tales, Myths and Legends, The F. W. Faxon Company, Boston, 1926. Supplement 1, 1937. Supplement 2, 1952.

Index to Fairy Tales, 1949–1972, Including Folklore, Legends and Myths in Collections, 1973.

These volumes compile fairy tales, legends, fables, and myths. Until 1949, the stories appear in a title index. From 1949–1972 the stories are arranged in a subject index. This is a source to locate folk stories that appear in collections.

Index to Children's Poetry, John E. and Sara W. Brewton, compilers, The H. W. Wilson Company, New York, 1942. First Supplement, 1954; Second Supplement, 1965.

Index to Poetry for Children and Young People: 1964–1969, 1972; *1970–1975,* 1978.

These volumes provide a dictionary index to collections of poems for children and youth with title, subject, author, and first-line entries. The volumes serve as a guide to locate poems to accompany specific topics.

Index to Children's Songs, Carolyn Sue Peterson and Ann D. Fenton, compilers, The H. W. Wilson Company, New York, 1979.

This is an index to more than 5,000 songs and variations that primarily include both music and lyrics found in children's books published between 1909 and 1977. The three sections are a list of the books, titles, and first-line and subject indexes.

Children's Literature Textbooks

General

Cullinan, Bernice E., in collaboration with Karrer, Mary K. and Pillar, Arlene M., *Literature and the Child,* Harcourt Brace Jovanovich, Inc., New York, 1981.

The preface of this children's literature text states that the approach "is child-centered and is based on Piagetian developmental principles, language learning research, and reader response theory." The text is organized into three major parts: "The Child," "The Books," and "The Child and the Books." Features of the book include the "Teaching Idea," information useful to the teacher to engage student interest; "Activity: Teacher to Student," activities addressed to the student; and "Profile," biographical vignettes of authors and illustrators. The appendices include "A Year of Holiday Books" and "Birthdays of Selected Authors and Illustrators."

Glazer, Joan I. and Williams III, Gurney, *Introduction to Children's Literature,* McGraw-Hill Book Company, New York, 1979.

    This children's literature textbook is divided into two parts. Part One, "Exploring the Realm of Literature," surveys the genres and states criteria for evaluating the categories. Part Two, "Literature and Children Together," suggests practical ways to bring books and children together. Case studies serve as models for organizing units and expanding units into year-long projects. Special features include "Issue" boxes in which experts give contrasting viewpoints on one subject. Anecdotes about authors and artists begin the chapters. Also, a color section depicts differences in media and style.

Huck, Charlotte S., *Children's Literature in the Elementary School,* 3rd ed., updated, Holt, Rinehart and Winston, New York, 1979.

    One special strength of this book is the author's ability to show how literature can become an integral part of the ongoing program. Three chapters are devoted to this. Another focus is "to recommend the right book to the right child." To meet this goal, characteristics of children's development with accompanying appropriate books are placed in an extensive chart, preschool through grade six. The book is divided into three sections: "Learning About Children and Books," "Knowing Children's Literature," and "Developing a Literature Program" Two-color sections include illustrations from picture books and photographs of learning environments and children's work.

Sutherland, Zena, Monson, Diane L., and Arbuthnot, May Hill, *Children and Books,* 6th ed., Scott, Foresman and Company, Glenview, Illinois, 1981.

    The first two chapters are new to this edition. Chapter 1 concerns the state of children's literature and chapter 2 concerns the understanding of children's needs in terms of the developmental theories. The book is divided into five parts; the longest is Part Three, "Exploring the Types of Literature." Extensive bibliographies conclude each chapter, separating adult references from children's books. A special feature called "Viewpoint" suggests issues to explore by quoting from books and articles on a variety of related topics.

Young Child

Cullinan, Bernice E. and Carmichael, Carolyn W., *Literature and Young Children,* National Council of Teachers of English, Urbana, Illinois, 1977.

    This volume consists of essays written by specialists in early childhood education to promote and state the value of literature for young children. Topics include poetry, traditional literature, audio-visual materials, and responses to and strategies for presenting literature. An annotated list of a basic collection of good books for young children concludes this volume.

Glazer, Joan I., *Literature for Young Children,* Charles E. Merrill Publishing Company, Columbus, Ohio, 1981.

    This practical resource tells why and how to use literature as the center of the curriculum. Books are shown to be valuable in the child's language, intellectual, personality, social and aesthetic development.

Lamme, Linda Leonard, ed., *Learning to Love Literature: Preschool through Grade 3,* National Council of Teachers of English, Urbana, Illinois, 1981.

This book focuses on the methods and materials available to help early childhood teachers to use literature as the core of their curriculum. From theory to practice, the authors suggest ways to create a literature environment and expose children to literature through a variety of techniques.

Adolescent

Donelson, Kenneth L. and Nielson, Alleen Pace, *Literature for Today's Young Adults,* Scott, Foresman and Company, Glenview, Illinois, 1980.

This textbook provides a framework and background information for young-adult literature (which is "any book freely chosen for reading by a person between the ages of twelve and twenty"). The chapters include an introduction, history of the field, a look at the books (fiction and nonfiction), and the professional's role in promoting the literature. Criteria for evaluating different kinds of books are presented by contrasting desired and undesired features of each genre.

Specialized Topics in Children's Literature

Cianciolo, Patricia, *Illustrations in Children's Books,* 2nd ed., Wm. Brown Company, Publishers, Dubuque, Iowa, 1976.

This volume discusses the varieties of illustrated books for children, art styles, media, and techniques, and criteria for appraising the illustrations. Suggestions for using illustrations in the school are of particular value to the teacher, as is the annotated bibliography.

Cianciolo, Patricia, *Picture Books for Children,* 2nd ed., revised and enlarged, American Library Association, Chicago, 1981.

This annotated bibliography of picture books for children from nursery school through junior high school is divided into four categories: "Me and My Family," "Other People," "The World I Live In," and "The Imaginative World." Each of the categories includes fiction, nonfiction, and poetry published before September, 1980. "The introduction explores the values and uses of picture books, examines and describes current trends, and discusses evaluation criteria."

Terry, Ann, *Children's Poetry Preferences: A National Survey of Upper Elementary Grades,* National Council of Teachers of English, Urbana, Illinois, 1974.

Findings of this research report about the poetry preferences of fourth-, fifth-, and sixth-grade students include the fact that children's enthusiasm for poetry declines from fourth to sixth grade. Also, children prefer narratives, humorous poems, and poems with rhythm and rhyme about familiar topics that are contemporary. They do not like poems with complex imagery or subtle emotion. Teachers may want to replicate the study with their students.

Guides for Using Children's Literature
> *Celebrating with Books,* Nancy Polette and Marjorie Hamlin, The Scarecrow Press, Metuchen, N.J., 1977.
>
> Arranged according to the school year, holidays are presented with information about the day, an annotated list of appropriate books, and activity suggestions for using the books. It is primarily for use with preschool through elementary children.

> *E is for Everybody,* Nancy Polette, The Scarecrow Press, Metuchen, N.J., 1976.
>
> This manual summarizes 147 picture books and details activities to accompany the titles that are appropriate for students in elementary through junior high school. Part Two gives specific suggestions for integrating art and literature experiences.

> *Response Guides for Teaching Children's Books,* Albert B. Somers and Janet Evans Worthington, National Council of Teachers of English, Urbana, Illinois, 1979.
>
> This guide gives teachers specific suggestions for integrating literature, reading, and language arts. The 27 works of fiction (10 picture books, four transitions, and 13 longer novels) are included because of their high literary quality and appeal to children. Each title follows the same format of "Summary," "Themes," "Appraisal," "Reading Considerations," "Initiating Activities," "Composing," and "Instructional Resources."

Children's Classroom Resources

Language-Arts Textbooks

A commonly used resource in the classroom is the language-arts textbook. The textbook is usually selected by a committee and adopted by the district. Typically, the language-arts textbook will already be there for the teacher.

Criteria for Assessing Language-Arts Textbooks. A teacher may have the opportunity to serve on a textbook selection committee and needs to be aware of the kinds of criteria used to evaluate books. The criteria can also be used to assess the value of currently used textbooks.

> *Guide for Assessing Language-Arts Textbooks*
>
> What are the qualifications of the authors?
>
> What are the features of the book? Do they meet my school's language-arts goals?
>
> Do the illustrations enhance the meaning?
>
> Does the book along with its pages look inviting?
>
> Is the book organized so that the students can look up needed information?
>
> Is language arts considered an integral part of the curriculum?
>
> Does the book foster integrated language experiences?
>
> Is the information given about language accurate?
>
> Does the book use clear, direct, and vivid language?
>
> Does the book avoid stereotypes?
>
> Are the concepts, as revealed by the scope and sequence chart, appropriate for the intended grade level?
>
> Is the book readable for the intended grade level?
>
> Does the book ask for reader involvement?
>
> Do the students have an opportunity to use their own language?
>
> Does the book use quality literature of interest to the student?
>
> Is there a handbook of skills accessible for student use?
>
> What supplemental aids are available?
>
> Does the teacher's edition provide suggestions for extending activities? Are the ideas innovative?

Using a Textbook. A teacher can organize the use of the textbook to get optimum benefit rather than beginning on page one and proceeding page by page to the end of the book. By using the index and scope and sequence chart, the teacher can identify lessons valuable for specific students. For instance, if a group of children needs examples in the use of capitalization, the appropriate pages throughout the book may be identified. This kind of organization assures an opportunity to have several experiences with the same concept. If a workbook is part of a language-arts series, it is most efficiently used in the same manner. Neither the textbook nor the workbook need to be used in the publisher's sequence. All children do not need to do all of the pages in their textbook or workbook. It is difficult for children to see the purpose of writing if they are asked to practice skills unnecessarily.

The scope and sequence chart is a valuable resource to the language-arts teacher. In addition to organizing the kinds of lessons available in the textbook, it allows the teacher to know what came before the current grade level and what follows. Single copies of textbooks at different adjacent grade levels may prove valuable to meet the needs of all levels of students. For example, a handbook of skills is only accessible for independent student use if the student can read the information. Also, a student may want to write a business letter that is introduced in a level above the present grade level.

Previewing copies of textbooks can reveal interesting aspects. For example, the Glencoe Publishing Company divides its text into three components: "Language," "Composition," and "Dramatic Expression." The three parts are color coded for quick identification as to the type of lesson. A strong section in this series is "Dramatic Expression." The sample pages "Moving in Different Shoes" (see pages 486–487) show the sequence for developing dramatic expression. The lesson consists of "Warming Up," "Working It Out," "Acting It Out," and "Talking It Over." This circular format could move easily into "Writing It Out" since drama leads to written expression. The lesson meets the criteria of involving students and giving them opportunities to use their own language. Other activities in the "Dramatic Expression" sections include stories to act out and stories to finish. The authors of this series are aware of the need to give students opportunities for listening, reading, talking, and writing. The Glencoe series meets the criteria of integrating language arts into the curriculum and provides integrated language experiences.

Another valuable feature of language-arts textbooks is the handbook section located at the end of the books. For example, the excerpt on pages 488–489 from *SERIES E: Macmillan English* gives the rules for capitalization and punctuation and applies them in the sample sentences. The student is also referred to the page where the rule was introduced and to lessons for more practice. Other sections of this handbook include forms for letters, invitations, book reports, and outlines. This series meets the criteria of organizing material so students can find needed information and for providing a handbook organized for easy student use.

The textbook is an often-used resource in the language-arts curriculum. It is important to remember that the textbook is a resource, not the entire curriculum.

Moving in Different Shoes

Warming Up

Look at the pictures on these pages.

- Tell what kinds of shoes are in each picture.

Think about how you would walk in each.

- Make believe you are wearing the rain boots. Show how you walk through a deep puddle.
- Now make believe you are wearing the roller skates. Show how you skate.
- Make believe you are wearing the running shoes. Show how you race in them.

Working It Out

Look at the pictures again. Choose any pair of shoes to wear.

You are going to wear those shoes on a walk. Think about how the shoes will make you feel. Think about how you will move in them.

- You start in a big field. You walk across it fast.
- You come to a steep hill. It is very hard to climb. You get tired as you walk up the hill.
- At the top, you stop to rest. Then you skip down the other side of the hill. You skip faster and faster.

54

Instructional Resources 487

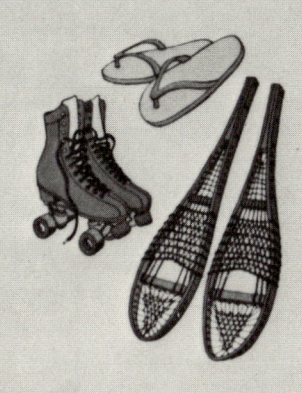

- At the bottom, you start to walk again. Then you come to some thick mud. Your feet stick in the mud. You have to lift them high as you walk.
- At last you get out of the mud. But then you come to a fence. There is no gate. You have to climb over the fence.
- When you get to the top of the fence, you jump down. Then you run.
- You get more and more tired. You run more and more slowly. Finally you can stop. You are home.

Acting It Out

■ Choose a pair of shoes from the pictures.

Think about how you will move in them.

—How will you move your legs?
—How will you move your feet?
—What will you do—walk? run? skate? play? dance?

Show how you move in the shoes. Have others in the class tell which shoes you are wearing.

Talking It Over

How did you move your legs to show what shoes you were wearing?
How did you move your feet?

55

Albert R. Kitzhaber, Coordinating Editor, *Spectrum of English, Yellow,* pp. 54, 55, Glencoe Publishing Co., Encino, California, 1978.

II. MECHANICS

Capitalization

Use a **capital letter** to begin the first word of every sentence. page 6 MORE PRACTICE, pages 324, 338
A sword was stuck in a stone.   The young boy pulled at the sword.

Begin each important word in a proper noun with a **capital letter.** page 47 MORE PRACTICE, page 327
They named the baby Marie.   The student attended Drew College.

Begin a title with a **capital letter.** End most titles with a period. page 48 MORE PRACTICE, page 327
John's father sent Dr. Brown a check.
The check went to Mr. Brown instead.

Begin each shortened word with a **capital letter.** End each shortened word with a period. page 48 MORE PRACTICE, page 327
Third Ave.   Oak St.   Wilson Ave.   Broad St.

Punctuation

Use a **period** (.) at the end of a declarative or an imperative sentence. page 6 MORE PRACTICE, pages 324, 338
The moon circles the earth every twenty-eight days.

Use a **question mark** (?) at the end of an interrogative sentence. page 6 MORE PRACTICE, pages 324, 338
When did the thieves break in?

Use an **exclamation mark** (!) at the end of an exclamatory sentence. page 6 MORE PRACTICE, pages 324, 338
What a day this has been!   How high the kite flies!

Use a **comma** (,) to separate each noun in a series of three or more nouns. page 168 MORE PRACTICE, page 333
Beets, radishes, and carrots are root crops.
I put tomatoes, beans, onions, and cheese in the salad.

HANDBOOK 313

Handbook

Use a **comma** (,) to separate each verb in a series of three or more verbs. page 168 MORE PRACTICE, page 333
Anita weeded, mowed, and raked the lawn.
We plant, grow, pick, and eat our own vegetables.

Use a **comma** (,) to set off words such as **yes, no,** and **well** when they begin a sentence. page 168 MORE PRACTICE, page 333
Yes, I read that book.   Well, I will write the report tonight.

Use a **comma** (,) to set off the name of a person who is spoken to directly in a sentence. page 168 MORE PRACTICE, page 333
David, please write a letter to me.   The telephone is ringing, Janie.

Use a **comma** (,) to separate the date from the year. page 168 MORE PRACTICE, page 333
My sister bought the radio on May 9, 1978.

Use a **comma** (,) before **and** when it joins two sentences. page 274 MORE PRACTICE, page 339
Mr. Lewis opened the door, and the children ran out.
Mrs. Lewis swept the porch, and James raked leaves.

Add an **apostrophe** and **s** (**'s**) to form the possessive of most singular nouns. page 52 MORE PRACTICE, page 327
The broom's handle broke into two pieces.
Mother washed Martha's apron.

Add an **apostrophe** (') to form the possessive of plural nouns that end with **s**. page 52 MORE PRACTICE, page 327
Jack cleaned the animals' cages.
The trainer trimmed the horses' tails.

Add an **apostrophe** and **s** (**'s**) to form the possessive of plural nouns that do not end with **s**. page 53 MORE PRACTICE, page 327
The group talked about women's rights.
The children's nurse attended the party.

Use an **apostrophe** (') in a contraction to show that one or more letters are missing. page 236 MORE PRACTICE, page 336
She's very fond of apples.   You're allowed one wish.

SERIES E: *Macmillan English*, Grade 4–Tina Thorburn, Rita Schlatterbeck, and Ann Terry (Copyright © 1982 Macmillan Publishing Co., Inc.).

Research by Graves (1977) supports our thesis that textbooks should not and cannot be the only basis for a language-arts curriculum.* Looking at only one of the language-arts strands, Graves reviewed approaches to writing by eight publishers in relationship to the research about the writing process. He sought to discover how much writing was an activity actually incorporated in the textbook and in what ways writing was taught. He found that 14 percent of the textbook is given to teaching composition in both grades two and five, while 72 percent is allotted in grade two and 75 percent in grade five is devoted to grammar and punctuation. Graves concludes that teachers need to stimulate the motivation for writing and then respond to the mechanical errors. No attention is given to the precomposing, composing, and postcomposing activities that are necessary in the writing process. A teacher depending solely on a textbook to teach writing may be depriving students of effective instruction as the student continues to think that writing consists of grammar and punctuation.

Magazines

Magazines written for children are resources for the language-arts classroom. They are compact, colorful, and attract the students' attention while providing a different source for reading and for acquiring current information about the world. The stories, poems, art ideas, games, and articles can enhance a classroom topic or provide the stimulus for further study. These periodicals often feature holiday-related material. Students can see and read work by their peers and also submit their own work for publication. A subscription to a magazine adds a dimension to the classroom materials and a focus as the students anticipate the arrival of the monthly issue.

Adult magazines can be used in a variety of ways in the classroom; they provide sources for collages and concrete and found poetry. Magazines with glossy, colorful pictures, such as *National Geographic* or *Smithsonian*, appeal to children.

A selected annotated list of pertinent children's magazines follows:

Cobblestone, The History Magazine for Young People, 28 Main Street, Peterborough, N.H., 03458.
    A thematic approach is used for this monthly magazine devoted to the subject of history. Included are poems, articles, stories, cartoons, and book reviews. The magazine accepts letters and drawings from children.

*Graves, Donald H., "Research Update: Language Arts Textbooks: A Writing Process Evaluation," *Language Arts* 54: 817–823, October, 1977.

Cricket, Manuscripts: Editor-in-Chief, P.O. Box 100, LaSalle, Ill. 61301; Subscriptions: Box 2670, Boulder, Colorado 80302.

Contributors to this monthly literary magazine for children are known authors and illustrators in the children's literature field. Stories, articles, poems, songs, biographical sketches, and activities are included. Also, monthly story, poetry, and drawing contests are sponsored by the magazine and described in the "Cricket League" section. The winners' works are published.

Highlights for Children, Manuscripts: 808 Church Street, Honestdale, Pennsylvania 18431; Subscriptions: P.O. Box 269, Columbus, Ohio 43216.

This monthly (except bimonthly June-July, August-September, and semimonthly December) magazine features articles, stories, poems, activities, and craft projects. The editorial board accepts original stories, articles, and craft ideas from children.

Jack and Jill, P.O. Box 567B, Indianapolis, Indiana 46206.

This magazine is published monthly, except bimonthly April/May, June/July, and August/September by Children's Health Publications. Articles reflect the health theme. Also included are activities, stories, cartoons, recipes, crafts, and jokes. The magazine accepts children's art, letters, and poetry pertaining to health subjects (exercise, safety, and nutrition). Children's Health Publications also publishes *Children's Digest* and *Child Life.*

McGuffey Writer, McGuffey Laboratory School, Miami University, Oxford, Ohio, 45056.

This is a collection of children's writing published three times a year at Miami University. Theme issues are planned and contributions in the form of short stories, essays, poems, cartoons, and black-and-white illustrations to accompany the writing are welcomed. "Items are accepted on the basis of merit, originality, and appropriateness to the overall balance and theme of the issue."

National Geographic World, 17th and M Streets, N.W., Washington, D.C. 20036.

Published monthly by the National Geographic Society, this magazine includes beautifully illustrated articles on a variety of topics and activities. It is also a magazine to which one can submit photojournalism.

Ranger Rick Nature Magazine, National Wildlife Federation, 1412 16th Street, N.W., Washington, D.C. 20036.

Articles in this profusely illustrated monthly magazine are concerned with some aspect of nature. Letters, manuscripts, art, and photographs are accepted.

Stone Soup, the Magazine by Children, Children's Art Foundation, P.O. Box 83, Santa Cruz, California 95063.

The Children's Art Foundation was founded in 1973 "for the purpose of encouraging children to develop their literary and artistic talents." Published five times a year (September, November, January, March, and May), the magazine accepts children's stories, book reviews, poems, and artwork. *The Editors' Notebook,* a companion periodical, is intended to help teachers find ways to use *Stone Soup* as the basis for a writing and art program.

Newspapers

In addition to subscribing to magazines, a teacher may want to add yet another dimension and focus to classroom reading materials by subscribing to commercial classroom newspapers. The typical arrangement is that for a yearly fee, all of the students receive the same weekly or biweekly issue designated by their grade level, but this procedure is blind to individual interests and reading levels. The teacher can change this standard arrangement and use the same amount of collected money to subscribe to a variety of magazines and newspapers. Publishers are usually willing to supply sample copies for preview so that the teacher, with the help of students, can make selections.

Two companies that publish newsmagazines for students in grades kindergarten through sixth are:

My Weekly Reader
Xerox Education Publication
1250 Fairwood Avenue
P.O. Box 2639
Columbus, Ohio

Scholastic Book Services
904 Sylvan Avenue
Englewood Cliffs, New Jersey 07632

Local newspapers often provide an educational service that sponsors workshops to help the teacher to use the newspaper as part of the curriculum and that supplies the class members with the newspaper free of charge. In any event, the teacher can bring newspapers from home so that features for children or of interest to children can be used on a regular basis. The local newspaper is also a place where children's work can be published. Many papers have weekly sections devoted to poems, stories, riddles, and art submitted by children of the area.

Knowledge of the sections of local newspapers helps the students to publish their own class newspaper. Publishing a class newspaper allows students to apply their knowledge and provides a forum for their work (see chapter 10). This newspaper informs parents and other students about news and work accomplished in their classroom.

Book Clubs

Owning books is an important aspect of the reading process because children tend to read more often the books in their personal collection. Paperback book publishing has made ownership within the reach of all children. Good children's literature is available inexpensively in paperback editions at bookstores and through classroom book clubs. The typical book club sends grade-level lists of titles available that month to distribute to the students. From the selected lists, students are able to make their choices from a variety of kinds and subjects of books. This provides the teacher with opportunities to recommend titles of high quality and for children to purchase the same book for small-group discussions.

Book clubs for children include:

Scholastic Book Club
904 Sylvan Avenue
Englewood Cliffs, New Jersey 07632

Book Clubs by Grade Levels

Seesaw	kindergarten/first grade
Lucky	second/third grades
Arrow	fourth/fifth/sixth grades
Campus	seventh through twelfth grades
T.A.B. (Teenage Book Club)	seventh through ninth grades

Troll Associates
320 Rt. 17
Mahwah, New Jersey 07430

All Grade Levels

Book Fairs and Book Stores

Books can also be purchased through book fairs sponsored by the school or parent groups. Prior to the book fair dates, the children are given a list of titles and prices that will be available. Some schools also have a "browsing only" day to give all students a chance to see the available books. These fairs provide opportunities for parents to see a variety of books that are suitable for their children. The quality of the titles in the book fair is a concern for teachers. They may wish to ask the school and public librarian to check the list of titles before the school or parent group contracts with the book fair company. Sponsoring a book fair gives students a chance to add to their personal collections and the sponsor to take its profit in cash or merchandise.

In addition to the book stores in shopping centers is the increasing number found in remodeled closets in the schools. Often a parent group has seen the need and taken the responsibility of opening a paperback book store. While it may be open a limited number of hours, the store provides a welcome source for books and can also be a place for students to buy books, pencils, and paper.

Resources from Outside the Classroom

Television

Commercial television is not a classroom resource, but language-arts teachers can take advantage of its influence on children in their classrooms. While television does not use book language or require children to use their imagination because it provides the visual images, it can be used as an impetus for reading. Children often want to read for themselves the classic stories and novels presented on television. The televising of *Little Women* leads directly to a volume of requests for the Louisa May Alcott book in libraries. The teacher can direct and guide the students' viewing by keeping abreast of worthwhile programs and recommending them to the students. Watching the television version of *The Great Gilly Hopkins* (Paterson; see chapter 8) can add an interesting dimension to a discussion for students who have already read the book. Comparing the book to the program may lead students into making their own generalizations about the place for television and reading. Teachers also need to know what programs are popular with students and watch some of them so they can capitalize on the students' interest to promote other activities and materials.

Parents and Grandparents

Parents and grandparents, in addition to sharing their specific talents from their careers, hobbies, and life experiences, can add helpful hands to classroom learning. They can type children's stories, bind books, record language experience stories, and listen to children read. A mother in one second-grade classroom took the responsibility for organizing and maintaining a weekly cooking center. She was also on hand during the preparation stage to give guidance to the young chefs. To minimize frustrated feelings by students, another teacher asked for parent help when the children do involved art projects. The list is endless and, of course, includes accompanying the class on field trips. Retired people are also good sources for this kind of assistance, especially if the majority of the parents work outside of the home or have younger children who limit their availability. The grandparent in the classroom can fulfill a role missing in the children's lives when children do not live near their own grandparents. The role also serves to fulfill the grandparents if their grandchildren live out of town. The lives of both the adults and students are enriched. Involving community members in the school provides another benefit, as it is one way to keep them informed and aware of the school's ongoing activities.

Library Media Centers

Library media centers provide both professional personnel who serve as resources and a variety of instructional materials to aid the teacher and student. Getting to know the librarian or media specialist can be valuable for the teacher. These professionals are able to select materials to help the teacher accomplish instructional goals, prepare bibliographies in areas of interest to the teacher, inform the teacher of new materials available in the language-arts field, locate needed materials from outside sources, and coordinate library programs with classroom units. The instructional materials include books, pamphlets, periodicals, study and art prints, slides, filmstrips, cassettes, records, 8-mm film loops, 16-mm films, videotapes, microfilms, models, realia, and computers.

The school library media center provides immediate access to instructional materials that will enrich the total curriculum. The teacher and media specialist can work together to find the best available materials to meet instructional goals. Prior planning assures them that they will have time to explore, locate, and preview relevant materials. Compiling bibliographies of topics provides a basis for future work and a source to revise. To become independent library media center users, students need opportunities to use the facilities in purposeful ways.

As with other learning, learning isolated library skills is meaningless. Students, in addition to their assigned library time, need access to the center at unassigned times to select recreational reading, to pursue personal interests, or to work in small groups on classroom projects.

Not as immediately accessible as the school media center, but as valuable, is the public library. The public librarian is available to help the teacher gather instructional materials to take to the classroom. Notifying librarians of assignments helps them to be prepared with materials students will need after school. The public librarian may be willing to visit the school to promote new materials, special programs, or to do storytelling. Many public libraries have special borrowing arrangements that allow the teacher to have a number of books for an extended period of time to support classroom collections.

In addition to the school and public library media centers, the teacher can get materials from an intermediate school district with a centralized instructional materials center, county and state libraries, and libraries that serve the needs of special groups such as the blind and learning disabled. Many local companies and organizations have quality materials for loan or distribution. Telephone books and guides to community resources are available in

These children are working on projects as a follow-up to a theme on architecture in the city. Notice how some are interacting with each other and with their teacher while others choose to work alone. A media center provides the opportunity to select study modes. (Douglas Alternative Elementary School, Columbus, Ohio)

libraries to locate materials distributed by such groups. Planning allows the teacher to exhaust all available resources.

Summary

The language-arts teacher is a professional who makes decisions about instruction. To aid in the decision-making process, the teacher has many resources available. These include both human and commercial resources. The teacher, students, school staff, and community members provide the human resources. Commercial resources include professional journals, books, textbooks, and library materials. Within the availability of commercial resources are some designed especially for student use, such as children's magazines, newspapers, book clubs, and book fairs. Professional organizations, college and community classes, and libraries provide a combination of human and commercial resources. The development of the language-arts teacher is a continuing process and an integral part of teaching. The teacher builds confidence and gains expertise by keeping current with research and resources.

Suggested Learning Experiences

1. Visit a school library media center. Observe the activity in the center to find how the center is used by both teachers and children. Ask the librarian how his or her knowledge might be put to better use. How do you think you might use a media center and work with a librarian/media specialist?

2. Examine as many of the children's magazines and newspapers listed in this chapter as possible. Try to categorize them in several ways; for example, journals for younger readers/for older readers; to be used for recreational reading/to be used for study resources; skill-oriented materials/literary materials; written for children/written by children. If you were to ask your school librarian to subscribe to four magazines, which would you choose? Why? Which would you want in your classroom? Why?

3. Select a current high-quality children's book, such as a book that has received an honor or an award, or one that was written by an outstanding author. Find as many reviews of that book from different sources as you

can. Compare these reviews. Which reviews give you the most information about the book? Which reviews are ones children would enjoy reading? Which reviews are the most useful in deciding whether the book was one you wanted to use in your classroom for a specific purpose?

4. Examine a series of children's language-arts textbooks that are used in your area. Using the guide in this chapter, look for the strengths in this series. Which sections of this text would you use? Which sections would you omit?

Index

Aardema, V., 354
ABC (Wildsmith), 417
ABC of Things (Oxenbury), 349
Abel's Island (Steig), 9, 441
Abstract experiences, content of language arts derived from, 13–15
Accommodation, 81–82
Across Five Aprils (Hunt), 93
Activities
   following reading aloud, 332
   from literature, 345–346
   in-class, and integration, 284–286
   leading to talk, 353–356
   out-of-class, and integration, 286–294
   see also specific activity
Adaptation, 78, 80–82
Adkins, J., 336, 420
Adults, language use of, with children, 40
Adventuring with Books: A Booklist for Pre-K–Grade 6 (White), 477
Advertisements
   language of, 311–321
   writing, 225
After the Goat Man (Byars), 335
Age, and children's interests, 338–339
Alexander and the Terrible, Horrible, No Good, Very Bad Day (Viorst), 359
Alexander and the Wind-Up Mouse (Lionni), 350
Allen, V. G., 410
Alliteration, 229–230
Allophones, 34
Alphabet Art: Thirteen ABCs from Around the World (Fisher), 249
Alphabet charts, 188
Amelia Bedelia (Parrish), 250
Amos and Boris (Steig), 6

And Then What Happened, Paul Revere? (Fritz), 328
Anecdotal records
   of day's work, 281, 282
   in language assessment, 144–145
   for writing, 234
Angel, M., 335
Animal communication, 32
Animals Should Definitely Not Wear Clothing (Barrett), 417
Animism, 84
Anne Frank: The Diary of a Young Girl (Frank), 94, 207
Annie and the Old One (Miles), 220, 421
Anno, M., 349, 416
Anno's Counting Book (Anno), 349, 416
Antisocial behavior, in puberty, 102, 103
Antonyms, 315
Applebee, A. N., 332
Arbuthnot, M. H., 481
Art from Many Hands (Schuman), 220
Art projects, 345–346, 354
Artistry, of writers, 327
Artwork
   and handwriting, 185
   and second-language learning, 400
   and writing, 209–210, 216, 218, 220, 222
Asimov, I., 314
Assessing response, teacher's, 133
Assessment
   of language-arts textbooks, 483–484
   of oral language of LEP child, 401–407
   of theme studies, 298–302
   see also Evaluation
Assimilation, 80–81
Associative writing, 212

499

Atmosphere, social, for writing, 244
Attitudes, toward language differences, 65
Atwater, F., 335
Atwater, R., 335
Audience
  and beginning writing, 195–196
  distant, 134
  intimate, 134
  see also Literature
Award-winning literature, 340

Babbitt, N., 328, 336, 337, 350
Babbling, infant, 38
Barnes, D., 122, 125, 132, 133, 134, 138, 147, 151, 208, 431, 476
Barret, J., 417
Basal reading text approach to reading
  and LEP child, 412
  and writing, 206
Baskin, B. H., 479
Baylor, B., 278, 334
Beach, R., 338, 339
Bear's Heart (Supree), 220, 421
Bergman, D., 361
Berko, J., 39, 144
Best Books for Children: Preschool through the Middle Grades (Gillespie and Gillespie), 478
Bettelheim, B., 94, 95, 96, 106
Bibliography cards, 262, 264
Biemiller, A., 183
Big Anthony and the Magic Ring (dePaola), 406
Biggest House in the World (Lionni), 350
Bilingual education programs, 383, 384–385
Binh, D. T., 386
Birnbaum, J. C., 195
Black, J. K., 144, 145
Black English, 65, 332
Blank booklets, 242
Bloom, L. M., 39
Blos, J. W., 207
Blume, J., 335, 369
Bogart, G. L., 478
Bond, N., 337
Book clubs, 493
Book discussions, 9, 344, 350–353
  as act of discourse, 114–120
  and accommodation, 81
  and reading aloud, 336
Book fairs, 493–494
Book stores, 494
Book talk
  activities leading to, 353–356
  stages in, 349–350
Bookbinding, 244, 245
Bookfinder: A Guide to Children's Literature About the Needs and Problems of Youth Aged 2–15, The (Dreyer), 479
Books
  assessing interaction with, 367–370
  extending use of words by, 362–363
  motivating writing by, 363–365
  number read, 343–344
  owning, 493
  professional, 476–483
  rereading, and equilibration, 83
  selecting, for classroom library, 338–341

  selecting, for LEP child, 416
  story frame provided by, 359–362
  suggestions of, for LEP child, 416–421
  text, 483–490
  as themes, 218–223
  writing about, 346
  see also Literature
Boreas, J., 303
Born to Talk (Weeks), 477
Borrowers, The (Norton), 329
Boston, L. M., 337
Brewton, J. E., 480
Brewton, S. W., 480
Bridge to Terabithia (Paterson), 103
Briggs, R., 361
Britton, J., 61, 69, 208, 209, 233
Brown, E. J., 339
Brown, J. S., 80
Brown, M., 362
Brown, M. W., 181, 330
Bucks, B. L., 420
Building belief, 213
Bulletin of the Center for Children's Books, 475
Bully of Barkham Street, The (Stolz), 350
Burke, C. L., 160
Burningham, J., 182, 416
Burton, W. H., 338, 339
Byars, B., 335, 339

Calendar, The, 475
Calkins, L. M., 195, 227
Call It Courage (Sperry), 363
Cameras, 288, 294
Can't You Make Them Behave, King George? (Fritz), 328
Carmichael, C. W., 481
Case grammar, 305
Castle (Macauley), 420
Causley, C., 335
Cay, The (Taylor), 114–120, 135, 351
Cazden, C. B., 39, 144, 387
Celebrating with Books (Polette and Hamlin), 483
Center activities, for integration, 284–286
Center for Applied Linguistics, 382, 387
Checklists, in language assessment, 144, 145–146
"Cherry, or the Frog Bride," 348
Child, as learner, 5–6, 11
Child development, 18–20
  and planning, 431
  see also Cognitive development; Moral development; Social development
Children
  planning by, 436–439, 441
  views of, about teachers, 471
Children and Books (Sutherland, Monson and Arbuthnot), 481
Children of Greene Knowe, The (Boston), 337
Children and Poetry, Annotated Bibliography (Haviland and Smith), 479
Children's Book Review Index (Tarbert), 479–480
Children's Catalog (Dill), 478
Children's Language and Learning (Lindfors), 477

Children's Literature in Education: An International Quarterly, 475
Children's Literature in the Elementary School (Huck), 481
Children's Poetry Preferences: A National Survey of Upper Elementary Grades (Terry), 482
Choice
 and poetry, 340
 and writing, 195
Chomsky, C., 44, 161, 255, 305, 319, 332
Choral reading
 and accommodation, 81–82
 in encouraging discourse, 139–140
Chukovsky, K., 32, 38, 94, 95
Cianciolo, P., 482
Cicourel, A. V., 145, 146
Clark, E. V., 37
Clark, M. M., 161, 331
Classroom climate, 10
Classroom environment
 and beginning reading, 197
 and growth in discourse, 142–143
 and managing space, 279–280
 and reading, 342
 and second-language learning, 398–399
 and writing, 242
Clauses, 43
Clay, M. M., 36, 49, 182, 183, 185, 199
Cleary, B., 335
Cleaver, B., 309
Cleaver, V., 309
Cleworth, M. C., 339
Clichés, 312
Close reading, 344
Cloud Book, The (dePaola), 286
Cobblestone, The History Magazine for Young People, 490
Cognitive development, 18–20, 76–88
 and language acquisition, 78
 and language arts teacher, 87–88
 see also Piagetian theory
Cognitive theories of moral development, 90–94
Cohen, D. H., 332
Cole, B., 399
Coles, R. E., 186
Collins, A., 80
"Colonel Fazackerly" (Causley), 335
Communication
 animal, 32
 and feedback, 56–57
Communication act, 15–18, 390
Communicative competence, 40, 90
Communicative speech, 122, 207, 272
Comparison, and creating images, 312
 topics inviting, 135
Competition, 104, 344
Composing speech, 122
Concepts, devlopment of, 19
Concrete experiences, 123
 content of language arts derived from, 13–15
 and second-language learning, 391, 399–401
 as source of writing, 210–212
Concrete operations stage, 84–86

Conferences
 for group work, 280
 parent-teacher, 234, 449
 writing (*see* Writing conferences)
Conger, J. J., 97, 104
Consonants, nasal, spelling, 50
Content area(s)
 and in-class experiences and activities, 284–286
 integration of language arts in, 273–302
 and interpreting the experience, 294–296
 language as (*see* Language, as content area)
 and opportunities for assessing, 298–302
 and organizing work, 278–280
 and out-of-class experiences and activities, 286–294
 and planning for theme, 276–278
 rationale for language arts in, 272–273
 and recordkeeping, 280–284
 and selecting topic or theme, 273–276
 and sharing experiences, 296–298
Context
 and discourse, 122, 123–124
 of language learning, 55–57
 and language functions, 60, 61, 147
 literacy, building, 195–197
 for reading, 341–346
 and second-language learning, 389–391
 writing, 242–244
Conventional level of moral development, 92–93
Conversation(s)
 interruption of, 126–127
 of school-age child, 42–43
 structure of, 42
Cook-Gumperz, J., 40
Cookbooks, 225
Cooper, S., 216, 336, 350
Copying
 and beginning reading and writing, 174–176
 and handwriting, 247
Craig, G. J., 82
Creepy Castle (Goodall), 419
Cricket, 491
Crictor (Ungerer), 353
Crow Boy (Yashima), 89, 421
Cuckoo's Reward: El premio del cuco: A Folktale from Mexico in Spanish and English, The (Kouzel), 420–421
Cullinan, B. E., 332, 480, 481
Culture
 and handwriting, 249
 and helping LEP children, 385–388
 and language, 66–67
 and learning styles, 386
Cummins, J., 390

Dale, E., 319
Dale, P. S., 38
Dark Is Rising, The (Cooper), 216, 336, 350
Data charts, in report writing, 262
Davis, B., 393
Davis, E. A., 120, 121
Dawn (Shulevitz), 334, 418
Day, E. J., 120
Dazzle (Viorst), 328, 329
de la Mare, W., 139

502 Index

Debates, 136
Deep in the Forest (Turkle), 419
Deep structure, 304, 305
DeFord, D., 206
dePaola, T., 354, 405, 406, 419
Descriptive grammar, 304
DeStefano, J. S., 43, 63, 476
Development, child (*see* Child development)
Developmental spelling errors, 251
Dialects, 19, 34, 64–65, 68
 attitudes toward, 308
 social, 65, 127, 128
 and spelling errors, 252
 power and beauty of, 308–309
Dialogue
 beginning use of, 51–54
 contribution of, to monologue, 208
 improvising, 357–358
 use of, 214–215
Diaries, motivated by books, 363–365
Dictation
 accepting, 169, 172–176
 ways of using, 176–180
Dictionaries
 personal spelling, 195, 258
 as writing source, 242–243
Dill, B. E., 478
Diller, A.-M., 386
Dillon, D., 152, 229
Dioramas, 354
Directive language, 61
Discourse, 121–150
 activities that encourage, 136–142
 assessment of, 144–150
 basic competencies in, 123–126, 129
 book discussion as act of, 114–120
 and classroom environment, 142–143
 and context, 122, 123–124
 and experiences, 123
 planning for growth in, 130–143
 and small-group discussion, 133–136
 study of, 15–18
 and teacher's role, 130–133
 see also Speaking
Discussion(s)
 book (*see* Book discussions)
 formal types of, 136
 small-group (*see* Small-group discussions)
 techniques, 136
Displays
 and beginning writing, 168–169
 in communicating language-arts program, 443
 as form of sharing, 225
 for integration, 284, 294, 296–297
 as "publishing," 244
Doctors and Nurses, 182
Dog on Barkham Street, A (Stolz), 350
Donelson, K. L., 482
Dorothy Heathcote: Drama as a Learning Medium (Wagner), 477
Downing, J., 63
Drama
 as bridge to writing, 359
 differentiating from theater, 141, 213, 356
 in encouraging discourse, 141–142
 reading strengthened by, 215

 in second-language learning, 400
 as source of writing, 212–225
Drawing (*see* Artwork)
Dreyer, S. S., 479
Duckworth, E., 79, 87, 106
Dumont, R. V., Jr., 387
Durkin, D., 161, 331
Duvoisin, R., 399

E is for Everybody (Polette), 483
Early childhood, social development in, 99–101
Ed Emberly's Great Thumbprint Drawing Book (Emberly), 420
Edelsky, C., 422
Edge of Two Worlds (Jones), 119–120
Egocentric speech, 101, 207, 208, 210
Egocentrism, 84, 91, 349
18th Emergency, The (Byars), 335
Elementary School Library Collection: A Guide to Books and Other Media, The (Winkel), 478
Elkind, D., 78, 88, 107
Emberly, E., 420
Emotional development, 20
Emotional theories of moral development, 94–96
Endless Steppe, The (Hautzig), 94
English Journal (NCTE), 472, 473–474
English as a second language, teacher of, 407–410: *see also* Limited English Proficiency (LEP children; Second-language learning
Environment, formal, 396–397
 informal, 396–397
 and language learning, 55–56
 and second-language learning, 396–399
 see also Classroom environment
Equilibration, 82–83
Ethnic community, 387
Evaluation, as response to writing, 229
 in a conference, 228
 observation guides, 129, 145–148, 170–171, 192, 231–232, 368–369, 402–404, 484
 self- (*see* Self-evaluation)
 of writing, 231–233
 see also Assessment
Evaluation, program, 449–451
 NCTE guidelines for, 451–464
Evaluation forms, for writing, 234, 237, 238–239
Events
 leading to book talk, 353–354
 as response to writing, 229, 230–231
 and selection of theme, 273–274
Everyone Knows What a Dragon Looks Like (Williams), 335
Expectations, teacher, and children's productivity, 105
Experiences, and book talk, 349–350
 and discourse, 123
 group, and reading aloud, 215–216
 in-class, and integration, 284–286
 interpreting, and integration, 294–296
 literature as, 328–330
 new, and new vocabulary, 315
 out-of-class, and integration, 284–286
 see also Abstract experiences; Concrete experiences; Shared experiences

Exploratory language, 125
  and field trips, 138
  and reply situation, 133
  and small-group discussions, 133
Eyes of the Amaryllis, The (Babbitt), 337

Fables, 361
Fables (Lobel), 334, 361
Fairy tales, and moral development, 94–96
Family, and social development, 99–101
Fantasy for Children: An Annotated Checklist (Lynn), 479
Fat Cat, The (Kent), 418
Favat, F. A., 339
Feedback
  classroom sources of, 57
  and communication, 56–57
  and discourse, 17–18
Fenton, A. D., 480
Field trips
  and assimilation, 80–81
  in encouraging discourse, 124, 138
  and second-language learning, 399–400
Files, of writing work, 234
Fillmore, L. W., 391, 393, 397
Fish Is Fish (Lionni), 350
Fisher, A., 335
Fisher, L. E., 249
Fitzgerald, J., 256, 258, 268
Flack, M., 6
"Flashlight" (Thurman), 329
Fleming, J. D., 32
FLES, 389
Flexibility principle, 185
Flexibles, in sentences, 121
Flood, J. E., 332
Florio, S., 196, 197
Folk tales, child's version of, 324–327
  and moral development, 94–95
  retelling, 349
Food Market, The (Spier), 417
Foreign Language in the Elementary Schools (FLES), 389
Formal operations stage, 86–87
Fox, S., 70
Frank, A., 94, 207
Frederick (Lionni), 6, 9
Freed, B., 393
Freidlander, B., 393
Fritz, J., 328
Frog Goes to Dinner (Mayer), 419
From Communication to Curriculum (Barnes), 476
From the Mixed-up Files of Mrs. Basil E. Frankweiler (Konigsburg), 339

Games
  competitive, regulatory language in, 61–62
  leading to talk, 353–356
Gangs, and social development, 101
Gasztold, C. B. de, 206
Gathering of Days, A (Blos), 207
General Language: English and Its Foreign Relations (Lindquist and Wachner), 315
Genishi, C., 26, 70
Gennaro, J., 420

George, J. C., 358, 363
Gilbert, S. S., 420
Gillespie, C. B., 478
Gillespie, J. T., 478
Glazer, J. I., 481
Goals, of language-arts program, 430, 431, 432–435
Good boy–nice girl orientation, 92–93
Goodall, J. S., 419
Goodman, Y., 186
Goodnight, Moon (Brown), 181, 330
Graffiti board, clichés for, 312
Grammar
  child's model of, 37, 78
  ineffectiveness of study of, 303
  types of, 304–305
  what children learn about, 305–309
  what teachers need to know about, 303–305
Grandpapa and Ellen Aroon (Monjo), 361
Grandparents, as resource, 494–495
Graves, D. H., 185, 192, 195, 209, 490
Great Gilly Hopkins, The (Paterson), 365–367, 494
Greene, B., 93
Greene, E., 478
Grenfeld, H., 314
Griego, M. C., 420
Griffin, W. J., 43, 121
Grillone, L., 420
Group projects
  and egocentrism, 84
  and moral development, 91
Grouping(s), 22
  by achievement level, 134–135
  self-selected, 279
  and social development, 104–105
  teacher-selected, 279
  teacher's role in, 104–105
  for work, 279
Groups
  influence of, on members, 98–99
  for spelling programs, 258
Guide to Periodical Literature, The, 261

Hall, E. L., 386
Hall, M. A., 160, 199, 331
Halliday, M. A. K., 38, 60, 61
Hamlin, M., 483
Handwriting, 184–192, 244, 246–249
  and art experiences, 185
  cursive, 246–249
  individual styles of, 247, 249
  manuscript versus cursive, 246
  italic calligraphy, 249
  in other cultures, 249
  self-evaluation of, 249
  speed of, 249
Handwriting programs, commercial, 247
Hanna, G., 339
Harris, A. J., 338, 339
Harris, K. H., 479
Harste, J. C., 160
Hautzig, E., 94
Haviland, V., 479
Heathcote, D., 213, 358, 477
Henderson, E. H., 193

Index 503

Hennings, D. G., 319
Henry Huggins (Cleary), 335
Hepler, S. I., 344, 345
Herman the Helper (Kraus), 418
Hersh, R. H., 91, 93
Hetherington, E. M., 90, 99, 104, 105
Heuristic language, 60, 62, 63, 272
Hickman, J., 367
Highlights for Children, 491
Highwater, J., 220
Hillocks, G., Jr., 210
Hispanic children, 387
Hoban, T., 417, 419
Hoberman, M. A., 362
Hogrogian, N., 418
Holman, F., 312
Home
 beginning literacy in, 159–161
 and social development, 99–101
Home language, 64, 252
Home visits
 and LEP child, 388, 394
 by teacher, 388, 394, 472
 to teacher, 471–472
Homework, in communicating with parents, 447–448
Homographs, 315
Homonyms, 315–316
Homophones, 315
 spelling, 253, 254
Horn, E., 256
Horn Book Magazine, The, 475
Horowitz, E., 314
Horwitz, E. L., 336
Horwitz, H. E., 362
House Is a House for Me, A (Hoberman), 362–363
Huck, C. S., 329, 365, 371, 481
Hudelson, S., 422
Hunt, B. K., 315
Hunt, I., 93
Hunt, K. W., 43
Hunter, M., 307, 336
Hurlock, E., 98, 99, 101, 102
Hutchins, P., 399, 417, 418
Hymes, D., 40, 60

"I Saw a Jolly Hunter" (Causley), 335
Illustrations in Children's Books (Cianciolo), 482
Imagery, 362–363
Imaginative language, 60–61, 62, 63
Immersion program, for second-language learning, 385
Improvisation, 357–358
In-class experiences and activities
 and integration, 284–286
 and reading context, 345–346
In the Land of Small Dragon: A Vietnamese Folktale (Kha), 421
Inch by Inch (Lionni), 441
Index to Children's Poetry (Brewton and Brewton), 480
Index to Children's Songs (Peterson and Fenton), 480
Index to Collective Biographies for Young Readers: Elementary and Junior High School Level (Silverman), 479

Index to Fairy Tales, Myths and Legends, 480
Index to Fairy Tales, 1949–1972, Including Folklore, Legends and Myths in Collections, 480
Index to Poetry for Children and Young People: 1964–1969, 480
Index to Poetry for Children and Young People: 1970–1975, 480
Infant(s)
 babbling of, 38
 and language acquisition, 40
 and mother's language, 40
Informative language, 61, 62, 63, 272
Inner speech, 207–208
Input, linguistic, and second-language learning, 392–395
Inside: Seeing Beneath the Surface (Adkins), 336, 420
Instruction, as response to writing, 229
Instructional resource(s), 468–498
 children's classroom, 483–494
 from outside classroom, 494–497
 professional, 472–483
 teacher as, 470–472
 see also specific resource
Instrumental language, 60
Instrumental-relativist orientation, 92
Integration, example of, 4–10
Interactional Competency Checklist, 145–146
Interactional experiences, 123
Interactional language, 60, 61
Interest centers, 84
Interest groups, and social development, 104
Interests, children's
 and second-language learning, 394
 and selecting books for classroom library, 338–340
 and selection of theme, 273
Interests, teacher's, 432, 471
Interlanguage, 406
International Reading Association (IRA)
 journals published by, 473, 474
 as professional resource, 472, 473
Interpretive language, 61
Interruptions, of conversations, 126–127
Intonation, and learning to read second language, 412
Introduction to Children's Literature (Glazer and Williams), 481
Inventory principle, 49
"Inventory of Children's Literary Background," 332
IRA (*see* International Reading Association)
Irregular forms, spelling of, 252, 253–254, 256
Iser, W., 330
Island of the Blue Dolphins (O'Dell), 358

"Jack and the Beanstalk," 95
Jack and Jill, 491
Jack and the Wonderful Beans (Still), 308–309
Jacobs, A., 393
Jaggar, A., 332
Japanese children, 386
Jim and the Beanstalk (Briggs), 361
John, V., 387

Johns, J. L., 339
Jones, H., 220
Jones, W., 120
Journal keeping, 207
Journal of Reading (IRA), 473, 474
Journals
 professional, 473–476
 reading and writing, 223
Journey to Topaz (Uchida), 120, 220, 330
Julie of the Wolves (George), 358, 363
Junior High School Library Catalog (Bogart), 478
Justice, 89
 immanent, 91
 redistributive, 96

Kagan, J., 97, 104
Karrer, M. K., 480
Keats, E. J., 170, 350
Kent, J., 418
Kha, D. M., 421
Kickle Snifters and Other Fearsome Critters (Schwartz), 363
Kimball, L. H., 420
King, M. L., 46, 70
Knee Knock Rise (Babbitt), 337
Kohlberg, L., 91, 93, 94
Konigsburg, E. L., 339
Kouzel, D., 420
Krashen, S. D., 393, 396
Kraus, R., 349, 418
Krzesni, J. S., 186

Labov, W., 144
Laird, C., 315
Laird, H., 315
Lamme, L. L., 371, 482
Language
 arbitrary quality of, 32, 33
 assessment of, 144–150
 categories of, 60–63
 as content area, 303–316
 and context, 60, 61, 147, 389–391
 functions of, 39–41, 58–63, 138, 233, 272
 history of, books on, 314–315
 home, 43
 juxtaposition of elements of, 328
 literature as input to, 327–328, 347–349
 as medium for learning, 272
 nature of, 32–37
 new words entering, 313–315
 oral versus written, 309–310
 as part of message, 327–328
 persuasive, 311–312
 playing with, 307
 and register, 53–54, 63–64
 school, 43
 spontaneous observations of, 144–148
 standardized tests for, 144
 time to acquire, 388–389, 392
 use of, growth of, 20, 21
 variations in, 57–68
 what children should learn about, 305–309
 see also Dialects; Oral language; Written language

Language acquisition, 40, 78
 sex differences in, 120, 121
 of siblings, 121
 of twins, 121
Language Across the Curriculum (Marland), 477
Language arts
 areas of, 11
 interrelationships of, 11–15
Language arts, in content areas
 integration of, 273–302
 rationale for, 272–273
Language Arts (NCTE), 472, 473
Language-arts program
 communicating, 443–444
 developing, 439–442
 integrating literature into, 365–370
 see also Evaluation; Goals, of language-arts program; Objectives, of language-arts program; Planning
Language-arts textbooks, 483–490
 criteria for assessing, 483–484
 using, 484–485
Language boxes, 408–410
Language change, 313–315
Language explorations
 for primary-grade children, 305–307
 for middle-grade children, 307–309
Language, the Learner and the School (DeStefano), 476
Language learning, 28–73, 160
 contextual and integrated nature of, 12–13
 and knowledge of social situation, 97
 second (*see* Second-language learning)
 see also Oral language learning; Written language development
Language output, literature as stimulus to, 330–331
Language of Primary School Children, The (Rosen and Rosen), 477
Language program, reasons for literature in, 327–331
Language systems, 33–37
Larkin, K. M., 80
Law-and-order orientation, 93
Learner
 child as, 5–6, 11
 teacher as, 5–6, 11
Learning
 advancing, 79
 interactive, 10–11
 styles of, cultural differences in, 386
Learning to Love Literature: Preschool through Grade 3 (Lamme), 482
Left-handed child, 190, 247
LeGuin, V. K., 350
L'Engle, M., 217, 328, 337, 351, 362
Leo, the Late Bloomer (Kraus), 349–350
LEP (*see* Limited English Proficiency [LEP] children)
Let's Be Enemies (Udry), 92
Letter names, 50, 251
Letter play, 162
Letters
 efficient ways of making, 187
 grouping, in writing, 188
 plastic and wooden, 184

Letters (*continued*)
  reading, 223
  shapes of, 184–185
  silent, and spelling, 255
  writing, 223, 247
Levstik, L. S., 320
Lexicon, 42
  and learning to read second language, 412
Library, and report writing, 262–262
Library, classroom
  grouping books in, 342
  number of books in, 340
  selecting books for, 338–341
Library media centers, 495–497
Limited English Proficiency (LEP) children, 383
  assessment of oral language of, 401–407
  and cultural considerations, 385–388
  and linguistic considerations, 388–391
  selecting books for, 416
  and social considerations, 391–392
  suggestions of books for, 416–421
  see also Second-language learning
Lindfors, J. W., 33, 37, 40, 44, 399, 477
Lindquist, L., 315
Lindsay, V., 139
Linguistic awareness sessions, 305
Linguistic differences
  and infant babbling, 38
  and scribbling, 46
Linguistic input, and second-language learning, 392–395
Lionni, L., 327, 350, 363, 441
Lisp, 41
Listening, 9, 11, 12
  directing, for specific purposes, 126
  research on, 120
  and social conventions, 128
  see also Discourse
Listening attitude, 134
Listening comprehension, and LEP child, 402
Literacy, beginning, at home, 159–161
Literacy context, building, 195–197
Literary language, 172, 307
Literature
  award-winning, 340
  in classroom, 331–359
  as experience, 328–330
  as input to language, 327–328, 347–349
  integrating, into language-arts program, 365–370
  in language program, reasons for, 327–331
  reading in, 338–346
  selecting, 333–337
  sharing, 330–331, 334, 337–338
  as source of writing, 215–225
  as stimulus to language output, 330–331
  talking about, 346, 347–359
  writing from, 346, 359–365
  see also Books
Literature and the Child (Cullinan, Karrer and Pillar), 480
Literature for Today's Young Adults (Donelson and Nielson), 482
Literature and Young Children (Cullinan and Carmichael), 481
Literature for Young Children (Glazer), 481

"Little Red Hen, The," 349
Little Red Riding Hood, 20
Living things, and integration, 284
Loban, W. D., 121
Lobel, A., 334, 361
Local school system, and planning, 432
Look Again! (Hoban), 419
Lundsteen, S. W., 120
Lynn, R. N., 479

Macauley, D., 420
Macauley, W. J., 303
Mackay, D., 188
Magazines, 225, 490–492
Magician of Cracow, The (Turska), 334
"Man Who Was Going to Mind the House, The," 148–150
Mapping, 220
Marland, M., 130, 135, 477
Massie, D. R., 328
Materials
  for out-of-class activities, and integration, 288, 294
  and second-language learning, 398–399, 400
  writing, 186, 187, 242–243
May, F. B., 134, 135
Mayer, M., 419
McAllister, M. K., 339
McCarthy, D. A., 120
McClosky, R., 350
McCord, D., 139
McCracken, M. J., 341
McCracken, R. A., 341
McGovern, A., 418
McGuffey Writer, 491
McKenzie, G. R., 262
McKenzie, M. G., 89, 93, 161, 199
McLenighan, V., 361
Meaning(s)
  and new experiences, 315
  sensitivity to nuances of, 307, 308
Mearnes, H., 266
Media center, library, 495–497
Mendoza, G., 224
Menyuk, P., 37, 78
Merriam, E., 334
Merrill, J., 361
Message
  in communication act, 15–17
  language as part of, 327–328
  shape of, 15–16, 17–18
Message writing, development of, 46–48
Metalinguistic system, 127
Metaphor, 312
  and observation, 211
Middle childhood, social development in, 101–102
Miel, A., 308
Migrant children, 392
Miles, M., 220, 421
Miller, H. R., 303
Minimal distance principle, 44
Minimal pairs, 34
Mitchell, E. P., 92
Modeling, revision behavior, 228
Modeling experiences, 123
Moffett, J., 17, 122, 134, 135, 350, 358, 359

Monjo, F. N., 361
Monologue, and writing, 208
Monson, D. L., 481
Moonsong Lullaby (Highwater), 220
Moral absolutism, 90–91
Moral development, 89–96
  cognitive theories of, 90–94
  emotional theories of, 94–96
  and language arts, 89–90
Moral realism, 90
Moral reciprocity, 90, 91
Moretz, S. A., 160, 331
Morphemes, 35
  bound, 35, 42
  derivational, 35
  free, 35
  inflectional, 35
Morphett, M. V., 246
Morphological generalizations, 251, 252, 254–255
Morphology, 35, 39, 41–42
Motivation, of LEP child, 392
Motor skills, and handwriting, 184, 186
Mr. Gumpy's Outing (Burningham), 182
Mr. and Mrs. Pig's Evening Out (Rayner), 349
Mr. Popper's Penguins (Atwater and Atwater), 335
Mrs. Frisby and the Rats of NIMH (O'Brien), 9, 214, 335
Multimedia Approach to Children's Literature, A (Greene), 478
Mussen, P. H., 97, 104
My Cat Has Eyes of Sapphire Blue (Fisher), 335
My Side of the Mountain (George), 363

National Clearinghouse for Bilingual Education, 382
National Council of Teachers of English (NCTE)
  guidelines for program evaluation, 451–464
  journals published by, 472, 473–474
  as professional resource, 472–473
National Geographic, 490
National Geographic World, 491
Navaho children, 386, 387, 392
NCTE (*see* National Council of Teachers of English)
Ness, E., 93
Newsletters, 492
  and communicating language-arts program to other teachers and principal, 443, 444
  and communicating language-arts program to parents, 444–447
Newspapers, commercial classroom
  as resource, 492
  influence of, on writing, 225
Newspapers, local, as resource, 492
Nielson, A. P., 482
No More Baths (Cole), 399
Noah's Ark (Spier), 419
Norris, R. C., 43, 121
Norton, M., 329
Norvell, G. W., 339
Note taking, for report writing, 262, 264
Notes, to parents, 449

Notes from a Different Drummer: A Guide to Juvenile Fiction Portraying the Handicapped (Baskin and Harris), 479

Obedience, and moral development, 92
Objectives, of language-arts program, 432–435
O'Brien, R. C., 9, 214, 335
Observation guides (*see* Evaluation)
Observational activities, as source of writing, 210–211
Observations
  and beginning writing, 170
  and books, 171–172
  focused, with study trip booklets, 288
  language, 144–148
O'Dell, S., 218, 219, 220, 222, 358
O'Donnell, R. C., 43, 121
Once a Mouse (Brown), 6, 9
One Fine Day (Hogrogian), 418
One Morning in Maine (McClosky), 350
One-word utterances, 38
O'Neill, M., 315
Oral language, 12
  assessment of LEP child's, 402–407
  differentiating from written language, 309–310
  and equilibration, 83
  fluency in, 56
  and punctuation, 310
  sharing of, 9
  see also Language
Oral language learning, 37–45
  context of, 55–57
  implications of, 55–57
  of school-age children, 41–44
  of young children, 37–41
  see also Language learning
Oral sharing, and integration, 296, 297–298
Oral speech form, 212
Ortony, A., 80
Outlines, in report writing, 262, 264
Over, Under and Through (Hoban), 417
Overenunciation, 252
Overgeneralization, 41, 49, 50, 51, 251, 253
Oxenbury, H., 349

Pancakes for Breakfast (dePaola), 419
Panel discussions, 136
Pantomime, 356–357
Paolitto, D. P., 94
Paper, special, 186
Parents
  communicating language-arts program to, 444–449
  conferences with, 234, 449
  goals of, 432
  and homework, 447–448
  and language learning, 56
  and LEP child, 388
  newsletters for, 444–447
  notes to, 449
  and planning, 432
  reading to children by, 331, 332
  as resource, 494–495
  school visits by, 444
Parke, R. D., 90, 99, 104, 105
Parnall, P., 334
Parrish, P., 250

Parts of speech, 304, 306, 307
Paterson, K., 103, 339, 365, 494
Peck, S., 395
Peer conferencing, 227
Peers
  authority of, 20
  influence of, as source of writing, 225
  and moral development, 91
  and social development, 102
Pencils, beginner, 186
Penmanship (see Handwriting)
Pepinsky, H. B., 43
Personal language, 60, 62, 63
Personal reaction response, 229, 230
Personality, and social development 97–99
Persuasive language, 311–321
Peter's Chair (Keats), 170, 350
Peterson, C. S., 480
Petunia (Duvoisin), 399
Phillips, J. L. Jr., 80
Phonemes, 34, 41
Phonics approach to reading
  effect of on writing, 206
  and LEP child, 411–412
Phonological generalizations, 251–252
Phonological spelling cues, 255
Phonology, 33–34, 39
Piaget, J., 19, 78, 90, 91
Piagetian theory,
  major principles of, 78–83
  of moral development, 90–91
  stages of development in, 83–87
"Pickety Fence, The" (McCord), 139
Picture books, and older children, 334
Picture Books for Children (Cianciolo), 482
Pillar, A. M., 480
Pinnell, G. S., 61, 62, 63, 138, 152
Planning
  by children, 436–439, 441
  and evaluation, 449–450
  examples of, 6–10, 432–433, 436–439
  long-term, 431–435
  and parents, 432
  rationale for, 430–431
  short-term, 435–439
  for theme, 276–278
  weekly, 439, 440
Planning sheets, 281, see also Webbing
Plante, P., 361
Platt, N. G., 14, 26, 320
Play
  categories of language used in, 61–62
  and language learning, 56
  and second-language learning, 399
Playground, as sensory base for integration, 286–287
Poems, as themes, 222–223
Poetic language, 211, 233
Poetry
  appreciation of, 335
  choices of, 340
  and choral reading, 139–140
  memorizing, 338
  reading aloud, 334–335
  sharing, 338
  styles, as source of writing, 223–225
Poetry tree, 338

Poetry Troupe, The (Wilner), 335
Polette, N., 483
Pomerantz, C., 421
Postconventional level of moral development, 93–94
Postwriting phase, 209
  and reading aloud, 216
Potter, B., 92
Prayers from the Ark (Gasztold), 206
Preconventional stage of moral development, 92
Preoperational stage, 79, 84
Preschool, and social development, 99
Prescriptive grammar, 304
Preston, E. M., 349
Prewriting talk, 205, 227
Primary-grade children, language explorations for, 305–307
Principal, communicating language-arts program to, 443–444
Print
  conventions of, 158, 163, 174, 184–195
  LEP child's background with, 411
  organization of, 160, 161–172
Print settings, 160
Productivity, and teacher expectations, 105
Professional resources, 472–483
Projective language, 61
Projects, in encouraging discourse, 137–138
Pronunciation spelling errors, 252
Proofreading, 253
Propaganda techniques, 311
Prose, poetic quality of, 335–336
"Proud Mysterious Cat" (Lindsay), 139
Puberty, social development in, 102–103
Punctuation
  and beginning writing, 190–191
  and context, 195
  and oral language, 310
Punishment, and moral development, 92
Puns, 316
Puppetry, 141, 358
Purves, A. C., 338, 339
Push Pull, Empty Full (Hoban), 417
"Puss in Boots," 95

"Questions" (Ridlon), 139–140

Ranger Rick Nature Magazine, 491
Rankin, P. T., 120
Rayner, M., 349
Read, C., 50, 51, 70, 79, 193
Reader and text, interaction between, 330
Readers
  early, 160–161
  parents reading to, 331
Reading, 11, 12
  basal reading series approach to, 206, 412
  close, 344
  context for, 341–346
  drama strengthening, 215
  learning from children's attempts at, 181–183
  in literature, 338–346
  as meaning-gaining procedure, 41
  and organization, 344
  phonics approach to, 206, 411–412
  races in, 344
  a second language, 410–412

signs of knowledge of, in classroom, 170–172
time for, 341, 344
whole language approach to, 206
wide, 344
and writing, relationship between, 205–207
Reading
beginning, overlap of with writing, 160–161
teacher-initiated, 172–184
Reading achievement, and children's interests, 339
Reading aloud, 331–338
art of, 337
and group experience, 215–216
at home, 159, 160
and imagery, 363–365
to LEP child, 407
and level of reading, 215, 333–334
in school, 170–171
as source of writing, 215–218
Reading behavior, early, 181–183
Reading Ladders for Human Relations (Tway), 478
Reading materials, children's choice of, 223–225
Reading register, 63
Reading Research Quarterly (IRA), 473, 474
Reading Teacher, The (IRA), 473, 474
Realistic thinking, 91
Reality, creating, 79
Receiver, in communication act, 15–17
Recordkeeping
on group work, 280–284, 294
and language assessment, 144–146
and writing, 234, 238–239
Red Riding (Merrill), 361
Reflective speech, 122, 208, 272
Regional dialects, 64–65
Register, 63–64, 124, 356
Regulatory language, 60, 61–62
Relational language, 61
Reply response, of teacher, 133
Report writing, 259–265
approaches to, 261
aspects of, 259
bibliography cards for, 262, 264
library resources in, 261–262
and note taking, 262, 264
outline for, 262, 264
Reportive language, 211
Research in the Teaching of English (NCTE), 472, 474
Resources, instructional (*see* Instructional resources)
Response Guide for Teaching Children's Books (Somers and Worthington), 483
Responses
reply, 133
to writing, 229–231
Retelling stories (*see* Story retelling)
Revision
of beginnings, 209
role of, 228–229
unnecessary, 229
Richardson, E. S., 212, 266
Ridlon, M., 139
Rinsland, H. D., 256
Rockwell, A., 417
Rockwell, H., 417

Rodrigues, R. J., 423
Role-playing, 214, 358
and accommodation, 81
in encouraging discourse, 141
Rosen, C., 10, 122, 477
Rosen, H., 10, 122, 477
Rosenblatt, L. M., 330
Rosie's Walk (Hutchins), 399, 418
Ross, A., 421
Ross, R. R., 372
Rossetti, C., 139
Rummelhart, D. E., 80

Sager, C., 239
Sam, Bangs, and Moonshine (Ness), 93
Sanders, T. S., 43
Saville, M., 391, 412, 423
Schemata, 79–80, 81
Schlager, N., 340
Schlatterbeck, R., 485
School Library Journal, 475–476
School register, 63–64
Schuman, J. M., 220
Schwartz, A., 315, 363
Scribbling, 46, 165
infant, 161–162
Search for Delicious, The (Babbitt), 337
Searle, D., 229
Seasons (Burningham), 416–417
Second-language learning, 19, 33, 66–67, 380–425
bilingual approaches to, 383, 384–385
child–adult interaction in, 393–395
child–child interaction in, 394–395
need for all teachers to know about, 383–384
and reading, 410–412
and register, 64
and writing, 412–416
see also Limited English Proficiency (LEP) children
Seeing Stick, The (Yolan), 335
Self-concept, 97–98
Self-correction
and beginning to read, 182–183
of spelling errors, 253
Self-evaluation
of handwriting, 249
of writing, 239–242
Self-initiated writing, example of, 204–205
Selinker, L., 406
Semantic generalizations, 251, 252
Semantics, 36–37, 42
Sendak, M., 92, 418
Sender, in communication act, 15–17
Sensorimotor stage, 83–84
Sentences, flexibles in, 121
SERIES E: Macmillan English (Thorburn, Schlatterbeck, and Terry), 485, 488, 489
Sex differences
in children's interests, 339
in language skills, 120, 121
and peer groups, 99
in sexual maturity, 102
and socialization, 99
Sex roles, 339
Shared experiences
and assimilation, 81

Shared experiences (*continued*)
  as base of interactions, 13–14
  and distance between listener and speaker, 19
  and study trips, 287, 296–298
Sharing
  in encouraging discourse, 136–137
  literature, 170–171, 181, 330–331, 334, 337–338
  and peer influence in writing, 225
Sheet music, 225
"Shoemaker and the Elves, The," 347
"Show and Tell," 136–137
Shugar, G. W., 40
Shulevitz, U., 334, 418
Shuy, R. W., 13, 26, 127, 394
Siblings, and language skills, 121
Sign-up sheet, for group work, 280
"Silver" (de la Mare), 139
Silver Pony, The (Ward), 419
Silverman, J., 479
Sima, J., 188
Sing Down the Moon (O'Dell), 218–220, 221, 222
Slang, 313
Slobin, D. I., 37
Small-group discussions
  and achievement level, 134–135
  and growth in discourse, 133–136
  and size of group, 134
  and techniques of discussion, 136
  and time, 135
  and topics, 135
Small Worlds Close Up (Grillone and Gennaro), 420
Smith, F., 199, 333
Smith, M. E., 120
Smith, W. J., 479
Smithsonian, 490
Snow, C. E., 40
Snowy Day, The (Keats), 170
Social-contract, legalistic orientation, 93
Social conventions
  listening aspects of, 128
  of speaking, 126–128
Social development, 20, 96–105
  and grouping, 104–105
  and personality, 97–99
  stages of, 99–103
Social dialects, 65, 127, 128
Social relationships, development of, 20
Social situation, knowledge of, and language learning, 97
Social speech, 207, 208
Socialization
  essentials of, 98
  and sex differences, 99
Socioeconomic level
  and language skills, 121
  and reading interests, 339–340
Somers, A. B., 372, 483
Songbooks, 225
Sostarich, J., 332
Sound of Chariots, A (Hunter), 307
Space
  managing, 279–280
  writing, 185, 186
Spacing
  in beginning writing, 158–159, 163
  within and between words, 190–191

Speaking, 11, 12
  directing, for specific purposes, 125–126
  research on, 120–121
  social convention of, 126–128
  and writing, link between, 207–209
  see also Discourse
Speech
  as communication, 122, 207, 272
  egocentric, 101, 207, 208, 210
  purposes of, 122, 125, 272
  as reflection, 122, 272
  social, 207, 208
  telegraphic, 39
  see also Exploratory language, Reflective speech
Spelling, 250–258
  beginning, 50–51
  and beginning writing, 192–195
  careless errors, 251, 253
  children's invented, 181
  development of, stages of, 193–195
  focus, time for, 193, 195
  forming own rules for, 50
  generalization errors, 251–252, 254–256
  and overgeneralization, 49, 50, 51, 251, 253
  and pressure for accuracy, 181, 192–193
Spelling acquisition, 79
Spelling analysis worksheet, 251–253
Spelling dictionaries, personal, 195, 258
Spelling patterns, 195
Sperry, A., 363
Spier, P., 417, 419
Standard English, 127–128, 332
State requirements, and planning, 432
Staton, J., 160, 331
Steig, W., 441
Still, A., 308
Stolz, M., 350
Stone Soup, the Magazine by Children, 491–492
Story, sense of, 332–333
Story frame, books providing, 359–362
Story retelling, 347–349
  as assessment tool for LEP child, 405–407
  in language assessment, 148–150
  and signs of reading knowledge, 170–171, 172
  and understanding story, 216–217
Story Theater, 358–359
Storytelling, 337–338
  in encouraging discourse, 141
  at home, 159
  as type of drama, 141
Stranger Came Ashore, A (Hunter), 336
Strategies, of second-language learners, 391–392, 397–398
Strega Nona (dePaola), 354, 356–358, 405–407
Strickland, D., 127, 332
Strickland, R. G., 43, 120, 121
String in the Harp (Bond), 337
Structural grammar, 304
Study trip booklets, 288, 289–293
Study trips
  for integration, 287–288, 296
  with several classes, 444
Subject Guide to Children's Books in Print, 479
Summer Is Icumen In: Our Ever Changing Language (Grenfeld), 314
Summer of My German Soldier (Greene), 93
Summer of the Swans (Byars), 335

Supree, B., 220, 421
Surface structure, 304, 305
Sustained Silent Reading (SSR), 341
Sutherland, K., 386
Sutherland, Z., 481
Swiftly Tilting Planet, A (L'Engle), 217
Swimmy (Lionni), 327, 350, 362
Symbols, in writing, 336
Sympathetic Understanding of the Child: Birth to Sixteen, A (Elkind), 88
Synonyms, 315
Syntax, 35–36, 43–44

T-unit measurement, 43, 121
Tale of Peter Rabbit, The (Potter), 92
Tales of a Fourth Grade Nothing (Blume), 335, 369
Talk, invitation to, 131
Talking about literature, 347–359; *see also* specific aspect
Tall Talk and Other Talk (Schwartz), 315
Tamarindo Puppy and Other Poems, The (Pomerantz), 421
Taping, in language assessment, 146, 147
Tarbert, G. C., 479
Taylor, T., 114, 351
Teacher(s)
 and beginning writing, 168–170
 children's views of, 471
 classroom, role of in second-language learning, 392–401
 communicating language-arts program to other, 443–444
 and discourse, 130–133
 ESL, 407–410
 and grammar knowledge, 303–305
 interests of, 432, 471
 as learner, 5–6, 11
 and need to know about second-language learning, 383–384
 as professional, 472
 responses of, 133
Teacher talk, types of, 130, 131–133
Telegraphic speech, 39
Television, as resource, 494
Templin, M. C., 120, 121
Terry, A., 340, 482, 485
Tests, standardized, 144
Text and reader, interaction between, 330
Text approximation, 161
Textbooks, language-arts (*see* Language-arts textbooks)
Theater, differentiating from drama, 141, 213, 356
Theme(s)
 and assessing, 298–302
 books as, 218–223
 differentiating from unit, 441–442
 planning for, and integration of language arts in content area, 276–278
 resources for, 274–276
 selection of, and integration of language arts in content area, 273–276
 webbing, 276–278
Thesaurus, as writing resource, 243
Thorburn, T., 485
Thought, choosing words to shape, 311–312
Thought ramblings, 212
Thought writing, 212

"Three Billy Goats Gruff, The," 141, 349
"Three Little Pigs, The," 95–96, 172
Thurman, J., 329
Time, managing, 280
Titch (Hutchins), 417–418
Too Much Noise (McGovern), 418–419
Toolbox, The (Rockwell and Rockwell), 417
Toolchest (Adkins), 420
Topics, 135, 273
Tortillitas Para Mama (Griego et al.), 420
Tough, J., 60, 61, 131, 152, 402
Tracing, and beginning reading and writing, 174
Traditional grammar, 304
Transactional language, 233
Transformational-generative grammar, 304–305
Tree of Language, The (Laird and Laird), 315
Trees Stand Shining, The (Jones), 220
Trips (*see* Field trips; Study trips)
Troike, R. C., 391, 412
Tuck Everlasting (Babbitt), 328, 336, 337, 350
Turkle, B., 419
Turn-taking, 40
Turska, K., 334
Turtle and the Two Ducks: English Retelling of La Fontaine's Fables, The (Plante and Bergman), 361
Tway, E., 267, 478
Twins, and language skills, 121

Uchida, Y., 120, 330, 330
Udry, J. M., 92
Ungerer, T., 353
Universal-ethical-principle orientation, 94
Unit, differentiating from theme, 441–442
Urzuá, C., 423
Usage, and social conventions, 127–128

Vietnamese children, 382–383, 386, 392
Viorst, J., 328, 359
Vocabulary
 basic, 256, 258
 books expanding, 362–363
 growth in, 36–37, 42
 words entering, 315
Volunteers, and second-language learning, 407–408, 414
Vowels, and spelling, 50–51
Vygotsky, L., 46, 161, 207

Wachner, C., 315
Wadsworth, B. J., 84, 86
Wagner, B. J., 17, 122, 134, 213, 358, 359, 477
Walk with Your Eyes (Brown), 362
Walter the Lazy Mouse (Flack), 5, 6, 9
Ward, L., 419
Washbourne, C. W., 246
Watchamacallit Book, The (Hunt), 315
Way, B., 356
Way to Start a Day, The (Baylor), 278, 334
WEB: Wonderfully Exciting Books, The, 476
Webs, 7–10
 book discussion, 351, 352
 literature, 220–222, 365–367
 planned with class, 276, 277
 and short-term plans, 435
 teacher-planned, 276, 278
 theme, 276–278
 word, 243, 256, 256, 257, 316, 317

Weekly planning, 439, 440
Weeks, T. E., 477
Weir, R. H., 38, 48
Wells, G., 40, 389
Welsh, C. A., 37
Wepman, J. M., 41
Wetstone, H., 393
"What Is Pink?" (Rossetti), 139
When the Sky Is Like Lace (Horwitz), 336, 362
Where Did My Mother Go? (Preston), 92, 349
Where the Lilies Bloom (Cleaver and Cleaver), 309–310
Where the Wild Things Are (Sendak), 92, 418
Whistle for Willie (Keats), 170
White, M. L., 477
White, R. H., 423
Why Don't You Get a Horse, Sam Adams? (Fritz), 328
Why Mosquitoes Buzz in People's Ears (Aardema), 354
Wide reading, 344
Wild Mouse (Brady), 6, 10
Wildsmith, B., 417
Wiles, M. E., 186
Williams, G., III, 481
Williams, J., 335
William's Doll (Zolotow), 339
Winer, I., 335
Wilt, M. E., 120
Winch, W. H. 246
Wind at the Door, A (L'Engle), 328
Winkel, L., 478
"Winter Alphabet" (Merriam), 334
Wizard of Earthsea (LeGuin), 350
Woodward, V. A., 160
Word banks, 180–181
Word classes, functional, 304, 306–307
Word distribution, and learning to read second language, 412
Word order, 305–306, 412
Word webbing, 243, 256, 257, 316
Words
 entering language, 313–315
 entering vocabulary, 315
 grouping information about, and spelling, 254–256, 257
 high-frequency, spelling, 195
 history of, books on, 314–315
 interest, spelling, 195
 irregular forms of, spelling, 252, 253–254, 256
 relationship of, 315–316
 sensitivity to, 307, 308
 to shape thought, 311–312
 spacing within and between, 190–191
 use of, books extending, 362–363
 what children should learn about, 313–316
Words Come in Families (Howowitz), 314
Words from History (Asimov), 314
Words Words Words (O'Neill), 315
Work
 grouping for, 279
 and managing space, 279–280
 and managing time, 280
 organizing for, 278–280
Workbooks, 485
Worth, V., 312

Worthington, J. E., 372, 483
Wrinkle in Time, A (L'Engle), 217, 337, 351, 362
Writers, early, 331–332
Writing, 9, 11, 12
 about books, 346
 and artwork, 209–210, 216, 218, 220, 222
 books motivating, 363–365
 context for, 242–244
 drama as bridge to, 359
 and equilibration, 83
 evaluating, 231–233
 evaluation forms for, 234, 237, 238–239
 feedback in, 57
 from literature, 346, 359–365
 and LEP child, 412–416
 message, development of, 46–48
 modeling, and accepting dictation, 173–174
 "publishing," 244
 and reading, relationship between, 205–207
 and recordkeeping, 234, 238–239
 responding to, 229–231
 revising, 228–229
 self-evaluation of, 239–242
 self-initiated, 204–205
 sources of, 210–225
 and speaking, link between, 207–209
 time for, 242
 See also Handwriting: Report writing
Writing, beginning, 158–159, 161–170
 observation guide for, 170
 overlap of, with reading, 160–161
 and role of teacher, 168–170
 teacher-initiated, 172–184
Writing center, 242–243, 244
Writing conferences, 226–228
 purposes of, 226–227
 types of, 227–228
Writing explorations, 48–49
Writing guides, 243
Writing materials, 242–243
 special, 186, 187
Writing process, 207–210
 segments of, 209–210
 stages of, 209
Writing product, looking at, 228–242
Writing samples, as writing resource, 243
Writing skills, 244, 246–265
 development of, 158–159, 164–168
 see also specific skill
Writing style, similar, as response, 229, 230
Written language, 12
 arbitrary quality of, 33
 differentiating from oral language, 309–310
 fluency in, 56
 see also Language
Written language development, 44–55
 context of, 55–57
 implications of, 55–57

Yashima, T., 89, 421
Yolan, J., 335
You Can Go Jump (McLenighan), 361

Zolotow, C., 339
Zidonis , F., 70
Zutell, J. 267

DEC 6 1984
DISCHARGED

DISCHAR 1981

DISCHARGED

AUG 3 1989
DISCHARGED